Azure Machine Learning Engineering

Deploy, fine-tune, and optimize ML models using Microsoft Azure

Sina Fakhraee, Ph.D.

Balamurugan Balakreshnan

Megan Masanz

BIRMINGHAM—MUMBAI

Azure Machine Learning Engineering

Copyright © 2022 Packt Publishing

All rights reserved. No part of this book may be reproduced, stored in a retrieval system, or transmitted in any form or by any means, without the prior written permission of the publisher, except in the case of brief quotations embedded in critical articles or reviews.

Every effort has been made in the preparation of this book to ensure the accuracy of the information presented. However, the information contained in this book is sold without warranty, either express or implied. Neither the authors, nor Packt Publishing or its dealers and distributors, will be held liable for any damages caused or alleged to have been caused directly or indirectly by this book.

Packt Publishing has endeavored to provide trademark information about all of the companies and products mentioned in this book by the appropriate use of capitals. However, Packt Publishing cannot guarantee the accuracy of this information.

Group Product Manager: Gebin George
Publishing Product Manager: Ali Abidi
Content Development Editor: Priyanka Soam
Technical Editor: Devanshi Ayare
Copy Editor: Safis Editing
Project Coordinator: Farheen Fathima
Proofreader: Safis Editing
Indexer: Tejal Daruwale Soni
Production Designer: Prashant Ghare
Marketing Coordinator: Shifa Ansari, Vinishka Kalra

First published: Dec 2022

Production reference: 1291222

Published by Packt Publishing Ltd.
Livery Place
35 Livery Street
Birmingham
B3 2PB, UK.

ISBN 978-1-80323-930-9

www.packt.com

To my wife, Dr. Shabnam Behdin, for being my loving and supportive partner in every step of our lives. To my son Nickan and my daughter Nila, who are my entire world and motivation to conquer any challenges encountered in life. To my wonderful parents, Dr. Hossein Fakhraee and Soraya Golrokh, for the countless sacrifices they made for me growing up and that they still make now in my adulthood.

– Sina Fakhraee

To my wife, Nandini, and my daughter, Aarushi, who have been very supportive, and for the sacrifices they have made. To my wonderful mom, Sellamma, and aunt Vasantha, who I can't thank enough, and my family for supporting me throughout my career. To my friends who have helped me, for the support they have provided.

– Balamurugan Balakreshnan

To my daughter, LD Bobs – to becoming a woman of vision. To my husband, Joe, who picks up the slack. To my Dad, who consistently teaches me what it means to be a fighter, and to my Mom, who demonstrates leadership with love. Mom, thanks for all the edits and endless hours – we are appreciative of your efforts.

– Megan Masanz

Contributors

About the authors

Sina Fakhraee, Ph.D., is currently working at Microsoft as an enterprise data scientist and senior cloud solution architect. He has helped customers to successfully migrate to Azure by providing best practices around data and AI architectural design and by helping them implement AI/ML solutions on Azure. Prior to working at Microsoft, Sina worked at Ford Motor Company as a product owner for Ford's AI/ML platform. Sina holds a Ph.D. degree in computer science and engineering from Wayne State University and prior to joining the industry, he taught various undergrad and grad computer science courses part time. If you would like to know more about Sina, please visit his LinkedIn: https://www.linkedin.com/in/sina-fakhraee-ph-d-2798ba70/.

I would like to thank my manager, Rod Means, for his outstanding guidance, support, and leadership over the past few years. I would also like to thank Ali Abidi, Priyanka Soam, Kirti Pisat, and the rest of the team at Packt for their help and support throughout the process. I would like to thank my amazing team members, Bala and Megan, for their amazing collaboration and teamwork.

Balamurugan Balakreshnan is a principal cloud solution architect at Microsoft Data/AI Architect and Data Science. He has provided leadership on digital transformations with AI and cloud-based digital solutions. He has also provided leadership in terms of ML, the IoT, big data, and advanced analytical solutions.

A big thank you to my manager Shruti Harish for her guidance and support throughout the book. I also thank the publishers, Packt, and their team – Ali Abidi, Priyanka Soam, Kirti Pisat, and rest of the team. Thank you to all my friends and colleagues for providing me with this wonderful opportunity to collaborate on the book (Sina Fakhraee and Megan Masanz).

Megan Masanz is a principal cloud solution architect at Microsoft focused on data, AI, and data science, passionately enabling organizations to address business challenges through the establishment of strategies and road maps for the planning, design, and deployment of Azure Cloud-based solutions. Megan is adept at paving the path to data science via computer science given her master's in computer science with a focus on data science (https://meganmasanz.azurewebsites.net/).

I would like to thank my manager, Marc Grove, a wonderful source of support and guidance. I would like to thank the Packt team for their partnership in bringing this book forward, and for the opportunity they have provided. I would like to thank my team members for their amazing collaboration and teamwork.

About the reviewers

Vijender Singh is a certified multi-cloud expert with over 5 years of experience. He is currently working with the Amazon Alexa AI team to tackle the effective use of AI on Alexa. He completed an MSc with distinction at Liverpool John Moores University with research work on keyphrase extraction. He has completed MLPE GCP, 5x Azure, 2x AWS certification, and TensorFlow certifications. Vijender is instrumental in co-mentoring and teaching his colleagues about ML and TensorFlow, which is a fundamental tool for the ML journey. He believes in working toward a better tomorrow.

Remon van Harmelen started his career as a software developer. Later, he became intrigued by Azure and made a career change to become an Azure consultant. He worked for several consulting parties and as part of multiple multinational projects, ranging from lift-and-shift migration to creating data analytical platforms. Now working for Microsoft as a cloud solution architect, he spends his days supporting customers on their Azure journeys.

Olivier Mertens is a cloud solution architect for data and AI at the Microsoft EMEA HQ in Ireland. He is responsible for designing data and AI solutions at scale on Azure. After specializing in AML, Olivier was selected as an advanced cloud expert for ML and MLOps. He works on the most complex ML cases in the EMEA region and leads knowledge-sharing initiatives. Before Microsoft, Olivier worked as a data scientist in Belgium. Olivier is a guest lecturer at PXL Digital Business School and holds an MSc in information management, a postgraduate degree in AI business architecture, and BSc in business management.

Nirbhay Anand has worked in the role of technical program manager and completed a master's in computer science and an MBA, and has 16 years of industry experience in software product development. He has developed software in different domains such as investment banking, manufacturing, supply chains, power forecasting, railroad infrastructure, and contract management. Currently, he is associated with Cloudmoyo, a leading cloud and analytics partner for Microsoft. CloudMoyo brings together powerful BI capabilities using Azure Data Platform to transform complex data into business insights. He is a passionate blogger and book reviewer.

I would like to thank my wife, Vijeta and kids, Navya and Nitrika, for their support. I would also like to thank my friends, family, and well-wishers for their never-ending support.

Deepak Mukunthu is a customer-focused and results-oriented AI/ML leader with over 20 years of experience leading teams and driving product vision and strategy. He currently leads the AI platform and initiatives for DocuSign. Prior to joining DocuSign, Deepak led multiple critical initiatives at Microsoft, including AutoML and labeling in AML, the data platform for Bing/Cortana, and ML-powered personalized news feeds. Deepak is passionate about democratizing AI for everyone and drives customer adoption of AI/ML technologies for their business-critical needs. Deepak is the published author of *Practical Automated Machine Learning on Azure* and loves mentoring and sharing his knowledge via platforms such as Product School and Sharebird.

Table of Contents

Preface   xv

Part 1: Training and Tuning Models with the Azure Machine Learning Service

1

Introducing the Azure Machine Learning Service   3

Technical requirements	4	Adding a schedule to a compute instance	32
Building your first AMLS workspace	4	Creating a compute instance through the Azure CLI	32
Creating an AMLS workspace through the Azure portal	5	Creating a compute instance with ARM templates	33
Creating an AMLS workspace through the Azure CLI	7	Developing within AMLS	34
Creating an AMLS workspace with ARM templates	10	Developing Python code with Jupyter Notebook	34
Navigating AMLS	11	Developing using an AML notebook	35
Creating a compute for writing code	29	Connecting AMLS to VS Code	37
Creating a compute instance through the AMLS GUI	29	Summary	40

2

Working with Data in AMLS   41

Technical requirements	42	Default datastore review	43
Azure Machine Learning datastore overview	42	Creating a blob storage account datastore	45

Creating a blob storage account datastore through Azure Machine Learning Studio 45
Creating a blob storage account datastore through the Python SDK 48
Creating a blob storage account datastore through the Azure Machine Learning CLI 51

Creating Azure Machine Learning data assets 52

Creating a data asset using the UI 52

Creating a data asset using the Python SDK 59

Using Azure Machine Learning datasets 61

Read data in a job 62

Summary 65

3

Training Machine Learning Models in AMLS 67

Technical requirements 68
Training code-free models with the designer 68
Creating a dataset using the user interface 68
Training on a compute instance 81
Training on a compute cluster 93
Summary 105

4

Tuning Your Models with AMLS 107

Technical requirements 108
Understanding model parameters 109
Sampling hyperparameters 110
Understanding sweep jobs 112
Truncation policies 114
Median policies 115
Bandit policies 115

Setting up a sweep job with grid sampling 116
Setting up a sweep job for random sampling 118
Setting up a sweep job for Bayesian sampling 120
Reviewing results of a sweep job 121
Summary 128

5

Azure Automated Machine Learning — 129

Technical requirements	129	AutoML using the AML Python SDK	144
Introduction to Azure AutoML	131		
Featurization concepts in AML	132	Parsing your AutoML results via AMLS and the AML SDK	151
AutoML using AMLS	133		
		Summary	158

Part 2: Deploying and Explaining Models in AMLS

6

Deploying ML Models for Real-Time Inferencing — 161

Technical requirements	162	Deploying a model with managed online endpoints through the Python SDK v2	179
Understanding real-time inferencing and batch scoring	163		
Deploying an MLflow model with managed online endpoints through AML Studio	164	Deploying a model for real-time inferencing with managed online endpoints through the Azure CLI v2	182
Deploying an MLflow model with managed online endpoints through the Python SDK V2	175	Summary	188

7

Deploying ML Models for Batch Scoring — 189

Technical requirements	189	Deploying a model for batch inferencing through the Python SDK	200
Deploying a model for batch inferencing using the Studio	191		
		Summary	204

8
Responsible AI — 205

Responsible AI principles	205	Data explorer	220
Responsible AI Toolbox overview	207	What-if counterfactuals	221
Responsible AI dashboard	208	Fairness	223
Error analysis dashboard	214	Summary	230
Interpretability dashboard	217		

9
Productionizing Your Workload with MLOps — 231

Technical requirements	231	Setting up variables in Azure Key Vault	244
Understanding the MLOps implementation	232	Setting up environment variable groups	249
		Creating an Azure DevOps environment	254
Preparing your MLOps environment	234	Setting your Azure DevOps service connections	257
Creating a second AML workspace	235	Creating an Azure DevOps pipeline	263
Creating an Azure DevOps organization and project	235	Running an Azure DevOps pipeline	274
Connecting to your AML workspace	241	Summary	285
Moving code to the Azure DevOps repo	241	Further reading	285

Part 3: Productionizing Your Workload with MLOps

10
Using Deep Learning in Azure Machine Learning — 289

Technical requirements	289	Deploying the object detection model to an online endpoint using the Azure ML Python SDK	305
Labeling image data using the Data Labeling feature of Azure Machine Learning	291	Summary	313
Training an object detection model using Azure AutoML	301		

11
Using Distributed Training in AMLS 315

Technical requirements	316	Creating a training job Python file to process	318
Data parallelism	317		
Model parallelism	317	Distributed training with TensorFlow	324
Distributed training with PyTorch	318		
Distributed training code	318	Creating a training job Python file to process	325
		Summary	330

Index 331

Other Books You May Enjoy 338

Preface

Data scientists working on productionizing machine learning workloads face a breadth of challenges at every step owing to the countless factors involved in getting ML models deployed and running. This book offers solutions to common issues, detailed explanations of essential concepts, and step-by-step instructions to productionize ML workloads using the Azure Machine Learning service. You'll see how data scientists and machine learning engineers working with Microsoft Azure can train and deploy ML models at scale by putting their knowledge to work with this practical guide.

Throughout the book, you'll learn how to train, register, and productionize ML models by leveraging the power of the Azure Machine Learning service. You'll get to grips with scoring models in real time and batch, explaining models to earn business trust, mitigating model bias, and developing solutions using an MLOps framework.

By the end of this Azure machine learning book, you'll be ready to build and deploy end-to-end ML solutions into a production system using AML for real-time scenarios.

Who this book is for

Machine learning engineers and data scientists who want to move to ML engineering roles will find this AMLS book useful. Familiarity with the Azure ecosystem will help you understand the concepts covered.

What this book covers

Chapter 1, *Introducing the Azure Machine Learning Service*, introduces the basic concepts of the **Azure Machine Learning** (**AML**) service. You will create an AML workspace, create a compute instance, and connect AML to VS Code for further development in later chapters.

Chapter 2, *Working with Data in AMLS*, covers how to work with data in AMLS. In particular, you will learn how to load data, save data as datasets, and use datasets in later development projects.

Chapter 3, *Training Machine Learning Models in AMLS*, shows you how to train machine learning models using AMLS experiments as well as the code-free designer. You will see how to train jobs remotely and save models to the AMLS model registry for later use.

Chapter 4, *Tuning Your Models with AMLS*, demonstrates how to tune hyperparameters for your machine learning models using AMLS HyperDrive.

Chapter 5, *Azure Automated Machine Learning*, covers how to script an AutoML job to automatically train a machine learning model.

Chapter 6, *Deploying ML Models for Real-Time Inferencing*, teaches you how to deploy models in the AML to support real-time inferencing.

Chapter 7, *Deploying ML Models for Batch Scoring*, shows you how to apply batch scoring to models using AML batch endpoints.

Chapter 8, *Responsible AI*, teaches you how to explain your machine learning models using AMLS and Azure Interpret.

Chapter 9, *Productionizing Your Workload with MLOps*, has you setting up an Azure DevOps pipeline to orchestrate model training and deployment to multiple environments.

Chapter 10, *Using Deep Learning in Azure Machine Learning*, demonstrates how to label image data using Azure Machine Learning's Data Labeling feature, which we will use to train an object detection model. You will learn how to train an object detection model using AMLS AutoML and how to deploy the trained model for inferencing using AMLS.

Chapter 11, *Using Distributed Training in AMLS*, teaches how to perform distributed training in AMLS. In particular, you will learn how to train models in a distributed fashion using two popular deep learning frameworks, PyTorch and TensorFlow.

To get the most out of this book

To get the most out of this book, you will need to have an Azure subscription and the latest versions of Windows PowerShell and Command Prompt.

Software/hardware covered in the book	Operating system requirements
Windows PowerShell or Command Prompt	Windows, macOS, or Linux

If you are using the digital version of this book, we advise you to type the code yourself or access the code from the book's GitHub repository (a link is available in the next section). Doing so will help you avoid any potential errors related to the copying and pasting of code.

Download the example code files

You can download the example code files for this book from GitHub at `https://github.com/PacktPublishing/Azure-Machine-Learning-Engineering`. If there's an update to the code, it will be updated in the GitHub repository.

We also have other code bundles from our rich catalog of books and videos available at `https://github.com/PacktPublishing/`. Check them out!

Download the color images

We also provide a PDF file that has color images of the screenshots and diagrams used in this book. You can download it here: `https://packt.link/8s9Lt`.

Conventions used

There are a number of text conventions used throughout this book.

`Code in text`: Indicates code words in text, database table names, folder names, filenames, file extensions, pathnames, dummy URLs, user input, and Twitter handles. Here is an example: "The actual data file, which in this case is `titanic.csv`."

Any command-line input or output is written as follows:

```
az extension remove -n azure-cli-ml
az extension remove -n ml
```

Bold: Indicates a new term, an important word, or words that you see onscreen. For instance, words in menus or dialog boxes appear in **bold**. Here is an example: "The rest of the options are the default, and you can click on the **Review + create** button."

> Tips or important notes
> Appear like this.

Get in touch

Feedback from our readers is always welcome.

General feedback: If you have questions about any aspect of this book, email us at `customercare@packtpub.com` and mention the book title in the subject of your message.

Errata: Although we have taken every care to ensure the accuracy of our content, mistakes do happen. If you have found a mistake in this book, we would be grateful if you would report this to us. Please visit `www.packtpub.com/support/errata` and fill in the form.

Piracy: If you come across any illegal copies of our works in any form on the internet, we would be grateful if you would provide us with the location address or website name. Please contact us at `copyright@packt.com` with a link to the material.

If you are interested in becoming an author: If there is a topic that you have expertise in and you are interested in either writing or contributing to a book, please visit `authors.packtpub.com`.

Share Your Thoughts

Once you've read *Azure Machine Learning Engineering*, we'd love to hear your thoughts! Scan the QR code below to go straight to the Amazon review page for this book and share your feedback.

`https://packt.link/r/1-803-23930-1`

Your review is important to us and the tech community and will help us make sure we're delivering excellent quality content.

Preface   xix

Download a free PDF copy of this book

Thanks for purchasing this book!

Do you like to read on the go but are unable to carry your print books everywhere? Is your eBook purchase not compatible with the device of your choice?

Don't worry, now with every Packt book you get a DRM-free PDF version of that book at no cost.

Read anywhere, any place, on any device. Search, copy, and paste code from your favorite technical books directly into your application.

The perks don't stop there, you can get exclusive access to discounts, newsletters, and great free content in your inbox daily

Follow these simple steps to get the benefits:

1. Scan the QR code or visit the link below

https://packt.link/free-ebook/9781803239309

2. Submit your proof of purchase
3. That's it! We'll send your free PDF and other benefits to your email directly

Part 1: Training and Tuning Models with the Azure Machine Learning Service

Readers will learn how to use the Azure Machine Learning service to train and tune different types of models in *Part 1*, taking advantage of its unique job tracking capabilities.

This section has the following chapters:

- *Chapter 1, Introducing the Azure Machine Learning Service*
- *Chapter 2, Working with Data in AMLS*
- *Chapter 3, Training Machine Learning Models in AMLS*
- *Chapter 4, Tuning Your Models with AMLS*
- *Chapter 5, Azure Automated Machine Learning*

1
Introducing the Azure Machine Learning Service

Machine Learning (ML), leveraging data to build and train a model to make predictions, is rapidly maturing. **Azure Machine Learning** (**AML**) is Microsoft's cloud service, which not only enables model development but also your data science life cycle. AML is a tool designed to empower data scientists, ML engineers, and citizen data scientists. It provides a framework to train and deploy models empowered through **MLOps** to monitor, retrain, evaluate, and redeploy models in a collaborative environment backed by years of feedback from Microsoft's Fortune 500 customers.

In this chapter, we will focus on deploying an AML workspace, the resource that leverages Azure resources to provide an environment to bring together the assets you will leverage when you use AML. We will showcase how to deploy these resources using a **Guided User Interface** (**GUI**), followed by setting up your AML service via the **Azure Command-Line Interface (CLI) ml extension (v2)**, which is the ml extension for the Azure CLI, allowing model training and deployment through the command line. We will proceed with setting up the workspace by leveraging **Azure Resource Management** (**ARM**) templates, which are referred to as ARM deployments.

During deployment, key resources will be deployed, including **AML Studio**, a portal for data scientists to manage their workload, often referred to as your **workspace**; **Azure Key Vault** for storing sensitive information; **Application Insights** for logging information; **Azure Container Registry** to store docker images to leverage; and an **Azure storage account** to hold data. These resources will be leveraged behind the scenes as you navigate through the Azure Machine Learning service workspace, creating compute resources for writing code by leveraging the **Integrated Development Environments** (**IDE**) of your choice, including **Jupyter Notebook**, **Jupyter Lab**, as well as **VS Code**.

In this chapter, we will cover the following topics:

- Building your first AMLS workspace
- Navigating AMLS

- Creating a compute for writing code
- Developing within AMLS
- Connecting AMLS to VS Code

Technical requirements

In this section, you will sign up for an Azure account and use the web-based Azure portal to create various resources. As such, you will require internet access and a working web browser.

The following are the prerequisites for the chapter:

- Access to the internet
- A web browser, preferably Google Chrome or Microsoft Edge Chromium
- If you do not already have an Azure subscription, you can leverage the $200 Azure credit available for 30 days by following this link: https://azure.microsoft.com/en-us/free/.
- The Azure CLI >= 2.15.0
- The code leveraged throughout this book has been made available in the following repository: https://github.com/PacktPublishing/Azure-Machine-Learning-Engineering.git.
- You will be leveraging code from a GitHub repository:
    - https://github.com/Azure/azure-quickstart-templates/blob/master/quickstarts/microsoft.machinelearningservices/machine-learning-workspace/azuredeploy.json
    - https://github.com/Azure/azure-quickstart-templates/blob/master/quickstarts/microsoft.machinelearningservices/machine-learning-compute-create-computeinstance/azuredeploy.json

Building your first AMLS workspace

Within Azure, there are numerous ways to create Azure resources. The most common method is through the **Azure portal**, a web interface that allows you to create resources through a GUI. To automate the creation of resources, users can leverage the Azure CLI with the ml extension (V2), which provides you with a familiar terminal to automate deployment. You can also create resources using ARM templates. Both the CLI and the ARM templates provide an automatable, repeatable process to create resources in Azure.

In the upcoming subsections, we will first create an **AMLS workspace** through the web portal. After you have mastered this task, you will also create another workspace via the Azure CLI. Once you understand how the CLI works, you will create an ARM template and use it to deploy a third workspace. After learning about all three deployment methods, you will delete all excess resources before moving on to the next section; leaving excess resources up and running will cost you money, so be careful.

Creating an AMLS workspace through the Azure portal

Using the portal to create an AMLS workspace is the easiest, most straightforward approach. Through the GUI, you create a **resource group**, a container to hold multiple resources, along with your AMLS workspace and all its components. To create a workspace, navigate to https://portal.azure.com and follow these steps:

1. Navigate to https://portal.azure.com and type Azure Machine Learning into the search box as shown in *Figure 1.1* and press *Enter*:

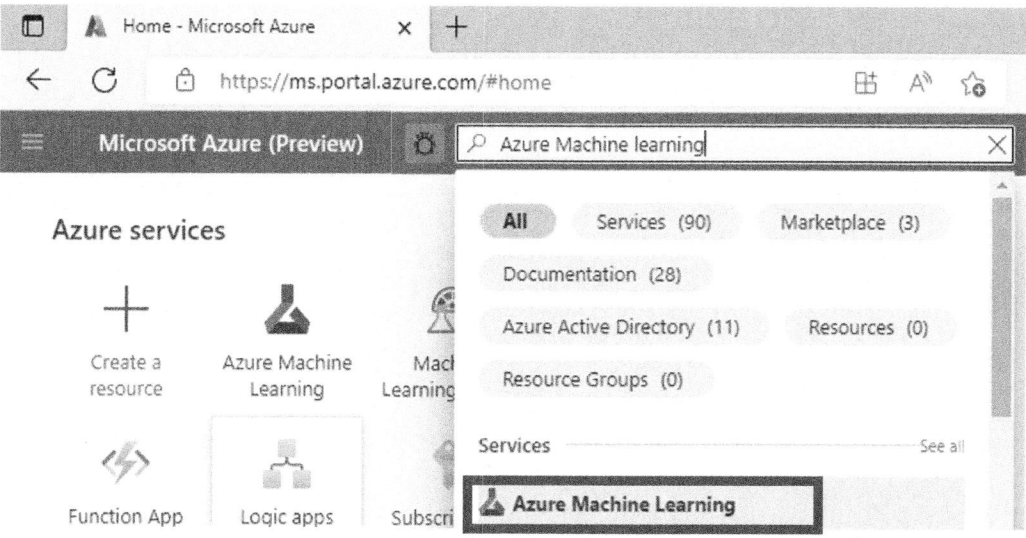

Figure 1.1 – Selecting resource groups

2. On the top left of the Azure portal, select the **+ Create** option shown in *Figure 1.2*:

Figure 1.2 – Creating an AML workspace

Selecting the **+ Create** option will bring up the **Basics** tab as shown here:

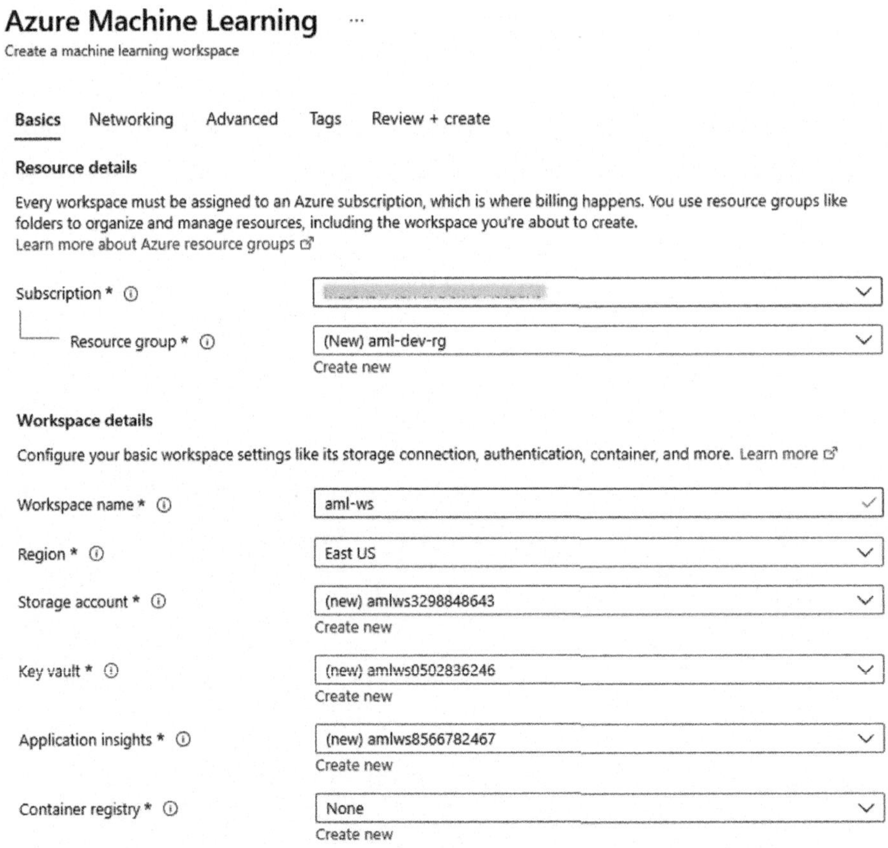

Figure 1.3 – Filling in the corresponding fields to create the ML workspace

3. In the **Basics** tab shown in *Figure 1.3* for creating your AML workspace, populate the following values:

    A. **Subscription**: The Azure subscription you would like to deploy your resource.

    B. **Resource group**: Click on **Create new** and enter a name for a resource group. In Azure, resource groups can be thought of as folder, or container that holds resources for a particular solution. As we deploy the AMLS workspace, the resources will be deployed into this resource group to ensure we can easily delete the resources after performing this exercise.

    C. **Workspace name**: The name of the AMLS workspace resource.

    D. The rest of the options are the default, and you can click on the **Review + create** button.

4. This will cause validation to occur – once the information has been validated, click on the + **Create** button to deploy your resources.

5. It usually takes a few minutes for the workspace to be created. Once the deployment is completed, click on **Go to resource** in the Azure portal and then click on **Launch studio** to go to the AMLS workspace.

    You are now on the landing page for AMLS as shown in *Figure 1.4*:

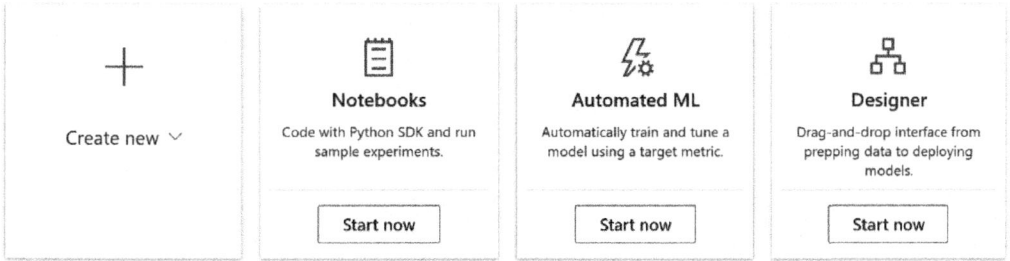

Figure 1.4 – AMLS

Congratulations! You have now successfully built your first AMLS workspace. While you can start by loading in data right now, take the time to walk through the next section to learn how to create it via code.

Creating an AMLS workspace through the Azure CLI

For people who prefer a code-first approach to creating resources, the *Azure CLI* is the perfect fit. At the time of writing, the AML CLI v2 is the most up-to-date extension for the Azure CLI available. While leveraging the Azure CLI v2, assets are defined by leveraging a YAML file, as we will see in later chapters.

> **Note**
> The Azure CLI v2 uses commands that follow a format of `az ml <noun> <verb> <options>`.

To create an AMLS workspace via the Azure CLI `ml` extension (v2), follow these steps:

1. You need to install the Azure CLI from https://docs.microsoft.com/en-us/cli/azure/install-azure-cli.

2. Find your subscription ID. In the Azure portal in the search box, you can type Subscriptions, and bring up a list of Azure subscriptions and the ID of the subscriptions. For the subscription that you would like to use, copy the **Subscription ID** information to use it with the CLI.

   Here's a view of **Subscriptions** within the Azure portal:

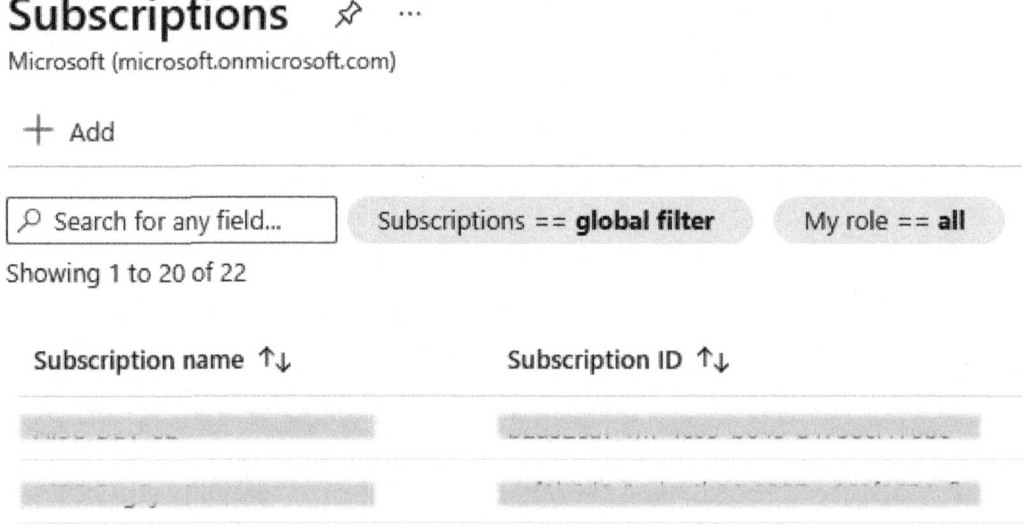

Figure 1.5 – Azure subscription list

3. Launch your **command-line interpreter** (**CLI**) based on your OS – for example, **Command Prompt** (**CMD**) or **Windows Powershell** (**Windows PS**) – and check your version of the Azure CLI by running the following command:

   ```
   az version
   ```

> **Note**
> You will need to have a version of the Azure CLI that is greater than 2.15.0 to leverage the `ml` extension.

4. You will need to remove old extensions if they are installed for your CLI to work properly. You can remove the old `ml` extensions by running the following commands:

   ```
   az extension remove -n azure-cli-ml
   az extension remove -n ml
   ```

5. To install the `ml` extension, run the following command:

   ```
   az extension add -n ml -y
   ```

6. Now, let's connect to your subscription in Azure through the Azure CLI by running the following command here, replacing xxxxxxxx-xxxx-xxxx-xxxx-xxxxxxxxxxxx with the **Subscription ID** information you found in *Figure 1.5*:

   ```
   az login
   az account set --subscription xxxxxxxx-xxxx-xxxx-xxxx-xxxxxxxxxxxx
   ```

7. Create a resource group by running the following command. Please note that `rg_name` is an example name for the resource group, just as `aml-ws` is an example name for an AML workspace:

   ```
   az group create --name aml-dev-rg --location eastus2
   ```

8. Create an AML workspace by running the following command, noting that `eastus2` is the Azure region in which we will deploy this AML workspace:

   ```
   az ml workspace create -n aml-ws -g aml-dev-rg -l eastus2
   ```

You have now created an AMLS workspace with the Azure CLI `ml` extension and through the portal. There's one additional way to create an AMLS workspace that's commonly used, ARM templates, which we will take a look at next.

Creating an AMLS workspace with ARM templates

ARM templates can be challenging to write, but they provide you with a way to easily automate and parameterize the creation of Azure resources. In this section, you will first write a simple ARM template to build an AMLS workspace and then deploy your template using the Azure CLI. To do so, take the following steps:

1. An ARM template can be downloaded from GitHub and is found here: https://github.com/Azure/azure-quickstart-templates/blob/master/quickstarts/microsoft.machinelearningservices/machine-learning-workspace/azuredeploy.json.

   This template creates the following Azure services:

   - **Azure Storage Account**
   - **Azure Key Vault**
   - **Azure Application Insights**
   - **Azure Container Registry**
   - **An AML workspace**

   The example template has three required parameters:

   - environment, where the resources will be created
   - name, which is the name that we are giving to the AMLS workspace
   - location, the Azure Region the resource will be deployed to

2. To deploy your template, you have to create a resource group first as follows:

   ```
   az group create --name rg_name --location eastus2
   ```

3. Make sure your command prompt is opened to the location to which you downloaded the azuredeploy.json file, and run the following command:

   ```
   az deployment group create --name "exampledeployment" --resource-group "rg_name" --template-file "azuredeploy.json" --parameters name="uniquename" environment="dev" location="eastus2"
   ```

   It will take a few minutes for the workspace to be created.

We have covered a lot of information so far, whether creating an AMLS workspace using the portal, the CLI, or now using ARM templates. In the next section, we will show you how to navigate the workspace, often referred to as the studio.

Navigating AMLS

AMLS provides access to key resources for a data science team to leverage. In this section, you will learn how to navigate AMLS exploring the key components found within the studio. You will learn briefly about its capabilities, which we will cover in detail in the rest of the chapters.

Open a browser and go to https://portal.azure.com. Log in with your Azure AD credentials. Once logged into the portal, you will see several icons. Select the **Resource group** icon and click on the **Azure Machine Learning** resource.

In the **Overview** page, click on the **Launch Studio** button as seen in the following screenshot:

Manage your machine learning lifecycle

Use the Azure Machine Learning studio to build, train, evaluate, and deploy machine learning models. Learn more

Launch studio

Figure 1.6 – Launch studio

Clicking on the icon shown in *Figure 1.6* will open AMLS in a new window.

The studio launch will bring you to the main home page of AMLS. The UI includes functionality to match several personas, including **no-code**, **low-code**, and **code-based** ML. The main page has two sections – the left-hand menu pane and the right-hand workspace pane.

The AMLS workspace home screen is shown in *Figure 1.7*:

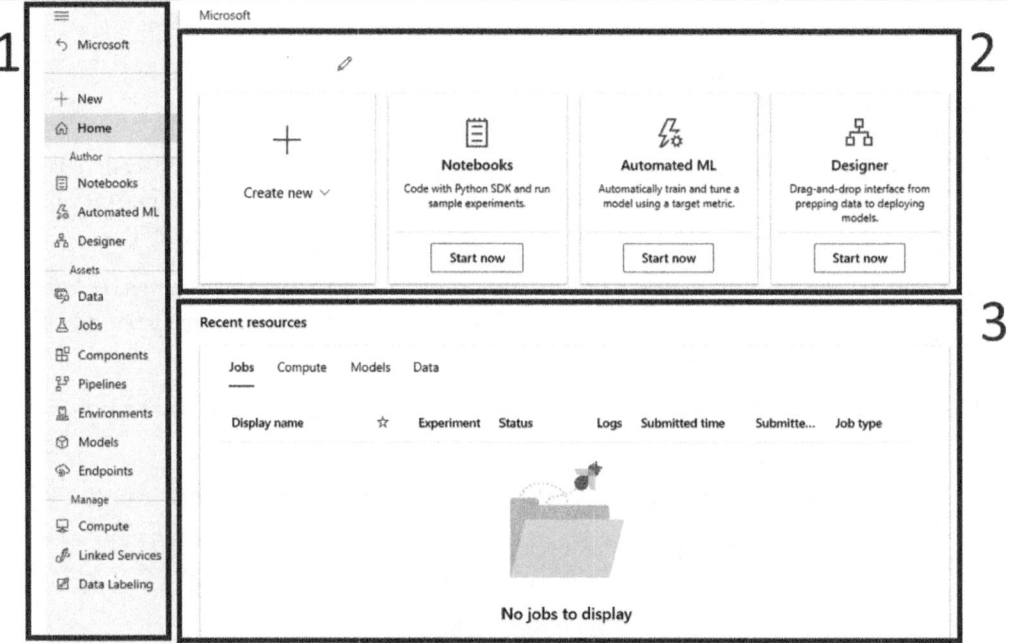

Figure 1.7 – AMLS workspace home screen

Now, let us understand the preceding screenshot in brief:

- In section **1** of *Figure 1.7*, the left-hand menu pane is displayed. Clicking on any of the words in this pane will bring up a new right workspace pane, which includes sections **2** and **3** of the screen. We can select any of these keywords to quickly access key resources within our AMLS workspace. We will drill into these key resources as we begin exploring the AMLS workspace.

- In section **2** of *Figure 1.7*, quick links are provided to key resources that we will leverage throughout this book, enabling AMLS users to create new items covering the varying personas supported.

- As we continue to explore our environment and dig into creating assets within the AMLS workspace, both with code-based and low-code options, recent resources will begin to appear in section **3** of *Figure 1.7*, providing users with the ability to see recently leveraged resources, whether the compute, the code execution, the models created, or the datasets that are leveraged.

The home page provides quick access to the key resources found within your AMLS workspace. In addition to the quick links, scroll down and you can view the **Documentation** section. In the **Documentation** section, we see great documentation to get you started in understanding how to best leverage your AML environment.

The **Documentation** section, a hub for documentation resources, is displayed on the right pane of the AMLS home screen:

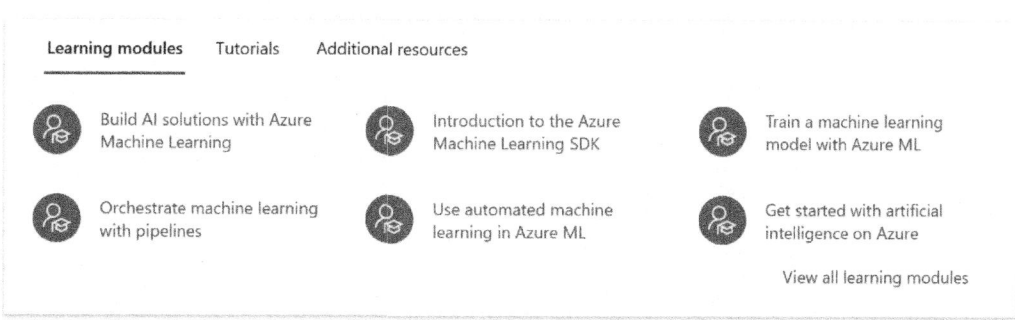

Figure 1.8 – Documentation

As shown in *Figure 1.8*, the AMLS home page provides you with a wealth of documentation resources to get you started. The links include training modules, tutorials, and even blogs regarding how to leverage AMLS.

On the top-right side of the page, there are several options available:

- **Notifications**: The bell icon represents notifications, which display the messages that are generated as you leverage your AMLS workspace. These messages will contain information regarding the creation and deletion of resources, as well as information regarding the resources running within your workspace.

Figure 1.9 – Top-right options

- **Settings**: The icon next to the bell that appears as a gear showcases settings for your Azure portal. Clicking on the icon provides the ability to set basic settings as shown in *Figure 1.10*:

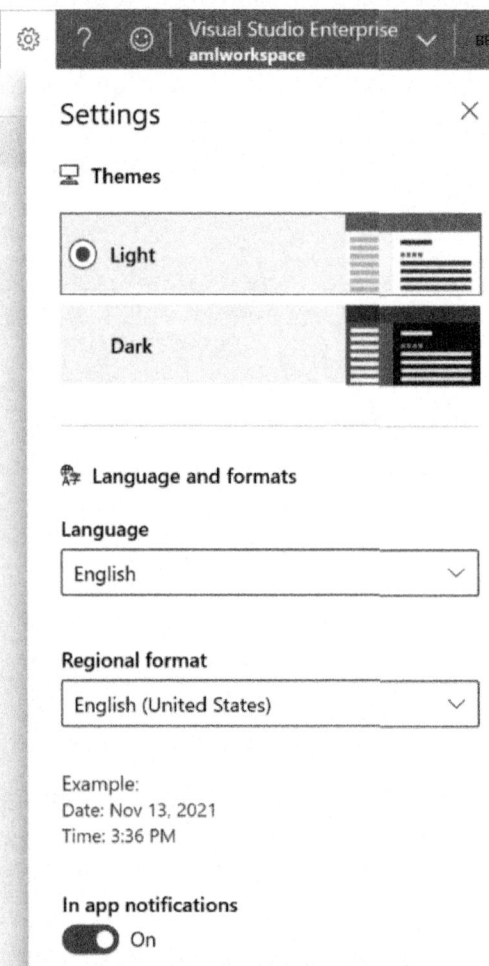

Figure 1.10 – Settings for workspace customization

Within the **Settings** blade, options are available to change the background of the workspace UI with themes. There are light and dark shades available. Then, there is a section for changing the preferred language and formats. Check the **Language** dropdown for a list of languages – the list of languages will change as new languages are added to the workspace.

- **Help**: The question mark icon provides helpful resources, from tutorials to placing support requests. This is where all the **Help** content is organized:

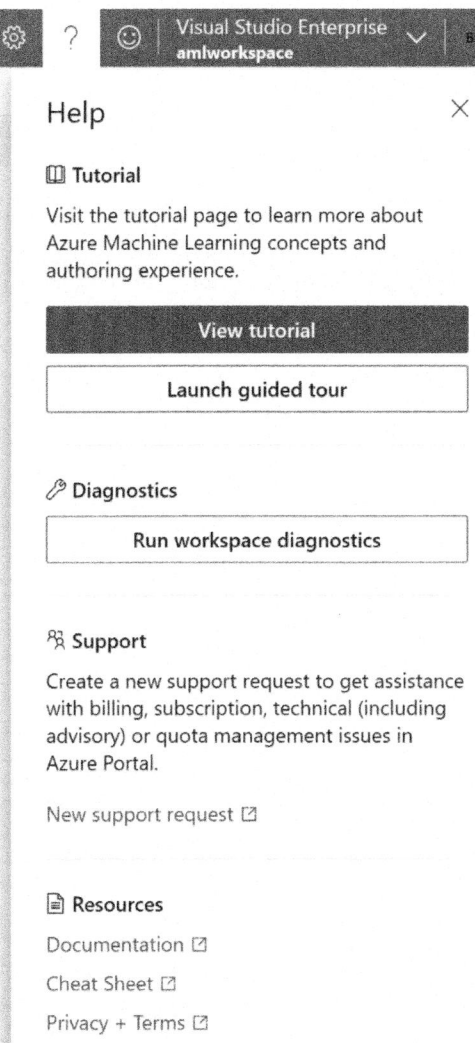

Figure 1.11 – Help for AMLS workspace support

Links are provided for tutorials on how to use the workspace and how to develop and deploy data science projects. Click on **Launch guided tour** to use the step-by-step guided tour.

To troubleshoot any issue with a workspace, click on **Run workspace diagnostics** and follow the instructions:

- **Support**: This is the section where technical and subscription core limits, and other Azure-related issues, are linked to create a ticket.
- **Resources**: This is the section that provides links to the AML documentation, as well as a useful cheat sheet that is hosted on GitHub. A link to Microsoft's **Privacy and Terms** is also available in this section.

Clicking on the smiley icon will bring up the **Send us feedback** section:

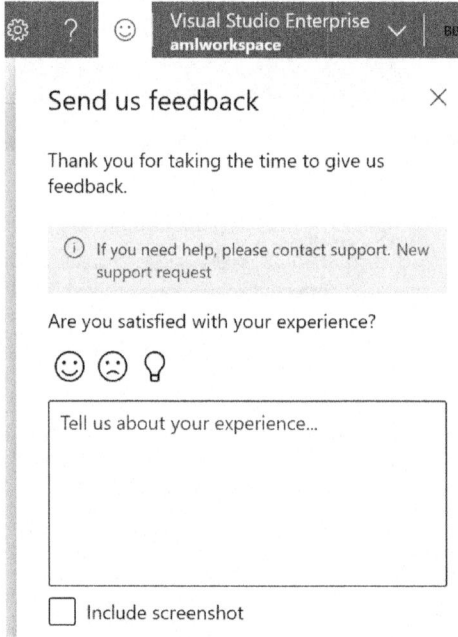

Figure 1.12 – Feedback page

Leveraging this section, an AMLS workspace user can provide feedback to the AMLS product team.

In the following screenshot, we can see the workspace selection menu:

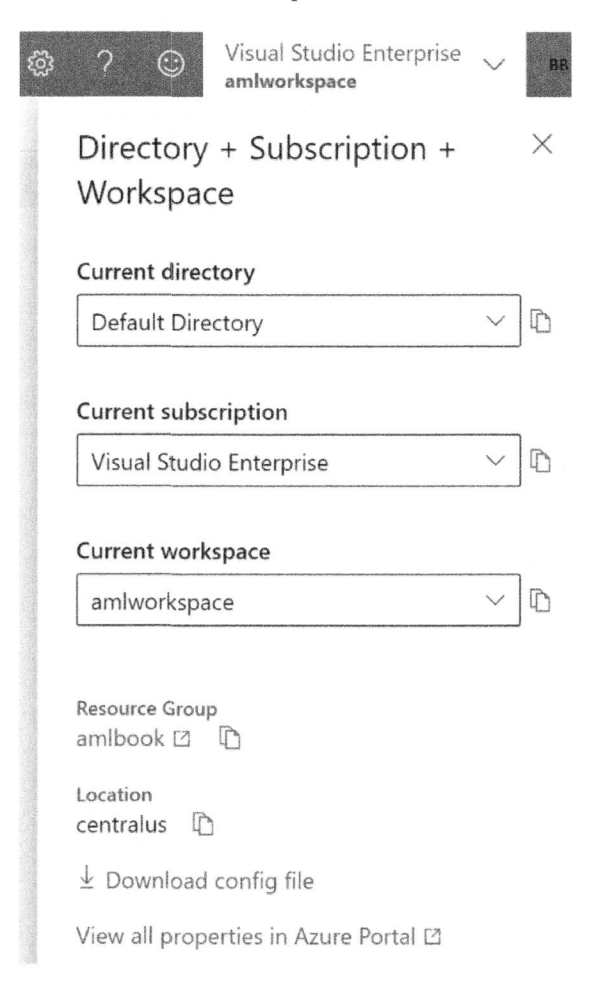

Figure 1.13 – Workspace selection menu

When working with multiple workspaces on multiple projects, there may be a need to switch the AMLS workspace between multiple Azure AD directories. This option is available via the selection of the subscription and workspace name as shown in *Figure 1.13*. Also note, under the **Resource Group** section, a link will open a new tab in your browser and bring you directly to your resource group in the Azure portal. This is a nice feature, allowing you to quickly explore the Azure resources that are outside of the AMLS workspace but may be relevant to your workload in Azure. The workspace `config` file, which holds the key information enabling authorized users to connect directly to the AMLS workspace through code, can be downloaded to use with the **Azure Machine Learning SDK for Python** (**AML SDK v2**) inside the workspace selection menu.

Next, we will discuss the AMLS left-hand navigation menu shown in *Figure 1.7* (**1**). This navigation menu will allow you to interact with your assets within your AML environment and is divided into three sections:

- The **Author** section, which includes **Notebooks**, **Automated ML**, and **Designer**
- The **Assets** section includes artifacts that will be created as part of your data science workload, which will be explored in detail in upcoming chapters.
- The **Manage** section, which includes resources that will be leveraged as part of your data science workload.

Let's review the sections as follows:

- **Author** is the section in which the data scientist selects the tool of choice for development:
    - **Notebooks**: This is a section within the **Author** portion of the menu that provides access to your files, as well as an AMLS workspace IDE, which is similar to a Jupyter notebook, but with a few extra features for data scientists to carry out feature engineering and modeling. Inside this IDE, with a notebook that has been created, users can select a version of Python kernel, connecting them to a Conda environment with a specified version of Python.

Figure 1.14 – Author menu items

Notebooks is an option within the **Author** section providing access to files, samples, file management, terminal access, and, as we will see later in this chapter in the *Developing within AMLS* section, a built-in IDE:

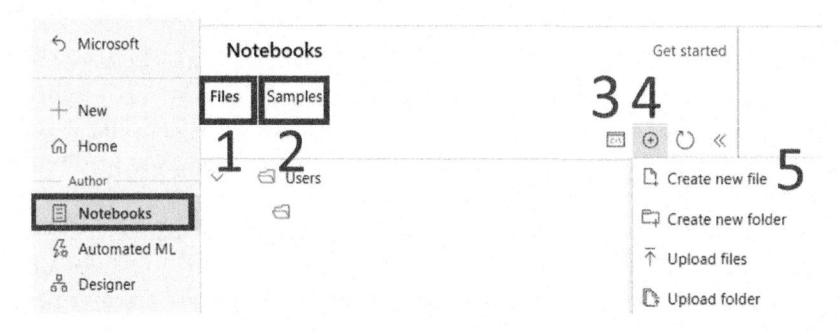

Figure 1.15 – Notebooks

We will highlight the different features found within the **Notebooks** selection:

  i. In section **1** of *Figure 1.15*, clicking on the **Files** label shows all the user directories within the collaborative AMLS workspace, in addition to files stored within those directories.

  ii. In section 2 of *Figure 1.15*, clicking on the **Samples** label provides AML tutorials for getting the most out of AMLS.

  iii. Additionally, there is the capability to leverage a terminal on your compute resource.

In this section, you can create new files. Clicking on the + icon gives you the ability to create new files. Note that both files and folder directories can be uploaded as well as created. This allows you to easily upload data files in addition to code.

Create **new file** has options to name the file and select what type of file it is, such as a Jupyter notebook or Python. Typically, data scientists will create new Jupyter notebooks, but in addition to the `.ipynb` extension, the menu for **File type** includes Jupyter, Python, R, Shell, text, and other, in which you can provide your own file extension.

In the left-hand navigation menu of *Figure 1.7*, we saw **Notebooks**, which we briefly reviewed, as well as **Automated ML** and **Designer**. We will next provide a high-level overview of the **Automated ML** section.

- **Automated ML**: This can also be selected from the **Author** section. **Automated ML** is a no-code-required tool that provides the ability to leverage data and select an ML model type and compute to accomplish model creation. In future chapters, we will go through this in more detail, but at a high level, this option provides a walk-through to establish a model based on the dataset provided. You will be prompted to pick classification, regression, or time-series forecasting; natural language processing (multi-class or multi-label classification); or compute vision (including multi-class, label, object detection, and instance segmentation) based on your data science workload. It's a guided step-by-step process. There are settings available to stop the model from overrunning past a set duration to ensure that unexpected costs are limited. **Automated ML** also provides the ability to exclude algorithms. AML will select a variety of algorithms and run them with a dataset to provide the best model available. In addition to the capability to run multiple algorithms to determine the best model based on a given dataset, **Automated ML** also includes model explainability, providing insight into which features are more or less important in determining the response variable. The timing required for this process is dependent on the dataset, as well as the compute resources allocated to the task. Automated ML uses an ad-hoc compute, so when the experiment is submitted to run, it starts the compute and then runs the experiment. Building the models is run inside an experiment as a job, which is saved as a snapshot for future analysis. After the best model is built with **Automated ML**, AMLS provides the ability to leverage the best model with a single-click deployment of a REST API hosted in an **Azure Container Instance** (**ACI**) for development and test environments. AMLS can also support production workloads with a REST API deployment to **Azure Kubernetes Services** (**AKS**) and leveraging the CLI v2 or the SDK v2 AMLS supports **endpoints** that streamline the process of model deployment.

Clicking on **Automated ML** in the left-hand menu tab opens the ability to create a new **Automated ML** job:

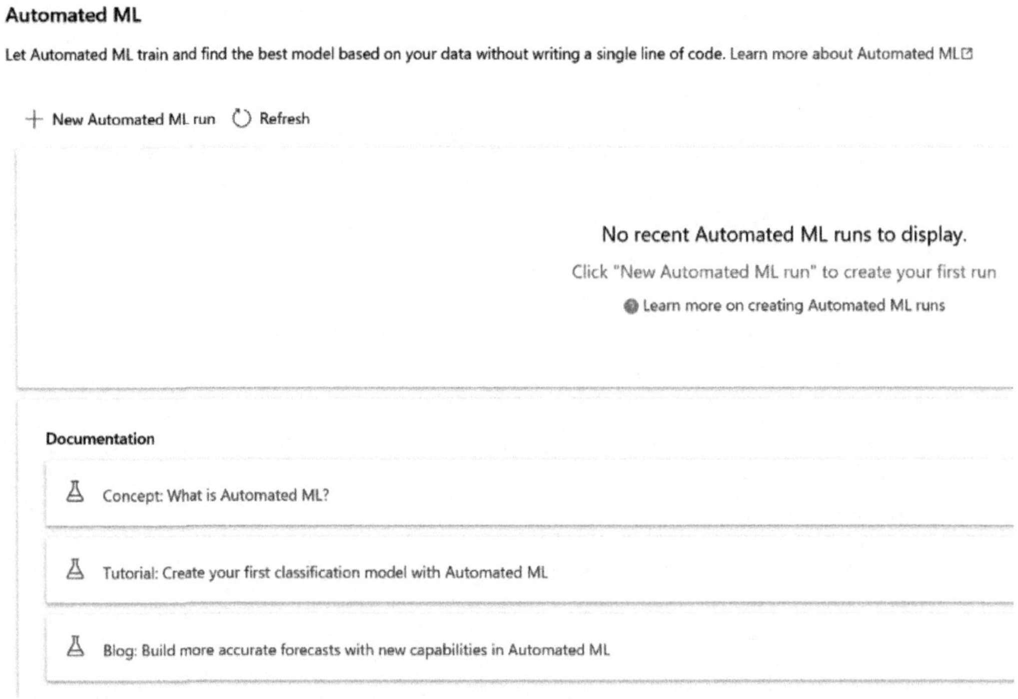

Automated ML

Let Automated ML train and find the best model based on your data without writing a single line of code. Learn more about Automated ML

+ New Automated ML run   ⟳ Refresh

No recent Automated ML runs to display.
Click "New Automated ML run" to create your first run
● Learn more on creating Automated ML runs

Documentation

⚗ Concept: What is Automated ML?

⚗ Tutorial: Create your first classification model with Automated ML

⚗ Blog: Build more accurate forecasts with new capabilities in Automated ML

Figure 1.16 – Automated ML screen with options

Now that we have seen the **Notebooks** and **Automated ML** sections, we will look at the **Designer** section for a low-code experience.

- **Designer**: This is the section where low-code environments are provided. Data scientists can drag and drop and develop model training and validation. **Designer** has two sections – to the left is the menu and to the right is the authoring section for development. Once the model is built, an option to deploy it in various forms is provided.

Here is a sample experiment built with **Designer**:

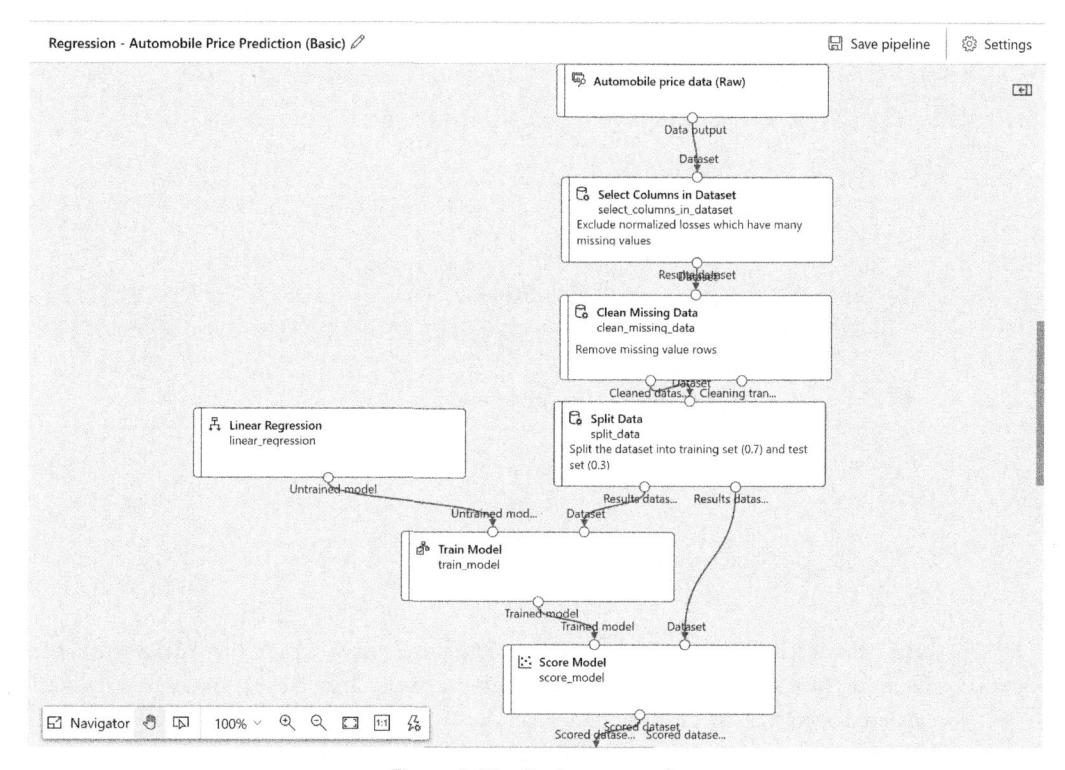

Figure 1.17 – Designer sample

Designer provides options to model with several types of ML models, such as classification, regression, clustering, recommendation, computer vision, and text analytics.

Now that we have reviewed the sections for authoring a model – **Notebooks**, **Automated ML**, and **Designer** – we will explore the concept of assets in the AMLS **Assets** navigation section.

- **Assets** is a section where all the experiment jobs and their artifacts are stored:

Figure 1.18 – Assets menu items

- **Data**: This section will display the registered datasets used within the AMLS workspace under the **Data assets** tab. Datasets manage the versions created every time a new dataset is registered. Datasets can be created through the UI, SDK, or CLI. When a dataset is created, a data store (the resource hosting the data) is also provided:

    - **Data assets**: This displays a list of the datasets leveraged within the workspace:

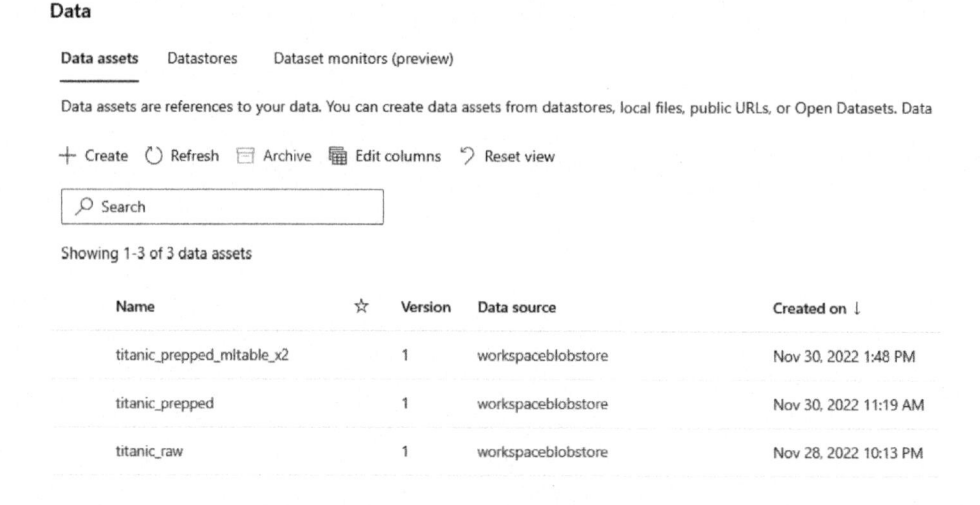

Figure 1.19 – The Datasets display

Click on **Data assets** and see the list of all data sets used. The UI displaying datasets can be customized by adding and deleting columns to your view. In addition to providing the ability to register datasets through the UI, there is also the ability to archive a dataset by clicking on **Archive**. The data in a repository may change over time as applications add in data.

- **Datastores**: Within the **Data** section of the left-hand pane menu, can also be selected. Data stores can be thought of as locations for retrieving data. Examples of data stores include Azure Blob storage, an Azure file share, Azure Data Lake Storage, or an Azure database, including SQL, PostgreSQL, and MySQL. All the security for connecting to a data store associated with your AMLS workspace and stored in Azure Key Vault. During the AMLS workspace deployment, an Azure Blob storage account was created. This Azure Blob storage account is your default datastore for your AMLS workspace.

- A registered dataset can be monitored with functionality that is currently in preview, which can be reviewed by clicking on the **Dataset monitors (preview)** label shown in *Figure 1.19*.

- **Jobs**: The **Jobs** screen shows all the experiments, which are groups of jobs, and the execution of code within your AMLS workspace:

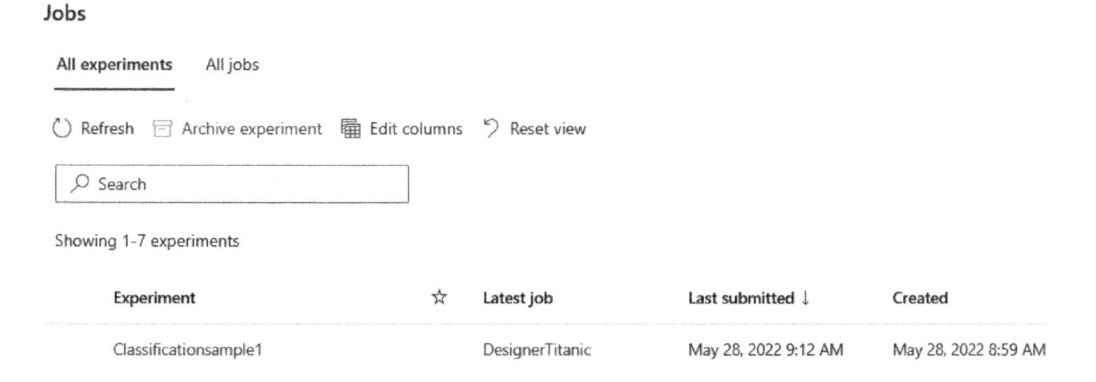

Figure 1.20 – The Experiments display

You can customize and reset the default view in the UI for jobs by adding columns or deleting columns, the properties of a given job.

Each experiment will display as blue text under **Experiment** as in *Figure 1.20*. Within the **Jobs** section, we can select multiple experiments and see charts on their performance.

- **Pipelines**: A pipeline is a sequence of steps performed within the job of an experiment:

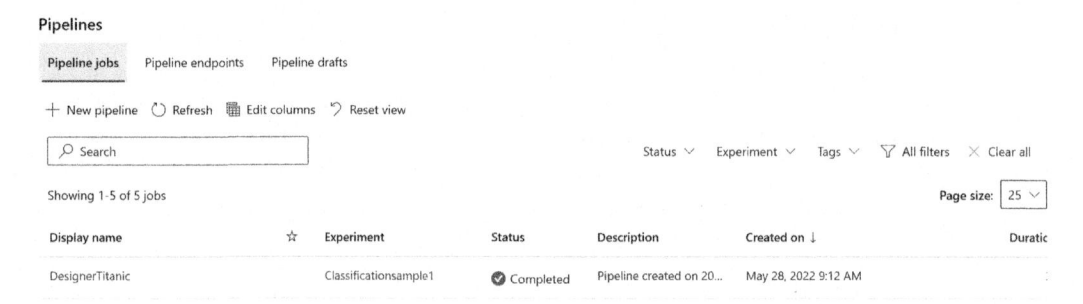

Figure 1.21 – The Pipelines display

Usually, designer experiments will show the pipeline and provide statuses for the job. As with the UIs for **Jobs** and **Datasets**, the UI provides customization when viewing pipelines. You can also display **Pipeline endpoints**. The **Pipeline drafts** option is also available. You can sort or filter the view by **Status**, **Experiment**, or **Tags**. Options to select all filters and clear filters are also available. The option to select how many rows to display is also available.

- **Environments**: Setting up a Python environment can be a difficult task, as with the value of leveraging open source packages comes the complexity of managing the versions of various packages. While this problem is not unique to the AMLS workspace, Azure has created a solution for managing these resources – in AMLS, they are called **environments**. **Environments** is a section in AMLS that allows users to view and register which packages, and which Docker images, should be leveraged by the compute resources. Microsoft has already created several of these environments, which are considered curated, and users can also create their own custom environments. We will be leveraging custom environments in *Chapter 3, Training Machine Learning Models in AMLS*, as we run experiment jobs on compute clusters.

The **Environments** section provides a list of environments leveraged by the AMLS workspace:

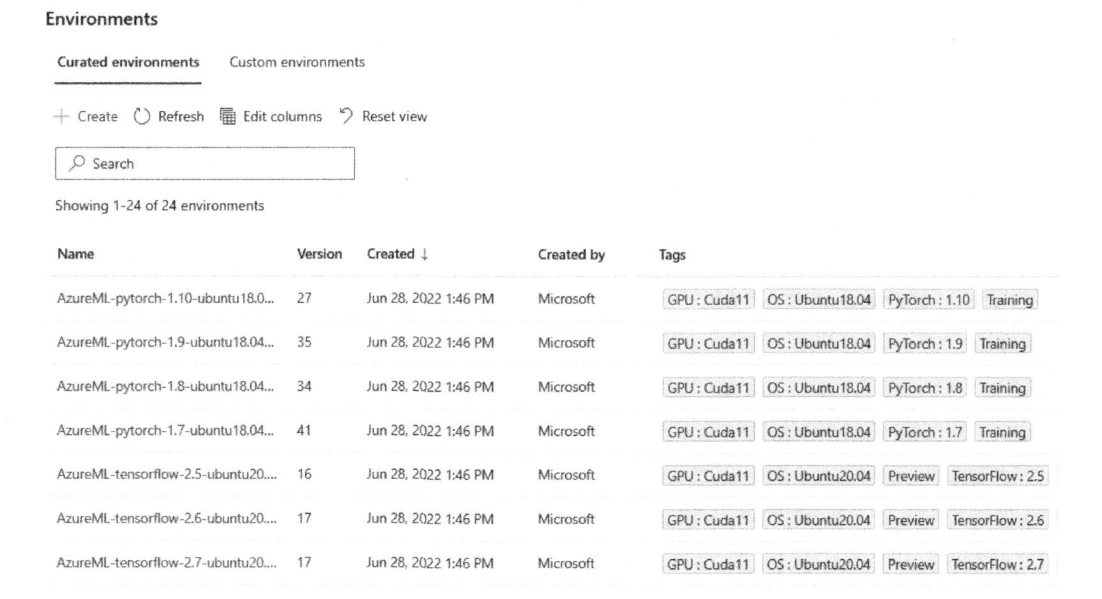

Figure 1.22 – Environments

In the **Curated environments** section, there is a wide variety of environments to select from. This is useful for applications that need specific environments with libraries. The list of environments created is available for selection. Click on each **Name** to see what is included in the environment. For now, most of the following environments are used for inference purposes.

- **Models**: The **Models** section shows all the models registered and their versions. The UI provides customization of columns as shown in the following screenshot:

Figure 1.23 – The Models display

Models can be registered manually, through the SDK, or through the CLI. The options to change how many models to display, to show the current version or all versions of the model, and the ability to sort and filter and then clear are all available.

- **Endpoints**: Models can be deployed as REST endpoints. These endpoints leverage the model, and with predicted values, provide a response based on the trained model. Leveraging the REST protocol, these models can easily be consumed by other applications. Clicking on **Endpoints** on the left-hand navigation menu of AMLS will bring these up.

The **Endpoints** section displays endpoints for both real-time and batch inferencing:

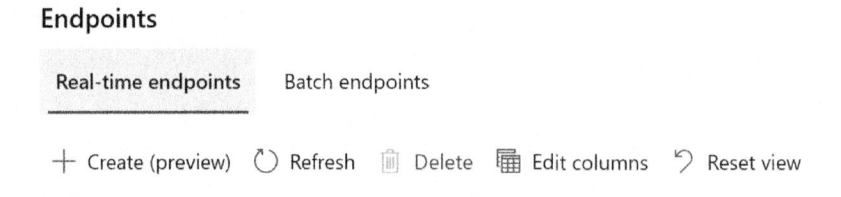

Figure 1.24 – The Endpoint display

Real-time endpoints are referred to as online endpoints and typically take a single row of data and produce a score output, and they are performant as a REST API. Batch endpoints are for batch-based execution, where we pass large datasets and are then provided with the predicted output. This is usually a long-running process. While CLI v1 and the SDK v1 allow AMLS users to deploy to ACI and Kubernetes, this book will focus on deployments leveraging CLI v2 and SDK v2, which leverage endpoints to deploy to managed online endpoints, Kubernetes online endpoints, and batch inference endpoints.

- **Manage** is the section in which users can manage resources leveraged by the AMLS workspace, including **Compute**, **Data Labeling**, and **Linked Services**:

    - **Compute**: This is where we manage various compute for developing data science projects. There are four types of compute resources found within the **Compute** section in AMLS. These four include **Compute instances**, **Compute clusters**, **Inference clusters**, and **Attached computes**.

The **Compute** section provides visibility into the compute resources leveraged with an AMLS workspace:

Figure 1.25 – Compute options

A compute can be a single node or include several **nodes**. A node is a **Virtual Machine** (**VM**) instance. A single node instance can vertically scale and will be limited to a **Central Processing Unit** (**CPU**) and **Graphics Processing Unit** (**GPU**). Compute instances are single nodes. These resources are great for development work. Compute clusters, on the other hand, can be scaled horizontally and can be used for workloads with larger datasets, as the workload can be distributed across the nodes. To enable scaling, jobs can be performed in parallel to effectively scale the training and scoring using our AML SDK.

Within the **Compute** section, as compute resources are created, the available quota for your subscription is displayed, providing visibility into the number of cores that are available for a given subscription. Most Azure VM SKUs are available for compute resources. For the GPU, depending on the region, users can create support requests to extend vCores if they are available in the region. When creating compute clusters, the number of nodes leveraged by the compute cluster can be set to from 0 to N nodes.

Compute resources in an AMLS workspace incur a cost per node on an hourly basis. On a compute cluster, setting the minimum number of nodes to 0 will shut down the compute resources when an experiment completes after the Idle seconds before scale down is reached. For a compute instance, there is the option to schedule when to switch on or off the instance to save money. In addition to compute instances and compute clusters, AMLS has the concept of inference clusters. **Inference clusters** in the **Compute** section allows you to view or create an AKS cluster. The last type of compute available within the compute section is under the **Attached computes** section. This section allows you to attach your own compute resources, including **Azure Databricks**, **Synapse Spark pools**, **HDInsights**, VMs, and others.

- **Data Labeling**: Data Labeling is a newer feature option added to AMLS. This feature is for projects that tag images for custom vision-based modeling. Images are labeled within an AMLS **Data Labeling** project. Multiple users can label images within one project. To further improve productivity, there is ML-assisted data labeling. Within a labeling project, both text and images can be labeled. For image projects, labeling tasks include **Image Classification Multi-class**, which involves classifying an image from a set of classes, and **Image Classification Multi-label**, which applies more labels from a set of classes. There is also **Object identification**, which defines a bounding box to each object found in an image, and finally, **Instance Segmentation**, which provides a polygon around an image and assigns a class label. **Text** projects, include **Multi-class** and **Multi-label** and **Text Named Entity Recognition** options. **Multi-class** will apply a single label to text, while **Multi-label** allows you to apply one or more labels to a piece of text. **Text Named Entity Recognition** allows users to provide one or more entities for a piece of text.

The **Data Labeling** feature requires a GPU-enabled compute, due to its compute-intensive nature. An option to provide project instructions is available. Every user will be assigned a queue and the user's progress in the project is also shown on a dashboard for each project.

The following screenshot shows how a sample labeling project is displayed:

Figure 1.26 – Data Labeling

- **Linked Services**: This provides you with integration with other Microsoft products, currently including Azure Synapse Analytics so that you can attach Apache Spark pools. Click on the **+ Add integration** button to select from an Azure subscription followed by a Synapse workspace.

    Linked Services, as seen in the following screenshot, provides visibility into established connections with other Microsoft products:

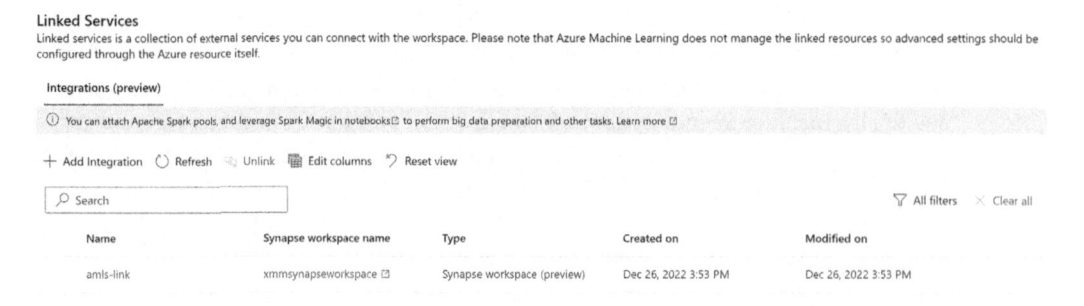

Figure 1.27 – Linked Services

Through this linked service, which is currently in public preview, AMLS can leverage an Azure Synapse workspace, bringing the power of an Apache Spark pool into your AMLS environment. A large component of a data science workload includes data preparation, and through **Linked Services**, data transformation can be delivered leveraging Spark.

With a basic understanding of the AMLS workspace, you can now move on to writing code. Before you do that, however, you need to create a VM that will power your jobs. **Compute instances** are AMLS VMs specifically for writing code. They come in many shapes and sizes and can be created via the AMLS GUI, the Azure CLI, Python code, or ARM templates. Each user is required to have their own compute instance, as AMLS allows only one user per compute instance.

We will begin by creating a compute instance via the AMLS GUI. Then, we will add a schedule to our compute instance so that it starts up and shuts down automatically; this is an important cost-saving measure. Next, we will create a compute instance by using the Azure CLI. Finally, we will create a compute instance with a schedule enabled with an ARM template. Even though you will create three compute instances, there is no need to delete them, as you only pay for them while they are in use.

> **Tip**
> When you're not using a compute instance, make sure it is shut down. Leaving compute instances up and running incurs an hourly cost.

In this section, we have navigated through AMLS, leveraging the left-hand navigation menu pane. We explored the **Author**, **Assets**, and **Manage** sections and each of the components found within AMLS. Now that we have covered navigating the components of AMLS, let us continue with creating a compute so that you can begin to write code in AMLS.

Creating a compute for writing code

In this section, you will create a compute instance to begin your development. Each subsection will demonstrate how to create these resources in your AMLS workspace following different methods.

Creating a compute instance through the AMLS GUI

The most straightforward way to create a compute instance is through AMLS. Compute instances come in many sizes and you should adjust them to accommodate the size of your data. A good rule of thumb is that you should have 20 times the amount of RAM as the size of your data in CSV format, or 2 times the amount of RAM as the size of your data in a **pandas DataFrame**, the most popular Python data structure for data science. This is because, when you read in a CSV file as a pandas DataFrame, it expands the data by up to a factor of 10.

The compute name must be unique within a given Azure region, so you will need to make sure that the name of your compute resources is unique or the deployment will fail.

Introducing the Azure Machine Learning Service

Now, let's create a compute instance – a single VM-type compute that can be used for development. Each compute instance is assigned to a single user in the workspace for them to develop.

To create a compute instance, follow these steps:

1. Log in to the AMLS workspace.
2. Click on **Compute** in the left-hand menu.
3. Click on **New**.

   A new tab will open to configure our compute instance. The following screenshot showcases the creation of a compute instance:

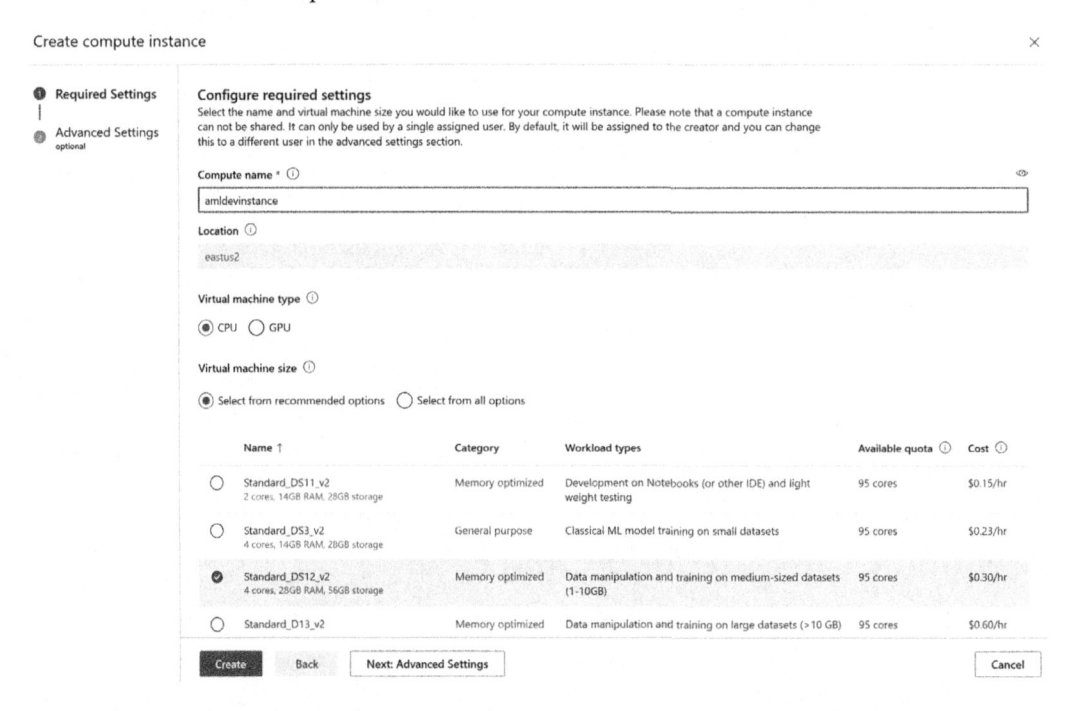

Figure 1.28 – Selecting the VM type and region

Under **Configure required settings**, shown in *Figure 1.28*, let's execute the following steps:

4. You need to provide a name for your compute instance. Let's name the compute instance `amldevinstance`. Note that the name of the compute instance will need to be unique for a given Azure region. Given that this name will likely already be used, in practice, you can provide a prefix or suffix to your compute name to ensure its uniqueness.

5. Set **Virtual machine type** to **CPU**. **GPU** can also be selected for high-power deep learning models. Now, set **Virtual machine size**. The size allocation will display the nodes based on the quota available.
6. Pick a VM size from the list of available CPUs.
7. Click on **Next: Advanced Settings**.
8. Turn on **Enable SSH access** if you want to use the compute instance from a remote machine. The **Enable virtual network** option is available to connect to a private network connected to a corporate network. An option to assign the compute to another user (**Assign to another user**) is also available. If there is any shell script to provision in the startup, please use the **Provision with setup script** option:

Create compute instance

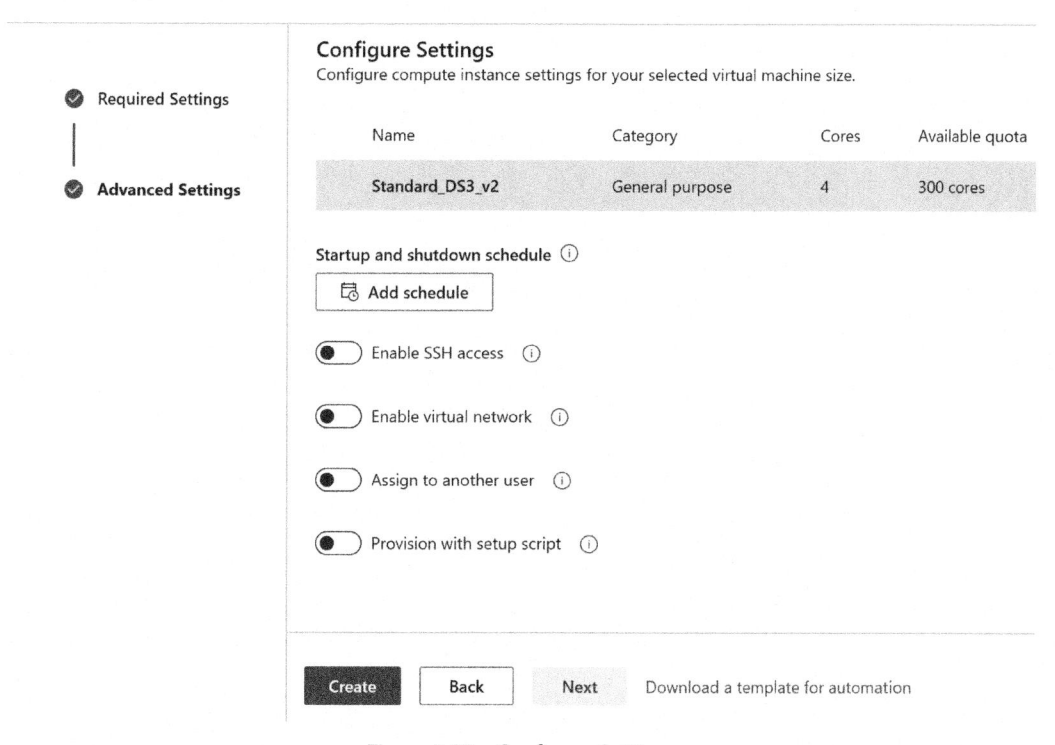

	Name	Category	Cores	Available quota
	Standard_DS3_v2	General purpose	4	300 cores

Figure 1.29 – Configure Settings

Now that we have the basic configurations provided for the compute, we can move to the next section on scheduling a time at which to shut down the instance to save money.

Adding a schedule to a compute instance

In the previous version of the AML service, data scientists had to manually spin up and shut down compute instances. Unsurprisingly, this led users to incur large bills when they forgot to shut them down over weekends and vacations. Microsoft added the ability to automatically start up and shut down compute instances in order to alleviate this problem. We recommend setting the shutdown schedule to just after your normal working hours conclude.

From *Figure 1.29*, click on the **Add Schedule** button to bring up the ability to set a start-up or shutdown automatic schedule.

Here's the **Startup and shutdown schedule** window for the compute instance:

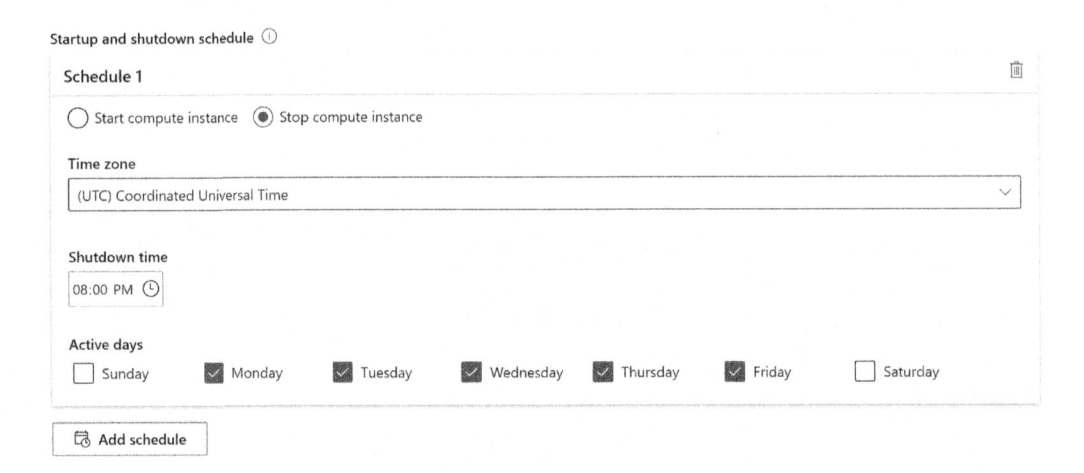

Figure 1.30 – Scheduling a shutdown for the compute instance

As shown in *Figure 1.30*, setting a schedule for the automatic shutdown of the compute will save on cost. Once scheduled, the system will automatically shut down to save money.

After setting your schedule, click on **Create** and wait for the instance to create. Once the instance has been created, it will automatically start and the compute instance page will be displayed.

Creating a compute instance through the Azure CLI

One major advantage of creating a compute instance with code is the ability to save your configuration file for later use.

Launch your command-line interpreter based on your OS (for example, CMD or Windows PS), connect the Azure CLI to your Azure subscription, and create a compute instance noting the name of the compute instance must be unique within an Azure Region by running the following commands:

```
az login
az ml compute create --name computeinstance01 --size STANDARD_
D3_V2 --type ComputeInstance--resource-group my-resource-group
--workspace-name my-workspace
```

Just as you created an AMLS workspace through the Azure CLI, you have now used it to create a compute instance. The next section will cover details on how to use ARM templates to create a compute instance.

Creating a compute instance with ARM templates

Upon creating your AMLS workspace with an ARM template, you can also instantiate compute instances at the same time, specifying their type, size, and schedule. This is an excellent strategy for large organizations that want to tightly control their compute instance configurations. It's also great for teams who are looking to create multiple compute instances in one step. In order to do so, follow these steps:

1. The ARM template can be downloaded from GitHub and is found here: https://github.com/Azure/azure-quickstart-templates/blob/master/quickstarts/microsoft.machinelearningservices/machine-learning-compute-create-computeinstance/azuredeploy.json.

   The template creates a compute instance for you.

   The example template has three required parameters:

   - `workspaceName`, which is the deployment location.
   - `computeName`, which is the name of the compute instance to create.
   - `objectId`, which is the object ID of the person to which to assign the compute instance. In your case, it will be yourself.

   To get your object ID, you can run the following command:

   ```
   az ad signed-in-user show
   ```

2. To deploy your template, you must deploy it into a workspace that has already been created in a resource group that already exists. Be sure to replace `objectId` with the object ID you found using the `az ad signed-in-user show` command. Make sure your command prompt is in the location at which you downloaded the `azuredeploy.json` file, and run the following command:

```
az deployment group create --name "exampledeployment"
--resource-group "aml-dev-rg" --template-file
"azuredeploy.json" --parameters workspaceName="aml-ws"
computeName="devamlcompute" objectId="XXXXXXXX-XXXX-
XXXX-XXXX-XXXXXXXXXXXX" schedules="{'computeStartStop':
[{'action': 'Stop','triggerType': 'Cron','cron':
{'startTime': '2022-07-06T23:41:45','timeZone': 'Central
Standard Time','expression': '00 20 * * 1,2,3,4,5'}}]}"
```

> **Tip**
> In order to create compute instances for users other than yourself, use the **create on behalf** option and specify a user ID.

Now you know how to create compute instances using the GUI, the Azure CLI, and ARM templates. You also know how to schedule startup and shutdown times for your compute instance, and are ready to use it to develop code, which will be the focus of the next section.

Developing within AMLS

With your compute instance VM created, you can use it to write code in either R or Python. Specifically, you can code in **Jupyter**, **JupyterLab**, **Visual Studio Code** (**VSCode**), or a terminal. Both Jupyter and JupyterLab are examples of IDEs for writing Python code. VS Code is Microsoft's recommended IDE that allows you to script in either R or Python, among many other languages.

In this section, you will begin by opening a Jupyter notebook and using it to connect to your AMLS workspace. Similarly, you will do the same thing with JupyterLab. Finally, you will learn how to use AML notebooks in order to develop code.

Developing Python code with Jupyter Notebook

Perhaps the most common way for data scientists to write code within the AMLS is through Jupyter Notebook, the most popularly used **Python IDE**. Jupyter Notebook does, however, come with many limitations; it lacks a lot of the most basic features of your traditional IDE, such as **linting** and code analysis to flag errors before you try running your code. Still, many data scientists prefer it for its streamlined, easy-to-use interface. In order to open Jupyter and create a notebook, follow these steps:

1. Go to the AML workspace UI.
2. Click on **Compute** in the left-hand navigation menu under the **Manage** section of the menu.

   The following screenshot shows us the list of all computes created:

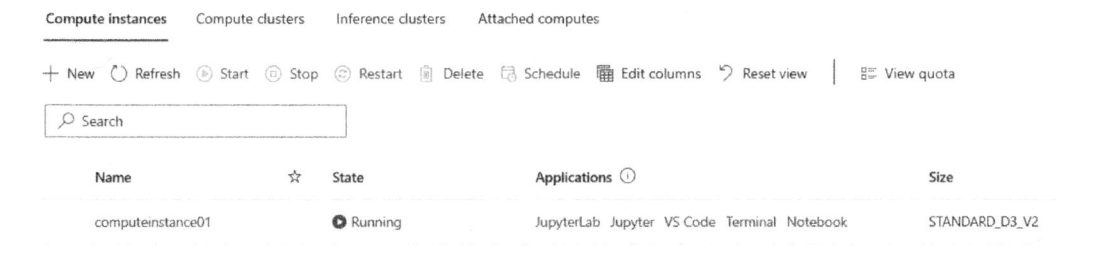

Figure 1.31 – List of compute instances

3. From the list, select your compute instance and click on **Start** (if it has not already started). Once the compute instance has started, a link to **Applications** will appear.
4. Click on the **JupyterLab** or **Jupyter** link to open the Jupyter notebook for further development.
5. To access the AMLS workspace notebook in the left-hand menu, go to the **Notebooks** section.
6. On the next screen, you should see the folders in the left-hand pane. Each user in an AMLS workspace will have a folder created for them by default. Inside your user folder, you can select a notebook to work on. Options to create folders and new notebooks are also available, as shown in *Figure 1.15*.

Now that you know how to use Jupyter Notebook within the AMLS, we will explore how to leverage an AML notebook.

Developing using an AML notebook

AML notebooks are similar to Jupyter notebooks and provide you with another option for developing code. Whether you choose to develop using Jupyter, JupyterLab, or AML notebooks is largely a matter of personal preference. Please try all three to determine which suits you best. In order to start developing with AML notebooks, follow the following steps:

1. Go to the AMLS workspace UI.
2. Click on **Notebooks** on the left-hand navigation menu under the **Author** section.

3. Expand the folder and select your notebook or create a new notebook:

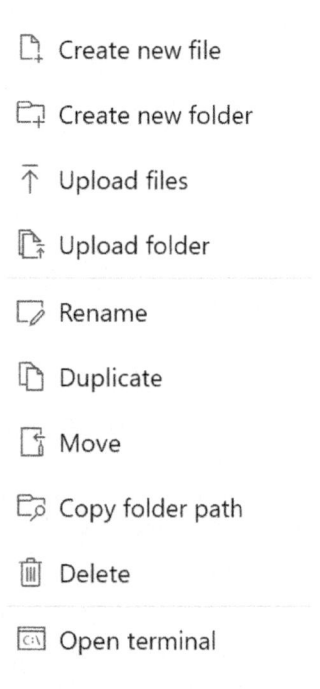

- Create new file
- Create new folder
- Upload files
- Upload folder
- Rename
- Duplicate
- Move
- Copy folder path
- Delete
- Open terminal

Figure 1.32 – File menu options

4. Click on **Create new file**.
5. Name the notebook file `amlbookchapter1.ipynb`.
6. Once you click on **Create**, the page in *Figure 1.33* should pop up. The preceding process will create a new notebook for us to start development:

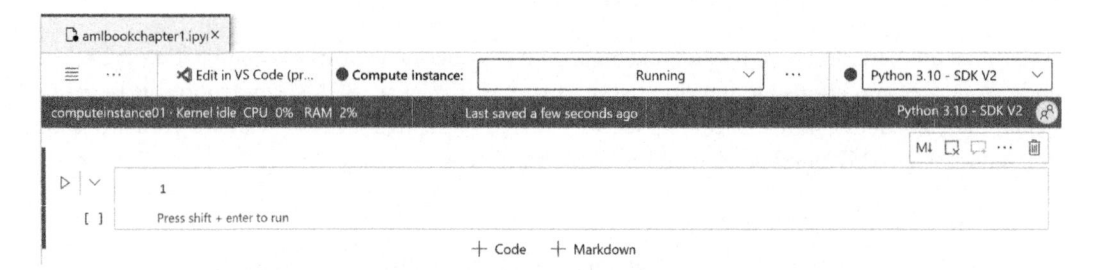

Figure 1.33 – New notebook

In your notebook, you will see the IDE default to the **Python 3.10 - SDK V2** environment. Each cell will allow you to execute code on your running compute instance.

There are two main ways to develop code within the AMLS: Jupyter and AML notebooks. However, a far more powerful IDE exists, which contains many features to improve your productivity – VS Code. In the next section, you will download VS Code and connect it to the AMLS.

Connecting AMLS to VS Code

VS Code is an IDE designed to work with Windows, macOS, or Linux. Its Git integration and debugging features make it a natural selection for a code editor. VS Code has an extension for working directly with your AMLS environment to build, train, and deploy ML models. In order to leverage this powerful tool, install and configure VS Code by following these steps:

1. Download and install VS Code at https://code.visualstudio.com/download.
2. From within VS Code, click on the **EXTENSIONS** icon (*Ctrl + Shift + x*), search for Azure Machine Learning as shown in *Figure 1.34*, and select **Install**:

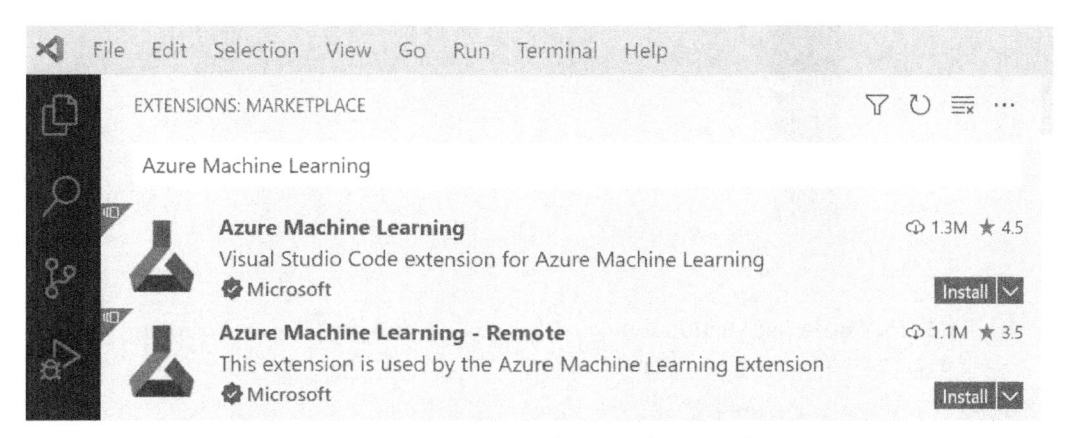

Figure 1.34 – Selecting the VS Code extension

3. Sign into your Azure account (*Ctrl + Shift + p*), and type the following:

    >Azure: Sign In

    A new browser window will open for you to supply your credentials to enable sign-in.

4. Set your default workspace, leveraging the command palette. In order to set your default AMLS workspace, you will need to have a folder open in which VS Code can store metadata. This can be done by selecting **File** from the menu and selecting **Open Folder**.

5. Choose your default workspace by leveraging the command palette (*Ctrl + Shift + p*) and type Azure ML: Set Default Workspace. This command will walk you through selecting your subscription and your workspace:

    >Azure ML: Set Default Workspace

38   Introducing the Azure Machine Learning Service

6. Go to the Azure icon (*Shift + Alt + A*), and go to **MACHINE LEARNING** as shown in *Figure 1.35*:

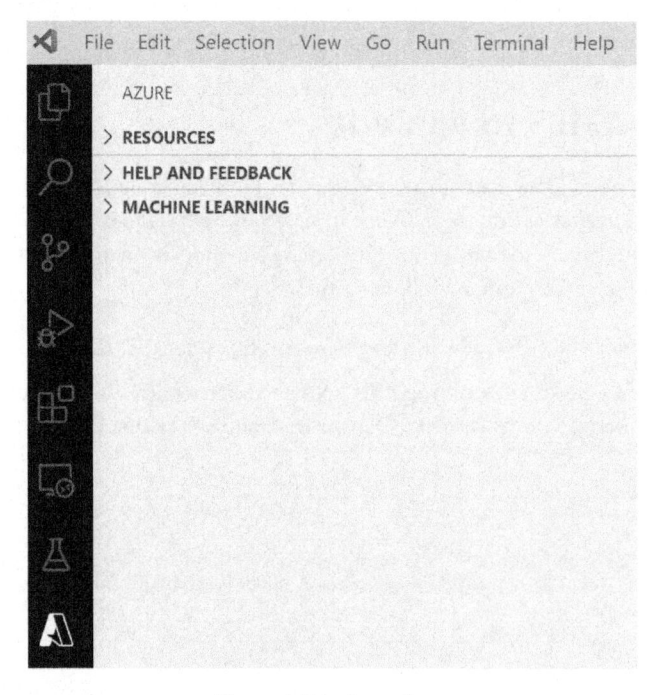

Figure 1.35 – Azure icon

7. Inside the **Machine Learning** section of the Azure icon, right-click as shown in *Figure 1.36* and select **Connect** for our compute instance:

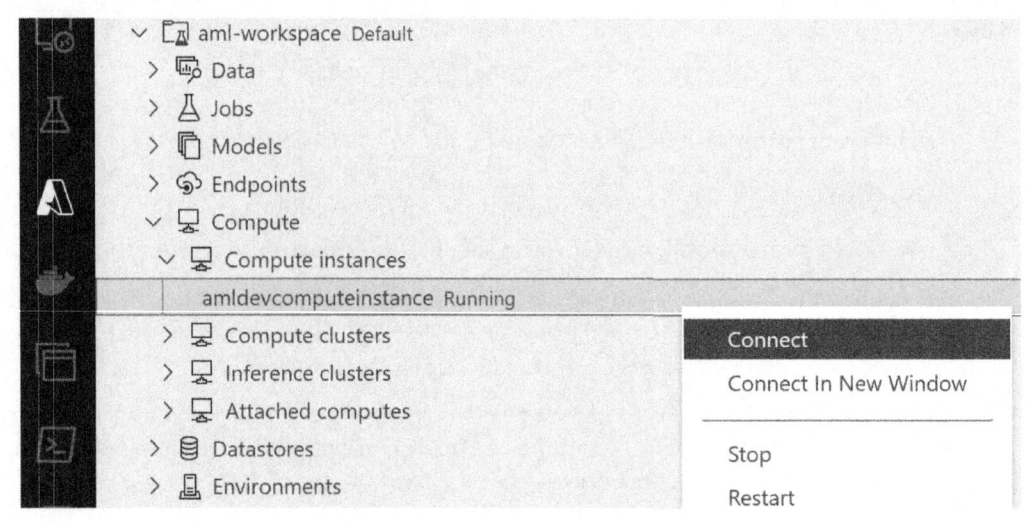

Figure 1.36 – Connect to compute instance

8. The VS Code extension will be installed on the compute instance you are connecting to and you will be asked whether you trust the authors of all files in the parent folder. Select **Yes, I trust the authors**.

9. This will open a new instance of VS Code on your local machine. In this new instance of VS Code, you will see the user directory and notebook previously created in the *Developing using an AML notebook* section as shown in *Figure 1.37*:

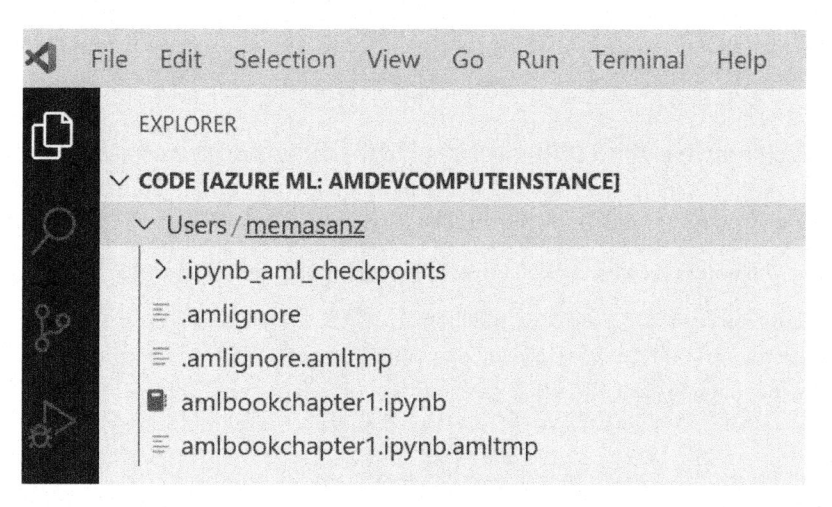

Figure 1.37 – Opening the notebook in VS Code

10. Select your Python interpreter from the top-right corner by clicking on **Select Kernel**. Please select the `azureml_py310_sdkv2` kernel:

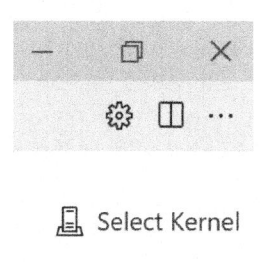

Figure 1.38 – Select Kernel

11. After the interpreter has been selected, you can create a `print` statement as shown in *Figure 1.39*:

```
import os
directory_path = os.getcwd()
print("My current directory is :" + directory_path)
```

```
My current directory is :/mnt/batch/tasks/shared/LS_root/mounts/clusters/amdevcomputeinstance/code
```

Figure 1.39 – Writing code

12. To execute this code, press the play button to the left of the cell (*Ctrl + Enter*). Note that the Python code supplied will print out the current working directory. Your code executes on the compute instance as shown by the directory path printed out.

Saving the notebook within VS Code will save the notebook to your AMLS workspace.

In this section, you have installed VS Code, the AML VS Code extension, and connected to your compute instance in your AMLS workspace to run your code. VS Code provides IntelliSense, the ability to run and debug your code, along with built-in Git integration. Combining these features with integration into your AMLS workspace makes this the ideal choice for development.

Summary

In this chapter, you have explored the options for creating an AMLS workspace, how to navigate in AMLS, how to create compute instances for developing code, and how to use your compute instance to develop code. You have dug into creating an AMLS workspace through the Azure portal, through the CLI, as well as through ARM templates. You have navigated through the AMLS workspace components, exploring the **Author**, **Assets**, and **Manage** sections of AMLS. You have explored a variety of IDEs, including Jupyter, AML notebooks, as well as VS Code, Microsoft's premier IDE, with the compute instance that you created either using the portal, the CLI, or via an ARM template. This foundation gives you everything you need to begin scripting ML solutions.

In the next chapter, you will import data into AMLS and connect to a variety of data sources. You will also learn how to automatically track changes to your data and roll back to earlier versions if necessary.

2
Working with Data in AMLS

In **Machine Learning** (**ML**), regardless of the use case or the algorithm we use, an important component that will always be used is data. Without data, you cannot build machine learning models. The quality of the data is very critical for building performant models. Complex models such as deep neural networks require a lot more data than simpler models. Data in an ML workflow will often come from a variety of data sources and require different methods to be leveraged for data processing, cleansing, and feature selection. During this process of feature engineering, your Azure Machine Learning workspace will be leveraged to empower you to collaboratively work with your data. This will ensure secure connectivity to a variety of data sources, as well as enable you to register your datasets for use in training, testing, and validation.

As an example of steps within this workflow, we may be required to take raw data, join with an additional dataset, cleanse data to remove duplicates, fill in missing values, and perform an initial analysis to identify outliers and skew in our data. This can be done even before an algorithm is selected to begin building a model to train leveraging our features and labels within our dataset.

Azure Machine Learning provides methods for connecting to a variety of data sources and registering datasets to be used to build a model, so you can use your data in a business context.

In this chapter, we will cover the following topics:

- Azure Machine Learning datastore overview
- Creating a Blob Storage account datastore
- Creating Azure Machine Learning data assets
- Using Azure Machine Learning data assets

Technical requirements

Read *Chapter 1, Introducing the Azure Machine Learning Service,* to get the environment workspace created to use.

These are the prerequisites for the chapter:

- Access to the internet.
- A web browser, preferably Google Chrome or Microsoft Edge Chromium.
- A supported storage service.
- Access to supported storage.
- To access the Azure machine learning service workspace, please go to `https://ml.azure.com`. Select the workspace from the drop-down list on the left in your web browser.

Azure Machine Learning datastore overview

Within an Azure Machine Learning workspace, a storage service that is the source of data is registered as a datastore for reusability. A datastore securely holds connectivity information for accessing data within the key vault that was created with your Azure Machine Learning workspace. The credentials supplied to the datastore are used to access the data within a given data service. These datastores can be created via the Azure Machine Learning Studio through the Azure Machine Learning SDK for Python, or the Azure Machine Learning **command-line interface** (**CLI**). Datastores enable data scientists to connect to data by name rather than passing connection information within scripts. This allows the portability of code through different environments (in different environments, a datastore may point to different services) and prevents the leaking of sensitive credentials.

Supported datastores include the following:

- Azure Blob Storage
- Azure SQL Database
- Azure Data Lake Gen 1 (deprecated)
- Azure Data Lake Gen 2
- Azure file share
- Azure Database for PostgreSQL
- Azure Database for MySQL
- Databricks File System

Each of the supported datastores will have an authentication type associated with the data service. When creating a datastore, the authentication type will be selected and leveraged within the Azure Machine Learning workspace. Note that Azure Database for MySQL is currently only supported for the `DataTransferStep` pipeline and thus cannot be created with Azure Machine Learning Studio. The Databricks File System is only supported for the `DatabricksStep` pipeline, and thus cannot be created leveraging Azure Machine Learning Studio.

The following table provides the authentication options for the Azure Storage types available for use with your Azure Machine Learning workspace:

Storage Type	Authentication Options Available
Azure Blob Container	SAS token, account key
Azure SQL Database	Service principal, SQL authentication
Azure Data Lake Gen 1	Service principal
Azure Data Lake Gen 2	Service principal
Azure File Share	SAS token, account key
Azure Database for PostgreSQL	SQL authentication
Azure Database for MySQL	SQL authentication
Databricks File System	No authentication

Figure 2.1 – Supported authentication for Azure Storage types

Now that you have an understanding of the types of supported datastores, in the next section, you will learn how to connect your Azure Machine Learning workspace to datastores that you can use within your ML workflow. The most common and recommended datastore is an Azure blob container. In fact, one was created for you in *Chapter 1*, *Introducing the Azure Machine Learning Service*, as part of the workspace deployment process.

Before continuing to the next section to create datastores using Azure Machine Learning Studio, the Python SDK, and the Azure Machine Learning CLI, we will briefly review the default datastore that was created for you.

Default datastore review

As noted in *Chapter 1*, *Introducing the Azure Machine Learning Service*, the left navigation includes a **Data** section, which you can use to access the datastores, as shown in *Figure 2.2*.

> **Tip**
> Clicking on the hamburger icon on the top of the left navigation within your workspace will include words with the icons in your navigation bar.

Working with Data in AMLS

If you click on the **Datastore** tab, you can see the storage accounts that have already been created for your workspace:

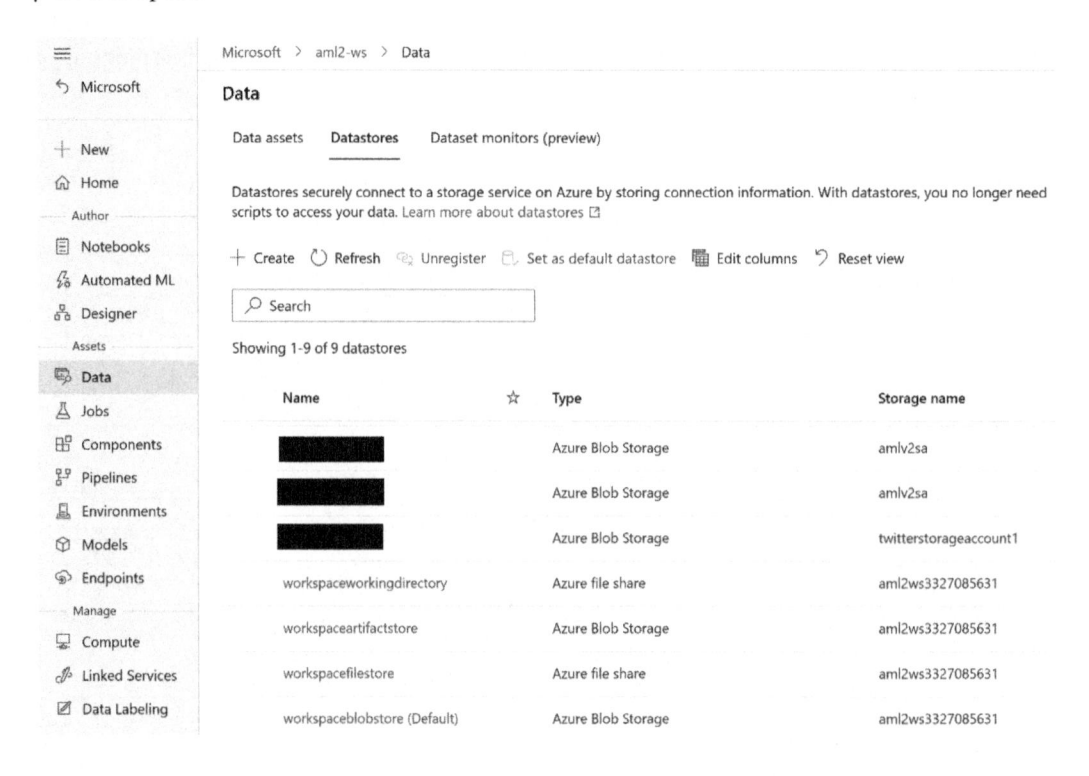

Figure 2.2 – Datastores

workspaceblobstore is the default Azure Machine Learning workspace datastore and holds experiment logs as well as workspace artifacts. Data can be uploaded to this default datastore, which will be covered in an upcoming section. **workspacefilestore** is used to store your notebooks that are created within your Azure Machine Learning workspace.

In the next section, we will see how to connect to a new datastore through Azure Machine Learning Studio, through the Azure Machine Learning Python SDK, as well as through the Azure Machine Learning CLI. This will enable you to use data where the data lives instead of bringing it into the default datastore associated with your Azure Machine Learning workspace.

Creating a blob storage account datastore

As mentioned in the previous section, *Default datastore review*, we can create a datastore through Azure Machine Learning Studio, through the Azure Machine Learning Python SDK, and through the Azure Machine Learning CLI. In the next section, we will walk through creating a datastore for a blob storage account with each of these methods.

Creating a blob storage account datastore through Azure Machine Learning Studio

In order to create a blob storage account datastore, first you need to create a storage account that contains a blob. Follow these steps to create an Azure storage account and create blob storage within that storage account:

1. Go to the Azure portal at `https://ms.portal.azure.com/#home`.
2. Find **Storage accounts** under **Azure Services**.
3. Click **Create** and follow the wizard for creating a storage account. Make sure to name the storage account `amlv2sa`.
4. Once the storage account is created, you can see it under **Storage accounts**.
5. Go ahead and click on the newly created storage account.
6. Then from the left side navigation click on **Containers** and then click **+ Container** to create a new container. Make sure to name it `datacontainer`.

Working with Data in AMLS

Now, go back to Azure Machine Learning Studio, click on the **Data** icon on the left navigation, go to the **Datastores** tab as shown in *Figure 2.2*, and click on **+Create**. A new **Create datastore** pane will open, as shown in *Figure 2.3*:

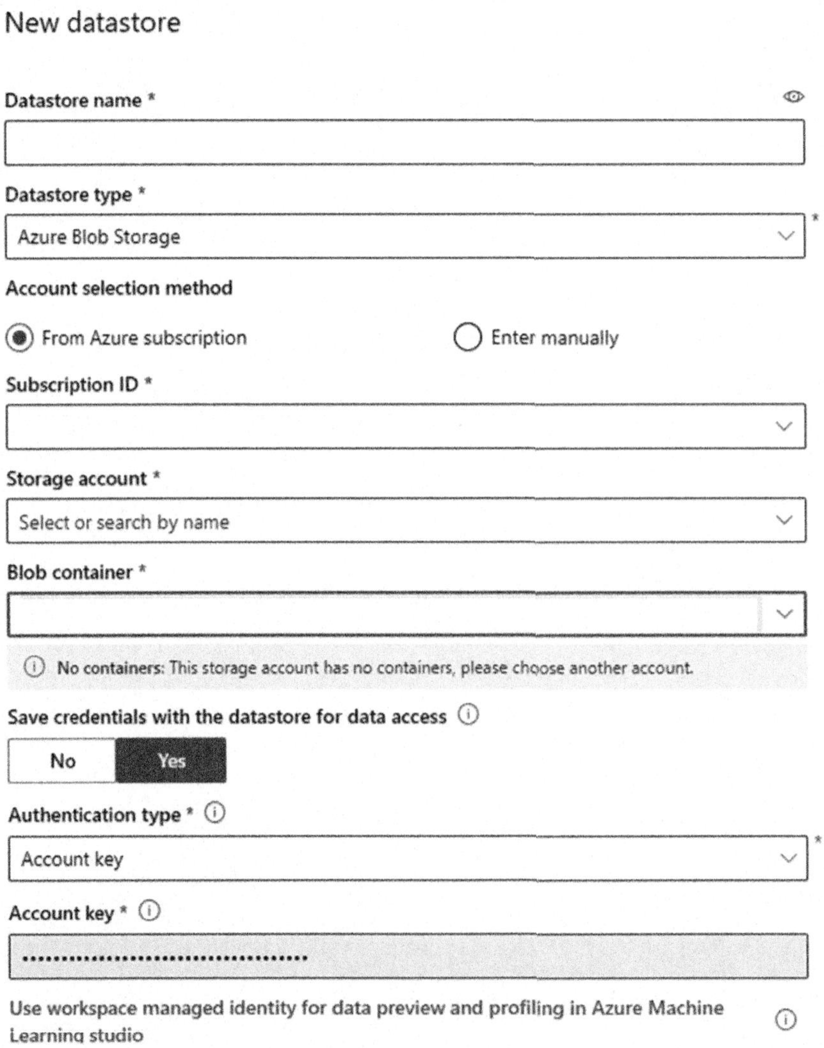

New datastore

Datastore name *

Datastore type *

Azure Blob Storage

Account selection method

● From Azure subscription   ○ Enter manually

Subscription ID *

Storage account *

Select or search by name

Blob container *

ⓘ No containers: This storage account has no containers, please choose another account.

Save credentials with the datastore for data access ⓘ

No **Yes**

Authentication type * ⓘ

Account key

Account key * ⓘ

••••••••••••••••••••••••••••••••

Use workspace managed identity for data preview and profiling in Azure Machine Learning studio

Figure 2.3 – Create datastore

On the **Create datastore** pane, configure the required settings:

1. Set **Datastore name** to `azureblobdatastore`.
2. Given that this is an Azure blob storage account, leave **Datastore type** as `Azure Blob Storage`.
3. Select your **Subscription ID** – note it should default to the Azure subscription of your workspace.
4. Find the storage account that you just created (`amlv2sa`) by clicking on the dropdown under **Storage account**.
5. Find the blob container that you just created (`datacontainer`) by clicking on the dropdown under **Blob container**.
6. Set **Save credentials with the datastore for data access** to **Yes**.
7. Set **Authentication type** to **Account key**.
8. Set the **Account key** by entering the value found in the **Access Keys** section of your storage account.
9. Set **Use workspace managed identity for data preview and profiling in Azure Machine Learning studio** to **Yes**.

    This will grant your Azure Machine Learning service workspace's managed **identity Reader** and **Storage Blob Data Reader** access.

10. Click on **Create**.

    You can verify that a datastore called `azureblobdatastore` has been created for you by viewing the **Datastores** tab shown in *Figure 2.2*.

Now that we have seen how to easily configure a datastore through the UI, we will continue with creating a datastore through the Python SDK.

Creating a blob storage account datastore through the Python SDK

In order to use the Python SDK, you need to run Python scripts in a Jupyter notebook. To start a Jupyter notebook, please click on the **Compute** tab on the left navigation, as shown in *Figure 2.4*:

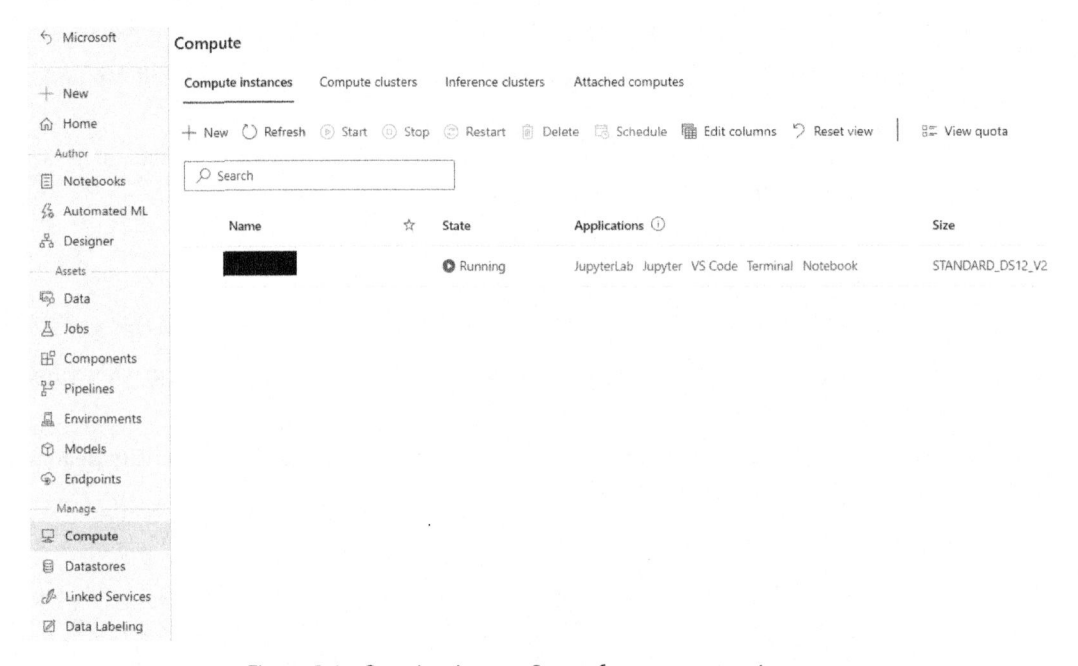

Figure 2.4 – Opening Jupyter Server from a compute instance

Next, from an existing compute instance click on **Jupyter** to open Jupyter Server. Under **New**, click on **Python 3.10 – SDKV2** in order to create a new Jupyter notebook, as shown in *Figure 2.5*:

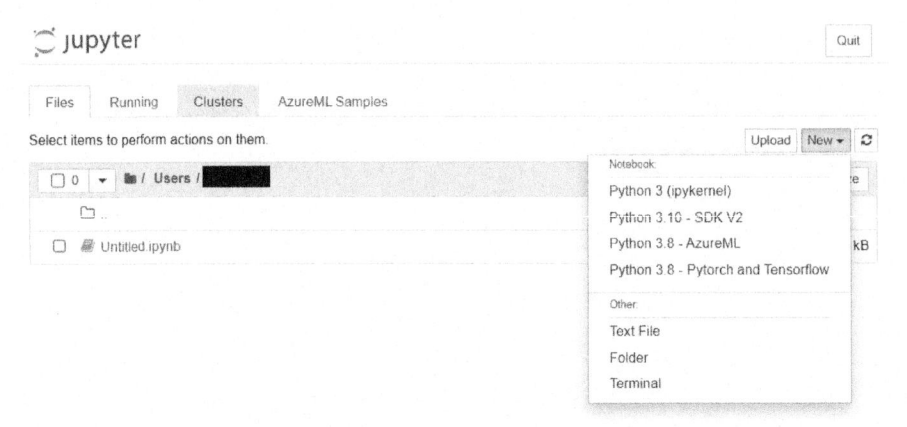

Figure 2.5 – Creating a new Jupyter notebook

Using the Azure Machine Learning Python SDK, an Azure blob container can be registered to your Azure Machine Learning workspace leveraging the following code in *Figure 2.6*. Recall from when we created a new datastore through the UI that the value of the account key can be found in the **Access Keys** section of your storage account:

```python
# import required libraries
from azure.ai.ml import MLClient
from azure.identity import DefaultAzureCredential
from azure.ai.ml import command, Input
from azure.ai.ml.entities import (
    AzureBlobDatastore,
    AzureFileDatastore,
    AzureDataLakeGen1Datastore,
    AzureDataLakeGen2Datastore,
)
from azure.ai.ml.entities import Environment
```

```python
# Enter details of your AML workspace
subscription_id = "XXXxxxXXXxXXXX"
resource_group = "aml-v2-book"
workspace = "aml2-ws"
```

```python
# get a handle to the workspace
ml_client = MLClient(
    DefaultAzureCredential(), subscription_id, resource_group, workspace
)
```

```python
# Create a datastore with account key
blob_datastore1 = AzureBlobDatastore(
    name="blobe_storage",
    description="AML Datastore pointing to a blob storgae.",
    account_name="amlv2sa",
    container_name="datacontainer",
    credentials={
        "account_key": "XXXxxxXXXXXxxxXXXXXxXXXXXXXxxXXXXXXXXXXXXxxXXXXXXXXXXXXXXXxxXXXXXXXXXXX"
    },
)
ml_client.create_or_update(blob_datastore1)
```

Out[24]: AzureBlobDatastore({'type': <DatastoreType.AZURE_BLOB: 'AzureBlob'>, 'name': 'blobe_storage', 'description': 'AML Datastore pointing to a blob storgae.', 'tags': {}, 'properties': {}, 'id': '/subscriptions/dcfc206a-203b-4c00-a236-bdf576a37896/resourceGroups/aml-v2-book/providers/Microsoft.MachineLearningServices/workspaces/aml2-ws/datastores/blobe_storage', 'base_path': './', 'creation_context': None, 'serialize': <msrest.serialization.Serializer object at 0x7f68069a6790>, 'credentials': <azure.ai.ml.entities._datastore.credentials.NoneCredentials object at 0x7f68069d1850>, 'container_name': 'datacontainer', 'account_name': 'amlv2sa', 'endpoint': 'core.windows.net', 'protocol': 'https'})

Figure 2.6 – Using the Python SDK to create a blob storage account datastore

You can verify that a new blob storage datastore called **blob_storage** has been created if you click on **Data** in the left navigation and then the **Datastores** option, as shown in *Figure 2.7*:

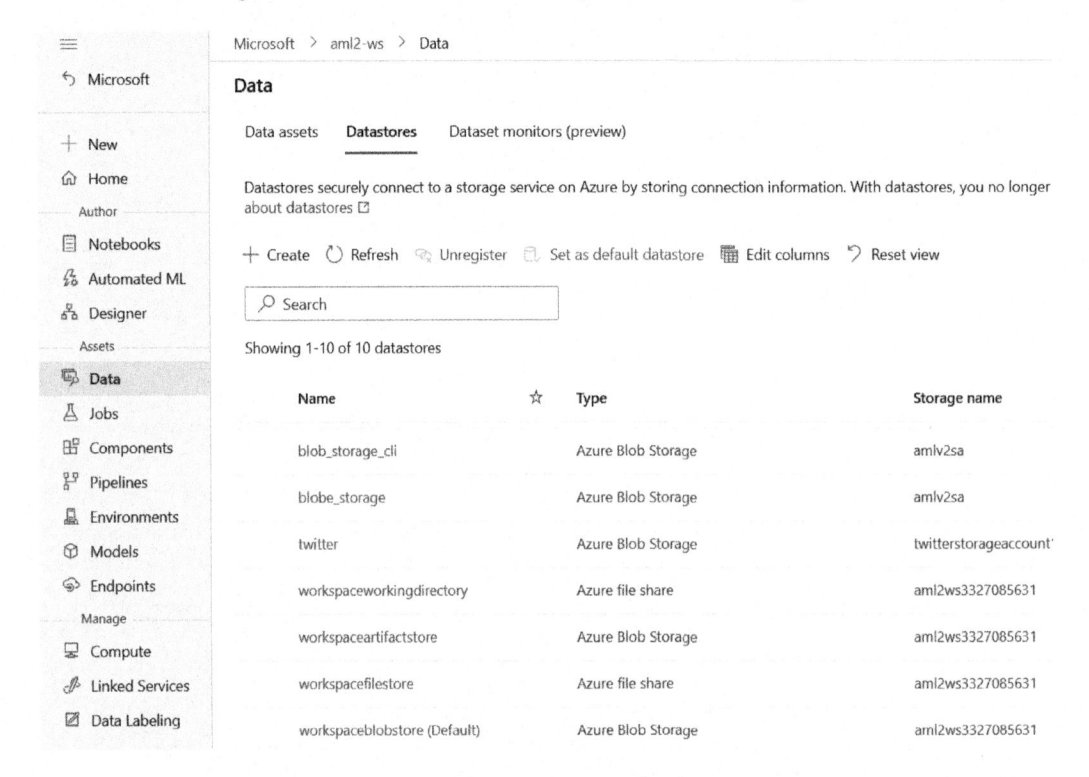

Figure 2.7 – List of datastores created in the workspace

Next, let's created a blob storage account datastore with the Azure Machine Learning CLI.

Creating a blob storage account datastore through the Azure Machine Learning CLI

Assuming you have followed the instructions in *Chapter 1, Introducing the Azure Machine Learning Service*, to install the Azure CLI and the machine learning extension in your local environment, you can run the following command to create a blob storage account datastore:

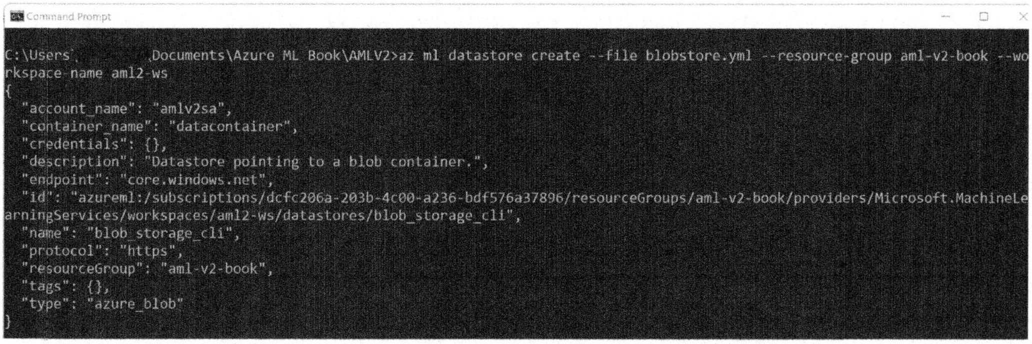

Figure 2.8 – CLI command to create a blob storage account datastore

In the preceding command, `blobstore.yml` is a YAML file schema specifying the datastore type, name, description, storage account name, and credentials for the storage account, as shown in *Figure 2.9*:

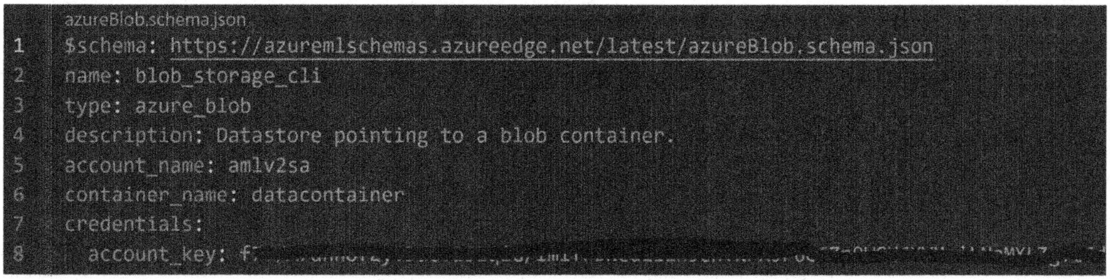

Figure 2.9 – Blob datastore YAML schema file

You can verify that a new blob storage datastore called `blob_storage_cli` has been created if you click on the **Datastores** tab, as shown earlier in *Figure 2.7*.

Now that you have successfully created a blob storage datastore, within your Azure Machine Learning workspace, you will be able to use this datastore for multiple data assets. The connection information to this datastore is securely held within your Azure key vault, and you have a location to store data as it is generated.

Creating Azure Machine Learning data assets

Once the previous datastore is created, the next step is to create a data asset. Please note that we will be using the terms "data asset" and "dataset" interchangeably throughout the chapter. A dataset is a logical connection to the datastore with versioning and schema management, such as choosing which columns of the data to use, the types of the columns in the dataset, and some statistics about the data. Data assets abstract the code from configuring data to be read. Also, data assets are very useful when we run multiple models as each model can be configured to read the dataset name instead of configuring or programming how to connect to the dataset and read it. This makes it easier to scale the model training.

In the following sections, you will learn how to create datasets using the Azure Machine Learning Python SDK, CLI, and UI. Datasets allow us to create versions based on schema changes without changing the underlying datastore that holds the data. Specific versions can be used within code. We can also create profiles on the data for each dataset created and stored for further data analysis.

Creating a data asset using the UI

Azure Machine Learning Studio provides a great interface for creating a dataset through a guided UI. In order to create a dataset using Azure Machine Learning Studio, follow these steps:

1. Go to `https://ml.azure.com`.
2. Select your workspace name.
3. In the workspace UI, click **Data** and make sure that the **Data assets** option is selected.
4. Next, click **+ Create** and fill out the **Create data asset** form, as shown in *Figure 2.10*, and make sure to select **Tabular** in the **Type** field:

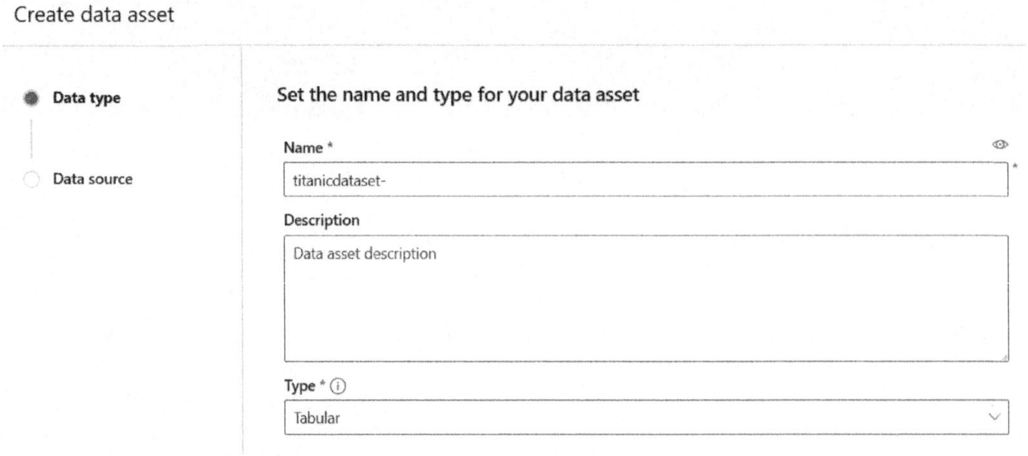

Create data asset

Figure 2.10 – Create data asset

5. On the next screen, select **From local files** and click **Next** to see the **Select a datastore** screen, as shown in *Figure 2.11*. Go ahead and select the **blob_storage** datastore that you created in the last section.

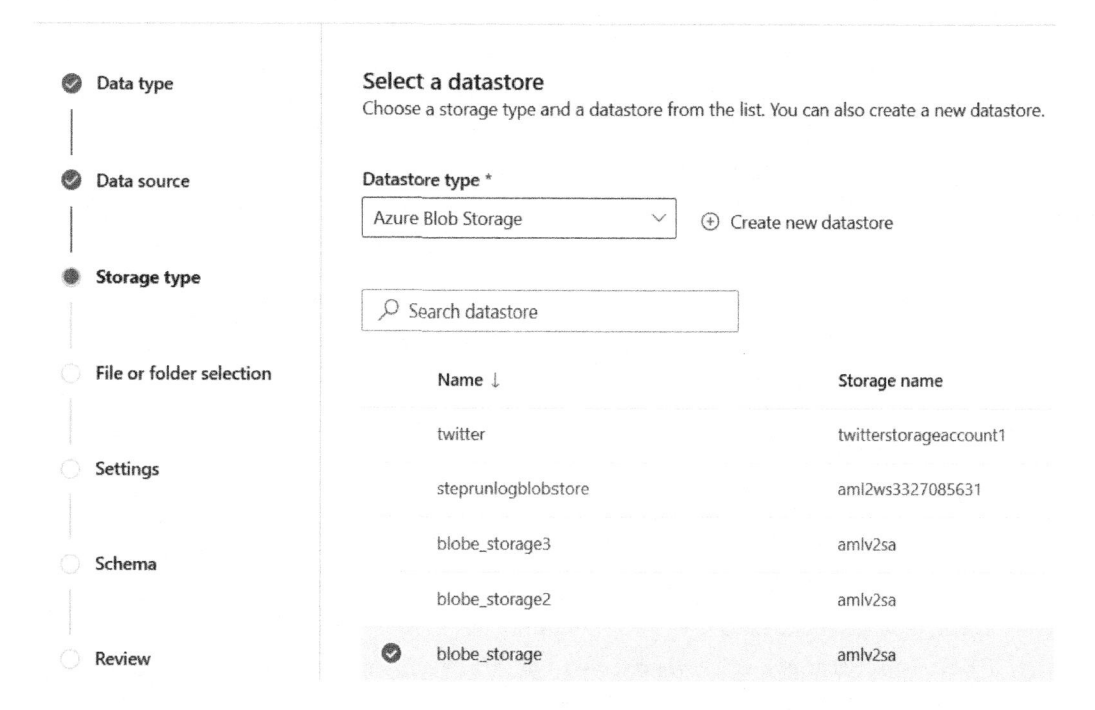

Figure 2.11 – Select a datastore

Once the datastore is selected, you are provided with the option to choose the path where the file is located, as shown in *Figure 2.12*. For this example, we will use the `titanic.csv` file, which can be downloaded from our GitHub repository. Enter the path where you downloaded and saved the file and then click **Next**:

54   Working with Data in AMLS

Create data asset

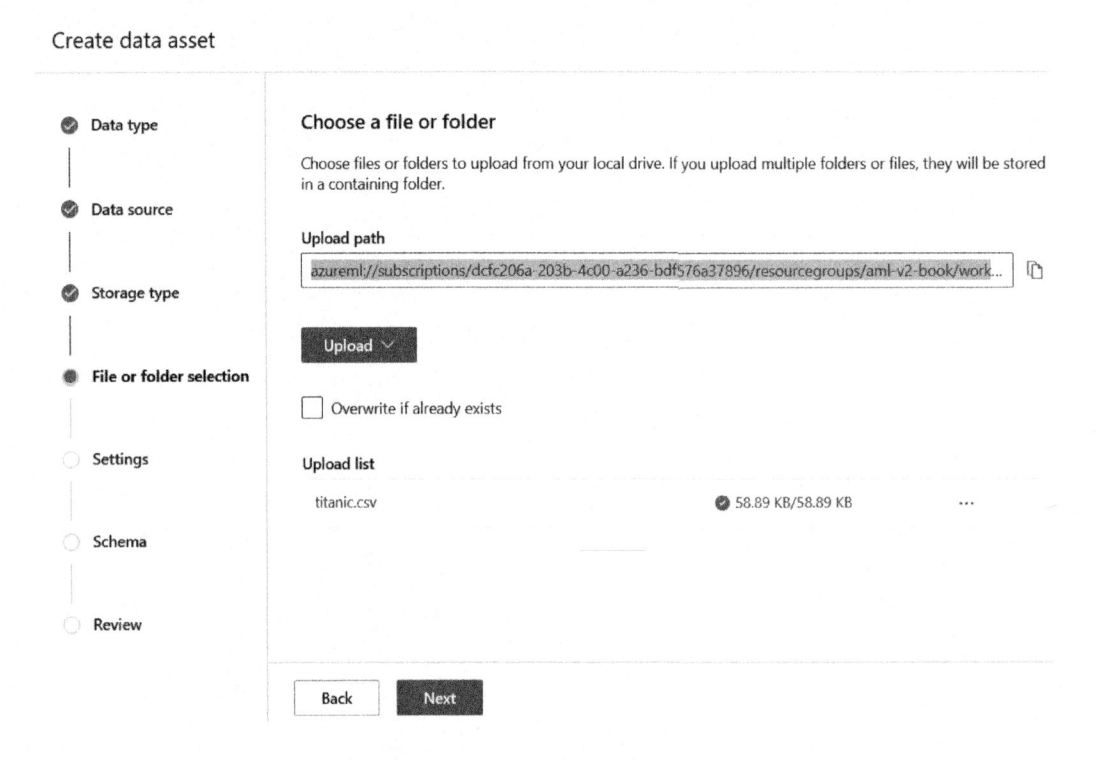

Figure 2.12 – Upload your data file

6. Next is the **Settings and preview** screen. On this screen, the file is automatically parsed, and options are displayed for the format detected. In our case, it's a CSV file, and settings for CSV file format are shown. Check the preview section to validate whether the dataset shows the data in the right format like identifying columns, header, and values. If the format is not detected, then you can change the settings for **File Format**, **Delimiter**, **Encoding**, **Column headers**, and **Skip rows**, as shown in *Figure 2.13*. If the dataset contains multi-line data, then check the option for **Dataset contains multi-line data**. Once the settings are configured properly for your dataset, click the **Next** button to go to the next section regarding schema:

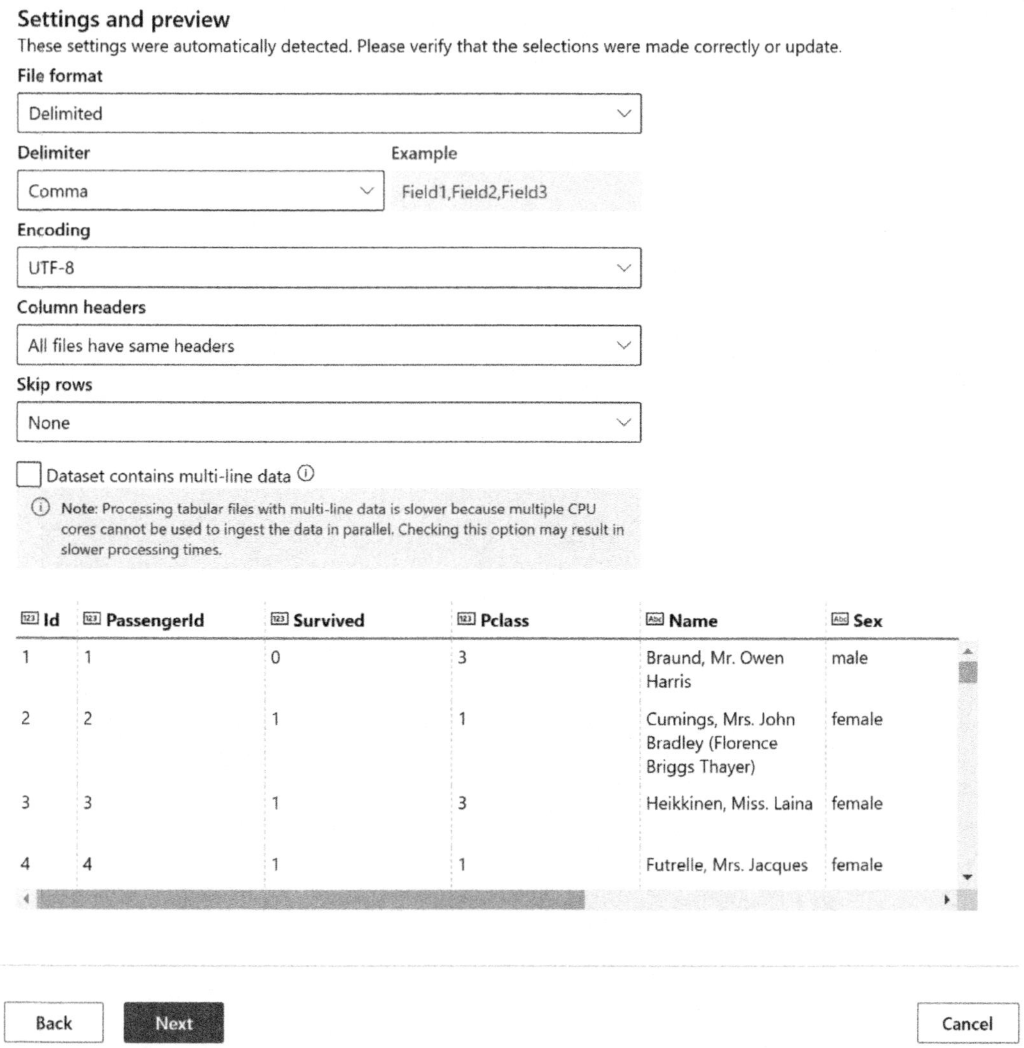

Settings and preview

These settings were automatically detected. Please verify that the selections were made correctly or update.

File format

| Delimited ⌄ |

Delimiter

| Comma ⌄ |

Example

Field1,Field2,Field3

Encoding

| UTF-8 ⌄ |

Column headers

| All files have same headers ⌄ |

Skip rows

| None ⌄ |

☐ Dataset contains multi-line data ⓘ

ⓘ **Note:** Processing tabular files with multi-line data is slower because multiple CPU cores cannot be used to ingest the data in parallel. Checking this option may result in slower processing times.

Id	PassengerId	Survived	Pclass	Name	Sex
1	1	0	3	Braund, Mr. Owen Harris	male
2	2	1	1	Cumings, Mrs. John Bradley (Florence Briggs Thayer)	female
3	3	1	3	Heikkinen, Miss. Laina	female
4	4	1	1	Futrelle, Mrs. Jacques	female

[Back] [**Next**]   [Cancel]

Figure 2.13 – Settings and preview screen

On this screen, the system will identify the schema of the data and display it for review, allowing changes as needed. Typically, a CSV or text file may require schema changes. As an example, a column may have an incorrect data type, so be sure to select the correct data type.

> **Important note**
> The first 200 rows are used to detect the column type. If the dataset has a column type mismatch, consider cleaning your dataset before registering using a Jupyter notebook.

Here are the available data type formats:

- **String**
- **Integer**
- **Boolean**
- **Decimal (dot '.')**
- **Decimal (comma ',')**
- **Date**

Figure 2.14 shows the schema information for your dataset. Check the **Type** header dropdown to see the available data types:

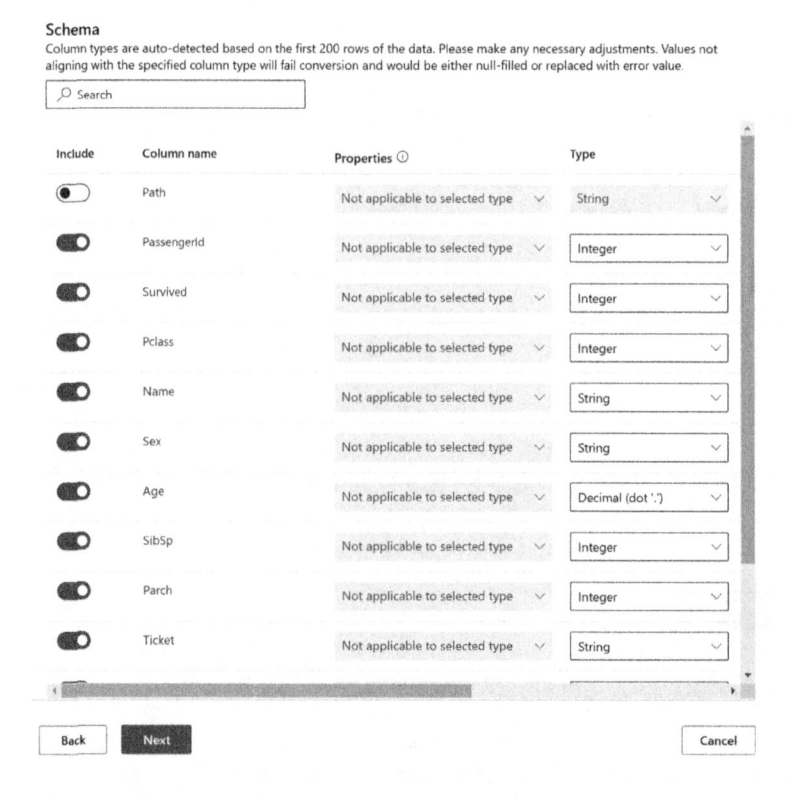

Figure 2.14 – Schema screen

7. Scroll down and review all the columns. For your registered data asset, you can choose to include or exclude a given column. The option to **Include** is available per column, as shown in *Figure 2.14*. This screen also includes the option to **Search** a column. Once the screen is properly configured for your data asset, click **Next**.

Creating Azure Machine Learning data assets   57

8. Next is the **Review** screen. Confirm all the settings that were selected previously are correct and then click **Create**:

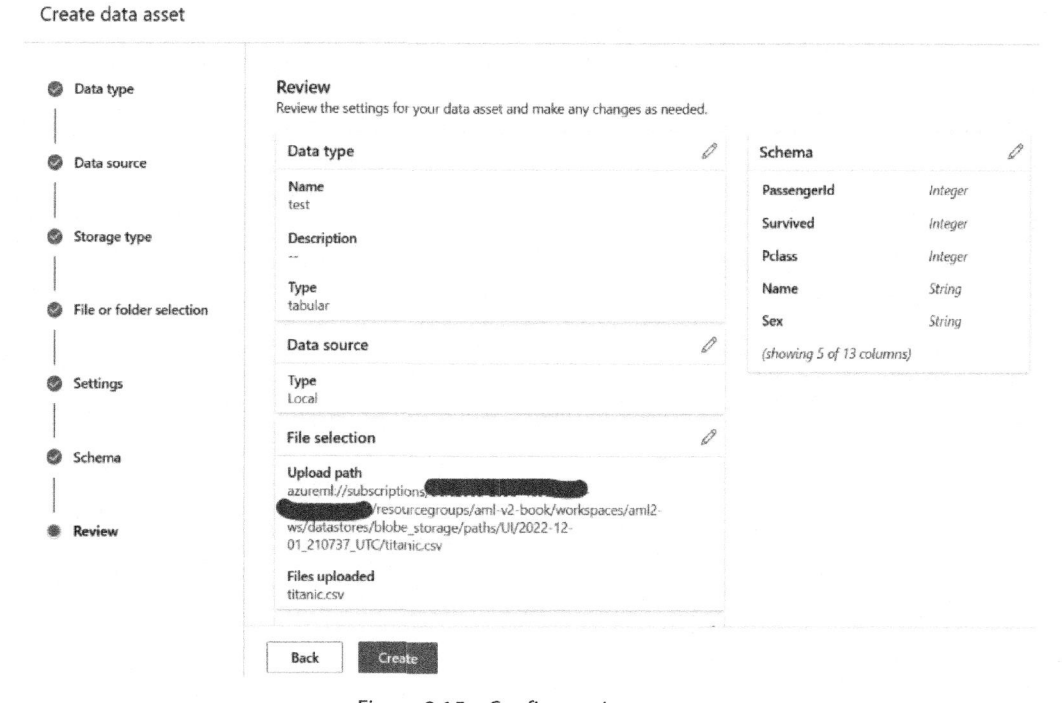

Figure 2.15 – Confirm review screen

During the review, if any changes are required, click the **Back** button and change the settings.

9. Once the data asset creation is complete, you will see the `titanicdataset` data asset page, which includes different options, such as **Explore**, **Consume**, and **Generate Profile**.

10. Click on the **Consume** option, as shown in *Figure 2.16*, to review the code for retrieving your registered dataset by name and displaying a pandas dataframe from your dataset:

58 Working with Data in AMLS

titanicdataset Version 1 (latest)

Details | **Consume** | Explore | Models | Jobs

New version | Refresh | ▶ Generate profile | Unregister

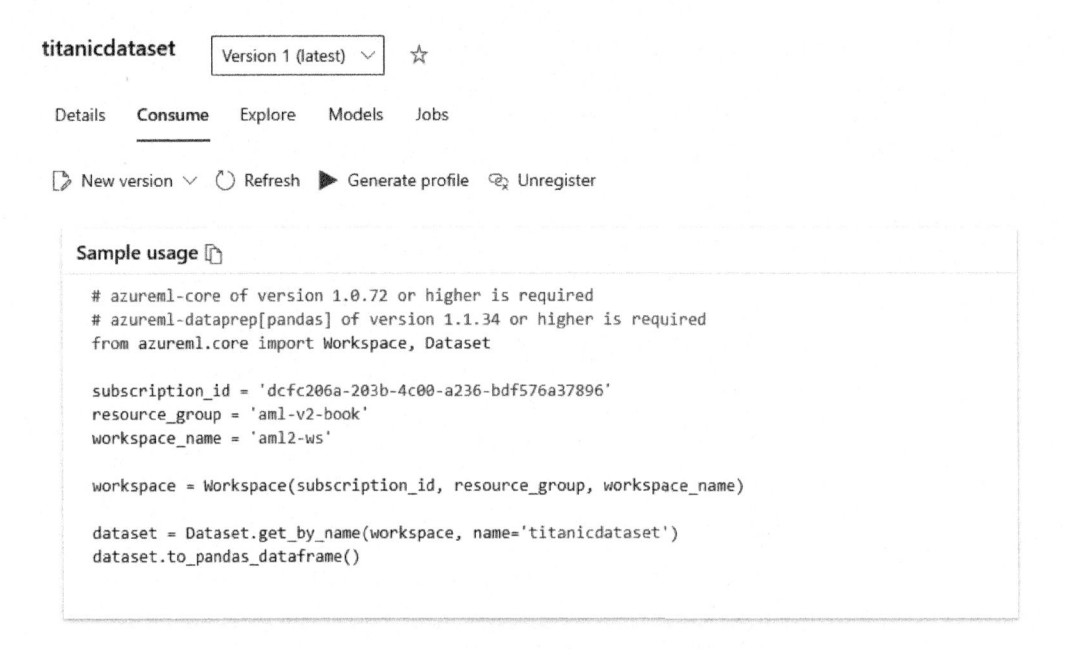

Sample usage

```python
# azureml-core of version 1.0.72 or higher is required
# azureml-dataprep[pandas] of version 1.1.34 or higher is required
from azureml.core import Workspace, Dataset

subscription_id = 'dcfc206a-203b-4c00-a236-bdf576a37896'
resource_group = 'aml-v2-book'
workspace_name = 'aml2-ws'

workspace = Workspace(subscription_id, resource_group, workspace_name)

dataset = Dataset.get_by_name(workspace, name='titanicdataset')
dataset.to_pandas_dataframe()
```

Figure 2.16 – Consuming the data asset using Python

The code shown in *Figure 2.16* can be copied and pasted directly into an Azure Machine Learning notebook and run on your Azure Machine Learning compute instance, as discussed later in the chapter.

11. Within the **Consume** option for the registered dataset, you can select the **Generate profile** option to begin a guided tour through profiling your dataset, as shown in *Figure 2.17*:

Generate profile

Select compute type

[Compute instance]

Select Azure ML compute instance

[devbox32 - Stopped]

Profile output location ⓘ

● Default workspace storage

○ Datastore

Select an existing Azure Blob datastore with credentials

[**Generate**] [Cancel]

Figure 2.17 – Generate profile screen

12. If you want to create a new version of the dataset, click **New Version**.
13. There is also the **Explore** option to view a sample of the data set. Only the first 50 rows are shown:

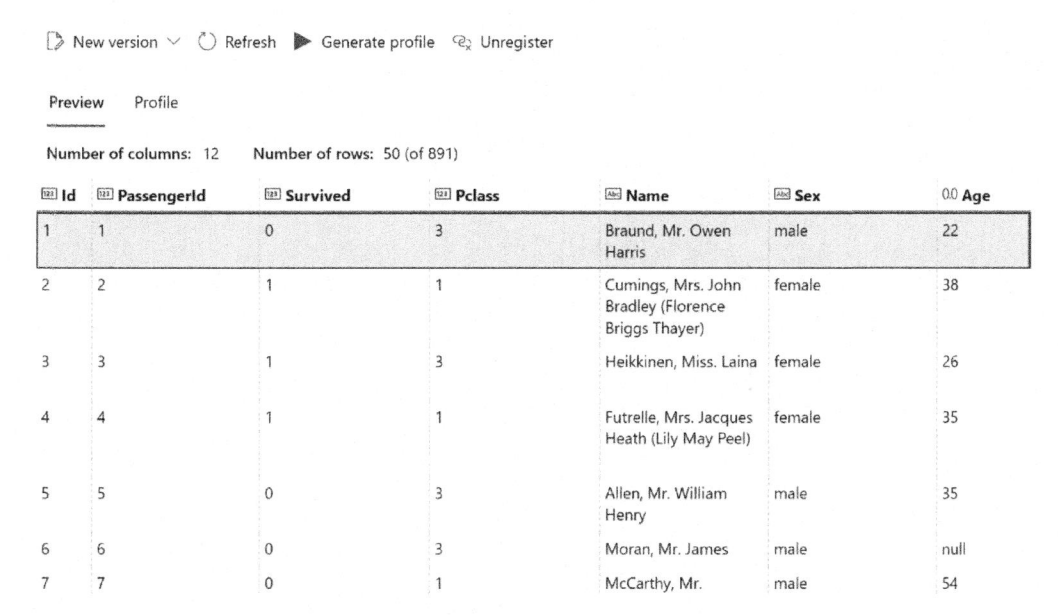

Id	PassengerId	Survived	Pclass	Name	Sex	Age
1	1	0	3	Braund, Mr. Owen Harris	male	22
2	2	1	1	Cumings, Mrs. John Bradley (Florence Briggs Thayer)	female	38
3	3	1	3	Heikkinen, Miss. Laina	female	26
4	4	1	1	Futrelle, Mrs. Jacques Heath (Lily May Peel)	female	35
5	5	0	3	Allen, Mr. William Henry	male	35
6	6	0	3	Moran, Mr. James	male	null
7	7	0	1	McCarthy, Mr.	male	54

Figure 2.18 – Explore screen

In this section, we showed you how to create data assets using the UI. In the next section, we will show you how to create data assets using the Python SDK.

Creating a data asset using the Python SDK

In this section, we will show you how to create a data asset using the Python SDK. As mentioned in the previous section, you can create data from datastores, local files, and public URLs. The Python script to create a data asset from a local file (for example, `titanic.csv`) is shown in *Figure 2.19*.

Working with Data in AMLS

Please note that in the following code snippet, `type = AssetTypes.mltable` abstracts the schema definition for the tabular data, making it easier to share datasets:

```python
from azure.ai.ml.entities import Data
from azure.ai.ml.constants import AssetTypes

# my_path must point to folder containing MLTable artifact (MLTable file + data
# Supported paths include:
# Local: './<path>'
# blob:  'https://<account_name>.blob.core.windows.net/<container_name>/<path>'
# ADLS gen2: 'abfss://<file_system>@<account_name>.dfs.core.windows.net/<path>/'
# Datastore: 'azureml://datastores/<data_store_name>/paths/<path>'

my_path = './my_data/'

my_data = Data(
    path=my_path,
    type=AssetTypes.MLTABLE,
    description="description",
    name="titanic-mltable-sdk",
    version='1'
)

ml_client.data.create_or_update(my_data)
```

```
Uploading my_data (0.06 MBs): 100%|████████| 60607/60607 [00:00<00:00, 976124.07it/s]

Data({'type': 'mltable', 'is_anonymous': False, 'auto_increment_version': False, 'name': 'titanic-mltable-sdk', 'descriptio
n': 'description', 'tags': {}, 'properties': {}, 'id': '/subscriptions/dcfc206a-203b-4c00-a236-bdf576a37896/resourceGroups/a
ml-v2-book/providers/Microsoft.MachineLearningServices/workspaces/aml2-ws/data/titanic-mltable-sdk/versions/1', 'base_path':
'./', 'creation_context': <azure.ai.ml._restclient.v2022_05_01.models._models_py3.SystemData object at 0x7f836df7c190>, 'ser
ialize': <msrest.serialization.Serializer object at 0x7f8382418130>, 'version': '1', 'latest_version': None, 'path': 'azurem
l://subscriptions/dcfc206a-203b-4c00-a236-bdf576a37896/resourcegroups/aml-v2-book/workspaces/aml2-ws/datastores/workspaceblo
bstore/paths/LocalUpload/3d965967cdc59f53b78e4c4a313ce4a1/my_data/', 'referenced_uris': None})
```

Figure 2.19 – Creating a data asset via the Python SDK

Inside the `my_data` folder, there are two files:

- The actual data file, which in this case is `titanic.csv`
- The `mltable` file, which is a YAML file specifying the data's schema so that the `mltable` engine can use it in order to materialize the data into an in-memory object such as pandas or DASK

Figure 2.20 shows the `mltable` YAML file for this example:

```yaml
type: mltable

paths:
    - file: ./titanic.csv

transformations:
    - read_delimited:
        encoding: ascii
        header: all_files_same_headers
        delimiter: ','
```

Figure 2.20 – The mltable YAML file for creating an mltable data asset

If you head back to the **Data** tab under **Data assets**, you will see that a new dataset called **titanic-mltable-sdk** has been created with its type set to **Table(mltable)** and its version to **1**.

In this section, we showed you how to create a data asset using the Python SDK. In the next section, you will learn how to consume a data asset.

Using Azure Machine Learning datasets

During this chapter, we have covered what an Azure Machine Learning datastore is and how to connect to a variety of supported data sources. We created connections to Azure Machine Learning datastores using Azure Machine Learning Studio, the Python SDK, and the Azure CLI. We have just covered Azure Machine Learning datasets, a valuable asset for your ML projects. We went through how to generate Azure Machine Learning datasets using Azure Machine Learning Studio and the Python SDK. Once an Azure Machine Learning dataset is created, it can be used throughout your Azure Machine Learning experiments, which are called **jobs**.

Figure 2.21 shows a code snippet for materializing the `mltable` artifact into a pandas dataframe. Please note that you need the `mltable` library installed in your environment (using the `pip install mltable` command).

```
import mltable
tbl = mltable.load(uri="./my_data")
df = tbl.to_pandas_dataframe()
df
```

	PassengerId	Survived	Pclass	Name	Sex	Age	SibSp	Parch	Ticket	Fare	Cabin	Embarked
0	1	0	3	Braund, Mr. Owen Harris	male	22	1	0	A/5 21171	7.25	None	S
1	2	1	1	Cumings, Mrs. John Bradley (Florence Briggs Th...	female	38	1	0	PC 17599	71.2833	C85	C
2	3	1	3	Heikkinen, Miss. Laina	female	26	0	0	STON/O2. 3101282	7.925	None	S
3	4	1	1	Futrelle, Mrs. Jacques Heath (Lily May Peel)	female	35	1	0	113803	53.1	C123	S
4	5	0	3	Allen, Mr. William Henry	male	35	0	0	373450	8.05	None	S
...	...	...	...	...	...	...	...	...	...	...	...	...
886	887	0	2	Montvila, Rev. Juozas	male	27	0	0	211536	13	None	S
887	888	1	1	Graham, Miss. Margaret Edith	female	19	0	0	112053	30	B42	S
888	889	0	3	Johnston, Miss. Catherine Helen "Carrie"	female	None	1	2	W./C. 6607	23.45	None	S
889	890	1	1	Behr, Mr. Karl Howell	male	26	0	0	111369	30	C148	C
890	891	0	3	Dooley, Mr. Patrick	male	32	0	0	370376	7.75	None	Q

891 rows × 12 columns

Figure 2.21 – Materializing the mltable artifact into a pandas dataframe

Now let's see how to use a data asset inside an ML job, which will be covered in the next section.

Read data in a job

An Azure Machine Learning job consists of a Python script, which could be simple data processing or a complex code for model development, a Bash command to specify tasks to be performed, the inputs and outputs of the job, the Docker environment specifying the runtime libraries required to run the job and a compute where the Docker container would run on. The code that is executed inside a job will probably need to use a dataset. The primary way to pass data to an Azure Machine Learning job is by using datasets.

Let's walk you through the steps needed to run a job that takes a dataset as input:

1. Create an Azure Machine Learning environment, which is where your process to train a model or process your data takes place. *Figure 2.22* shows the code snippet to create an environment called `env_docker_conda`, which will be used in *step 4*:

```python
from azure.ai.ml.entities import Environment

env_docker_conda = Environment(
    image="mcr.microsoft.com/azureml/openmpi3.1.2-ubuntu18.04",
    conda_file="env-mltable.yml",
    name="mltable",
    description="Environment created for consuming MLTable.",
)

ml_client.environments.create_or_update(env_docker_conda)
```

```
Environment({'is_anonymous': False, 'auto_increment_version': False, 'name': 'mltable', 'description': 'Environment created for consuming MLTable.', 'tags': {}, 'properties': {}, 'id': '/subscriptions/dcfc206a-203b-4c00-a236-bdf576a37896/resourceGroups/aml-v2-book/providers/Microsoft.MachineLearningServices/workspaces/aml2-ws/environments/mltable/versions/1', 'base_path': './', 'creation_context': <azure.ai.ml._restclient.v2022_05_01.models._models_py3.SystemData object at 0x7f836cdb8fd0>, 'serialize': <msrest.serialization.Serializer object at 0x7f836cda9760>, 'version': '1', 'latest_version': None, 'conda_file': OrderedDict([('channels', ['conda-forge']), ('dependencies', ['python=3.8', 'pip=21.2.4', OrderedDict([('pip', ['mltable', 'pandas==1.3.0'])])]), ('name', 'mltable-env')]), 'image': 'mcr.microsoft.com/azureml/openmpi3.1.2-ubuntu18.04', 'build': None, 'inference_config': None, 'os_type': 'Linux', 'arm_type': 'environment_version', 'conda_file_path': None, 'path': None, 'upload_hash': None, 'translated_conda_file': None})
```

Figure 2.22 – Creating the Azure Machine Learning environment

In the preceding code, `env-mltable.yml`, which is shown in *Figure 2.22*, is a YAML file defining the Python libraries that need to be installed in the environment:

```yaml
name: mltable-env
channels:
  - conda-forge
dependencies:
  - python=3.8
  - pip=21.2.4
  - pip:
    - mltable
    - pandas==1.3.0
```

Figure 2.23 – Environment specification YAML file

2. Write a Python script to process your data and build a model. For this chapter, we will show you a simple Python script that takes an input dataset, converts it to a pandas dataframe, and then prints it. *Figure 2.24* shows the script saved in a file called read_data.py, which will be used in *step 4*:

```python
import argparse
import mltable

parser = argparse.ArgumentParser()
parser.add_argument("--input_data", type=str)
args = parser.parse_args()

tbl = mltable.load(args.input_data)
df = tbl.to_pandas_dataframe()
print(df)
```

Figure 2.24 – Python script processing the input dataset

3. Create an Azure Machine Learning compute cluster where the Azure Machine Learning containerized job will be submitted. *Figure 2.25* shows the Python script to create a compute cluster called cpu-cluster by specifying its type and the minimum and maximum number of nodes:

```python
from azure.ai.ml.entities import ComputeInstance, AmlCompute

compute_cluster = AmlCompute(
    name="cpu-cluster",
    type="amlcompute",
    size="STANDARD_DS3_v2",
    location="eatus",
    min_instances=0,
    max_instances=2,
    idle_time_before_scale_down=120,
)
ml_client.begin_create_or_update(compute_cluster)
```

Figure 2.25 – Create Azure Machine Learning compute cluster

4. Now you have all the necessary pieces to construct an Azure Machine Learning job and submit it for execution. *Figure 2.26* shows the Python script for creating an Azure Machine Learning job called `job`. This job is essentially a Docker container containing your Python code in `read_data.py`, which is taking your previously created input dataset and is submitted to the compute cluster you created:

```python
from azure.ai.ml import command
from azure.ai.ml.entities import Data
from azure.ai.ml import Input
from azure.ai.ml.constants import AssetTypes


# Possible Paths for Data:
# Blob: https://<account_name>.blob.core.windows.net/<container_name>/<folder>/<file>
# Datastore: azureml://datastores/paths/<folder>/<file>
# Data Asset: azureml:<my_data>:<version>


# for example you can use either one of the following paths:
# inputs = {"input_data": Input(type=AssetTypes.MLTABLE, path="./my_data/")}
# or
inputs = {"input_data": Input(type=AssetTypes.MLTABLE, path="azureml:titanic-mltable-sdk:2")}

job = command(
    code=".",  # local path where the code is stored
    command="python read_data.py --input_data ${{inputs.input_data}}",
    inputs=inputs,
    environment=env_docker_conda,
    compute="cpu-cluster",
)

# submit the command
returned_job = ml_client.jobs.create_or_update(job)
# get a URL for the status of the job
returned_job.services["Studio"].endpoint
```

```
Warning: the provided asset name 'mltable' will not be used for anonymous registration
Warning: the provided asset name 'mltable' will not be used for anonymous registration
Uploading chapter 2 (0.09 MBs): 100%|██████████| 86455/86455 [00:00<00:00, 225024.44it/s]
```

'https://ml.azure.com/runs/boring_neck_jmc85444kw?wsid=/subscriptions/dcfc206a-203b-4c00-a236-bdf576a37896/resourcegroups/aml-v2-book/workspaces/aml2-ws&tid=72f988bf-86f1-41af-91ab-2d7cd011db47'

Figure 2.26 – Creating an Azure Machine Learning job

The output of the Jupyter notebook cell is a link to the job in Azure Machine Learning Studio, which displays the job's overview, its status, the Python code, and the output of the job. If you navigate to this link and click on **Outputs + logs**, then **std_log.txt** under **user_logs**, you will see the output generated by the Python code, which is printing the input dataset to the standard log, as shown in *Figure 2.27*:

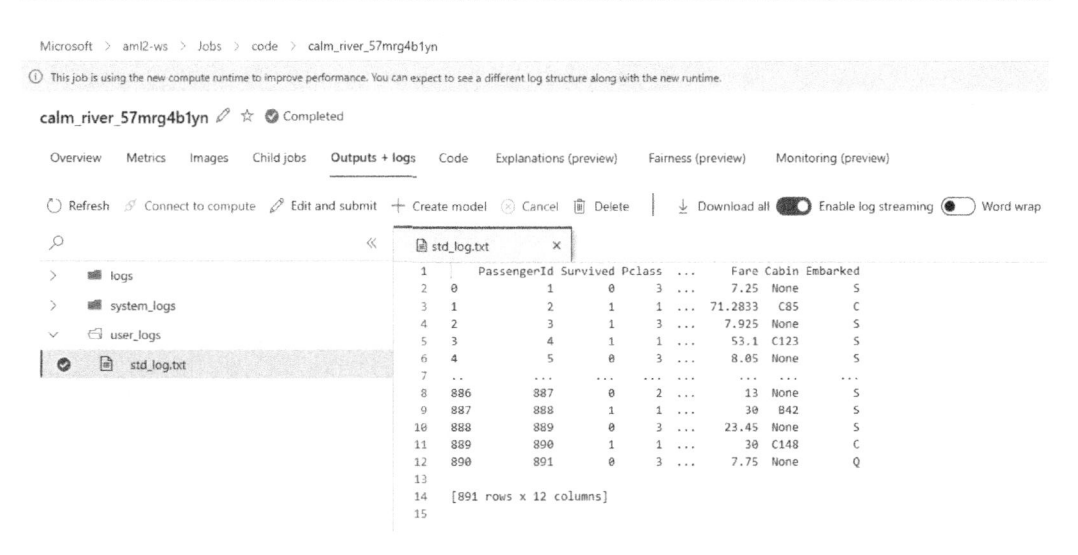

Figure 2.27 – Output of the Azure Machine Learning job after successful execution

Let's summarize the chapter now.

Summary

In this chapter, you have explored Azure Machine Learning datastores, which enable you to connect to datastore services. You have also learned about Azure Machine Learning datasets, empowering you to create a reference to a location within a datastore. These assets within Azure Machine Learning can be created through the UI for a low code experience, as well as through the Azure Machine Learning Python SDK or the Azure Machine Learning CLI. Once these references are created, datasets can be retrieved and used through the Azure Machine Learning Python SDK. Once the dataset has been retrieved, it can easily be converted into a pandas dataframe for use within your code. You have also seen how to use datasets within an Azure Machine Learning job by passing them as input to the job.

In *Chapter 3, Training Machine Learning Models in AMLS*, you will explore training models; experiments will become a key asset in your toolbelt, enabling traceability as you build your model in AMLS.

3
Training Machine Learning Models in AMLS

Training **Machine Learning** (ML) models in **Azure Machine Learning** (AML) is key to enabling your data science workload. Typically, during the model creation process, data is split into test and training datasets. Models are then built with the training data and evaluated using the test dataset. During this process, many algorithms are selected and used to answer the question: what model will provide the best results on an unseen dataset? AML has the capability to log metrics, taking snapshots of the code that produced a given model performance to enable answering this question. AML comes with a variety of accelerating capacities. During this chapter, we will focus on the creation of experiments to train models and on the basic functionality of AML experiments to unlock using compute instances, compute clusters, and registered datasets.

Model training can be established through the AML Python SDK or the designer for a low-code experience. During the model training process, different compute resources can be used to accomplish this task. In this chapter, we will explore using compute instances for basic model training and compute clusters for a repeatable training environment, as well as through the designer for a low-code experience.

In this chapter, we will learn how to use datasets to build ML models with AML compute and datasets.

We will cover the following topics:

- Training code-free models with the Designer
- Training on a compute instance
- Training on a compute cluster

Technical requirements

Refer to *Chapter 1, Introducing the Azure Machine Learning Service*, to create the environment workspace to use.

The following are the prerequisites for this chapter:

- Have access to the internet.
- Have a web browser, preferably Google Chrome or Microsoft Edge Chromium.
- To access the Azure Machine Learning Service workspace, please go to this address: `https://ml.azure.com`. Select the workspace from the drop-down list.

Training code-free models with the designer

In this section, let's see what options are available for code-free modeling using the **designer**. The Designer enables data scientists to create models without the need to write code. It makes it easy for any data scientist to build and compare models. Within the designer, the development environment is a graphical user interface that allows right-clicking to change the settings for a given step. The interface allows not only the development of the model but also one-click deployment to deploy to various styles of APIs, including real-time or batch endpoints, which are REST APIs that can be consumed by other business applications or downstream applications.

For example, drag a task to connect to a data source and configure the properties to connect to the data source. These properties include the dataset name and connection string parameters, including the username and password.

Creating a dataset using the user interface

Let's go through the steps to create a dataset using the user interface:

1. Go to `https://ml.azure.com`.
2. Select your workspace name.
3. On the left side of the workspace, select **Designer**, as seen in the following screenshot:

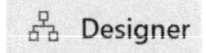

Figure 3.1 – Designer icon

4. Once you are on the **Designer** screen, you'll see that the screen is divided into two parts. The top part shows some examples or samples available for anyone to test. All samples use open source datasets, so anyone can test, develop, and learn from them. The bottom parts show the experiments you created, and if you click on an experiment, the graph will be shown in the canvas to the right.

Training code-free models with the designer   69

The designer experience is shown in the following screenshot:

Figure 3.2 – Designer experience

5. Before creating an experiment, make sure a compute cluster is created, as shown in *Chapter 1, Introducing the Azure Machine Learning Service*, or you can also find it in this chapter where we show how to create a cluster for remote jobs.

6. Click the + button to create a new experiment:

Figure 3.3 – Create a new designer experiment

7. Clicking **Create a new pipeline** will take you to the designer canvas. First and foremost, we give the experiment a name. I have provided `Classificationsample1` as the name. Now, we also have to provide a compute target. From the dropdown, select **Compute cluster** and then select the cluster that you have created. The cluster can be CPU-based or GPU-based.

> **Tip**
> A compute cluster provides a way to scale compute across multiple VMs to scale horizontally. Select CPU or GPU based on the use case. For example, most tabular datasets with less-than-TB size can use CPU-based clusters. For vision-based workloads, please choose GPU clusters.

8. Select the default data store, which usually would be the Azure Machine Learning service's underlying data store. Select **workspaceblobstore** as your choice and provide experiment details in the **Draft details** section. Then, click on the **X** icon on the right side to see the entire canvas:

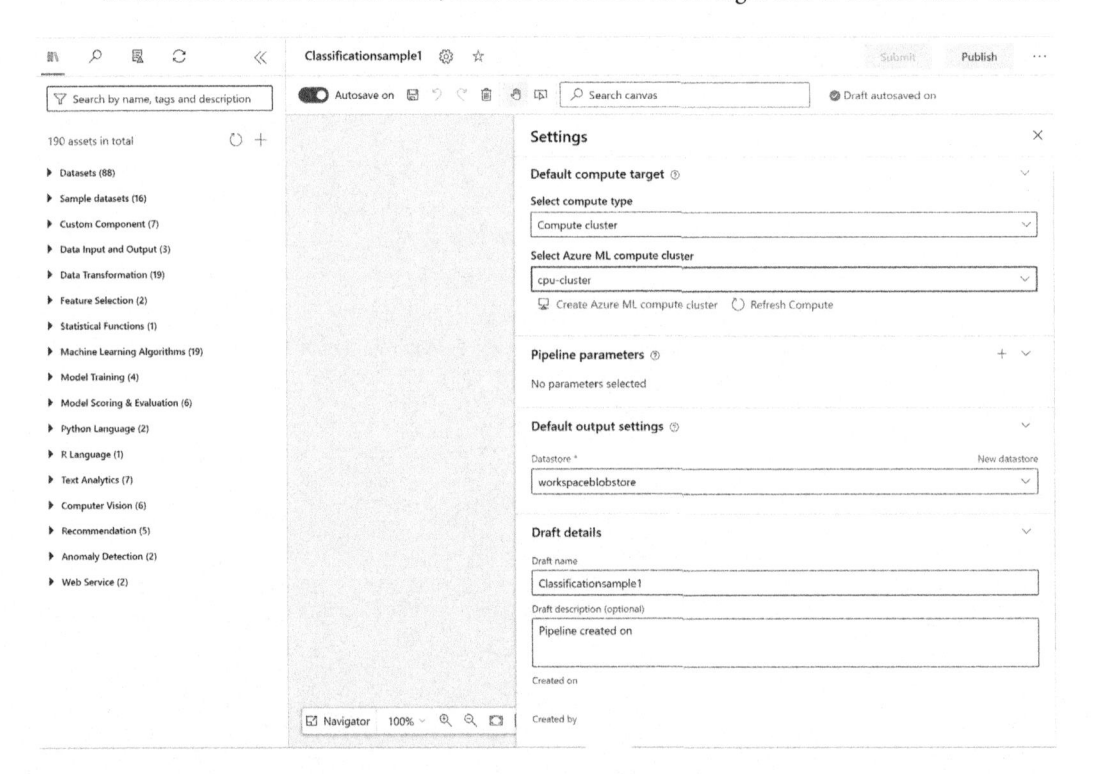

Figure 3.4 – Create a new designer experiment canvas

Note, from *Figure 3.4*, that on the left side you have the menu options. This is where we have all the tasks that can be dragged and dropped onto the canvas to build a model. The menu is categorized for different operations, such as datasets, data input and output, data transformation, and ML algorithms. Consider reading the product documentation online for each task and its properties and functionalities.

Let's build a model. The first thing you are going to bring is the dataset that you have it registered from *Chapter 2*, *Working with Data in AMLS*. In the left menu, expand **Datasets**, select the one to use, and drag and drop it to the canvas.

> **Important note**
> In this chapter, I am going to walk you through a basic ML modeling step.

9. For this chapter, I have created a Titanic open source data sample and configured as a dataset. Here is how it looks when you drag and drop it on the canvas. Right-click on the dataset and the property sheet will show on the right side of the screen. Select **Output** and view the dataset sample rows. An option to view the data profile will also be provided:

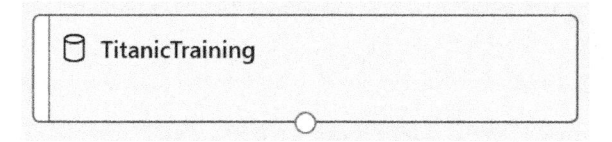

Figure 3.5 – Dataset on canvas

10. Now, in the search box of the left menu, type `Select Columns in Dataset` and drag and drop it on the canvas, then connect the previous dataset to **Select Columns in Dataset**. Now, click **Select Columns in Dataset**, go to **Select columns**, and select the **Edit columns** to use for modeling. This task allows us to choose which columns we can use:

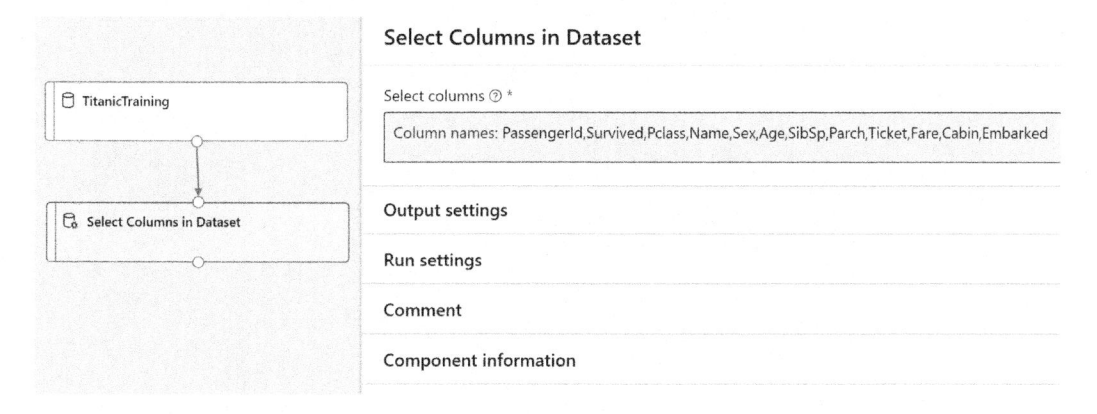

Figure 3.6 – Select Columns in Dataset

In the **Edit Columns** section, choose the columns we need. There are options to select all columns, all features, or all labels or choose by name. For the preceding sample, we chose to select by column name and selected columns from the list.

11. The next transformation is going to be for cleaning data. This is a common task to perform to get rid of unwanted rows that have no values, null values, and so on. Type `Clean Missing Data` in the search box and drop it on the canvas, then connect it to the previous task, in this case, **Select Columns in Dataset**:

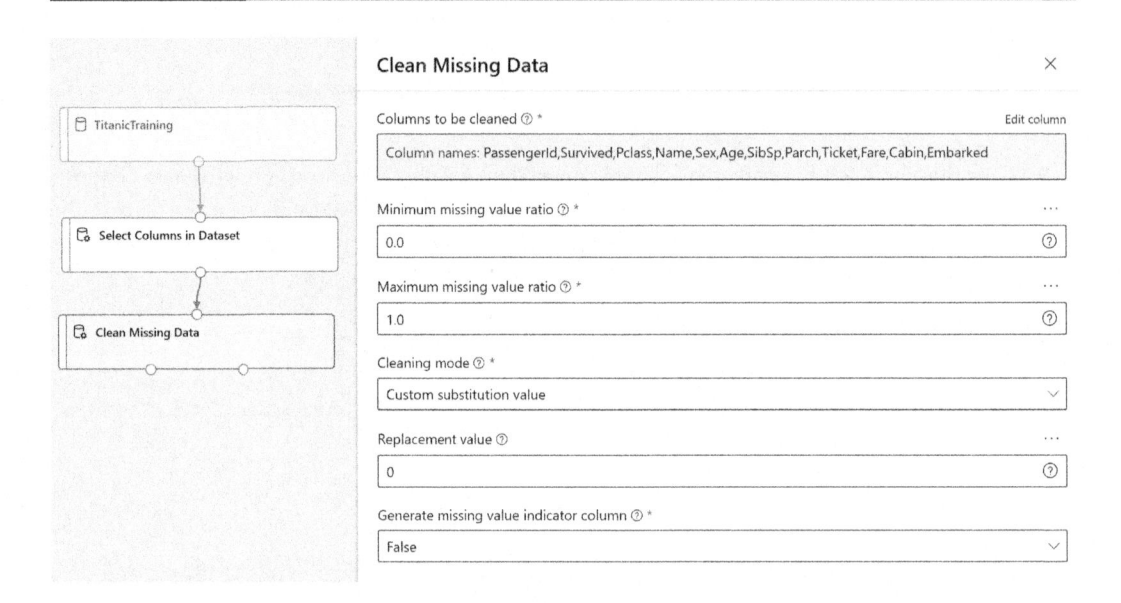

Figure 3.7 – Clean Missing Data

12. Click **Edit column** and select the columns or features to clean. Feature or column selection can be either by rule or by name. When you click on the text box, a list will pop up, as shown in *Figure 3.8*. Select the columns or features you need to model. In this example, select all the columns:

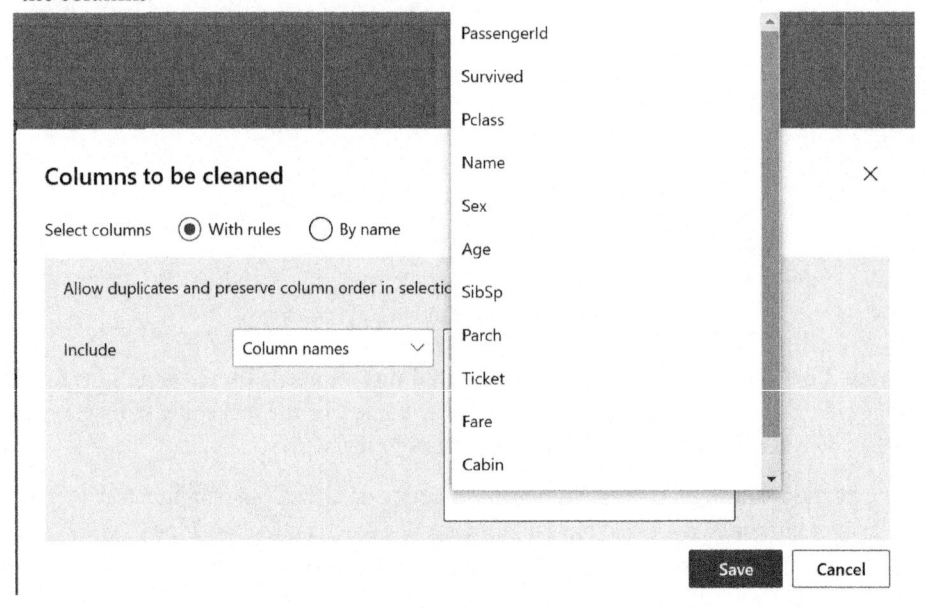

Figure 3.8 – Edit column

13. Now that we have done some feature engineering, it's time to split the data for training and testing. It's a very common practice during ML to split the dataset into training and testing. Usually, the split is 70% training and 30% testing. Type `Split Data` in the search box and drag and drop it on the canvas to connect it to the previous task. The property sheet will show up on the right. For **Splitting mode**, select **Split Rows**. For **Fraction of rows in the first output dataset**, type in `0.7`. This setting allows us to split the dataset into 70% for training and the remaining 30% for the test dataset.

The **Split Data** activity enables you to choose the split, whether the split should be randomized, the seed used for splitting, and whether the split should be stratified, as shown in the following screenshot:

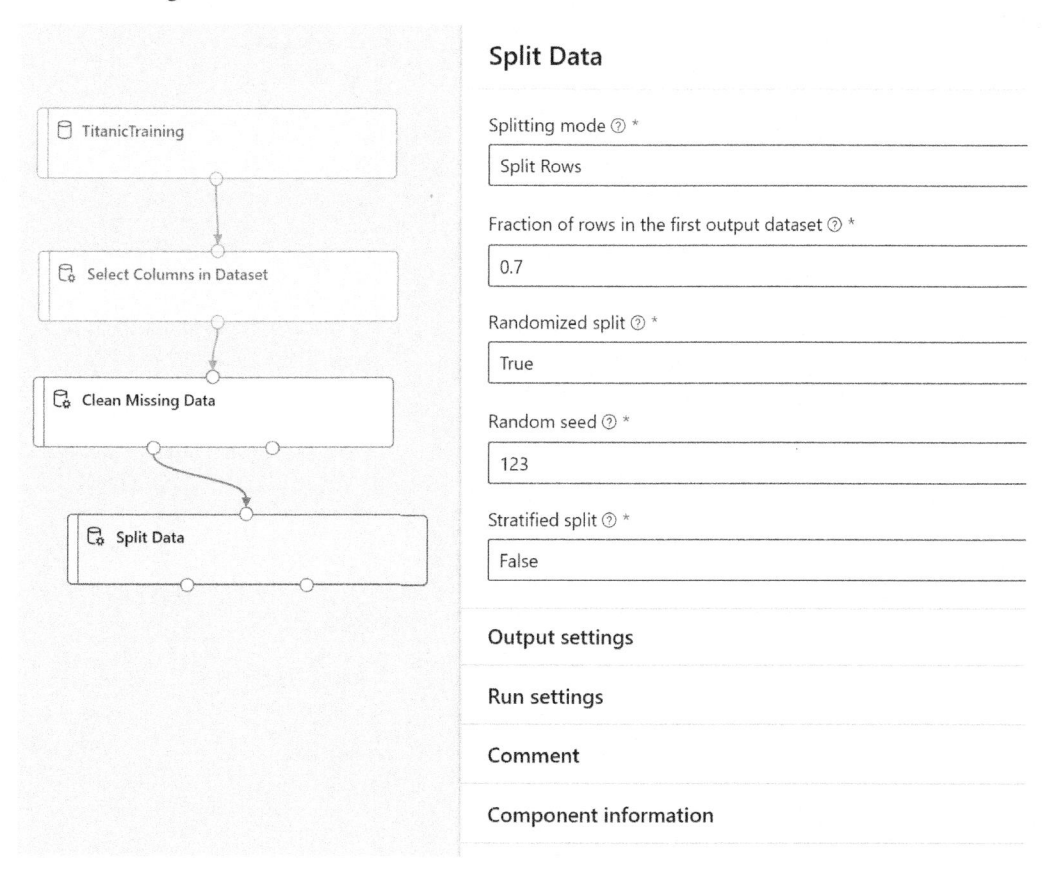

Figure 3.9 – Split Data

14. After **Split Data**, we need to add the ML algorithm to use for modeling. In the search box of the menu, type in `Two-Class Boosted Decision Tree` and drag and drop it onto the canvas. Since this is a simple survived ML task, we are choosing two-class boosted decision tree. You can select another two-class algorithm as needed. Once the algorithm is selected, we need to configure its parameters. Typically, you can leave most as the default values, as these parameters are chosen based on statistics of various model runs. You should ensure that you set your random seed as shown in *Figure 3.10*.

The following screenshot showcases the parameters to set for **Two-Class Boosted Decision Tree**:

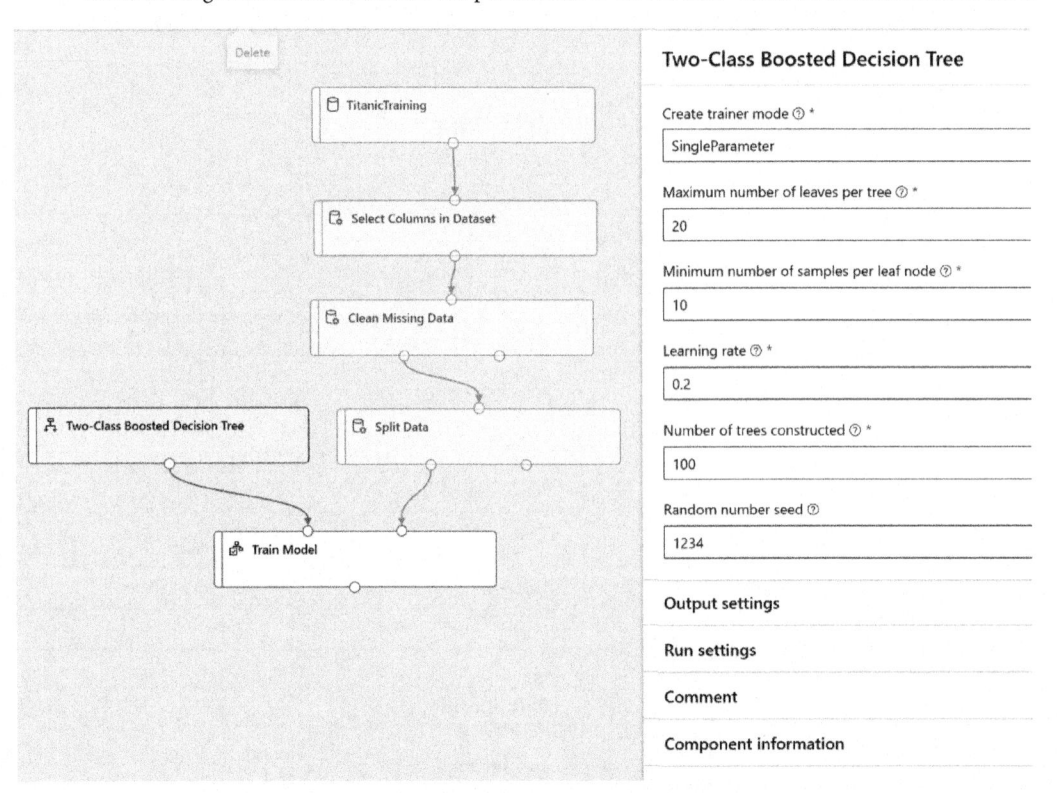

Figure 3.10 – Two-Class Boosted Decision Tree

15. Now, on the left menu, in the search box, type in `Train Model` and drop it onto the canvas. For **Train Model**, we need to connect to two inputs, which are one from the model output and the other from the first output of **Split Data**. Make sure the algorithm and training data are connected. Then, select **Train Model** and the label column to predict.
16. Select **Edit Column** and then set **Label column** to **Survived**. **Model explanations** is a feature that allows us to enable model expandability:

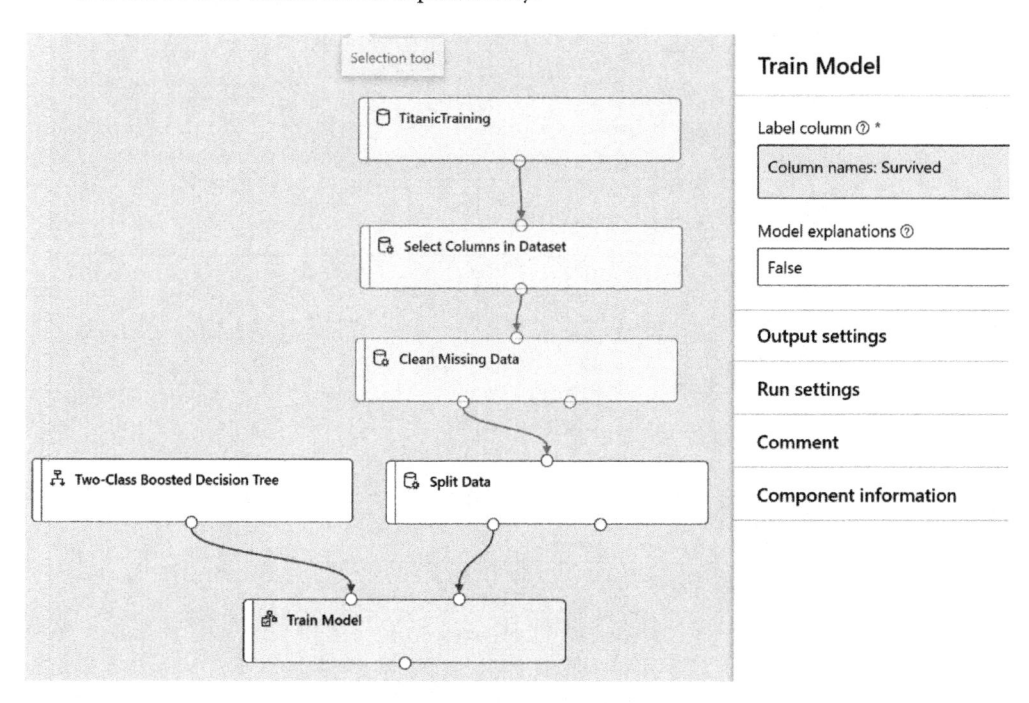

Figure 3.11 – Train Model

17. Now, you can score the model. Go to the left menu and in the search box, type in Score Model and drag and drop it onto the canvas. **Score Model** must be connected to two outputs. The first input should be connected to the output of **Train Model** and the second input has to be connected to **Split Data**'s second output. **Score Model** takes the training output model and then consumes the test dataset to score the test dataset:

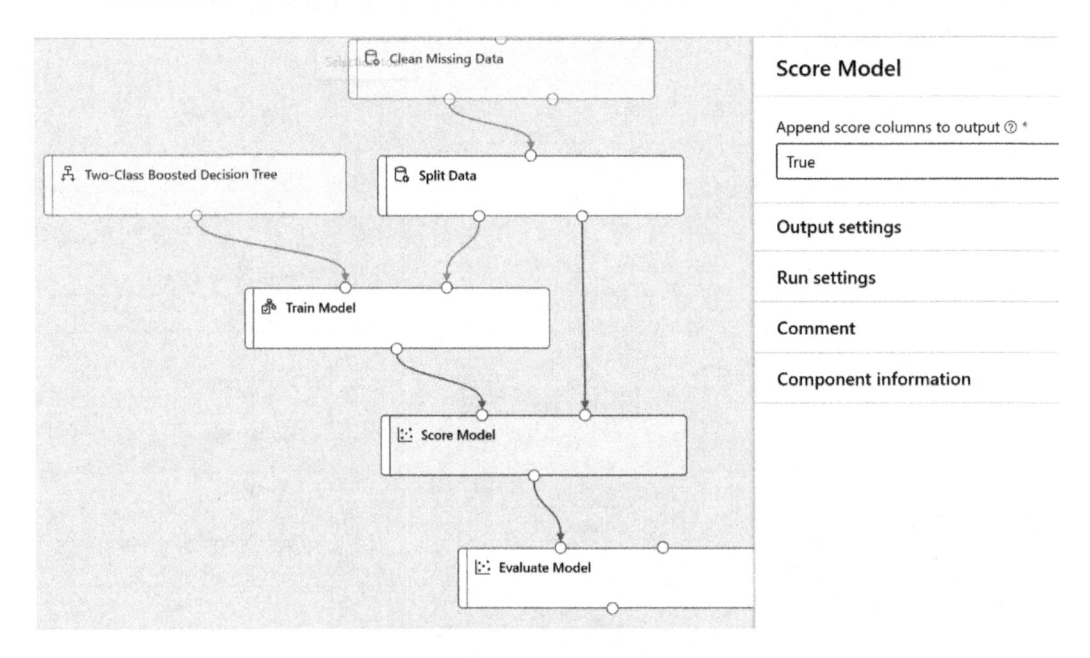

Figure 3.12 – Score Model

18. Now, the last step here is adding the **Evaluate Model** output and getting the model accuracy scores. For this, from the left menu, drag and drop **Evaluate Model** onto the canvas. For **Evaluate Model**, the first input should be connected to the **Score Model** output. There are no settings for this task:

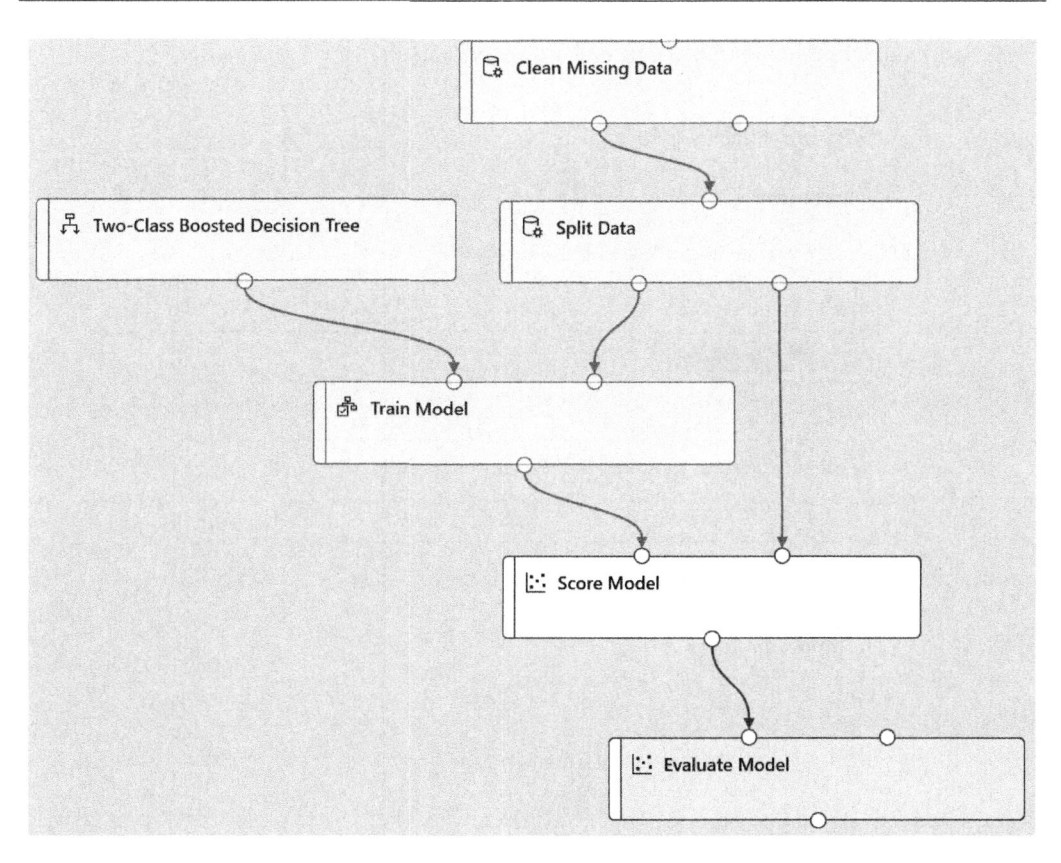

Figure 3.13 – Evaluate Model

19. Now, click **Save** on the canvas. We have now completed our development of the model. In the upper-right corner, you will see a button for **Submit**:

Figure 3.14 – Submit experiment

20. Click on **Submit** and provide a name for the experiment:

Set up pipeline run

Experiment

○ Select existing   ● Create new

New experiment name *

Classificationsample1

Job description

Pipeline created on 20220117

☑ Continue on failure step

Compute target

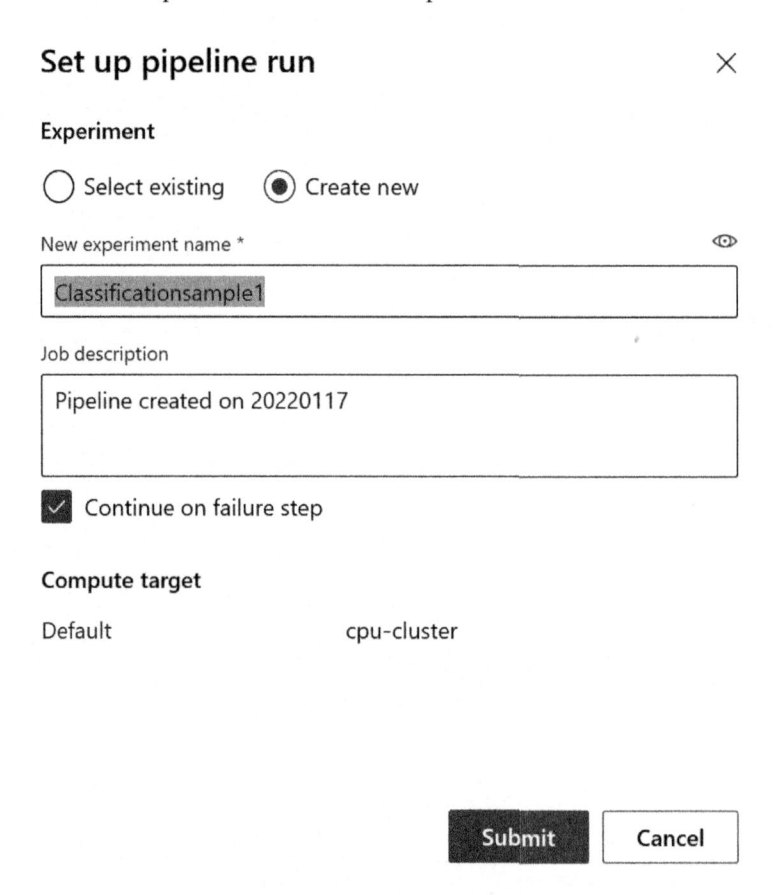

Default   cpu-cluster

Submit   Cancel

Figure 3.15 – New experiment

21. Then, click **Submit**. The system will take some time to start the compute cluster and then run the experiment. Provide the experiment name as `Classificationsample1`. Provide a job description for the experiment, which is optional. Leave **Compute target** as **Default** as we selected at the beginning of the experiment. Wait for the experiment to complete. Once the experiment is started, you should see the following screenshot:

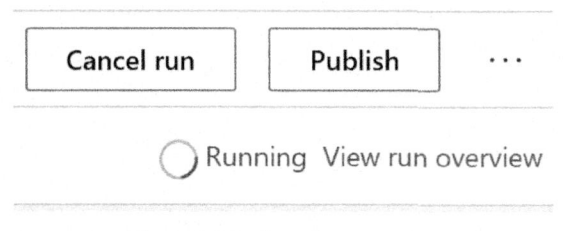

Cancel run   Publish   ...

◯ Running View run overview

Figure 3.16 – Experiment status

Optionally, you can also see the run details by clicking on **Jobs**, and then for **Classificationsample1**, click on its latest job.

22. Once the experiment is completed, you should see all the tasks in green, as per the following screenshot:

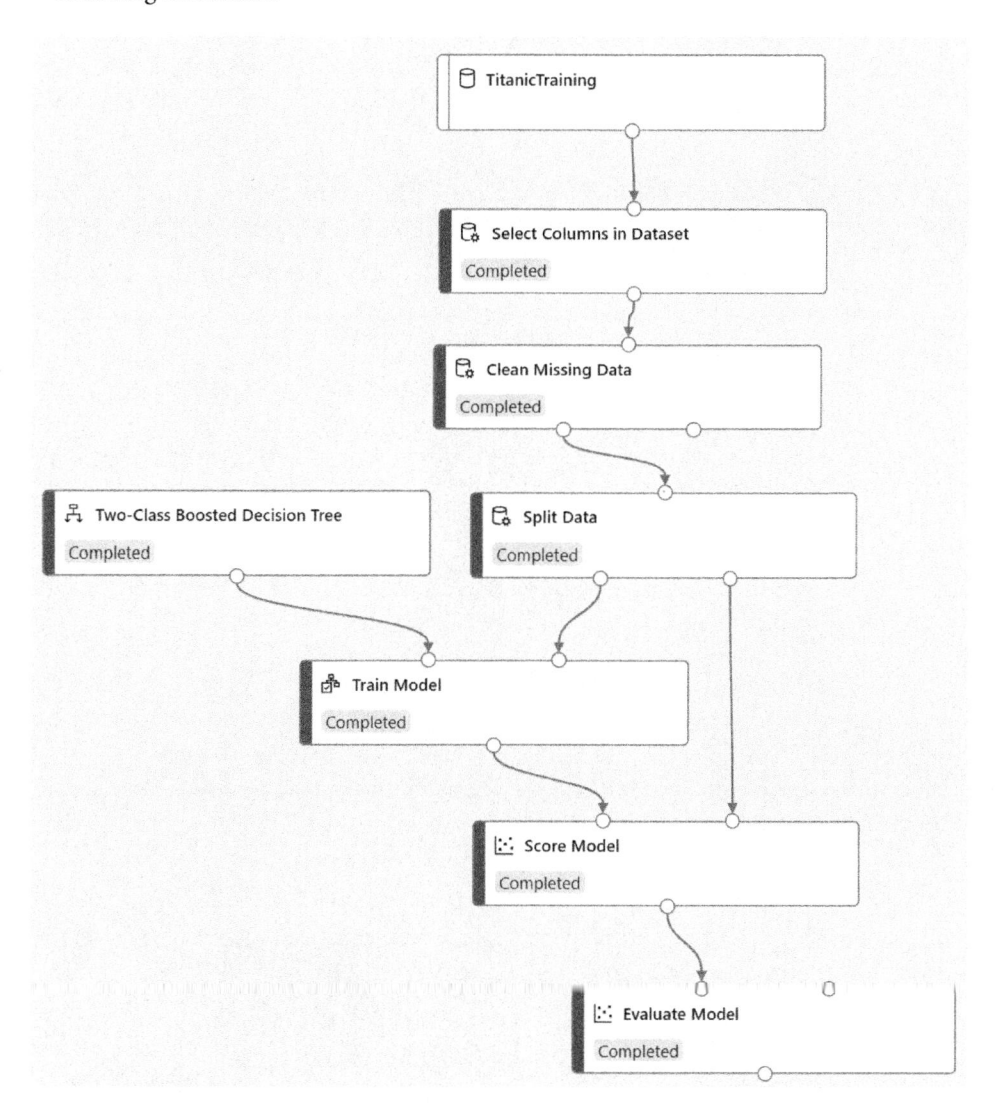

Figure 3.17 – Experiment completed

By clicking on the **Evaluate Model** task, we can review the results of the **Evaluate Model** task. In our case, I am only going to show **Evaluate Model** to see the confusion matrix and the **Receiver Operating Characteristic (ROC)** curve:

Figure 3.18 – ROC curve

In addition to reviewing the ROC curve, we can also review the confusion matrix, as shown in the following screenshot:

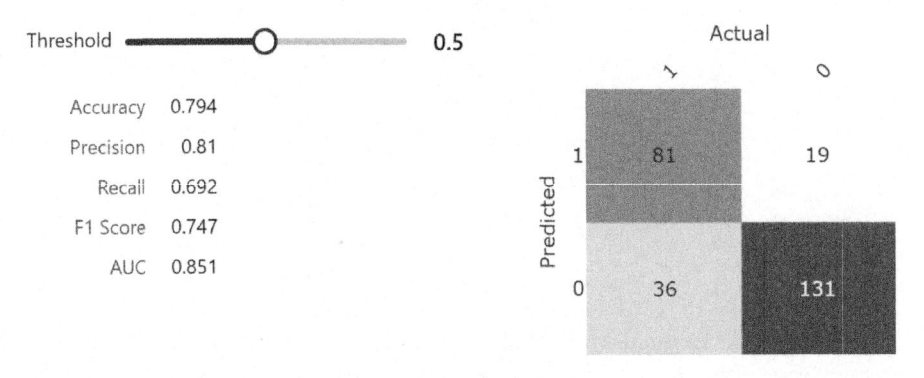

Figure 3.19 – Confusion matrix

In this section, we saw how to train a model using the Designer in AMLS. Using the Designer, we can train the model using the drag-and-drop interface, as well as carrying out feature engineering to provide an improved model. As a follow-up, take a look at each task in the user interface.

In the next section, you will learn how to train a model by writing Python code and running it on a compute instance.

Training on a compute instance

You can train a model on a compute instance or on a compute cluster. In this section, we will use our existing compute instance before continuing with training on a compute cluster.

To begin working with a compute instance, we will need to turn on the compute instance that was created in *Chapter 1, Introducing the Azure Machine Learning Service*.

Follow these steps to train a model on a compute instance within AMLS:

1. Go to https://ml.azure.com.
2. Select your workspace name.
3. On the left side of the workspace, click **Compute**:

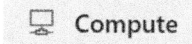

Figure 3.20 – Compute instance icon

4. On the **Compute** screen, select your compute instance and select **Start**:

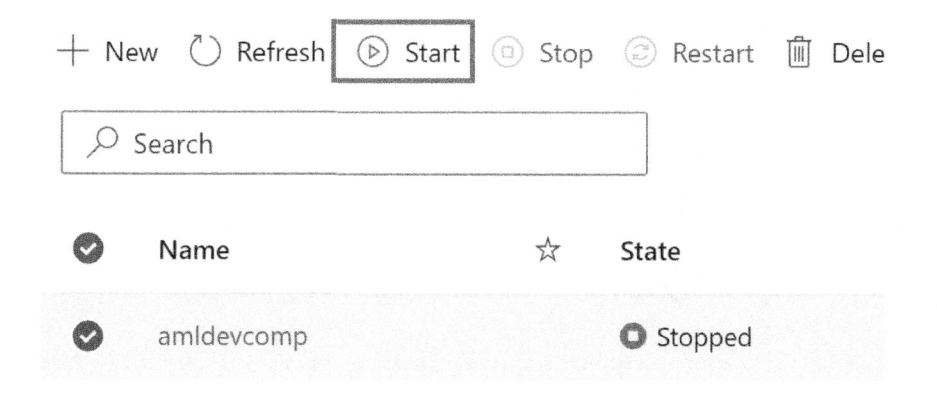

Figure 3.21 – Start compute

Your compute instance will change from **Stopped** to **Starting** status. Once the compute instance moves from **Starting** to **Running** status, it is ready for use.

5. Click on the Terminal blue hyperlink under applications.
6. This will open the terminal on your compute instance. Note your user will be included in the directory path. Type the following into the terminal to clone the sample notebooks into your working directory: `https://github.com/PacktPublishing/Azure-Machine-Learning-Engineering.git`.
7. Clicking on the refresh icon shown in *Figure 3.22* will display the repository in your working directory:

Figure 3.22 – Refresh

After clicking the refresh icon within AML, the cloned repository will be displayed in your working directory, as shown in the following screenshot:

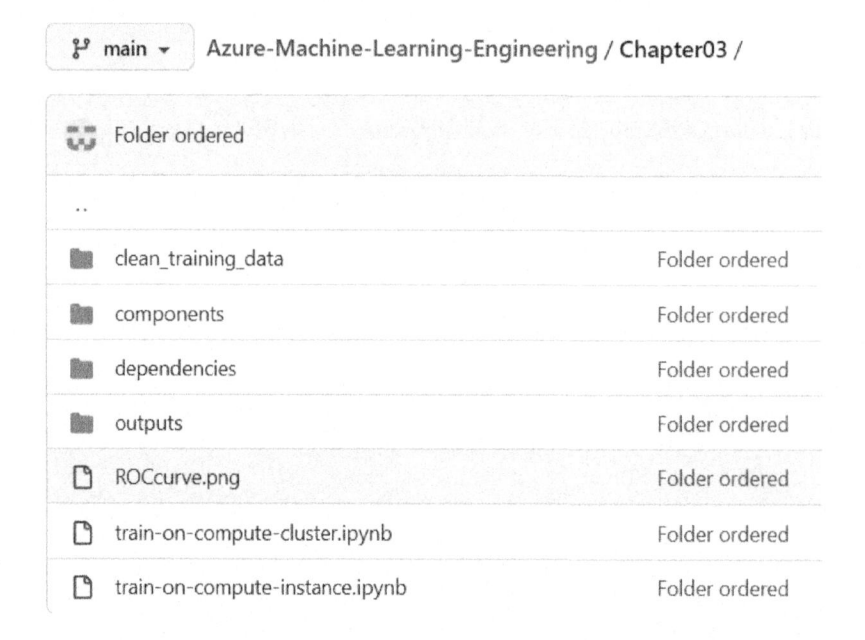

main ▾ Azure-Machine-Learning-Engineering / **Chapter03** /	
Folder ordered	
..	
clean_training_data	Folder ordered
components	Folder ordered
dependencies	Folder ordered
outputs	Folder ordered
ROCcurve.png	Folder ordered
train-on-compute-cluster.ipynb	Folder ordered
train-on-compute-instance.ipynb	Folder ordered

Figure 3.23 – Azure-Machine-Learning-Engineering

8. Clicking on the **train-on-compute-instance.ipynb** notebook will bring up the notebook.
9. The code snippet shown in *Figure 3.24* enables you to connect to the Azure ML workspace in your compute instance:

```python
import azure.ai.ml
```

```python
# import required libraries
from azure.ai.ml import MLClient
from azure.identity import DefaultAzureCredential
from azure.ai.ml import command, Input
from azure.ai.ml.entities import (
    AzureBlobDatastore,
    AzureFileDatastore,
    AzureDataLakeGen1Datastore,
    AzureDataLakeGen2Datastore,
)
from azure.ai.ml.entities import Environment
```

```python
# Enter details of your AML workspace
subscription_id = 
resource_group = "aml-v2-book"
workspace = "aml2-ws"
```

```python
# get a handle to the workspace
ml_client = MLClient(
    DefaultAzureCredential(), subscription_id, resource_group, workspace
)
```

Figure 3.24 – Connecting to the workspace

10. The code snippet shown in *Figure 3.25* uses pandas to read in the dataset that is located in the my_data folder and then view it:

```python
import pandas as pd
file_name = os.path.join('../chapter 2/my_data', "titanic.csv")
df = pd.read_csv(file_name)
print(df.shape)
print(df.columns)
```
```
(891, 12)
Index(['PassengerId', 'Survived', 'Pclass', 'Name', 'Sex', 'Age', 'SibSp',
       'Parch', 'Ticket', 'Fare', 'Cabin', 'Embarked'],
      dtype='object')
```

```python
df.head(5)
```

	PassengerId	Survived	Pclass	Name	Sex	Age	SibSp	Parch	Ticket	Fare	Cabin	Embarked
0	1	0	3	Braund, Mr. Owen Harris	male	22.0	1	0	A/5 21171	7.2500	NaN	S
1	2	1	1	Cumings, Mrs. John Bradley (Florence Briggs Th...	female	38.0	1	0	PC 17599	71.2833	C85	C
2	3	1	3	Heikkinen, Miss. Laina	female	26.0	0	0	STON/O2. 3101282	7.9250	NaN	S
3	4	1	1	Futrelle, Mrs. Jacques Heath (Lily May Peel)	female	35.0	1	0	113803	53.1000	C123	S
4	5	0	3	Allen, Mr. William Henry	male	35.0	0	0	373450	8.0500	NaN	S

Figure 3.25 – Data exploration: Reading in the dataset and viewing the data

The next cell checks to see what columns have null data have so that we can cleanse the dataset:

```
1  df.isnull().sum()
```

```
PassengerId      0
Survived         0
Pclass           0
Name             0
Sex              0
Age            177
SibSp            0
Parch            0
Ticket           0
Fare             0
Cabin          687
Embarked         2
dtype: int64
```

Figure 3.26 – Data exploration: View null values in the dataset

11. The **Age**, **Cabin**, and **Embarked** columns in the dataset will require cleansing. *Figure 3.27* shows populating the **Age** column with the median value for a given Pclass and Sex when the value is null:

```
1  df['Age'] = df.groupby(['Pclass', 'Sex'])['Age'].apply(lambda x: x.fillna(x.median()))
2  df.isnull().sum()
```

```
PassengerId      0
Survived         0
Pclass           0
Name             0
Sex              0
Age              0
SibSp            0
Parch            0
Ticket           0
Fare             0
Cabin          687
Embarked         2
dtype: int64
```

Figure 3.27 – Data cleansing: Populating the Age column's null values with the medians for Pclass and Sex

12. For `Cabin`, we can use the first character and treat it as a categorical variable during model creation to represent the location in the ship. If the value is `null`, we will replace it with X, representing an unknown `Cabin` type, as shown in *Figure 3.28*:

    ```
    df['Loc']= df['Cabin'].apply(lambda x: x[0] if pd.notnull(x) else 'X')
    ```

    Figure 3.28 – Feature engineering: Populating the Loc column

13. We will drop the `Cabin` column, given we have retrieved the useful information from it, and also remove the `Ticket` column, as the `Loc` column will now represent the location within the ship, as shown in *Figure 3.29*:

    ```
    df.drop(['Cabin', 'Ticket'], axis=1, inplace=True)
    ```

    Figure 3.29 – Data cleansing: Dropping unnecessary columns

14. Continuing with feature engineering, we will create a column called `GroupSize`, as groups of passengers that were family members may have had a greater chance at survival by working together:

    ```
    df.loc[:,'GroupSize'] = 1 + df['SibSp'] + df['Parch']
    ```

    Figure 3.30 – Feature engineering: Group size

15. Given the values for the `'Embarked'` column are limited, and we only have two rows with null values, we will arbitrarily set them to the value of `'S'`, as shown in *Figure 3.31*:

    ```
    df['Embarked'] = df['Embarked'].fillna('S')
    ```

    Figure 3.31 – Data cleansing: Populating null value with a default value

As shown in *Figure 3.32*, we will drop the columns that we won't be using during the training process:

```
1   LABEL = 'Survived'
2   columns_to_drop = ['Name','SibSp', 'Parch', 'Survived']
3   df_train = df
4   df = df_train.drop(['Name','SibSp', 'Parch', 'PassengerId'], axis=1)
5
6   df.head(5)
```

	Survived	Pclass	Sex	Age	Fare	Embarked	Loc	GroupSize
0	0	3	male	22.0	7.2500	S	X	2
1	1	1	female	38.0	71.2833	C	C	2
2	1	3	female	26.0	7.9250	S	X	1
3	1	1	female	35.0	53.1000	S	C	2
4	0	3	male	35.0	8.0500	S	X	1

Figure 3.32 – Data cleansing: Dropping columns not needed for model training

16. We will create a folder to hold our training data, as shown in *Figure 3.33*. This is not required but will keep our directories clear:

```
import os
script_folder = os.path.join(os.getcwd(), "clean_training_data")
print(script_folder)
os.makedirs(script_folder, exist_ok=True)
```

Figure 3.33 – Folder creation

Training on a compute instance   87

The directory can be seen on the left pane in the *Notebooks* section after clicking on the refresh button, as shown in *Figure 3.34*:

- clean_training_data
- components
- dependencies
- outputs
- ROCcurve.png
- train-on-compute-cluster.ipynb
- train-on-compute-instance.ipynb

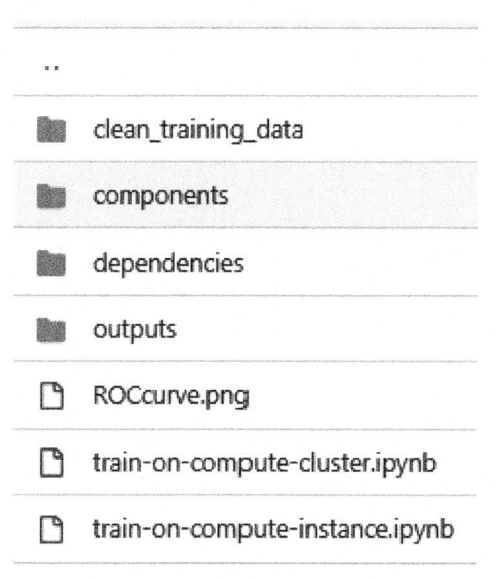

Figure 3.34 – View the clean_training_data folder in the directory

17. With the newly created directory, we can save the dataset to the `clean_training_data` directory, as shown in *Figure 3.35*:

```
df.to_csv('./clean_training_data/titanic.csv')
df.head(2)
```

Figure 3.35 – Saving the engineered dataset

18. We will begin with importing the needed libraries to create a logistic regression model, as shown in *Figure 3.36*:

```
1   import os
2   import sys
3   import argparse
4   import joblib
5   import pandas as pd
6   import numpy as np
7
8   from azureml.core import Run, Dataset, Workspace, Experiment
9   from sklearn.compose import ColumnTransformer
10  from sklearn.impute import SimpleImputer
11  from sklearn.linear_model import LogisticRegression
12  from sklearn.model_selection import train_test_split
13  from sklearn.pipeline import Pipeline
14  from sklearn.preprocessing import OneHotEncoder, StandardScaler
15  from sklearn.metrics import roc_auc_score,roc_curve, confusion_matrix
16  import matplotlib.pyplot as plt
```

Figure 3.36 – Import libraries

After importing the libraries required for our experiment, we will focus on the main method, which will be called as the code is executed on the compute instance:

```
def main():

    # Start Logging
    experiment_name = 'titanic_local_compute'
    mlflow.set_experiment(experiment_name)
    # Start Logging
    mlflow.start_run()

    # enable autologging
    mlflow.sklearn.autolog()

    df = pd.read_csv('./clean_training_data/titanic.csv')
    mlflow.log_metric("num_samples", df.shape[0])
    mlflow.log_metric("num_features", df.shape[1] - 1)

    model, auc, acc = model_train('Survived', df)

    os.makedirs('outputs', exist_ok=True)

    model_file = os.path.join('outputs', 'titanic_model.pkl')
    joblib.dump(value=model, filename=model_file)


    # Register the model
    # Stop Logging
    mlflow.end_run()

if __name__ == "__main__":
    main()
```

Figure 3.37 – Main module of the experiment

Using MLflow, which is an open source ML framework to manage an end-to-end ML life cycle and is fully integrated with AMLS, we will create an experiment named `'titanic_local_compute'`, which can be seen in *Figure 3.37* inside the main method. If it does not exist the first time the notebook is run, it will be created in the AML workspace. This experiment can be viewed on the **Jobs** tab. Next, we use the `mlflow.start_run()` method, which will begin a new run within the experiment. Using the `mlflow.sklearn.autolog()` and `mlflow.log_metric()` methods, we can log parameters and ML metrics for the current run.

Next, we will discuss the `model_train` function, as shown in *Figure 3.38*:

```python
def model_train(LABEL, df):
    y_raw = df[LABEL]
    X_raw = df.drop([LABEL], axis=1)
    # Train test split
    X_train, X_test, y_train, y_test = train_test_split(X_raw, y_raw, test_size=0.3, random_state=0)

    lg = LogisticRegression(penalty='l2', C=1.0, solver='liblinear')
    preprocessor = buildpreprocessorpipeline(X_train)

    #estimator instance
    clf = Pipeline(steps=[('preprocessor', preprocessor),
                          ('regressor', lg)])
    model = clf.fit(X_train, y_train)
    # calculate AUC
    y_scores = model.predict_proba(X_test)
    auc = roc_auc_score(y_test,y_scores[:,1])
    print('AUC: ' + str(auc))
    mlflow.log_metric("AUC:", auc)

    # calculate test accuracy
    y_hat = model.predict(X_test)
    acc = np.average(y_hat == y_test)
    print('Accuracy:', acc)
    mlflow.log_metric("Accuracy:", acc)
    # plot ROC curve
    fpr, tpr, thresholds = roc_curve(y_test, y_scores[:,1])
    fig = plt.figure(figsize=(6, 4))
    # Plot the diagonal 50% line
    plt.plot([0, 1], [0, 1], 'k--')
    # Plot the FPR and TPR achieved by our model
    plt.plot(fpr, tpr)
    plt.xlabel('False Positive Rate')
    plt.ylabel('True Positive Rate')
    plt.title('ROC Curve')
    plt.show()
```

Figure 3.38 – Model _train

A logistic regression model is created in the `model_train` function, as shown in *Figure 3.38*. The inputs and the response variable are separated and a train-test split is applied using the `sklearn` library. The model is fitted and the AUC and accuracy are printed as outputs in the notebook, but also leveraging the MLflow framework, they are logged to the experiment as output. In addition to logging key metrics and parameters as part of an experiment, figures associated with these metrics will be automatically logged using MLflow, which we will look at later in this section.

Given the training has been handled, we also want to include a preprocessor pipeline to handle data transformation as part of our pipeline, as shown in the following screenshot:

```python
def buildpreprocessorpipeline(X_raw):
    categorical_features = X_raw.select_dtypes(include=['object']).columns
    numeric_features = X_raw.select_dtypes(include=['float','int64']).columns

    categorical_transformer = Pipeline(steps=[('imputer', SimpleImputer(strategy='constant', fill_value="missing")),
                                              ('onehotencoder', OneHotEncoder(categories='auto', sparse=False, handle_unknown='ignore'))])
    numeric_transformer = Pipeline(steps=[('scaler', StandardScaler())])

    preprocessor = ColumnTransformer(
        transformers=[
            ('numeric', numeric_transformer, numeric_features),
            ('categorical', categorical_transformer, categorical_features)
        ], remainder="drop")

    return preprocessor
```

Figure 3.39 – Preprocessor

19. We have incorporated a preprocessor pipeline to handle data transformation, as shown in *Figure 3.39*. Creating a pipeline for data transformation ensures that when we score unseen data, the same transformations that were applied to our training dataset will be applied to the testing data, and to the new data the model hasn't seen before. This enables model deployment to use the same transformations in a deployed model when we get to that step.

20. Within the `model_train` method, after plotting the ROC curve, we use the `confusion_Matrix()` method to calculate the confusion matrix for the run of the experiment, which will also be logged automatically within AML, as shown later in the section.

21. This experiment was run directly on the AML compute instance as cells are executed in the notebook. Print statements and `plt.show` provide output directly in the notebook, as shown in *Figure 3.40*, but the Azure Machine Learning service has also captured this information within an experiment run, so when a notebook is cleared out, key metrics for model evaluation are not lost:

```
Starting experiment: titanic_local_compute
AUC: 0.8492261904761904
Accuracy: 0.8097014925373134
```

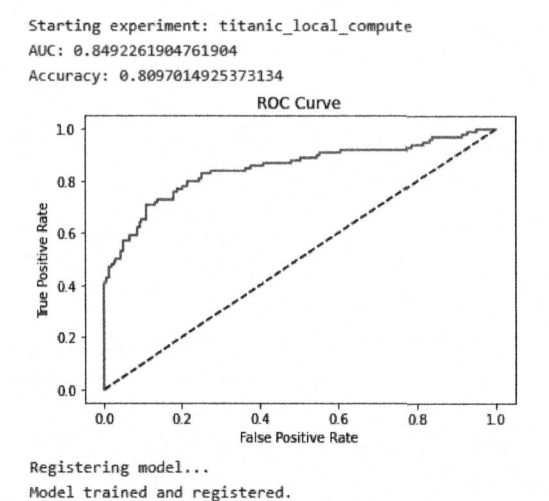

ROC Curve

```
Registering model...
Model trained and registered.
```

Figure 3.40 – Notebook output

22. On the left pane, by clicking on the **Jobs** icon, we can see **titanic_local_compute** under **Experiment** as a blue hyperlink. By clicking on this experiment, we can drill into an overview of the different runs of our experiment, as shown in *Figure 3.41*:

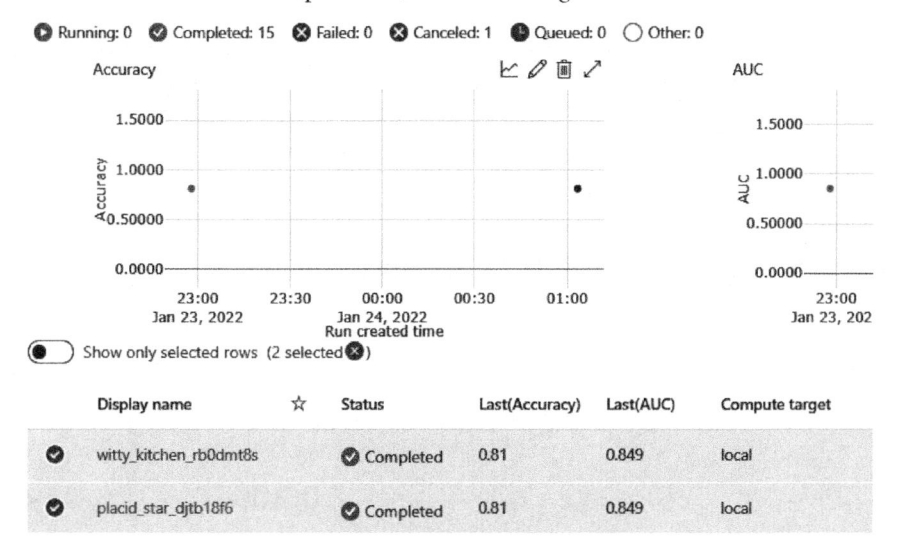

Figure 3.41 – Experiment run output

23. Clicking on the display name of a given run in the experiment provides details regarding the experiment run, as shown in *Figure 3.42*:

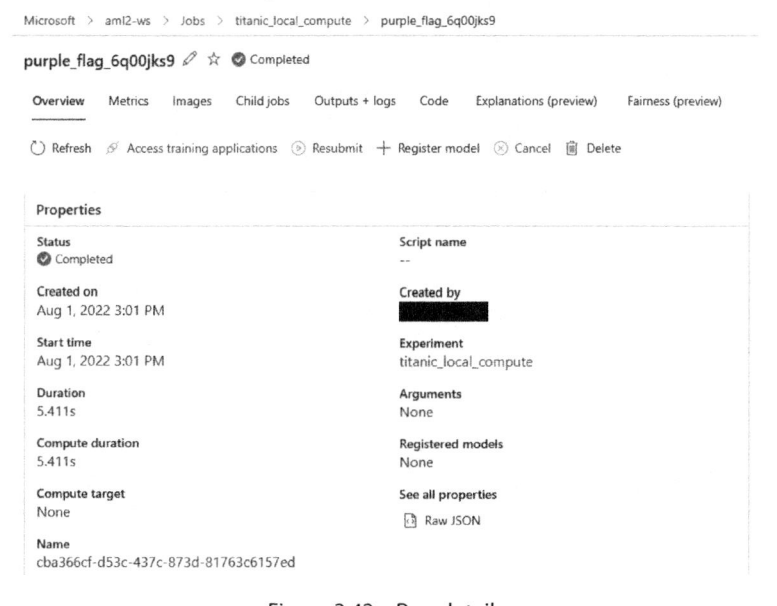

Figure 3.42 – Run details

24. By clicking on the **Metrics** tab, we can see our **AUC** and **Accuracy** values, as logged for the run of the experiment in *Figure 3.43*. This enables a data scientist to easily compare models to understand how changes to the model impact performance, accelerating model development:

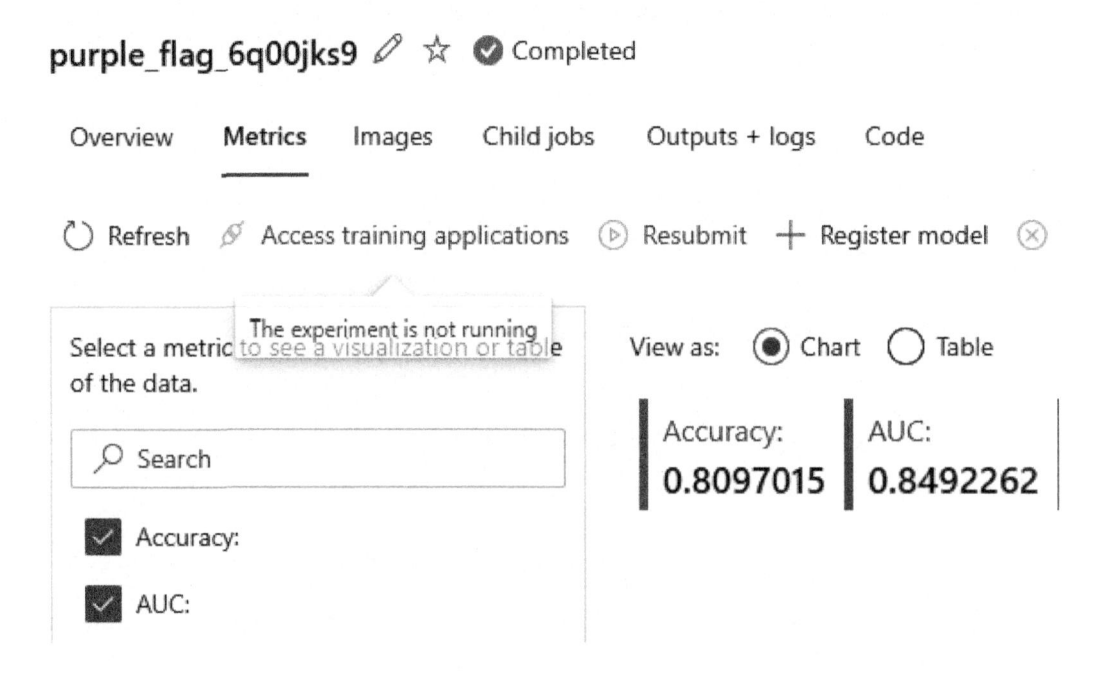

purple_flag_6q00jks9 ✎ ☆ ✓ Completed

Overview | **Metrics** | Images | Child jobs | Outputs + logs | Code

↻ Refresh   ✎ Access training applications   ▷ Resubmit   + Register model   ⊗

Select a metric to see a visualization or table of the data.

🔍 Search

☑ Accuracy:
☑ AUC:

View as: ● Chart ○ Table

Accuracy: 0.8097015

AUC: 0.8492262

Figure 3.43 – Run metrics

25. The **Images** tab captures the figures associated with model metrics, such as the ROC curve, precision-recall curve, and confusion matrix, as shown in *Figure 3.44*:

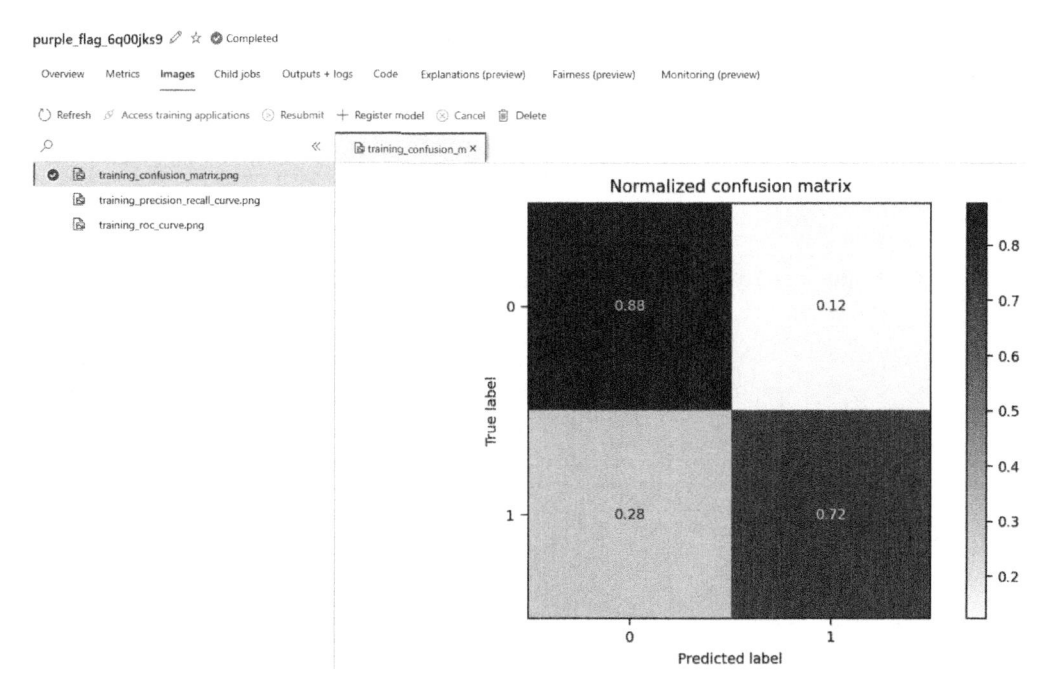

Figure 3.44 – Images tab

This section showed how to train a model using an AML compute instance. The objective is to show how we can train a model using a code-first approach with common open source libraries to tackle the task of data engineering, feature selection, and model development.

In the next section, we will use a compute cluster to train a model.

Training on a compute cluster

In the previous section, we showed how to train your model on a compute instance. In this section, we will show you how to submit your training job to a compute cluster when the training job needs to scale out. AML has made it extremely easy to run your training code on various compute targets without the need to change the training script. You need to create an AML pipeline that handles the data processing, the model training, and registering the trained model, as explained in this section.

The following are the steps to train your model on a compute cluster:

1. Go to `https://ml.azure.com`.
2. Select your workspace name.

94   Training Machine Learning Models in AMLS

3. On the left side of the workspace user interface, click **Compute**:

Figure 3.45 – Compute icon

4. On the **Compute** screen, click on the **Compute clusters** tab and then click on **+ New**, as shown in *Figure 3.46*:

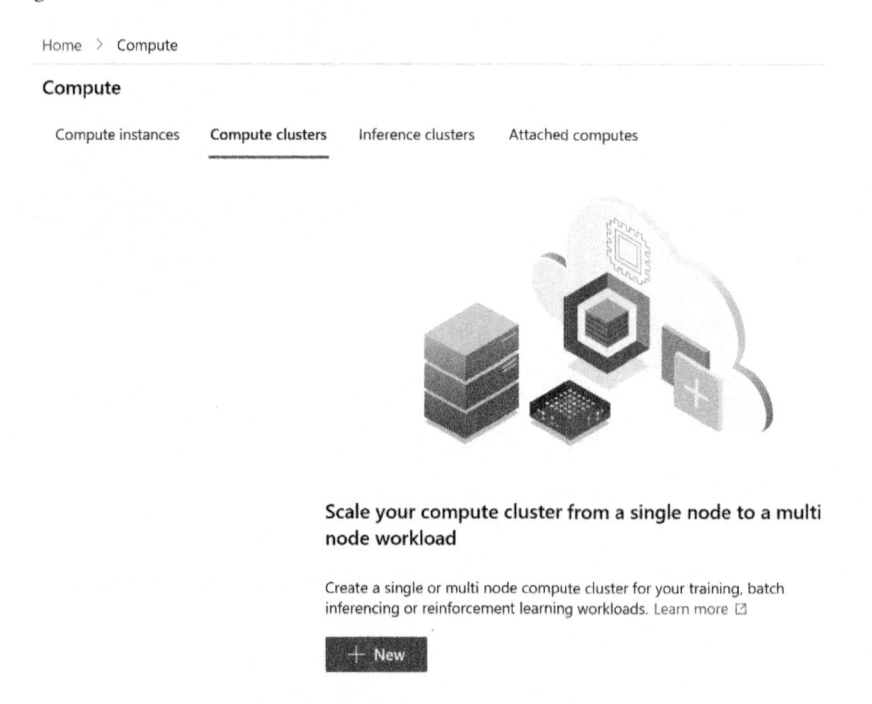

Figure 3.46 – Creating a new compute cluster

5. The next few screens allow you to create and configure a compute cluster based on your need. Once done, click on **Create**, as shown in *Figure 3.47*:

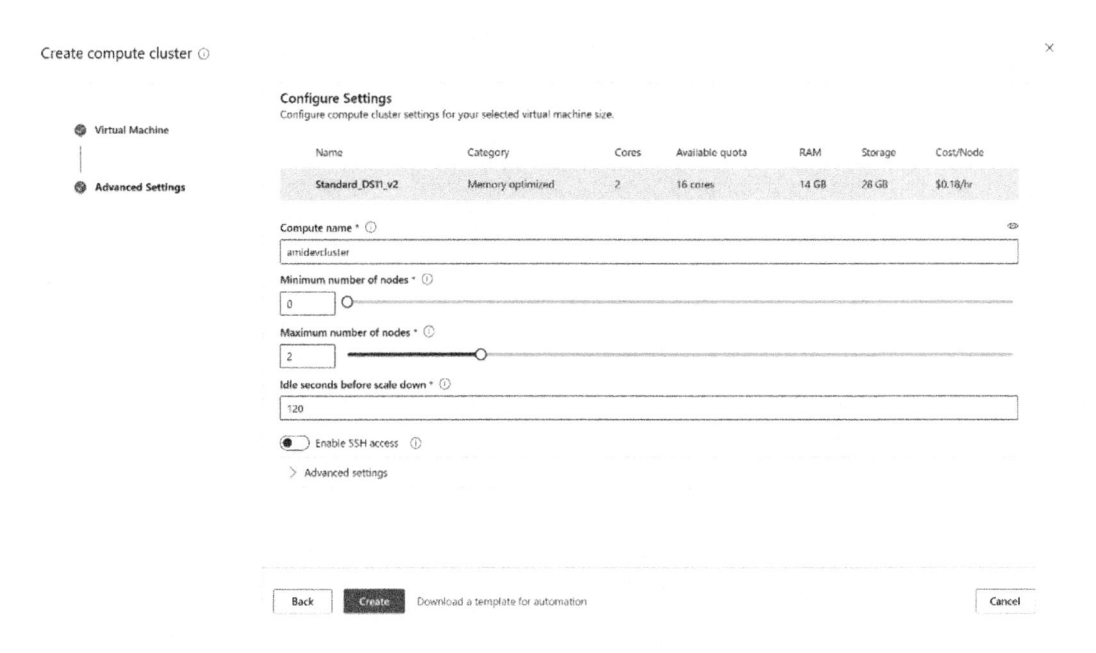

Figure 3.47 – Configuring a compute cluster

6. After a few seconds, your new compute cluster will be running, as shown in *Figure 3.48*:

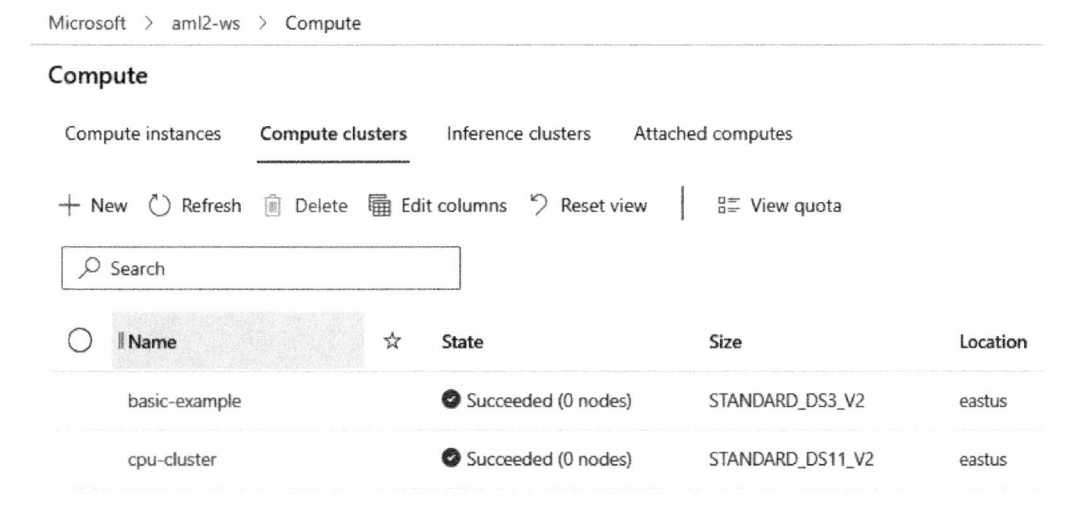

Figure 3.48 – List of compute clusters

7. Go to your working directory, as shown in *Figure 3.49*:

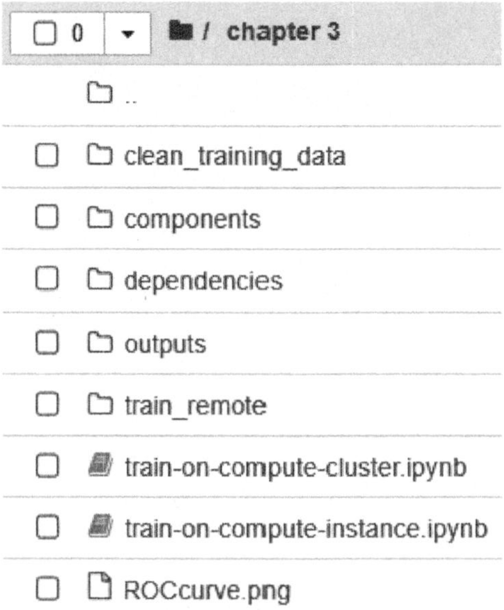

```
☐ 0  ▼   ▮ / chapter 3
         ▫ ..
    ☐    ▫ clean_training_data
    ☐    ▫ components
    ☐    ▫ dependencies
    ☐    ▫ outputs
    ☐    ▫ train_remote
    ☐    ▮ train-on-compute-cluster.ipynb
    ☐    ▮ train-on-compute-instance.ipynb
    ☐    ▫ ROCcurve.png
```

Figure 3.49 – Working directory

8. Clicking on **train-on-compute-cluster.ipynb** will bring up the notebook, which is very similar to the notebook in the previous section. We will not repeat all the steps here again and will only go through the steps needed to run the training on the remote cluster that you have just created. To learn more about AML pipelines and submitting remote jobs, please refer to https://github.com/Azure/azureml-examples.

The code snippet shown in *Figure 3.50* is used to create an object to access your AML workspace:

```
# Enter details of your AML workspace
subscription_id = "                                      "
resource_group = "aml-v2-book"
workspace = "aml2-ws"
```

```
# get a handle to the workspace
ml_client = MLClient(
    DefaultAzureCredential(), subscription_id, resource_group, workspace
)
```

Figure 3.50 – Working directory

9. Next, we will create an AML environment, which is an encapsulated Python environment where different steps of an ML pipeline, such as the training step, happen. *Figure 3.51* shows how to create a conda environment for your jobs, using a conda.yaml file:

```python
import os

dependencies_dir = "./dependencies"
os.makedirs(dependencies_dir, exist_ok=True)
```

```yaml
%%writefile {dependencies_dir}/conda.yml
name: model-env
channels:
  - conda-forge
dependencies:
  - python=3.8
  - numpy=1.21.2
  - pip=21.2.4
  - scikit-learn=0.24.2
  - scipy=1.7.1
  - pandas>=1.1,<1.2
  - pip:
    - inference-schema[numpy-support]==1.3.0
    - xlrd==2.0.1
    - mlflow== 1.26.1
    - azureml-mlflow==1.42.0
```

Overwriting ./dependencies/conda.yml

Figure 3.51 – conda environment

10. The preceding .yaml specification file contains Python packages, which are used in the pipeline. You can then use this .yaml file to create and register this custom environment in your AML workspace, as shown in *Figure 3.52*:

```python
from azure.ai.ml.entities import Environment

custom_env_name = "aml-scikit-learn"

pipeline_job_env = Environment(
    name=custom_env_name,
    description="Custom environment for Credit Card Defaults pipeline",
    tags={"scikit-learn": "0.24.2"},
    conda_file=os.path.join(dependencies_dir, "conda.yml"),
    image="mcr.microsoft.com/azureml/openmpi3.1.2-ubuntu18.04:latest",
    version="1.0",
)
pipeline_job_env = ml_client.environments.create_or_update(pipeline_job_env)

print(
    f"Environment with name {pipeline_job_env.name} is registered to workspace, the environment version is {pipeline_job_env.version}"
)
```

Figure 3.52 – Creating and registering a custom environment in AML

To create an AML component, you need to write a Python script to implement the ML task. This script can take input data and input parameters, which are used within the code, and output the results (for example, a transformed dataset or a trained model) to a persistent place, such as a mounted folder. An output of an ML component can be used as an input to the next step in the pipeline via its ML component's input. Once you have the Python script, you can create the component either programmatically or using a .yaml definition.

11. Next, we need to write a Python script for the data processing step of the pipeline, as shown in *Figure 3.53*:

```python
%%writefile {data_prep_src_dir}/data_prep.py
import os
import argparse
import pandas as pd
from sklearn.model_selection import train_test_split
import logging
import mlflow

def main():
    """Main function of the script."""
    # input and output arguments
    parser = argparse.ArgumentParser()
    parser.add_argument("--data", type=str, help="path to input data")
    parser.add_argument("--test_train_ratio", type=float, required=False, default=0.25)
    parser.add_argument("--train_data", type=str, help="path to train data")
    parser.add_argument("--test_data", type=str, help="path to test data")
    args = parser.parse_args()

    # Start Logging
    mlflow.start_run()

    print(" ".join(f"{k}={v}" for k, v in vars(args).items()))
    print("input data:", args.data)
    file_name = os.path.join(args.data)
    titanic_df = pd.read_csv(file_name)
    print(titanic_df.head(10))

    mlflow.log_metric("num_samples", titanic_df.shape[0])
    mlflow.log_metric("num_features", titanic_df.shape[1] - 1)

    titanic_train_df, titanic_test_df = train_test_split(
        titanic_df,
        test_size=args.test_train_ratio,
    )
    # output paths are mounted as folder, therefore, we are adding a filename to the path
    titanic_train_df.to_csv(os.path.join(args.train_data, "data.csv"), index=True)
    titanic_test_df.to_csv(os.path.join(args.test_data, "data.csv"), index=True)
    # Stop Logging
    mlflow.end_run()

if __name__ == "__main__":
    main()
```

Figure 3.53 – Python script for the data preparation step of the pipeline

12. Now that we have a script to perform the data processing task, we can create an AML component from it using the programmatic definition. To create an ML component, we will use the `command` class to specify the inputs and outputs of the Python script, the source code directory of the script, the command line to run the script, and the Python environment where this job will run, as shown in *Figure 3.54*:

```
from azure.ai.ml import command
from azure.ai.ml import Input, Output
from azure.ai.ml.constants import AssetTypes
data_prep_component = command(
    name="data_prep_titanic_survival",
    display_name="Data preparation for training",
    description="reads a .csv input, split the input to train and test",
    inputs={
        "data": Input(type=AssetTypes.URI_FILE),
        "test_train_ratio": Input(type="number"),
    },
    outputs=dict(
        train_data=Output(type="uri_folder", mode="rw_mount"),
        test_data=Output(type="uri_folder", mode="rw_mount"),
    ),
    # The source folder of the component
    code=data_prep_src_dir,
    command="""python data_prep.py \
            --data ${{inputs.data}} --test_train_ratio ${{inputs.test_train_ratio}} \
            --train_data ${{outputs.train_data}} --test_data ${{outputs.test_data}} \
            """,
    environment=f"{pipeline_job_env.name}:{pipeline_job_env.version}",
)
```

Figure 3.54 – Creating a data processing component using the command class

13. Next, we need to write a Python script for the model training step of the pipeline and then create an AML component from it. Please refer to our GitHub to use the Python code for the model training. To create an AML component from it, we will be using the `.yaml` definition this time, as shown in *Figure 3.55*:

```yaml
%%writefile {train_src_dir}/train.yml
# <component>
name: train_titanic_survival_model
display_name: Train Titanic Survival Model
# version: 1 # Not specifying a version will automatically update the version
type: command
inputs:
  train_data:
    type: uri_folder
  test_data:
    type: uri_folder
  learning_rate:
    type: number
  registered_model_name:
    type: string
outputs:
  model:
    type: uri_folder
code: .
environment:
  # for this step, we'll use an AzureML curate environment
  azureml:AzureML-sklearn-0.24-ubuntu18.04-py37-cpu:21
command: >-
  python train.py
  --train_data ${{inputs.train_data}}
  --test_data ${{inputs.test_data}}
  --learning_rate ${{inputs.learning_rate}}
  --registered_model_name ${{inputs.registered_model_name}}
  --model ${{outputs.model}}
# </component>
```

Figure 3.55 – Creating a model training component using the yaml definition

14. We can load the training component from the .yaml file and then register it to the workspace using the code snippet shown in *Figure 3.56*:

```python
# importing the Component Package
from azure.ai.ml import load_component

# Loading the component from the yml file
train_component = load_component(path=os.path.join(train_src_dir, "train.yml"))
```

```python
# Now we register the component to the workspace
train_component = ml_client.create_or_update(train_component)

# Create (register) the component in your workspace
print(
    f"Component {train_component.name} with Version {train_component.version} is registered"
)
```

Figure 3.56 – Loading and registering the model training component

15. Now that both the data processing and model training components have been created, we can start coding the pipeline definition, which will be called in a later step. We will use the @dsl.pipeline decorator to tell the SDK that we are defining an AML pipeline, as shown in *Figure 3.57*. As you can see, the compute target is specified here, which is our compute cluster that we created earlier in this section:

```python
# the dsl decorator tells the sdk that we are defining an Azure ML pipeline
from azure.ai.ml import dsl, Input, Output


@dsl.pipeline(
    compute=cpu_compute_target,
    description="Titanic data-prep and model training pipeline",
)
def titanic_survival_pipeline(
    pipeline_job_data_input,
    pipeline_job_test_train_ratio,
    pipeline_job_learning_rate,
    pipeline_job_registered_model_name,
):
    # using data_prep_function like a python call with its own inputs
    data_prep_job = data_prep_component(
        data=pipeline_job_data_input,
        test_train_ratio=pipeline_job_test_train_ratio,
    )

    # using train_func like a python call with its own inputs
    train_job = train_component(
        train_data=data_prep_job.outputs.train_data,  # note: using outputs from previous step
        test_data=data_prep_job.outputs.test_data,  # note: using outputs from previous step
        learning_rate=pipeline_job_learning_rate,  # note: using a pipeline input as parameter
        registered_model_name=pipeline_job_registered_model_name,
    )

    # a pipeline returns a dictionary of outputs
    # keys will code for the pipeline output identifier
    return {
        "pipeline_job_train_data": data_prep_job.outputs.train_data,
        "pipeline_job_test_data": data_prep_job.outputs.test_data,
    }
```

Figure 3.57 – Defining an AML pipeline using the @dsl.pipeline decorator

16. Now that we have defined our pipeline, let's instantiate it by passing our dataset, the split rate, and the name for the trained model, as shown in *Figure 3.58*:

```python
from azure.ai.ml.constants import AssetTypes

registered_model_name = "titanic_survival_model"

titanic_dataset = ml_client.data.get("titanic-clean-data", version='1')

# Let's instantiate the pipeline with the parameters of our choice
pipeline = titanic_survival_pipeline(
    # pipeline_job_data_input=credit_data,
    pipeline_job_data_input=Input(type=AssetTypes.URI_FILE, path=titanic_dataset.id),
    pipeline_job_test_train_ratio=0.2,
    pipeline_job_learning_rate=0.25,
    pipeline_job_registered_model_name=registered_model_name,
)
```

Figure 3.58 – Instantiating the pipeline by passing data and parameters

17. Now that we have instantiated the pipeline object, we can submit the job to run in AML, which uses the compute cluster to run the steps within the pipeline, as shown in *Figure 3.59*:

```python
import webbrowser

# submit the pipeline job
pipeline_job = ml_client.jobs.create_or_update(
    pipeline,
    # Project's name
    experiment_name="titanic_remote_cluster",
)
# open the pipeline in web browser
webbrowser.open(pipeline_job.services["Studio"].endpoint)
```

False

```
ml_client.jobs.stream(pipeline_job.name)
```

```
RunId: polite_stomach_4hv30w4x0d
Web View: https://ml.azure.com/runs/polite_stomach_4hv30w4x0d?wsid=/subscriptions/dcfc206a-203b-4c00-a236-bdf576a37896/resou
rcegroups/aml-v2-book/workspaces/aml2-ws

Streaming logs/azureml/executionlogs.txt
========================================

[2022-08-02 14:33:47Z] Completing processing run id 2fa11077-9980-47e1-b111-bcd1df50f195.
[2022-08-02 14:33:48Z] Completing processing run id ca4261c3-e8d9-466d-bdd7-2be9d1c4b694.
[2022-08-02 14:33:48Z] Finishing experiment: no runs left and nothing to schedule.

Execution Summary
=================
RunId: polite_stomach_4hv30w4x0d
Web View: https://ml.azure.com/runs/polite_stomach_4hv30w4x0d?wsid=/subscriptions/dcfc206a-203b-4c00-a236-bdf576a37896/resou
rcegroups/aml-v2-book/workspaces/aml2-ws
```

Figure 3.59 – Submitting a pipeline job to run in AML

18. To see the pipeline progress and details about each step of the pipeline, you can either click on the link shown in *Figure 3.61* or click on the **Jobs** tab, which will show you a list of experiments, including **titanic_remote_cluster**, as shown in *Figure 3.60*:

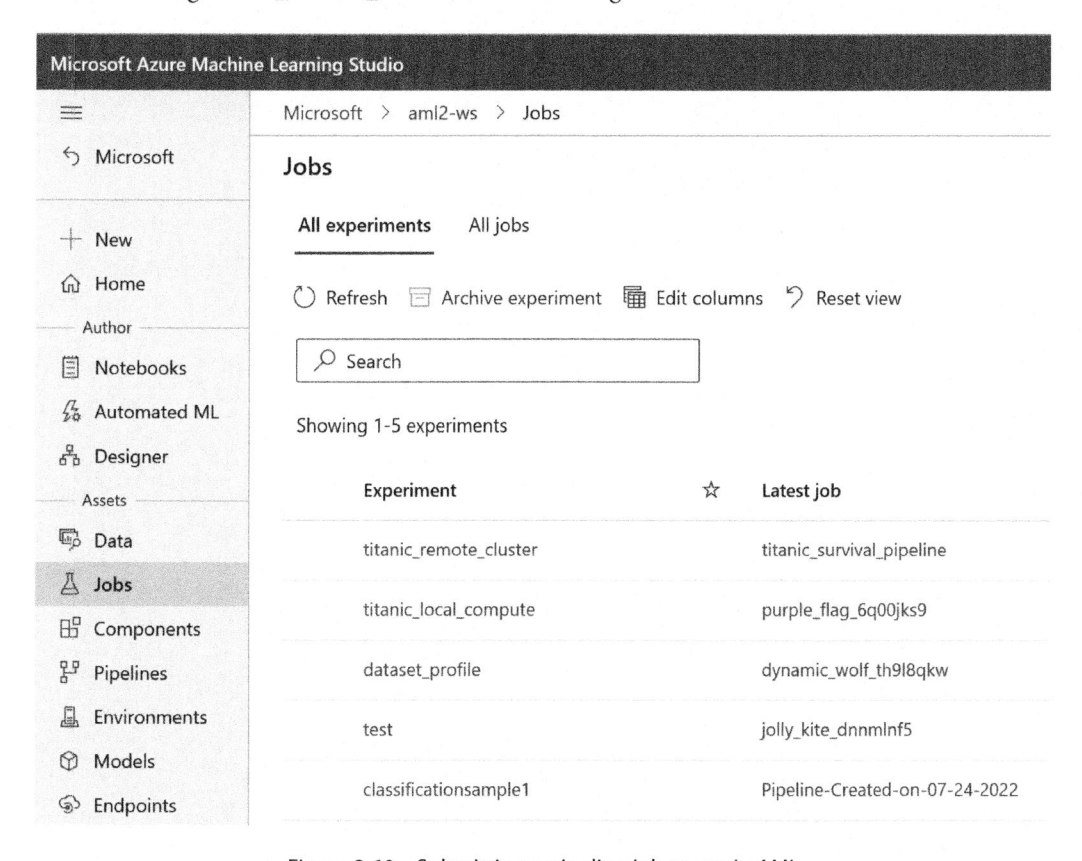

Figure 3.60 – Submitting a pipeline job to run in AML

19. Go ahead and click on the **titanic_remote_cluster** experiment to see a list of all the runs associated with this pipeline job. You should only see one run for this job, which we just ran in the notebook. Clicking on that will take you to a screen with a graphical representation of the pipeline, as shown in *Figure 3.61*:

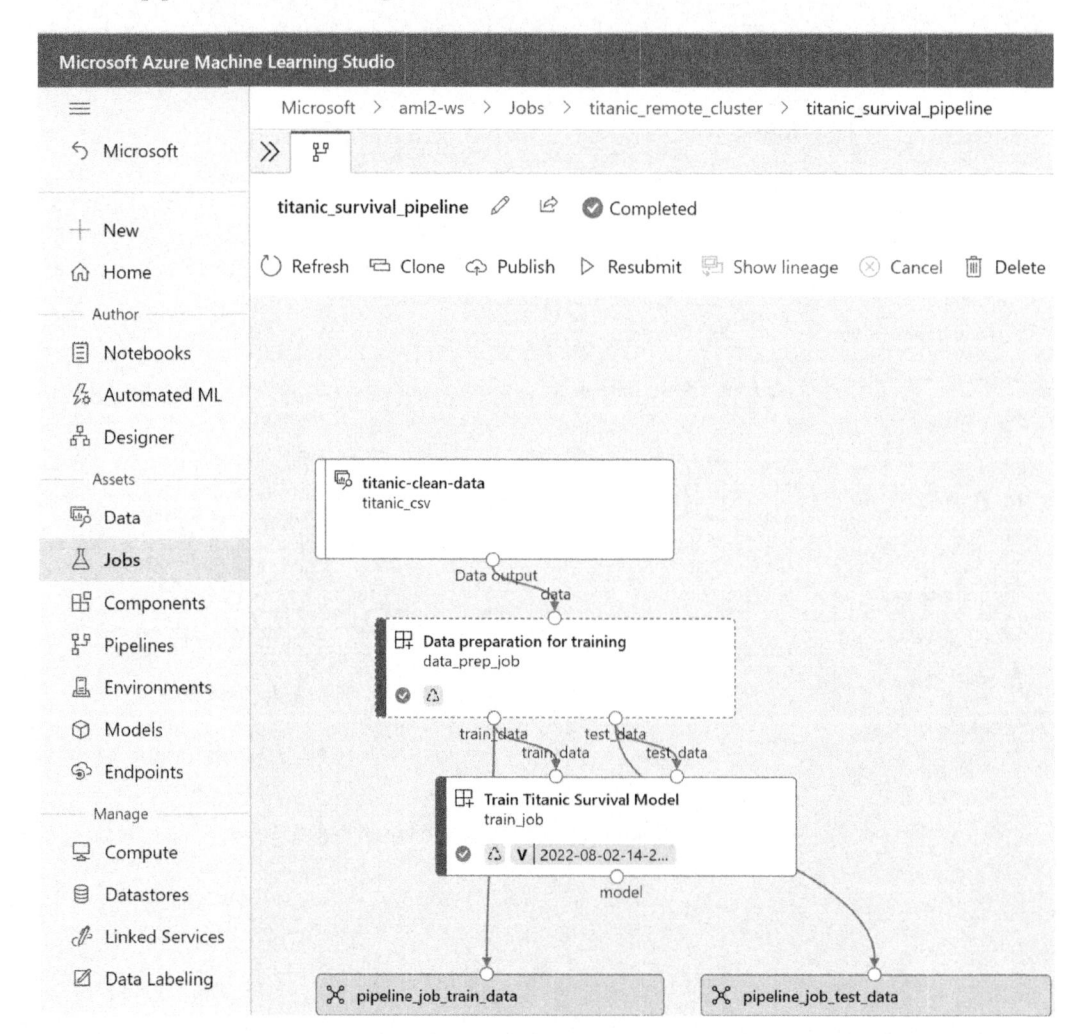

Figure 3.61 – Graphical view of an AML pipeline

20. Go ahead and click on different steps of the pipeline to see detailed information regarding each step. For instance, by clicking on the **Train Titanic Survival Model** step, you can see model metrics such as accuracy, precision, and recall, as shown in *Figure 3.62*:

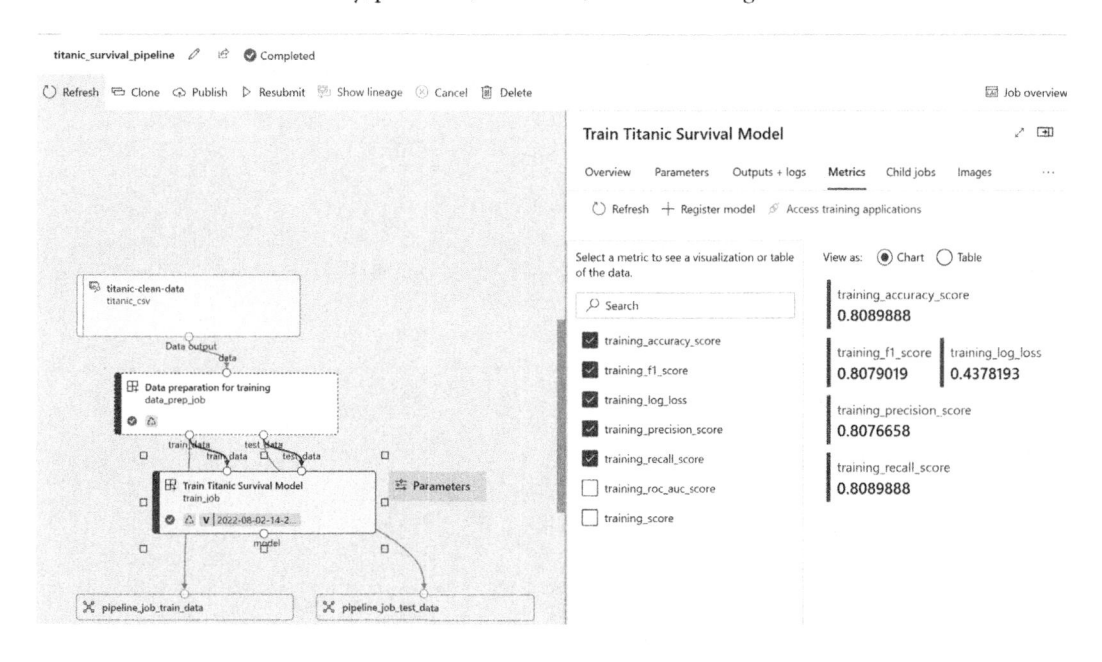

Figure 3.62 – Detailed view of pipeline steps

You have successfully trained a model and reviewed the metrics within your AML workspace using an AML compute cluster. Now, let's review the chapter.

Summary

We have covered a lot of topics in this chapter. We have shown you how to train an ML model using the AML Designer, which requires no coding. It is a great fit for citizen data scientists or advanced data scientists who would like to explore different algorithms quickly and evaluate their performance without having to write a lot of code to do so. Next, you learned how to train an ML model through the AML Python SDK, running on both a compute instance and a compute cluster for more compute-intensive ML jobs.

In the next chapter, you will learn how to tune hyperparameters for your ML models using AML HyperDrive.

4
Tuning Your Models with AMLS

Tuning your models is an important step in your data science journey. The objective of a data science workload is to provide the best model on unseen data in the shortest duration of time. In order to provide a reliable model, not only are you required to tune the features that are the inputs to your model but you also need to tune the parameters of your model itself. Model parameters, also known as **hyperparameters**, can have a significant impact on the performance of your trained model. Tuning a model can take a lot of effort and involves trial and error. Several frameworks can be leveraged to automate this task. AMLS provides this functionality, which we will explore in this chapter. AMLS allows you to define model parameters that should be tuned to find the best model through the use of a special type of job referred to as a **sweep job**. These hyperparameters will be defined for a given AMLS job, and AMLS will run many trials and determine the best model for the hyperparameters within the range of possible defined values.

In this chapter, we will explore how AMLS enables hyperparameter tuning through a sweep job.

In this chapter, we will cover the following topics:

- Understanding model parameters
- Sampling hyperparameters
- Understanding sweep jobs
- Setting up a sweep job with grid sampling
- Setting up a sweep job with random sampling
- Setting up a sweep job with Bayesian sampling
- Reviewing the results of a sweep job

Technical requirements

In order to access your workspace, recall the steps from the previous chapter:

1. Go to https://ml.azure.com.
2. Select your workspace name.
3. In the workspace **user interface** (**UI**), on the left-hand side, click on **Compute**.
4. On the **Compute** screen, select your compute instance and select **Start**:

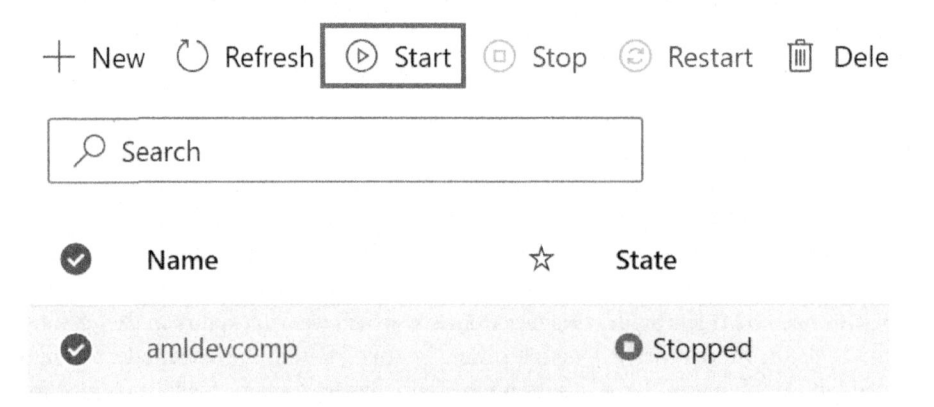

Figure 4.1 – Start compute

5. Your compute instance will change from a **Stopped** status to a **Starting** status.
6. In the previous chapter, we cloned the Git repository – if you have not already done so, continue to follow the steps provided here. If you have already cloned the repository, skip to *step 7*.

    Open the terminal on your compute instance. Note that the path will include your user in the directory. Type the following into the terminal to clone the sample notebooks into your working directory:

    ```
    git clone https://github.com/PacktPublishing/Azure-
    Machine-Learning-Engineering.git
    ```

7. Clicking on the refresh icon shown in *Figure 4.2* will update and refresh the notebooks displayed on your screen:

Figure 4.2 – The refresh icon

8. Review the notebooks in your `Azure-Machine-Learning-Engineering` directory. This will display the files cloned into your working directory as shown in *Figure 4.3*:

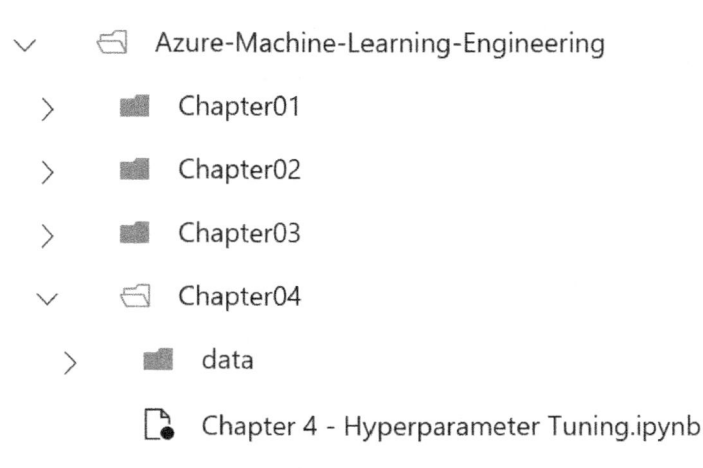

```
∨  📁 Azure-Machine-Learning-Engineering
   >  📁 Chapter01
   >  📁 Chapter02
   >  📁 Chapter03
   ∨  📁 Chapter04
      >  📁 data
         📄 Chapter 4 - Hyperparameter Tuning.ipynb
```

Figure 4.3 – Azure-Machine-Learning-Engineering

Understanding model parameters

In your data science workload, as you define your features, you determine which parameters should be leveraged by your model. However, depending on the algorithm selected, you can control the training behavior by altering the parameters of the model itself – this is known as **hyperparameter tuning**. Using hyperparameter tuning, we can explore a variety of model parameters to identify the best model parameters to establish the best model result. To evaluate the model results, a **primary metric** is selected. A primary metric is defined as the key metric for evaluating the model. Every time a hyperparameter is changed, the primary metric will either go up or down in value and based on the primary metric, that will yield a better or worse model.

In this chapter, we will create a logistic regression model by leveraging `sklearn`'s implementation of logistic regression with an `sklearn` pipeline. For a logistic regression model, there are several model parameters that we can tune to improve the performance of our model. For a logistic regression model, one parameter is the penalty term. Defining the penalty term as `l2`, referred to as ridge regression, is used by the logistic regression estimator to apply a penalty to a model when the model is overly complex. This uses the `l2` normalization on the coefficients of your model as the penalty. Typically, the `l2` normalization prevents the model from being overfitted by penalizing complex models. The `l2` norm squares the model coefficients, sums them, and takes the square root of the value. When creating the model, we can select the `l1` norm, referred to as lasso regression, which would be the sum of the absolute value of the coefficients as penalty terms. Changing the code from leveraging a `l2` normalization penalty to a `l1` normalization penalty would leverage the technique of hyperparameter tuning or tuning our model parameters. If we were not going to rely on hyperparameter tuning to select the penalty term, we would say that lasso regression generally performs better than ridge regression when few predictor variables are significant, and ridge regression generally performs better when there are many significant predictor variables.

In addition to the penalty term, we can also specify the value of `C`, which is the inverse of the regularization strength, as a hyperparameter to tune for our model.

The last hyperparameter we will tune is `max_iter`, which is the maximum iterations that the solver can take before converging. As you consider the model parameters you would like to explore when building your model, you are defining the search space. The **search space** is a concept that defines the parameters and the range of values possible during hyperparameter tuning.

Now that we have an understanding of hyperparameter tuning, and defining a search space, we will explore the method for selecting the combinations of model hyperparameters to leverage within an AMLS job designed to tune these parameters, known as a **sweep job**.

Sampling hyperparameters

Inside the search space, hyperparameters are either continuous or discrete values. Continuous hyperparameters can be in a continuous range of values, while discrete hyperparameters are only able to use certain values. For logistic regression, the penalty term can have one of two discrete values: `l1` or `l2`. AMLS can use either a list or a range for setting hyperparameters, as we will see when we dig into the code.

For the hyperparameter of `C`, we could define it as a discrete value, or we could define C to be a value in a continuous range with a specified distribution.

For the `max_iter` hyperparameter, the default value for the `sklearn` logistic regression model is `100`. We could set this to a discrete value such as `penality_term`, or a uniform value such as C.

The following code shown in *Figure 4.4* defines the search space for the penalty term, the inverse regularization strength of the model, and the maximum iterations as choices, which are discrete values for a defined job command:

```
grid_command_job_for_sweep = gridsamplingjobcommand(
    penalty_term=Choice(values=['l2', 'l1']),
    C=Choice(values=[0.01, .1, 1.0, 10]),
    max_iter=Choice(values=[10, 100, 150, 200]),
)
```

Figure 4.4 – Defining the search space

Once the search space has been defined, we can select what type of sampling we would like our sweep job to run. For each parameter defined in the search space, trials are created based on the sampled model hyperparameters. There are three types of sampling available with sweep jobs in AMLS: **random**, **grid**, and **Bayesian**.

Grid sampling will create a trial per hyperparameter combination. As an example, if we had specified our search space to check for l1 and l2, and we selected C to be discrete values of 0.01, .1, 1, and 10 and max_iter to be 10, 100, 150, and 200, then there would be 2x4x4=32 trials created. Given grid sampling will create a trial per hyperparameter combination, grid sampling only supports discrete hyperparameters.

When leveraging random sampling, the hyperparameter values are randomly selected during the trials.

Figure 4.5 shows the hyperparameters defined in the search space here for both discrete and continuous values. In this code, the value for C follows a uniform distribution between values of 0.01 and 10 for a defined job command, which shows how we can define C as a continuous value, as opposed to with the grid job, when C was defined as a value from a list as shown in *Figure 4.5*:

```
random_command_job_for_sweep = randomsamplingjobcommand(
    penalty_term=Choice(values=['l2', 'l1']),
    C=Uniform(min_value=0.01, max_value=10.0),
    max_iter=Choice(values=[10, 100, 150, 200]),
)
```

Figure 4.5 – Discrete and continuous hyperparameters

In the preceding example, since C is a continuous hyperparameter, we are not able to leverage grid sampling, but we can leverage either random or Bayesian sampling.

Bayesian sampling leverages the output on the primary metric of the previous trial to determine the next set of hyperparameters to run.

> **Note**
> Grid space sampling does not support continuous hyperparameters – it will only support choice hyperparameters containing discrete values.

Given that hyperparameters can be discrete or continuous, we will define how exhaustive the search on the grid space should be and, importantly, how to end a job that is searching across a search space to provide the best primary metric for a given model. In the next section, we will explore how to set up our job to effectively and efficiently search for the best hyperparameters.

Understanding sweep jobs

Sweep jobs in AMLS enable a data scientist to define the hyperparameters to explore in a single job. During the job, this will automate the task of searching for the hyperparameters that will provide a model with the best results for the primary metric-creating trials. In a run of a job, multiple trials are created and evaluated for the hyperparameters that are defined within the search space based on the sampling method selected. By defining the search space, we can create a single run of a job for testing multiple hypotheses at a single time rather than re-writing code and re-running jobs, reducing the time spent exploring the search space.

To leverage the hyperparameters in your job, your code needs to be updated to leverage these new parameters by passing them into your code through the Python ArgumentParser shown as follows:

```
parser.add_argument("--penalty-term", type=str, default='l1')
parser.add_argument("--C", type=float, default=0.01)
parser.add_argument("--max-iter", type=int, default=100)
parser.add_argument("--randomstate", type=int, default=42)
```

Figure 4.6 – Passing a parameter list into the job

Now that the arguments have been passed into the main function, they can be leveraged in the model training script by passing them into the `model_train` function.

Here's the code for passing parameters into the `model_train` function:

```
model = model_train('Survived', df, args.penalty_term, args.C, args.max_iter, args.randomstate)
```

Figure 4.7 – Passing parameters for model training

In the `model_train` function, you can leverage the hyperparameters as you build the logistic regression model.

Here's the code for passing parameters into the logistic regression model:

```
lg = LogisticRegression(penalty=penalty_term, C=C, max_iter=max_iter, solver='liblinear')
```

Figure 4.8 – Leveraging hyperparameters

As with all AML SDK v2 jobs, a sweep job is defined initially as a job command. In the job command, you specify the code, the location of the file, the command with its parameters, inputs, the environment, the compute, and a display name, but for the sweep job, we also specify the hyperparameters as we saw in *Figures 4.4* and *4.5*.

Once the job command is updated to include the hyperparameters, you can specify the sweep parameters for the command. In the sweep method, you specify the compute that you are going to leverage, the sampling algorithm, the primary metric, and the goal. The sampling algorithm can be set to random, bayesian, or grid as discussed earlier. The primary metric is the metric that is required to be logged in the job that you would like to evaluate the trials against. The goal specifies how you would like the primary metric to be evaluated. The goal can be to minimize or maximize the primary metric, which is used to judge your model's performance.

The code for the sweep of the job command is shown here:

```
grid_sweep_job = grid_command_job_for_sweep.sweep(
    compute="cpu-cluster",
    sampling_algorithm="grid",
    primary_metric="test_AUC",
    goal="Maximize",
)
```

Figure 4.9 – Setting the sweep parameters

In *Figure 4.9* here, you can see the values for sweep parameters being set. In this case, we will evaluate the test_AUC primary metric to be maximized by leveraging a grid sampling algorithm on the compute cluster named cpu-cluster.

To set the limits for a sweep job, we specify the maximum total trials – max_total_trials – which defaults to 1000. The maximum concurrent trials – max_concurrent_trials – which defaults to the number specified by max_total_trials if not set, will specify how many concurrent trials should be run at any given time. An additional parameter to set is the timeout: timeout. The timeout is in seconds. The timeout is for the entire sweep job, which defaults to a value of 100800:

```
grid_sweep_job.set_limits(max_total_trials=60,
                          max_concurrent_trials=10,
                          timeout=7200)
```

Figure 4.10 – Setting job limits for grid sampling

Note that in the grid sampling experiment explored in this chapter, the maximum number of total runs is actually 32, but if we added additional choices as hyperparameters, setting the trial limits will ensure the job does not exceed a total number of 60 trials in *Figure 4.10* here.

With random sampling, hyperparameters are selected at random, so the job limit here will be very important to set. As stated, `max_total_trials` defaults to `1000`, so we can see that running a job with `max_total_trials` equal to `120` will result in only `120` trials being created for a given job run.

Setting the maximum limits of the sweep job is shown as follows:

```
random_sweep_job.set_limits(max_total_trials=120,
                            max_concurrent_trials=10,
                            timeout=7200)
```

Figure 4.11 – Setting job limits for random sampling

When leveraging Bayesian sampling, previous trial information is leveraged to determine the next parameters for which to search in the search space. With grid and random sampling, each trial is independent of other trials. Given each trial for grid sampling and random sampling is independent, once the primary metric has been determined in a given trial, if it will not yield the best model, there is no need for the code to continue running. These trials can be terminated early, so compute resources can be used for the next trial primary metric evaluation instead.

To enable early termination, AMLS sweep jobs incorporate the concept of an **early termination policy**. An early termination policy will prematurely end a given trial after the primary metric is logged if the defined criteria are not met. For early termination, there are several policies that AMLS supports, including **none**, a **truncation** selection policy, a **median** stopping policy, and a **bandit** policy.

If no early termination policy is selected, the trial run will execute until completion – as explained earlier, this is required for Bayesian sampling. However, when grid or random sampling is leveraged, if a truncation policy is selected, AMLS will terminate trials based on the selected early termination policy.

Truncation policies

If a truncation policy is selected, AMLS will cancel a percentage of the lowest-performing runs based on the value in `truncation_percentage`.

The following is the sample code for an early termination policy that starts evaluations at an interval of 1, and terminates the lowest 75% of all trials using a truncation policy:

```
sweep_job.early_termination = TruncationSelectionPolicy(evaluation_interval= 1,
                                                        truncation_percentage= 75,
                                                        delay_evaluation= 1)
```

Figure 4.12 – Truncation early termination policy

When executing a sweep job with a truncation early termination policy, in the **Overview** tab in AMLS, you can review the policy on the **Job Overview** screen. Regardless of the early termination policy selected, it can be viewed on the **Job Overview** screen.

An early termination policy is shown as follows in the workspace:

Early termination policy

Early termination policy
TruncationSelection

Properties
{"evaluation_interval":1,"delay_evaluation":1,"truncation_percentage":75,"exclude_finished_jobs":false}

Figure 4.13 – Early termination policy for a sweep job

In addition to a truncation policy, we can also set a median policy, which we will look at next.

Median policies

Another type of early termination policy is the median stopping policy. This policy will prematurely end trials based on the median value across all the training trials. If a given trial is worse than the median average, it will be terminated.

Here is the sample code for an early termination policy that starts evaluation at an interval of 2, and terminates any trial that is below the median of all trials:

```
sweep_job.early_termination = MedianStoppingPolicy(evaluation_interval= 1,
                                                    delay_evaluation= 2)
```

Figure 4.14 – Median early termination policy

Bandit policies

An early termination policy known as the bandit policy will end runs prematurely when the primary metric is not within a certain range of the current most successful trial. This range is defined by `slack_factor`. At the time of evaluation, the best primary metric value is divided by (1+ `slack_factor`), and if a trial does not have a primary metric that is better than that value, it will be terminated early. If a data scientist would prefer to set a value rather than setting a ratio with `slack_factor`, `slack_amount` can be used instead:

```
sweep_job.early_termination = BanditPolicy(slack_factor = 0.1,
                                            delay_evaluation = 5,
                                            evaluation_interval = 1)
```

Figure 4.15 – Bandit early termination policy

To provide some context to the bandit policy, let us assume that the primary metric at the interval of 2 so far has the best metric of .85 for our `test_AUC`. In the example here, if the metric is below .85/1.1 or .773, then it will be terminated.

As the training becomes increasingly complex, establishing the ability to terminate trials prematurely ensures that compute resources are not consumed when the desired result will ultimately not be achieved.

In the next section, we will explore setting up a sweep job that leverages grid sampling to determine the best model hyperparameters.

Setting up a sweep job with grid sampling

Earlier in the chapter, we cloned our sample notebook to leverage this material. The notebook for this chapter, `'Chapter 4 - Hyperparameter Tuning'`, provides a review on creating a job command to create a logistic regression model by leveraging an `sklearn` pipeline and `mlflow` capabilities.

The code is then updated and placed into a new directory – the `hyperparametertune` folder. The code leverages python's `argparse` module, which enables you to pass parameters into scripts. To run the script that has been generated by this notebook, we will create a job command and update the job command to include the hyperparameters as shown in the following code snippet:

```python
from azure.ai.ml.sweep import Choice, Uniform, MedianStoppingPolicy, BanditPolicy, TruncationSelectionPolicy

grid_sampling_job_command = command(
    code="./hyperparametertune",  # local path where the code is stored
    command="python main.py --titanic ${{inputs.titanic}} --randomstate ${{inputs.randomstate}}",
    inputs={
        "titanic": Input(
            type="uri_file",
            path="azureml:titanic_prepped:1",
        ),
        "randomstate": 0,
        "penalty_term": 'l1',
        "C": 0.01,
        "max_iter": 100,
    },
    environment="job_base_env@latest",
    compute="cpu-cluster",
    display_name="GridSampling",
)

#Set Parameter expressions
grid_command_job_for_sweep = grid_sampling_job_command(
    penalty_term=Choice(values=['l2', 'l1']),
    C=Choice(values=[0.01, .1, 1.0, 10]),
    max_iter=Choice(values=[10, 100, 150, 200]),
)
```

Figure 4.16 – Job sweep command with hyperparameters for grid sampling

Note that the hyperparameters have been included as inputs to the command, but their values are added to the command in line 22 in the preceding figure. This could have been done as a single command, but for illustrative purposes, it is provided separately as an update to `grid_sampling_job_command`.

Once the command is prepared, we call the sweep method providing the compute, the sampling algorithm, the primary metric, and the goal. Recall that here we will expect to see 32 runs, so setting `max_total_trials` to 60 will not be a hit, but if we were to update the hyperparameters to include more choices, we could hit `max_total_trials`:

```python
# apply the sweep parameter to obtain the sweep_job
grid_sweep_job = grid_command_job_for_sweep.sweep(
    compute="cpu-cluster",
    sampling_algorithm="grid",
    primary_metric="test_AUC",
    goal="Maximize",
)

#2*4*4 = 32 trial runs, but we will explicity set the max total trials, to see it is not exceeded
grid_sweep_job.set_limits(max_total_trials=60,
                max_concurrent_trials=10,
                timeout=7200)
```

Figure 4.17 – Calling the sweep method during grid sampling

Later in the notebook when we look at random sampling and Bayesian sampling, we will define the value of C as a continuous value – however, to leverage grid sampling, we have defined it to be a choice, which is a list of discrete values.

To submit `grid_sweep_job`, we pass the command to `ml_client`, which was created to manage the connection to AMLS:

```python
# submit the sweep
returned_sweep_job = ml_client.create_or_update(grid_sweep_job)
# get a URL for the status of the job
returned_sweep_job.services["Studio"].endpoint
```

Figure 4.18 – Running the sweep job

As the sweep job is executing, it can be helpful to get the status of the running job. Given we are leveraging `mlflow` to log the metrics of the `sklearn` model, we can request all trials for a given parent `run_id` value, which is the run for `grid_sweep_job`.

In the following code snippet, we pass in our `experiment_id` and `run_id` values and get back the job status:

```python
def getStatus(experiment_id, run_id):
    df = mlflow.search_runs([experiment_id])
    rslt_df = df[(df['tags.mlflow.parentRunId'] == run_id )]
    rslt_df_finished = rslt_df[rslt_df['status'] == 'FINISHED']

    while rslt_df.shape[0] == 0:
        print('waiting for jobs to register')
        df = mlflow.search_runs([experiment_id])
        rslt_df = df[(df['tags.mlflow.parentRunId'] == run_id )]
        rslt_df_finished = rslt_df[rslt_df['status'] == 'FINISHED']
        time.sleep(5)

    while rslt_df_finished.shape[0] != rslt_df.shape[0]:
        df = mlflow.search_runs([experiment_id])
        rslt_df = df[(df['tags.mlflow.parentRunId'] == run_id )]
        rslt_df_finished = rslt_df[rslt_df['status'] == 'FINISHED']
        status = rslt_df["status"].unique()
        print(status)
        for x in status:
            rslt_df_status = rslt_df[rslt_df['status'] == x]
            print(returned_sweep_job.display_name + ', Number:' + str(x) + " " + str(rslt_df_status.shape[0]))
        time.sleep(5)

    print('Sweep Job for run:' + run_id + ' Complete')

getStatus(experiment_id, run_id)
```

Figure 4.19 – Getting the status of the sweep job

We search across the run for a given `experiment_id` value. Our `experiment_id` value will be `'chapter4'`, so we request all runs that have been made for `'chapter4'` and further refine that list based on `tags.mlflow.parentRunId`, which is the `run_id` value associated with the grid sampling run. In line 3 of *Figure 4.19*, we request runs that have a `run_id` value associated with the run of the grid sweep job. If we get back a value of 0, then we know that we have to wait for the run to be established in AMLS. Once there are runs provided, we move on to the next `while` loop, where we are checking whether all the runs have been completed. Once all the runs are completed for the grid sweep job, the message on line 24 will be printed.

Congratulations on leveraging a sweep job with grid sampling! Grid sampling works well when you have a search space that contains discrete values for your hyperparameters. Next, we will explore leveraging a sweep job with random sampling to enable use to explore continuous values for our hyperparameters.

Setting up a sweep job for random sampling

As we saw with setting up a command for grid sampling, a command for random sampling is simply a job command with the hyperparameters included in the command. One difference between the `grid` command and the `random` command is that the hyperparameters can be continuous in a random sampling sweep job.

Here's the code for the job command for random sampling:

Setting up a sweep job for random sampling   119

```
1  from azure.ai.ml.sweep import Choice, Uniform, MedianStoppingPolicy, BanditPolicy, TruncationSelectionPolicy
2
3  random_sampling_job_command = command(
4      code="./hyperparametertune",  # Local path where the code is stored
5      command="python main.py --titanic ${{inputs.titanic}} --randomstate ${{inputs.randomstate}}",
6      inputs={
7          "titanic": Input(
8              type="uri_file",
9              path="azureml:titanic_prepped:1",
10         ),
11         "randomstate": 0,
12         "penalty_term": 'l1',
13         "C": 0.01,
14         "max_iter": 100,
15     },
16     environment="job_base_env@latest",
17     compute="cpu-cluster",
18     display_name="RandomSampling",
19 )
20
21 # #Set Parameter expressions
22 # #choice, randint, qlognormal, qnormal, qloguniform, quniform, lognormal, normal, loguniform, uniform
23 random_command_job_for_sweep = random_sampling_job_command(
24     penalty_term=Choice(values=['l2', 'l1']),
25     C=Uniform(min_value=0.01, max_value=10.0),
26     max_iter=Choice(values=[10, 100, 150, 200]),
27 )
```

Figure 4.20 – Sweep job command with hyperparameters for random sampling

As shown in *Figure 4.20* in line 25, the value of C is defined to follow a uniform distribution from 0.01 to 10.0, making this a continuous hyperparameter across the search space.

Just as with the grid sampling sweep job, we set parameters for our sweep but specify them using a random sampling algorithm as shown here:

```
1  # apply the sweep parameter to obtain the sweep_job
2  random_sweep_job = random_command_job_for_sweep.sweep(
3      compute="cpu-cluster",
4      sampling_algorithm="random",
5      primary_metric="test_AUC",
6      goal="Maximize",
7  )
8
9  random_sweep_job.set_limits(max_total_trials=120,
10                             max_concurrent_trials=10,
11                             timeout=7200)
```

Figure 4.21 – Calling the sweep method during random sampling

Given the parameters for the sweep job and the limits have been set, we are ready to execute the sweep job. In order to execute the code, again we leverage an ml_client method to create or update a job as shown in *Figure 4.18*.

Now you have gone through grid and random sampling, there is an additional type of hyperparameter sampling that can be applied, which we will look at next.

Setting up a sweep job for Bayesian sampling

Earlier in the chapter, we cloned our sample notebook to leverage this material. The notebook for this chapter, 'Chapter 4 - Hyperparameter Tuning', provides a review on creating a job command to create a **logistic regression model** by leveraging an sklearn pipeline and mlflow capabilities.

The code is then updated and placed into a new directory – the hyperparametertune folder, which leverages Python's argparse module and enables you to pass parameters into scripts. To run the script that has been generated by this notebook, we will create a job command and update the job command to include the hyperparameters as shown in the code snippet here. Conveniently, the job command is the same as was found for the random sampling displayed in *Figure 4.16*.

The only difference here is that the sampling algorithm is defined as bayesian, as shown in the figure:

```
# apply the sweep parameter to obtain the sweep_job
sweep_job = command_job_for_sweep.sweep(
    compute="cpu-cluster",
    sampling_algorithm="bayesian",
    primary_metric="test_AUC",
    goal="Maximize",
)

# define the limits for this sweep
sweep_job.set_limits(max_total_trials=60, max_concurrent_trials=10, timeout=7200)
```

Figure 4.22 – Calling a sweep method using Bayesian sampling

In order to execute the code, again, we leverage the ml_client's method to create or update a job and continue by leveraging the get_job_status method as shown in *Figure 4.19*.

You have now made it through grid, random, and Bayesian hyperparameter tuning job commands in AMLS. We will continue reviewing the results of the job within AMLS.

Reviewing results of a sweep job

Recall that for a single trial of a sweep job, several trials will be created to determine the model that will provide the best primary metric. Clicking on **jobs** in the left-hand menu pane of your AMLS workspace will display a list of your jobs for review. By now, you have run the sample notebook provided for this chapter – let's review your results.

Clicking on the **chapter4** job brings you to the jobs that you have performed as part of this chapter. Selecting the display name will drill into a given job's details. Let us start by reviewing the results of the jobs that we have run as shown here:

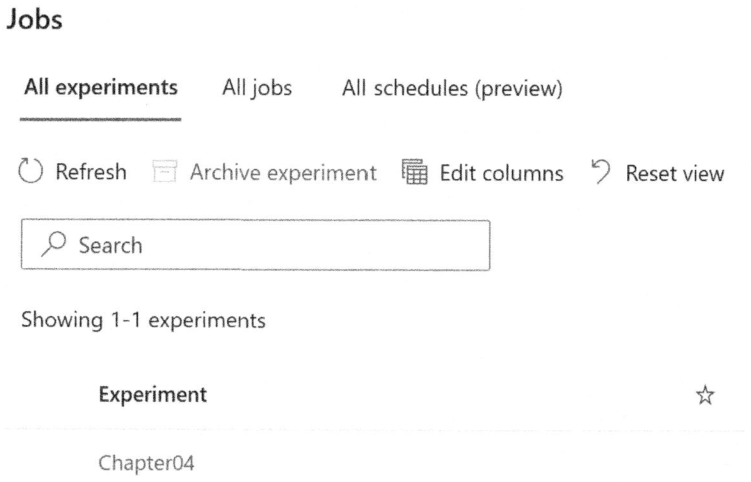

Jobs

All experiments   All jobs   All schedules (preview)

↻ Refresh   ▭ Archive experiment   ▦ Edit columns   ↺ Reset view

🔍 Search

Showing 1-1 experiments

Experiment   ☆

Chapter04

Figure 4.23 – Job results

To review the results of the job, follow the next steps:

1. Clicking on the **Experiment** name, **Chapter04**, will bring us to the different job sweeps that have been performed as part of this chapter.
2. Clicking on a given run of your experiment will provide the details for a given job run as shown in *Figure 4.24*:

Tuning Your Models with AMLS

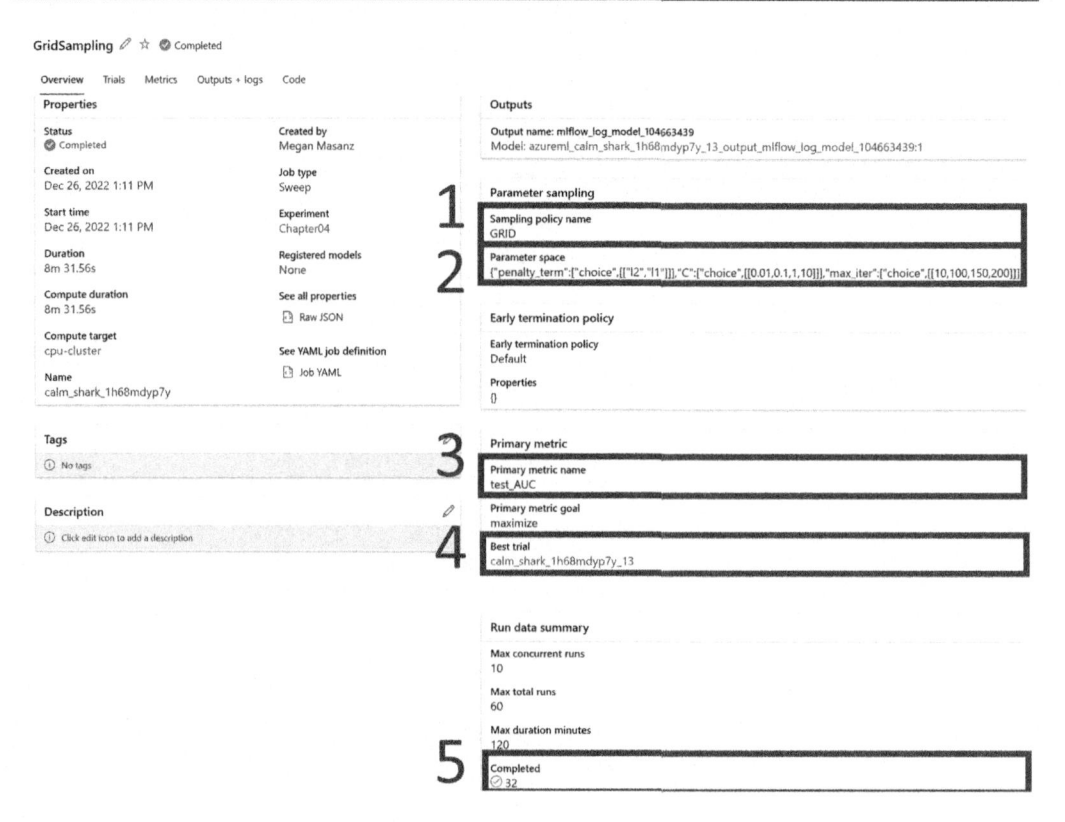

Figure 4.24 – Job sweep details

Key information was captured as metadata, providing traceability for a given job run. This information includes the following:

I. The sampling policy

II. The parameter space

III. The primary metric

IV. The best trial

V. The number of runs completed

3. Clicking on the trial hyperlink from the run details brings up the trial with the best results for the selected primary metric:

Reviewing results of a sweep job | 123

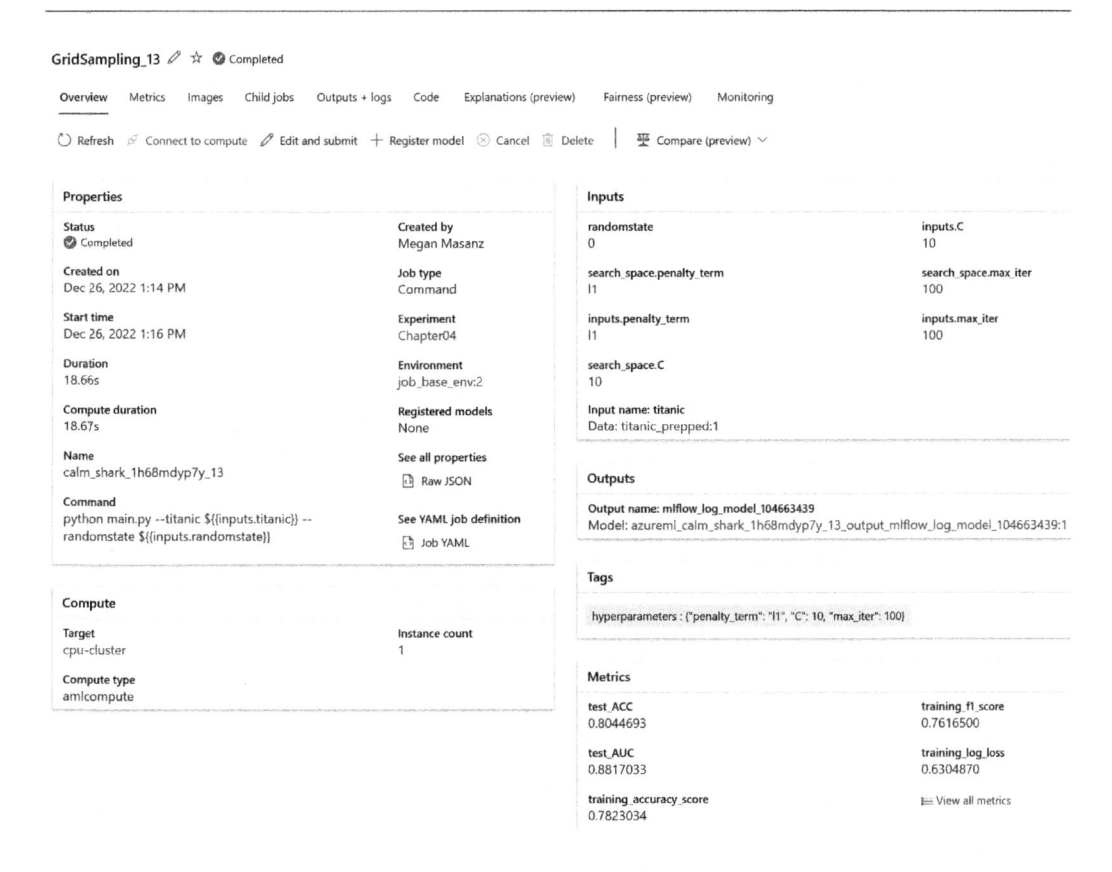

Figure 4.25 – Best trial run

4. Clicking on the **Metrics** tab for the best trial run provides the metrics for the evaluation of a given trial:

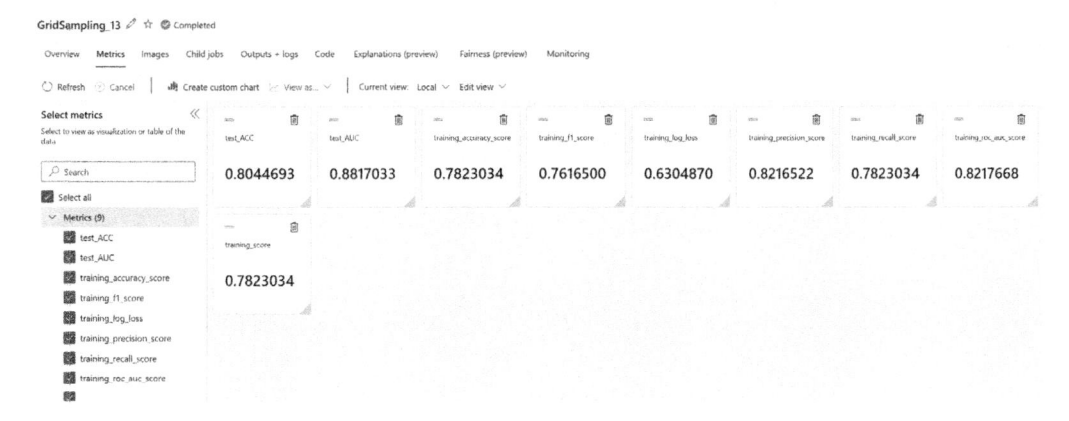

Figure 4.26 – Metrics for the best trial run of the sweep job

5. To review all the trials created for a job run holistically, you can click on the job run and head over to the **Trials** tab as shown in *Figure 4.27*:

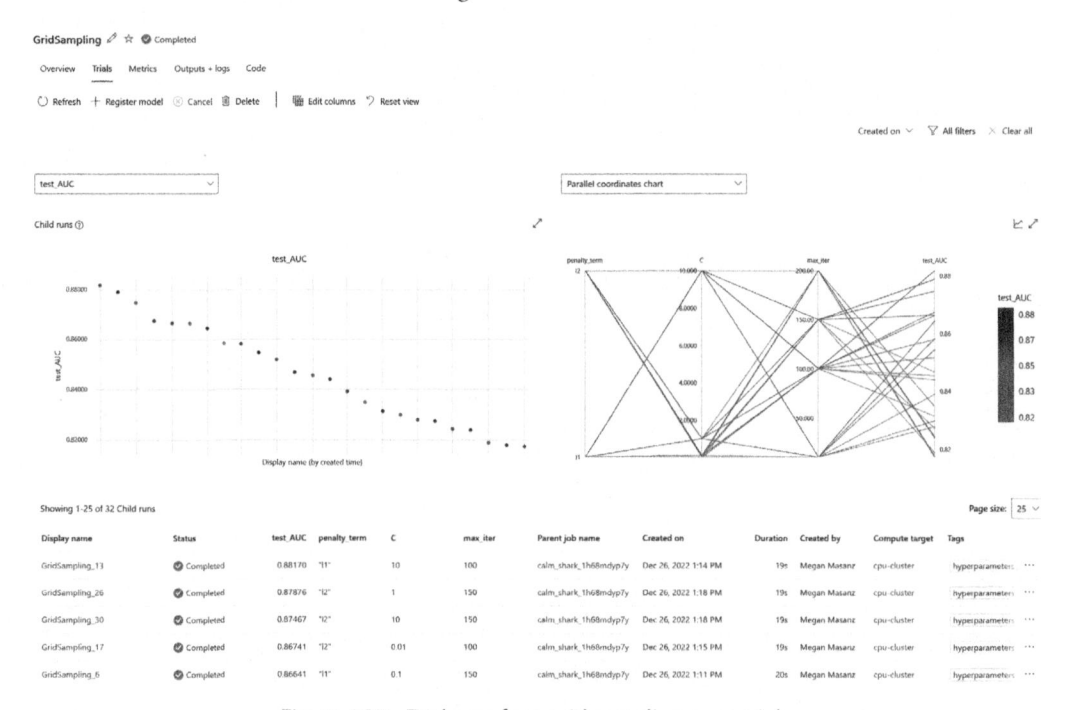

Figure 4.27 – Trial runs for a grid sampling sweep job

Not only are you able to review each metric individually through the AMLS workspace UI for a given run of a job but you can also view a parallel coordinates chart, displaying how the different hyperparameters selected impacted the primary metric.

To review the search space and its impact on the primary metric, review the parallel coordinates chart in the **Trials** tab:

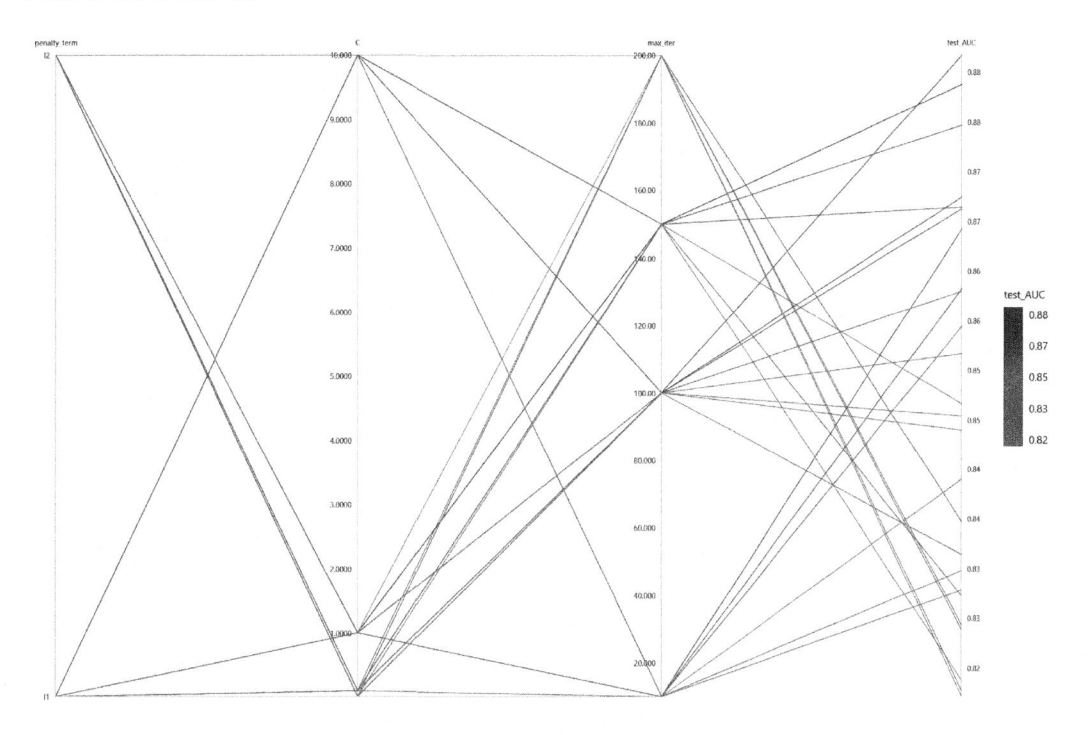

Figure 4.28 – Grid search space parallel coordinates chart

In addition to the parallel coordinates chart, AMLS provides a 2D scatter chart and a 3D scatter chart for evaluating hyperparameter tuning.

The 3D scatter chart for hyperparameter tuning is shown here:

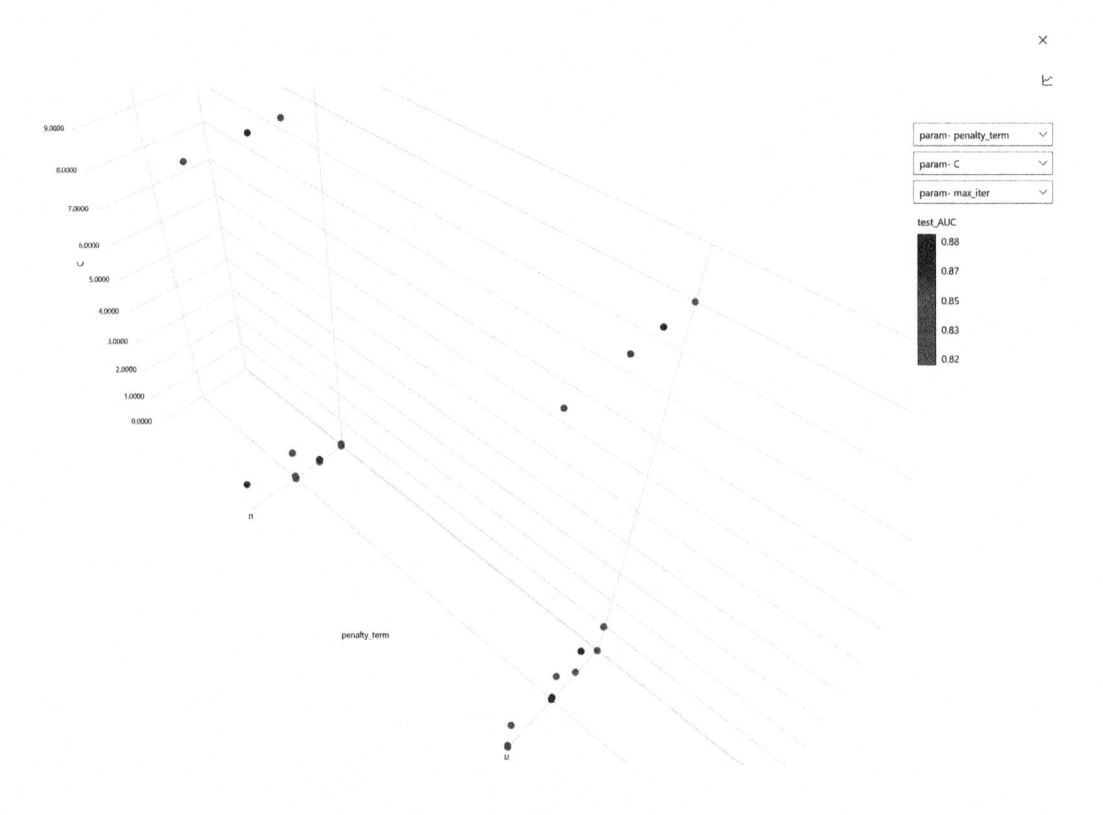

Figure 4.29 – 3D scatter chart

We have seen how to graphically view and compare models through charts in the AML Studio, but we are not limited to accessing this valuable information through the UI.

Not only are we able to retrieve the best trial of the sweep job through the AMLS Studio by reviewing results in the experiment tab but we are also able to access this information by leveraging the AMLS Python SDK v2.

Putting the results from the job run into a pandas DataFrame is shown as follows:

```
def get_job_run_results(experiment_id, run_id):
    df = mlflow.search_runs([experiment_id])
    rslt_df = df[(df['tags.mlflow.parentRunId'] == run_id )]
    rslt_df_finished = rslt_df[rslt_df['status'] == 'FINISHED']

    while rslt_df.shape[0] == 0:
        print('waiting for jobs to register')
        df = mlflow.search_runs([experiment_id])
        rslt_df = df[(df['tags.mlflow.parentRunId'] == run_id )]
        rslt_df_finished = rslt_df[rslt_df['status'] == 'FINISHED']
        time.sleep(5)

    while rslt_df_finished.shape[0] != rslt_df.shape[0]:
        df = mlflow.search_runs([experiment_id])
        rslt_df = df[(df['tags.mlflow.parentRunId'] == run_id )]
        rslt_df_finished = rslt_df[rslt_df['status'] == 'FINISHED']
        status = rslt_df["status"].unique()
        print(status)
        for x in status:
            rslt_df_status = rslt_df[rslt_df['status'] == x]
            print(returned_sweep_job.display_name + ', Number:' + str(x) + " " + str(rslt_df_status.shape[0]))
        time.sleep(5)

    rslt_df_status = rslt_df[rslt_df['status'] == 'FINISHED']
    return rslt_df_status

df = get_job_run_results(experiment_id, run_id)
df
```

Figure 4.30 – Getting the job results into a pandas DataFrame

At the end of the notebook, we have included the code for returning a pandas DataFrame for the completed job run:

```
df = df.sort_values(by='metrics.test_AUC', ascending=False)
```

Figure 4.31 – Sorting the job trials to get the highest test_AUC for trials

Given we have the pandas DataFrame properly sorted by the primary metric, we can easily pull out the `run_id` value for the best trial run as shown here:

```
best_run_id = df.iat[0, 0]
```

Figure 4.32 – Getting the best run_id value from the sorted pandas DataFrame

Now that we have the best run retrieved into the `best_run_id` variable as shown here, we can leverage the best model from the sweep job.

Loading the model from the best sweep job trial is shown as follows:

```
pipeline_model = mlflow.sklearn.load_model(f"runs:/{best_run_id}/model")
```

Figure 4.33 – Loading the best model

Once the model has been loaded and given we are using the virtual environment that was used to create the model, we can carry out inference using the loaded model as shown here:

```
results = pipeline_model.predict(X_raw)
```

Figure 4.34 – Inference using the best model from the sweep job

Congratulations – you have retrieved the best trial run for a given sweep job from the SDK v2! This run information can be viewed in the UI as well as programmatically.

Summary

In this chapter, we have explored what model parameters are and how a sweep job can be leveraged to tune hyperparameters that are defined for a given model. We have also explored options for setting up sweep jobs based on the search space and sampling methodology selected. AMLS provides the ability to sweep across the search space to tune a model, automating the process of hyperparameter tuning on a compute cluster, which will shut itself down in the idle period after the trials are completed, consuming compute resources wisely.

In addition to setting up a sweep job, you have been able to review your results in the Studio as well as in the code – providing intuitive insight into the best-performing model for your use case. Now that you have completed the chapter, be sure to turn off your compute resources to save cost.

In the next chapter, we will show you how to leverage AMLS to take over the time-consuming task of model development. This functionality is not only available through the SDK and the CLI, but in the AMLS Studio itself as well.

5
Azure Automated Machine Learning

Automated Machine Learning, also referred to as AutoML, is the automation of the iterative and time-consuming process of machine learning model development. AutoML enables data scientists and machine learning engineers to develop high-performing models in an efficient way allowing them to scale and build the best model quickly. Data scientists can rely on AutoML to perform tedious model development tasks such as feature engineering, algorithm selection, hyperparameter tuning, and model evaluation.

In this chapter, we will cover the following topics:

- Introduction to Azure AutoML
- Featurization concepts in AML
- AutoML using AMLS
- AutoML using AML Python SDK
- Parsing your AutoML results via AML and the AML SDK

Technical requirements

In this section, we are going to see how to create an automated machine learning model from start to end with step-by-step procedures.

In order to access your workspace, recall the steps from the previous chapter:

1. Go to https://ml.azure.com.
2. Select your workspace name.
3. In the workspace **User** interface on the left-hand side, click **Compute**.

4. On the **compute** screen, select your compute instance and select **Start**:

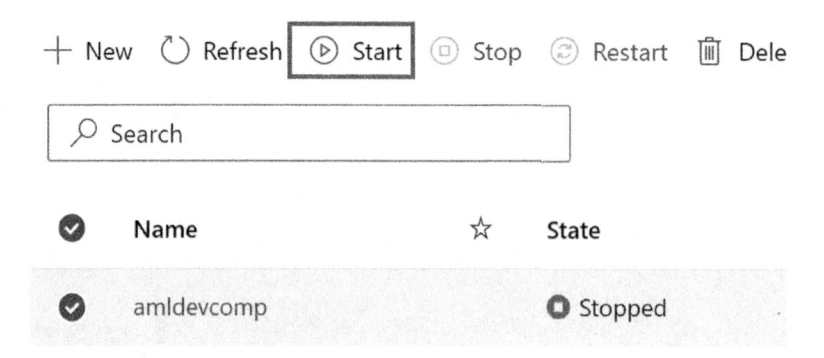

Figure 5.1 – Start compute

5. Your compute instance will change from having a **Stopped** status to a **Starting** status.

6. In *Chapter 2, Working with Data in AMLS*, we cloned the Git repository – if you have not already done so, continue to follow the steps provided here. If you have already cloned the repository, skip to *step 7*.

7. Open the Terminal on your compute instance. Note the path will include your user in the directory. Type the following into the Terminal to clone the sample notebooks into your working directory:

```
git clone (https://github.com/PacktPublishing/Azure-
Machine-Learning-Engineering.git)
```

8. Clicking on the refresh icon shown in *Figure 5.2* will update and refresh the notebooks displayed on your screen:

Figure 5.2 – Refresh

9. Review the notebooks in your Azure-Machine-Learning-Engineering directory. This will display the files cloned into your working directory as shown in *Figure 5.3*:

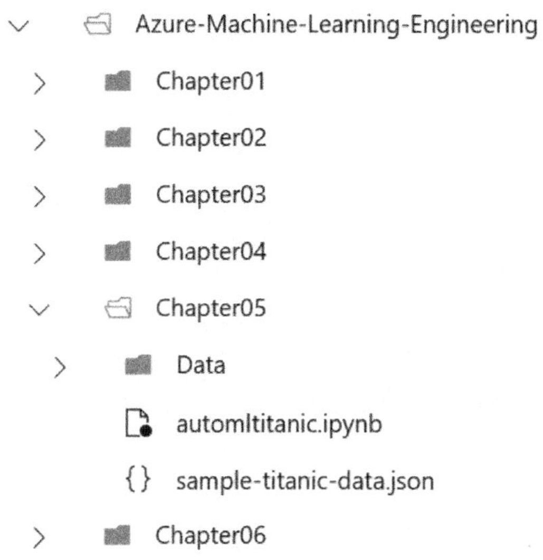

Figure 5.3 – Azure-Machine-Learning-Engineering

Now, let's learn about what **Azure Machine Learning** (**AML**) AutoML is, some of its benefits, and how to consume them.

Introduction to Azure AutoML

AutoML is a powerful solution that enables not only data scientists but also citizen data scientists to build machine learning models supporting a variety of use cases. AutoML currently supports classification, regression, time-series forecasting, and computer vision in preview. Classification involves a response variable that identifies a category. The input training dataset will be leveraged to build a model to predict which category a new sample will fall into. Leveraging the Titanic dataset, we can leverage the classification model to predict whether a passenger will survive on the Titanic. In addition to supporting classification model creation, AutoML is also able to generate a regression model. A regression model will provide a continuous value as the output of the model. An example of a regression model would be to predict gas prices or taxi fares. AutoML can also predict values based on time with time-series forecasting. Not only this but AutoML also supports image classification, object detection, and instance segmentation using the **AML Studio** (**AMLS**) Python SDK.

While AMLS supports a variety of AutoML tasks, the AMLS Python SDK supports a variety of features for developers and data scientists to leverage that are not currently available via AMLS alone.

With the Python SDK, not only do we find support for computer vision tasks but also for viewing featurization information, enabling voting ensemble models, showing the best model based on non-primary metrics, as well as enabling and disabling **Open Neural Network Exchange** (**ONNX**) model compatibility.

Featurization concepts in AML

In order to provide the best model, regardless of whether AutoML is being leveraged, an important step in model creation is the engineering features. AutoML in AMLS will default to leverage featurization. This can be disabled in the UI as well as the SDK if the feature engineering step has already been accomplished. These featurization transformations on your dataset can not only be enabled or disabled but they can also be customized or excluded from specific columns. There are several featurization steps applied to your dataset based on the type of column, and the column's data type.

During training, AutoML leverages scaling or normalization to ensure model performance. AutoML leverages a variety of techniques, including scaling to unit variance, scaling by quantile range, scaling by the maximum absolute value, scaling by a column's minimum and maximum, by applying **Principle Component Analysis (PCA)** for dimensionality reduction, **Singular Value Decomposition (SVD)** for dimensionality reduction, as well as rescaling each sample to a norm of 1.

Provided that featurization is enabled, certain columns will be dropped during the training process. Columns that have no variance – meaning all rows have the same value – or rows with high cardinality – meaning they have a very high variance, such as a column with GUID values – will be dropped. If a column has a numeric value but a low variance, AutoML will transform that value into a categorical feature and apply one-hot encoding. If a categorical column has high variance, one-hot hash encoding will be leveraged.

AutoML will also generate a k-means clustering model for each numeric column. Each sample will have its distance from the centroid of the cluster added to the dataset.

Often, datasets will include missing values. AutoML will replace missing values with averages if the column is numeric or impute values using the most common value for a given column if it is categorical. This can actually be customized by leveraging a `FeaturizationConfig` in AutoML. The imputer for missing values can replace values with the mean, median, or mode of a value.

For features that are date-time values, additional features will be generated including year, month, day, day of the year, day of the week, quarter, hour, minute, and second.

Specific to the forecasting task, the `TimeIndexFeaturization` class is leveraged to generate many different features. Examples include an integer value specifying whether it is before or after a certain date (July 1st, for example), the year, calendar quarter, calendar month, day, hour, minute, second, an a.m. or p.m. indicator, the day of the week, the day of the quarter (1 through 92), the day of the year (1 through 366), as well as an ISO week and year defined by the ISO 8601 standard.

For features that are text, term frequency will be added based on trigrams, bigrams, and unigrams. Text features are converted into document feature vectors. AutoML can be configured to leverage **Bidirectional Encoder Representations from Transformers (BERT)** during the featurization process by enabling deep learning.

AutoML not only can handle a variety of featurization steps to prepare models for training but can also handle classification, regression, and time-series forecasting directly in AMLS and accomplish these same modeling tasks, as well as compute vision tasks through the AML Python SDK.

In the next section, we will explore how to leverage AMLS to accomplish classification for the well-known Titanic dataset. The dataset link will be available in the book's GitHub repository.

AutoML using AMLS

As mentioned earlier in the chapter, there are two ways to use AutoML in AML. For citizen data scientists or data scientists who prefer a no-code approach, AMLS can be used; for data scientists with coding experience, the AML Python SDK can be used. In this section, we will show you how to use AMLS to train a classification model on your Titanic dataset with AutoML to predict whether a passenger would survive the Titanic disaster or not.

Please sign in to AMLS at `https://ml.azure.com` and follow these instructions:

1. Select your subscription and the workspace you have been using throughout the book.
2. On the left-hand side of the studio, click on **Automated ML** as shown in *Figure 5.4*:

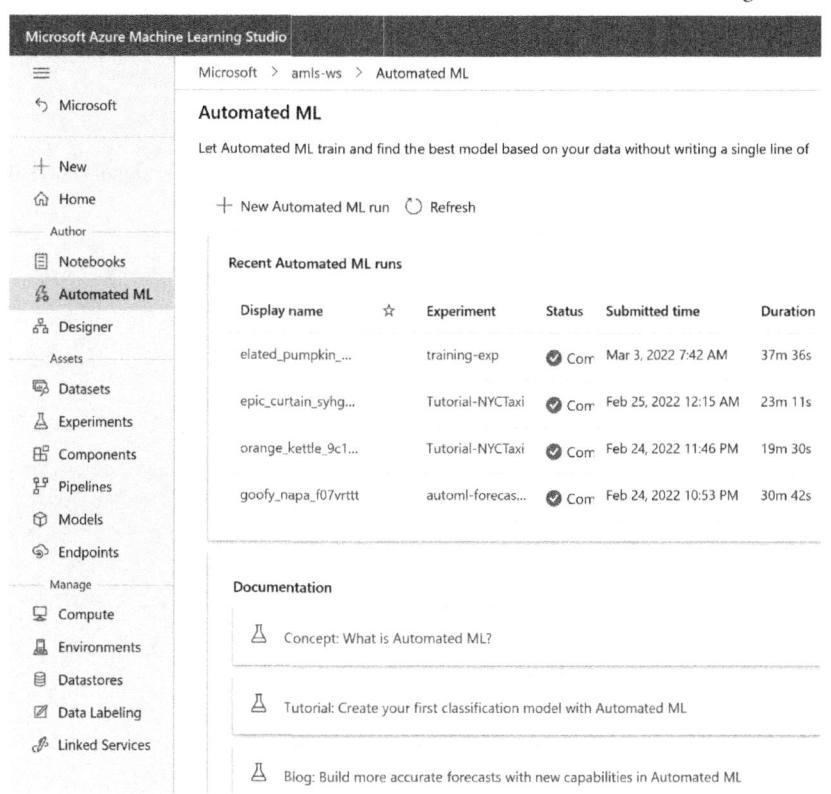

Figure 5.4 – Importing AutoMLConfig

3. Select **+ New Automated ML run**, which takes you to the screen to select your dataset for the model. If you don't have the dataset for training, you can click on **+ Create dataset** to upload `titanic.csv` from your local computer to Azure as shown in *Figure 5.5*:

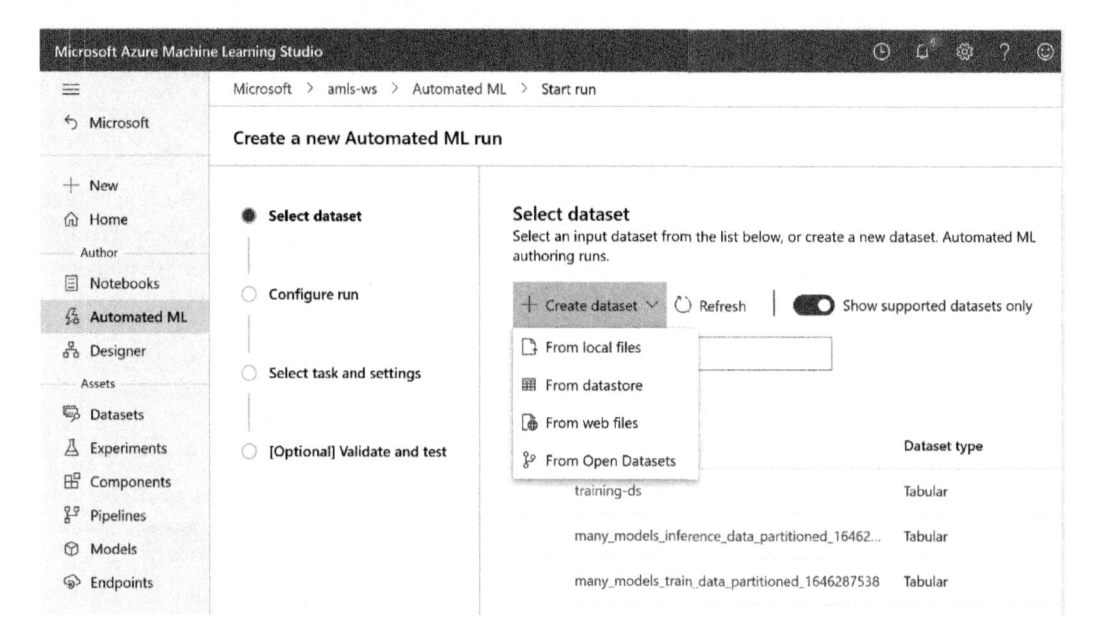

Figure 5.5 – Creating a new dataset by uploading titanic.csv from your local computer

4. Provide basic information for the dataset as shown in *Figure 5.6*:

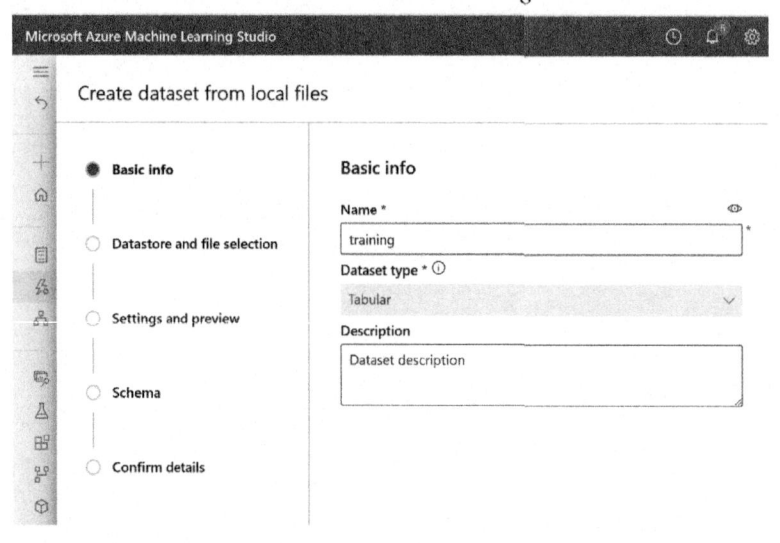

Figure 5.6 – Providing basic information for the dataset

5. On the next screen, click on **Browse** to locate and upload `titanic.csv` as shown in *Figure 5.7*. The dataset is available in the GitHub repo for this book:

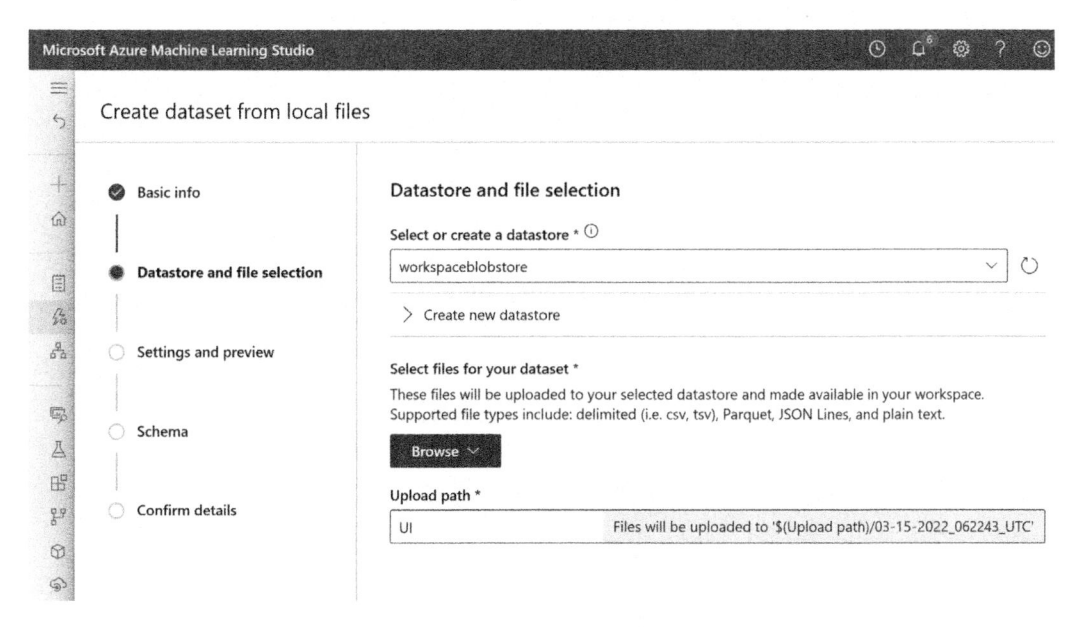

Figure 5.7 – Providing the location of stored data files

6. Once uploaded, the next screen will show you the settings and preview based on the upload file. The only setting you need to change is under **Column headers**, which you should set to **Only first file has headers** as shown in *Figure 5.8*:

Create dataset from local files

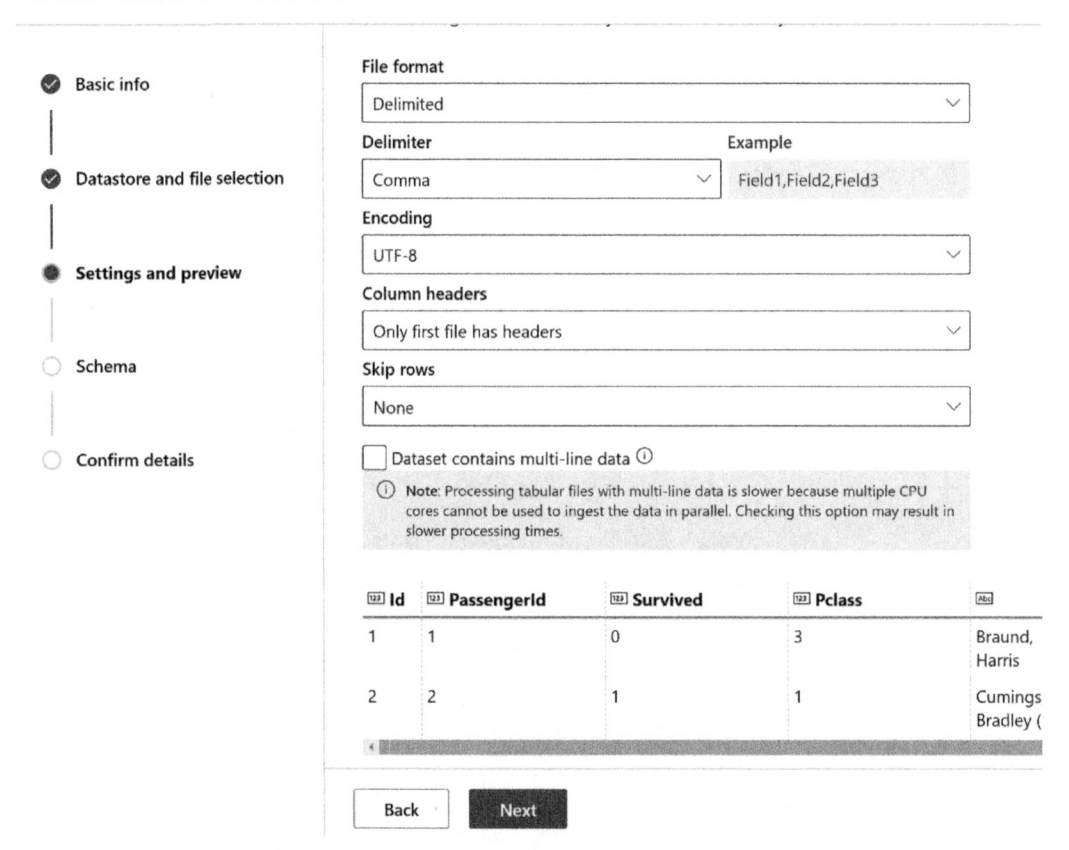

Figure 5.8 – Dataset preview

7. The next screen will show the dataset's schema, which has been autodetected from the file as shown in *Figure 5.9*:

Create dataset from local files

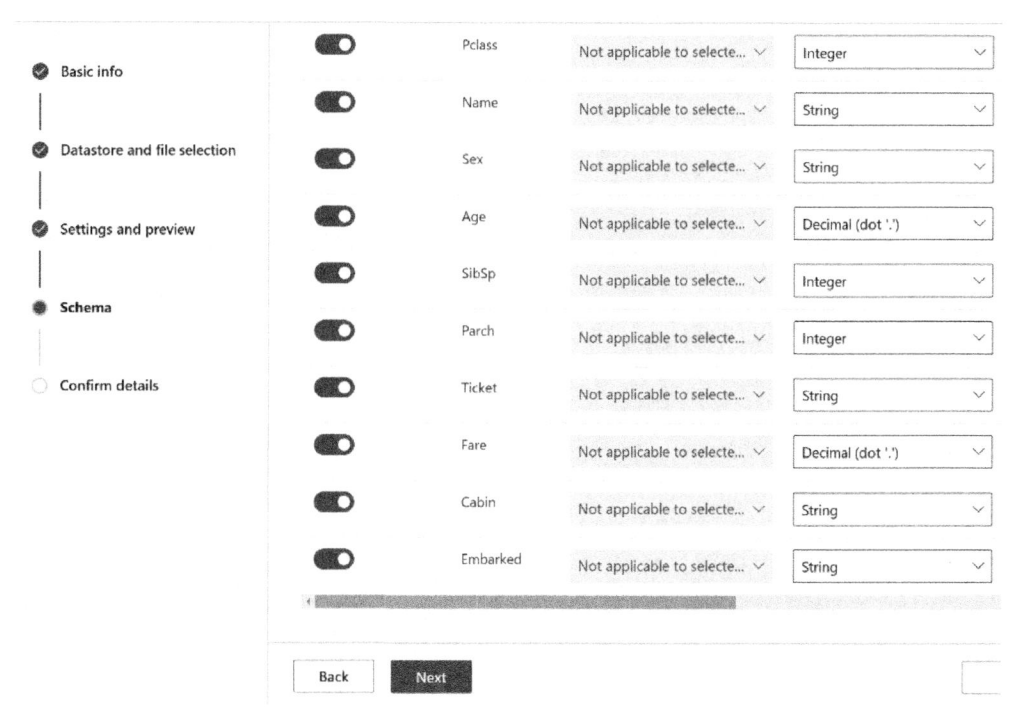

Pclass	Not applicable to selecte...	Integer	
Name	Not applicable to selecte...	String	
Sex	Not applicable to selecte...	String	
Age	Not applicable to selecte...	Decimal (dot '.')	
SibSp	Not applicable to selecte...	Integer	
Parch	Not applicable to selecte...	Integer	
Ticket	Not applicable to selecte...	String	
Fare	Not applicable to selecte...	Decimal (dot '.')	
Cabin	Not applicable to selecte...	String	
Embarked	Not applicable to selecte...	String	

Figure 5.9 – Dataset settings

8. The last step is to review and confirm the details and click on **Create** as shown in *Figure 5.10*:

Create dataset from local files

- ✓ Basic info
- ✓ Datastore and file selection
- ✓ Settings and preview
- ✓ Schema
- ● Confirm details

Basic info

Name
training

Dataset type
Tabular

File settings

File format
Delimited

Delimiter
Comma

Encoding
UTF-8

Column headers
Only first file has headers

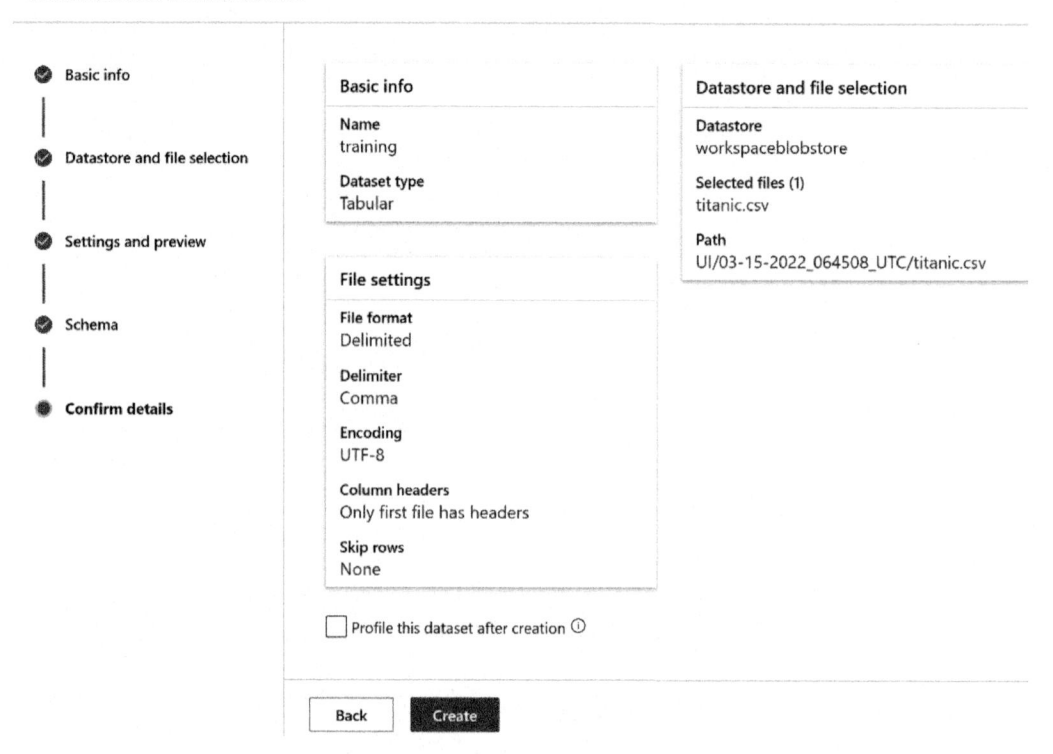

Skip rows
None

Datastore and file selection

Datastore
workspaceblobstore

Selected files (1)
titanic.csv

Path
UI/03-15-2022_064508_UTC/titanic.csv

☐ Profile this dataset after creation ⓘ

[Back] [Create]

Figure 5.10 – Reviewing and confirming the creation of the dataset

9. You will be taken back to the list of the datasets. You should see your Titanic dataset, which we named **training**, at the top of the list. Go ahead, select it, and click on **Next** as shown in *Figure 5.11*:

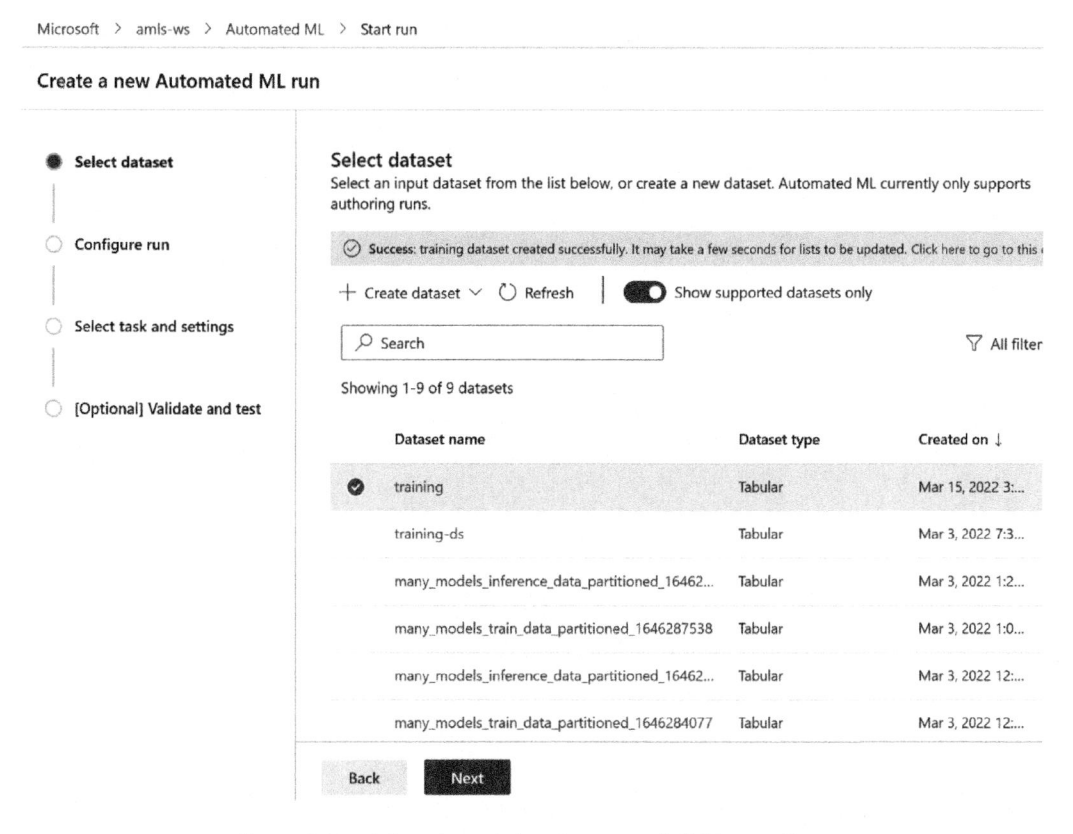

Figure 5.11 – Select the training dataset and clicking on Next

10. In this step, you need to create an experiment for your AutoML run and then select the target column, sometimes called the *dependent variable*, and lastly, select a compute cluster for the model training as shown in *Figure 5.12*:

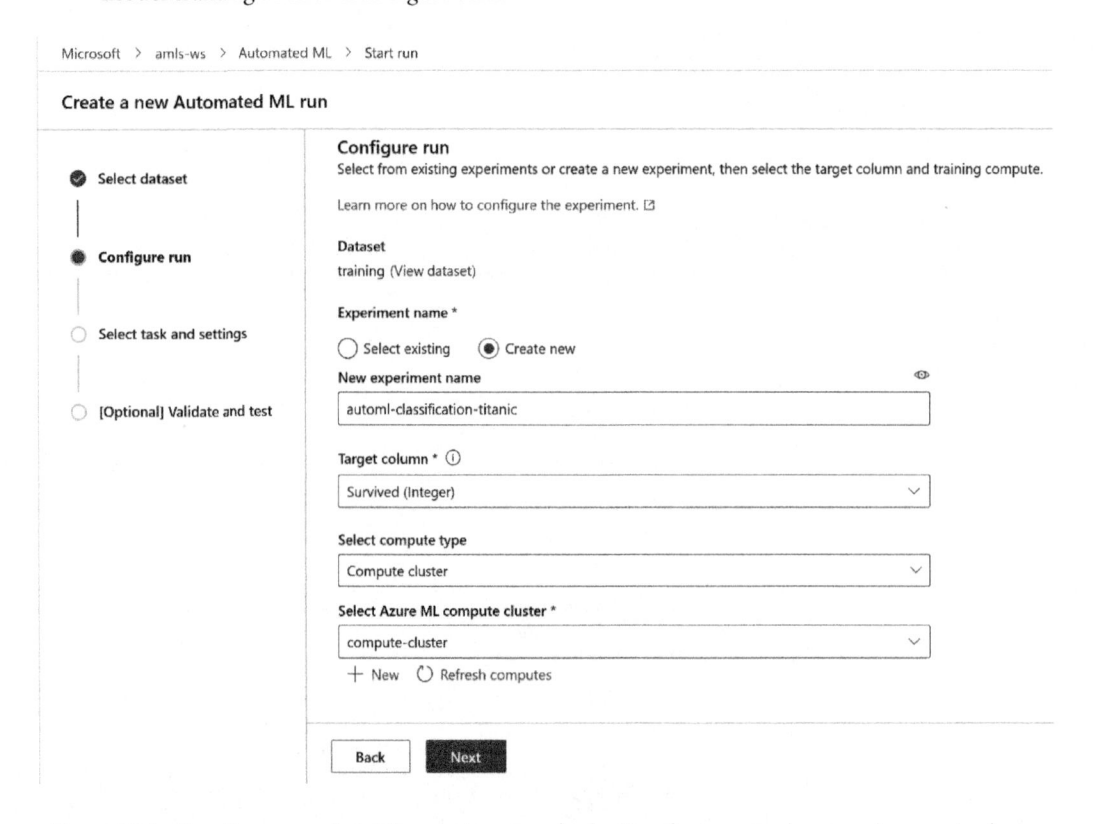

Figure 5.12 – Creating a new AutoML experiment and selecting the target column and compute cluster

11. On the next screen, you can select the machine learning task. AutoML has auto-detected the task based on the target column. In this case, it should be **Classification** as shown in *Figure 5.13*:

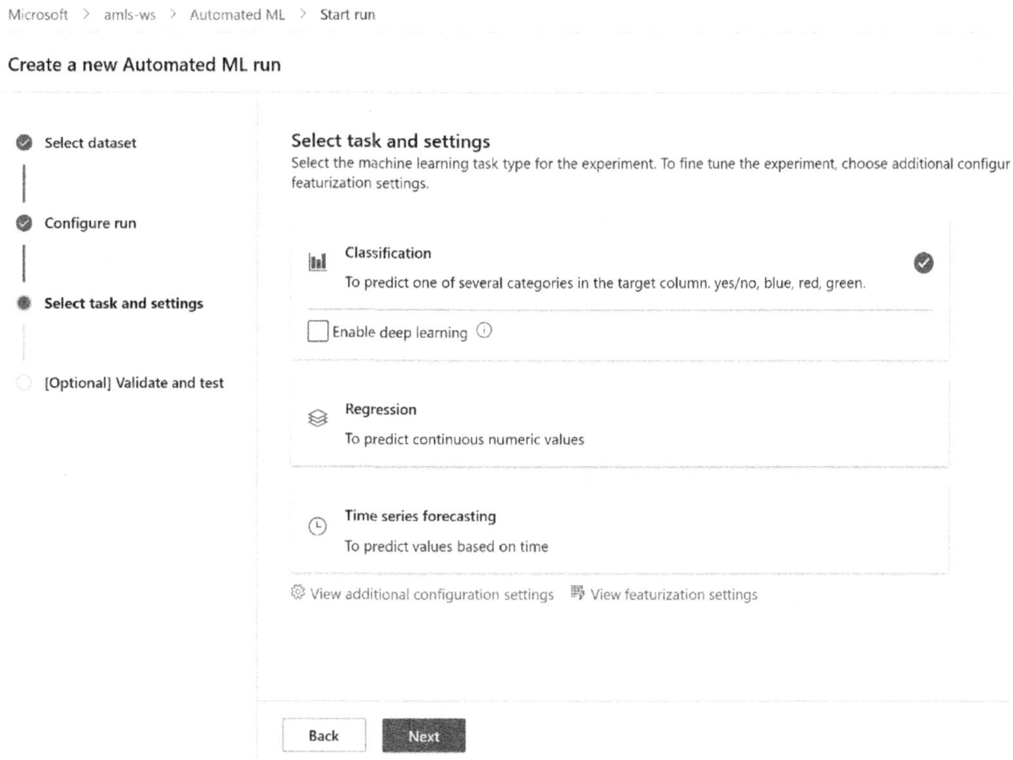

Figure 5.13 – Selecting the machine learning task (for example, in this case, Classification)

12. Next, click on **View additional configuration settings** to open a window to set **Additional Configurations**, such as the **Primary metric** configuration for the model performance and the exit criteria. We use the **Area Under the Curve** (**AUC**) for the metric and set the training job to terminate if no further performance is gained in 30 minutes (0.5 hours). Click **Save** to exit as shown in *Figure 5.14*:

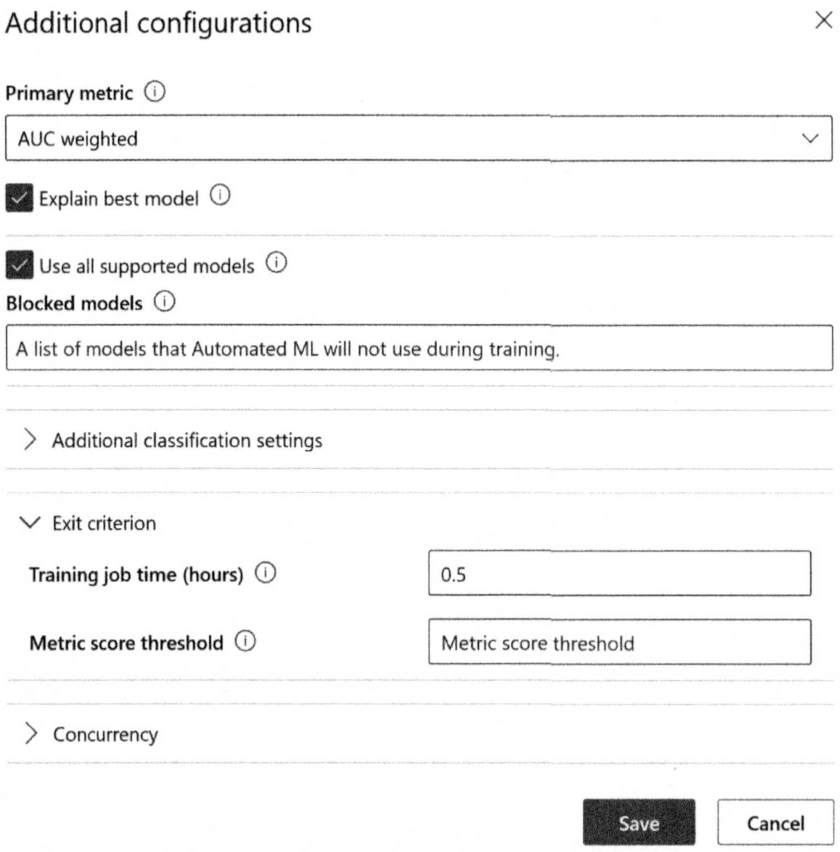

Figure 5.14 – Configuring settings for the training job

13. Click **Next** to be taken to the next screen. To validate the performance of the trained model thus far, please select **k-fold cross validation**, and make the **Number of cross validations** setting 3. For the **Test dataset (preview)** option, select **Test split (choose a percentage of the training data)**, set **Percentage test of data** to 10, and finally, click on **Finish** as shown in *Figure 5.15*:

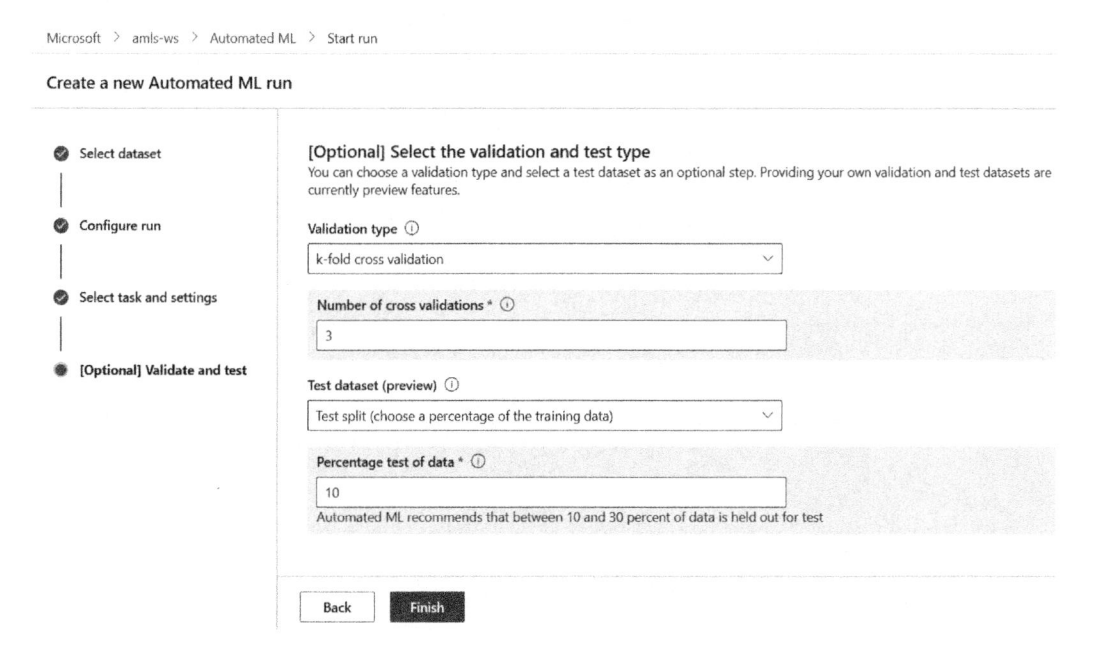

Figure 5.15 – Setting the validation type and test dataset

14. Once the model training is done, you will be presented with a screen summarizing the training statistics, such as the duration of the training, a link to the **training** dataset, and a summary of the best-performing model, with the name of its algorithm and its performance metric (for example, **AUC weighted**) as shown in *Figure 5.16*:

Microsoft > amls-ws > Automated ML > automl-classification-titanic > kind_glove_v8ztms12

kind_glove_v8ztms12

⟳ Refresh   ▶ Edit and submit (preview)   ⊗ Cancel   🗑 Delete

Details   Data guardrails   Models   Outputs + logs   Child runs   Snapshot

Properties

Status
✅ Completed ∨

⚠ Warning: No scores improved over last 20 iterations, so experiment stopped early. This early stopping behavior can be disabled by setting enable_early_stopping = False in AutoMLConfig for notebook/python SDK runs.

See more details

Created
Mar 16, 2022 10:19 AM

Started
Mar 16, 2022 10:19 AM

Duration
24m 44.07s

Compute duration
24m 44.07s

Compute target
compute-cluster

Run ID

Best model summary

Algorithm name
VotingEnsemble

Ensemble details
≡ View ensemble details

AUC weighted
0.87978   ≡ View all other metrics

Sampling
100.00 % ⓘ

Registered models
No registration yet

Deploy status
No deployment yet

Run summary

Task type
Classification   ≡ View configuration settings

Featurization

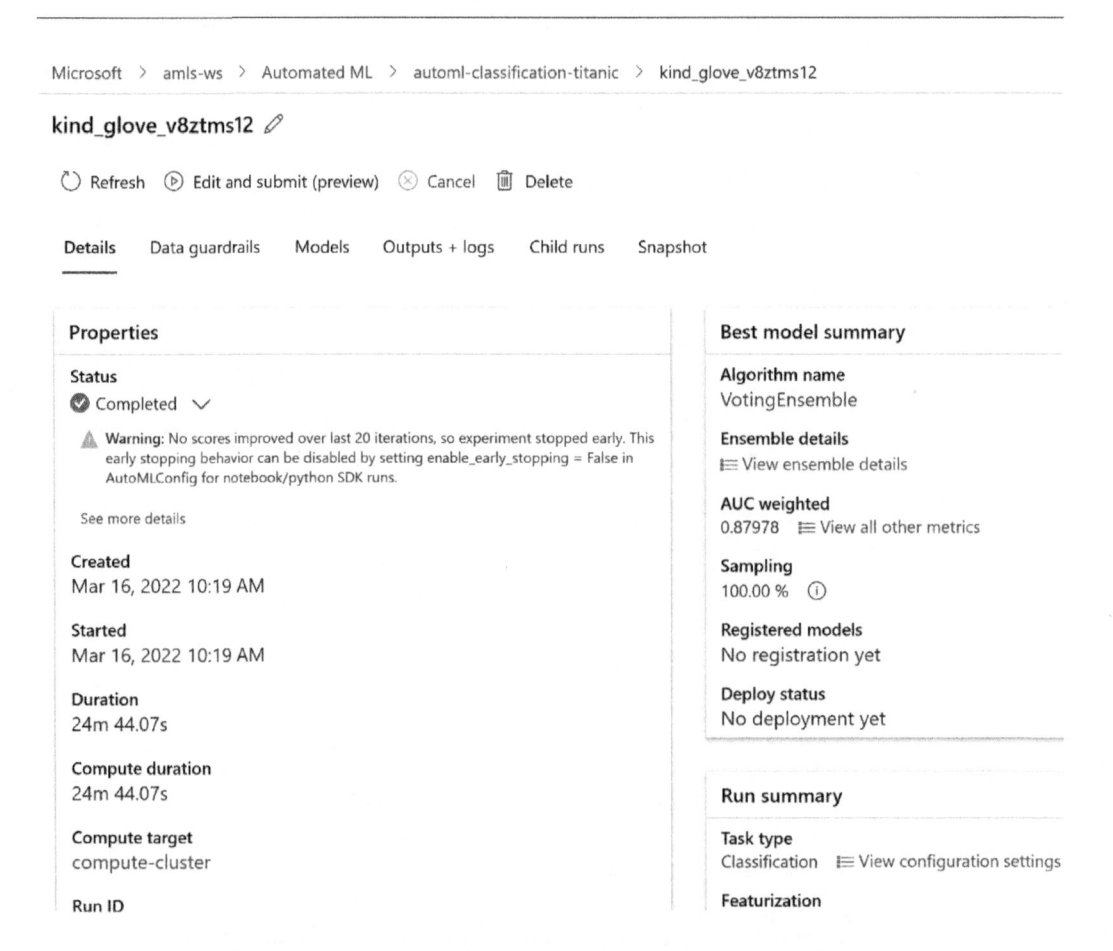

Figure 5.16 – Model and run summary after training is completed

Now that you have seen how to leverage AutoML through AMLS, take a moment to review the output not only in the **Details** section as shown in *Figure 5.16* but also review each tab and explore the wealth of information provided during an AutoML experiment run.

Next, we will explore leveraging AutoML through the AML Python SDK. The AML Python SDK provides fine-grained control over your experiment, as we will see in the next section.

AutoML using the AML Python SDK

Now that you have seen how to leverage AutoML inside AMLS, we will explore creating a model leveraging the AML Python SDK.

Earlier in the chapter, in *Introduction to AutoML*, we cloned our sample notebooks to leverage this material. For this chapter, note that there is a single notebook titled `Chapter5_Titanic_AutoML`.

The initial code should look familiar, as the preparation of the dataset has not changed. However, when we run the experiment, we will now be leveraging an AutoML experiment.

In order to run an AutoML experiment, we will need to import `AutoMLConfig` as shown in *line 8* of the following figure.

Here's `AutoMLConfig` being imported with the Python SDK:

```
1    import azureml.core
2    from azureml.core import Workspace
3    import pandas as pd
4
5    from azureml.core.experiment import Experiment
6    from azureml.core.workspace import Workspace
7    from azureml.core.dataset import Dataset
8    from azureml.train.automl import AutoMLConfig
9
10   # Load the workspace from the saved config file
11   ws = Workspace.from_config()
12   print('Ready to use Azure ML {} to work with {}'.format(azureml.core.VERSION, ws.name))
```

Figure 5.17 – Importing AutoMLConfig

As part of an AutoML experiment, we are required to specify a training dataset, but we are not required to specify a validation or testing dataset. However, we can specify the training and validation datasets, and the test datasets in preview. In our sample, we will separate the dataset into a training, test, and validation dataset.

Leveraging the `train_test_split` method from `sklearn`, we will break the dataset into three datasets used for training, validation, and testing.

Let's now look into how we can split the data for training the model and also test the model to analyze the accuracy of the model built:

1. The following code is going to split the dataset between model training and model evaluation. We are also specifying which column is used for prediction – in the following case, it's `Survived`. Then, we will print the output to validate whether the split worked or not. Here's the dataset being split for model training, testing, and validation:

```
1   from sklearn.model_selection import train_test_split
2
3   print(df.shape)
4   x_train, X_test = train_test_split(df, test_size=0.2, random_state=223)
5
6   # Use the same function above for the validation set
7   X_train, X_val = train_test_split(x_train,  test_size=0.2, random_state= 8)
8
9
10  print("X_train shape: {}".format(X_train.shape))
11  print("X_test shape: {}".format(X_test.shape))
12  print("X_val shape: {}".format(X_val.shape))
13
14  label = "Survived"
15
16  X_train.to_csv('./automl_train/train.csv', index = False)
17  X_test.to_csv('./automl_train/test.csv', index = False)
18  X_val.to_csv('./automl_train/validate.csv', index = False)
```

Figure 5.18 – Dataset splitting

Once the dataset has been split, we can upload the datasets from our local directory where they have been saved in the **AML** default data store. The local directory where the CSV files are saved is the `automl_train` folder, and when placed into blob storage, they will be placed into a directory called `titanic-auto-ml`.

2. In the following screenshot, the directory is uploaded into the default data store:

```
1   default_ds = ws.get_default_datastore()
2   default_ds.upload(src_dir='./automl_train', target_path='titanic-auto-ml',
3                    overwrite=True, show_progress=True)
4
```

Figure 5.19 – Uploading datasets to the data store

3. Given that the data is now in blob storage, we can leverage the files to create tabular datasets with the AML Python SDK, noting their location in blob storage as shown here:

```
1   from azureml.core import Dataset
2
3   #Create a tabular dataset from the path on the datastore
4   train_dataset      = Dataset.Tabular.from_delimited_files(default_ds.path('titanic-auto-ml/train.csv'))
5   test_dataset       = Dataset.Tabular.from_delimited_files(default_ds.path('titanic-auto-ml/test.csv'))
6   validation_dataset = Dataset.Tabular.from_delimited_files(default_ds.path('titanic-auto-ml/validate.csv'))
```

Figure 5.20 – Creating AML tabular datasets

4. Using the AML Python SDK, we can create an experiment as shown in the following code block in *line 4*:

```
1    # choose a name for experiment
2    experiment_name = 'automl-classification-titanic'
3
4    experiment=Experiment(ws, experiment_name)
```

Figure 5.21 – Creating an Azure ML experiment

An AutoML experiment can be run on a compute instance but given the duration of an experiment will be longer than we have seen up to this point, we will run it on a compute cluster. The following code shows how to create a compute cluster as we saw in *Chapter 1, Introducing the Azure Machine Learning Service*.

5. Next, we will create a compute cluster for us to write out code:

```
from azureml.core.compute import ComputeTarget, AmlCompute
from azureml.core.compute_target import ComputeTargetException

cluster_name = "aml-cluster"

try:
    # Check for existing compute target
    training_cluster = ComputeTarget(workspace=ws, name=cluster_name)
    print('Found existing cluster, use it.')
except ComputeTargetException:
    # If it doesn't already exist, create it
    try:
        compute_config = AmlCompute.provisioning_configuration(vm_size='STANDARD_DS11_V2', max_nodes=2)
        training_cluster = ComputeTarget.create(ws, cluster_name, compute_config)
        training_cluster.wait_for_completion(show_output=True)
    except Exception as ex:
        print(ex)
```

Figure 5.22 – Compute cluster creation for running the AML experiment run

For an AutoML experiment, we are able to provide fine-grained control over the experiment that is being run with the Python SDK.

6. An AutoML experiment run through the SDK can specify its behavior during the experiment run:

```
1   automl_settings = {
2       "experiment_timeout_hours" : 0.3,
3       "enable_early_stopping" : True,
4       "iteration_timeout_minutes": 5,
5       "max_concurrent_iterations": 4,
6       "max_cores_per_iteration": -1,
7       #"n_cross_validations": 2,
8       "primary_metric": 'AUC_weighted',
9       "featurization": 'auto',
10      "verbosity": logging.INFO,
11  }
```

Figure 5.23 – AutoML experiment settings

As shown in *Figure 5.23*, we are able to specify experiment_time_hours. If no value is provided, the experiment run will time out after 6 days. enable_early_stopping, which defaults to True, will stop the experiment early if the model is not improving after n_interations. This behavior ensures that at a minimum, 20 iterations are run before an experiment run is stopped early.

iteration_timeout_minutes is the number of minutes each iteration can run before it is terminated. If it is not specified, a default value of 1 month is used. Another setting that can be configured is max_concurrent_iterations. An AML compute cluster can handle a single iteration per node. Specifying this value will expand the number of active nodes in a given cluster. If max_concurrent_iterations is greater than the node count in a given cluster, then the experiment runs will be queued and will execute once a node is available within a cluster. Setting max_cores_per_iteration to a value of -1 indicates that all the cores available from the compute running the iteration should be leveraged. This value defaults to 1. It is acceptable to provide values of -1, 1, or a number that is less than or equal to the number of cores that are on the compute running the training experiment.

We can specify n_cross_validations, and that will ensure the validation dataset will be extracted from the training data. However, in our experiment, we are explicitly passing a validation dataset, so this is commented out in *line 7* of *Figure 5.23*. If neither n_cross_validations is set nor is a validation dataset provided, AutoML will use its own validation techniques. If neither is provided and an AutoML experiment run is working with a dataset greater than 20,000 rows, 10% of the data will be used as a validation dataset. If a dataset is smaller than 20,000 rows, then cross-validation is leveraged. If the dataset is less than 1,000 rows, 10 folds are used for cross-validation, and if the dataset is between 1,000 and 20,000 rows, then 3 folds are used for cross-validation.

primary_metric is the metric used to evaluate the model. Each task type has a list of valid metrics. The code here provides a list of the metrics available to use for a classification model evaluation:

```
1    azureml.train.automl.utilities.get_primary_metrics('classification')
```
✓ <1 sec

```
['norm_macro_recall',
 'precision_score_weighted',
 'AUC_weighted',
 'accuracy',
 'average_precision_score_weighted']
```

Figure 5.24 – Primary metrics for classification

Another property of an AutoML experiment run that can be set is featurization. The value here can either be set to auto, off, or FeaturizationConfig. If the value of FeaturizationConfig is specified, you can provide custom featurization, which will allow you to specify column transformer properties that support an imputer using the mean, median, or mode, as well as a one-hot hash encoding. For our example, we will leave the featurization as auto.

By setting the value of verbosity in *Figure 5.23*, we specify how granular the information logged in a given experiment will be. Keeping the logging at the INFO level will provide fine-grained logs inside the run of an AutoML experiment.

The next thing that needs to be done is creating the AutoMLConfig object for running the experiment. There are many properties to support an AutoML experiment run. The first property we will review is the property *task*. The supported task types include classification, regression, and forecasting. Currently, in public preview, multi-class and multi-label image classification, object detection, and instance segmentation are available. For our task type, we will select 'classification' as shown in the following screenshot:

```
13    automl_config = AutoMLConfig(task = 'classification',
14                                debug_log = 'automl_errors.log',
15                                compute_target=training_cluster,
16                                experiment_exit_score = 0.9984,
17                                blocked_models = ['KNN','LinearSVM'],
18                                enable_onnx_compatible_models=True,
19                                training_data = train_dataset,
20                                label_column_name = label,
21                                validation_data = validation_dataset,
22                                test_data=test_dataset,
23                                **automl_settings
24                                )
```

Figure 5.25 – AutoMLConfig object

The `debug_log` property specifies the log file to which the debug information is written. If not specified, the value of `'automl.log'` is used as the log file name.

`compute_target` is specified, which can be either a compute instance or a compute cluster. Leveraging a compute cluster enables concurrent runs for an AutoML experiment run, which cannot be leveraged by a compute instance.

`blocked_models` is a list of models to exclude from a given AutoML experiment run. For a classification model, the following is a list of models that can be excluded from a given experiment:

Classification Model	AutoMLConfig Value
Averaged Perceptron Classifier	`AveragedPerceptronClassifier`
Bernoulli Naïve Bayes	`BernoulliNaiveBayes`
Decision Tree	`DecisionTree`
Extreme Random Trees	`ExtremeRandomTrees`
Gradient Boosting	`GradientBoosting`
K-Nearest Neighbors Classifier	`KNN`
Light GBM Classified	`LightGBM`
Linear Support Vector Machine	`LinearSVM`
Logistic Regression	`LogisticRegression`
Multinomial Naïve Bayes	`MultinomialNaiveBayes`
Random Forest	`RandomForest`
SGD Classifier	`SGD`
Support Vector Machine	`SVM`
TabNet Classifier	`TabNetClassifier`
TensorFlow DNN Classifier	`TensorFlowDNN`
TensorFlow Linear Classifier	`TensorFlowLinearClassifier`
XGBoost Classifier	`XGBoostClassifier`

Figure 5.26 – List of models available to block

`enable_onnx_compatible_models` defaults to a value of `False`. If this value is set to `True`, then you can export models in the ONNX format to leverage them for high-performance gains during inference.

`training_data` can be a pandas DataFrame, an AML dataset, or a tabular dataset. *Figure 5.20* showcases how to create the tabular training dataset, which is passed to the `AutoMLConfig` object in *Figure 5.25* on *line 19*. Note that the training dataset does include the response variable, `Survived`, which is specified as the response variable in the `label_column_name` property on *line 20*.

Note that the validation dataset is provided in `AutoMLConfig` in the property named `validation_data`, which means that `n_cross_validations` cannot be provided in `automl_settings`. As mentioned earlier, it is not valid to supply both.

As part of the AML Python SDK, you can specify `test_data`. This feature is currently in preview. Metrics are calculated by using this dataset.

`experiment_exit_score` is the value to hit for the primary metric. If the primary metric hits that value, then the experiment will terminate early.

In order to run the experiment, the `automl_config` object is submitted to the experiment as shown in the following code:

```
1    remote_run = experiment.submit(automl_config, show_output = False)
```

Figure 5.27 – Submitting the AutoML experiment run

In the notebook, while not required, we can specify to hold off on the execution of future cells until the run is complete by executing the following code:

```
1    # Wait for the remote run to complete
2    remote_run.wait_for_completion()
```

Figure 5.28 – Waiting for completion

Wait for the experiment to complete and then move on to see the output of the model training. We can also view the metric to understand how the model performed.

Parsing your AutoML results via AMLS and the AML SDK

When the experiment run is completed, we are able to extract valuable information from the AutoML experiment run by leveraging the AML Python SDK:

1. For an AutoML experiment run, each run is executed as a child run of the AutoML experiment run. This means that we can get the best run for the experiment run by looking at the child runs for a given run as shown in *Figure 5.29*:

```
1    # Retrieve the best Run object
2    best_run = remote_run.get_best_child()
3    best_run
```

Figure 5.29 – Retrieving the best child run for an AutoML experiment run

2. As we can view the information programmatically, we are also able to retrieve the best model through AMLS. In the studio, by clicking on the `automl-classification-titanic` experiment, we can see the run created for the experiment.

3. Clicking on the run hyperlink brings us to the details of the experiment run. If we move over to the **Models** tab, we can see the models by their values for the primary metric, and an explanation provided for the best model:

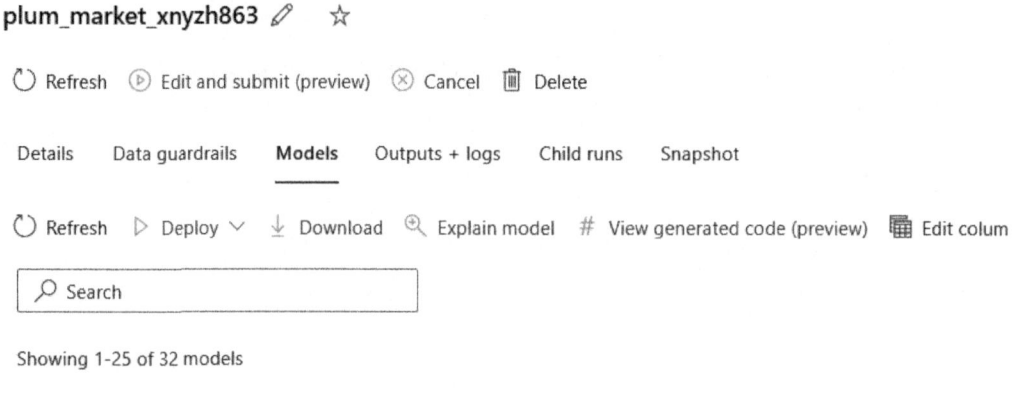

plum_market_xnyzh863

Refresh Edit and submit (preview) Cancel Delete

Details Data guardrails **Models** Outputs + logs Child runs Snapshot

Refresh Deploy Download Explain model View generated code (preview) Edit colum

Search

Showing 1-25 of 32 models

Algorithm name	Explained	AUC weighted ↓	Sampling
VotingEnsemble	View explanation	0.90023	100.00 %
StandardScalerWrapper, XGBoostClassifier		0.89524	100.00 %
MaxAbsScaler, XGBoostClassifier		0.88546	100.00 %
StandardScalerWrapper, XGBoostClassifier		0.87942	100.00 %
MaxAbsScaler, ExtremeRandomTrees		0.87099	100.00 %

Figure 5.30 – Retrieving the best child run for an AutoML experiment run in AMLS

From *Figure 5.30*, if we click on the **View explanation** hyperlink, we can explore information about the best model that AutoML was able to create.

4. By clicking on the **Aggregate feature importance** tab, we can see the features that had the highest impact on the model. We can see that **Sex**, **Pclass**, **Age**, and **Fare** were the top four features by importance for the model that was created:

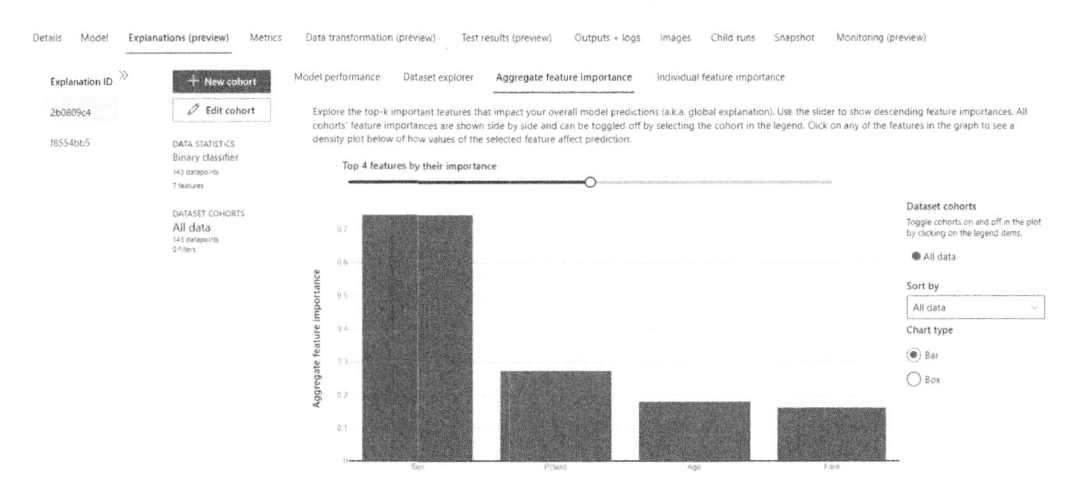

Figure 5.31 – Aggregate feature importance

5. From the `best_run` object, we can pull back the featurization that occurred on the dataset programmatically by downloading the `featurization summary json` file from the `outputs` directory. This gives us insight into the automated featurization that occurred on the dataset to provide the best model:

```
# Download the featurization summary JSON file locally
import json
best_run.download_file("outputs/featurization_summary.json", "featurization_summary.json")

# Render the JSON as a pandas DataFrame
with open("featurization_summary.json", "r") as f:
    records = json.load(f)

pd.set_option('display.width', 1000)
pd.set_option('display.max_colwidth', 1000)
pd.DataFrame.from_records(records)
```

Figure 5.32 – Retrieving the featurization results

6. The featurization results can not only be reviewed programmatically but the explanation of the best model within AMLS can also be reviewed as shown here:

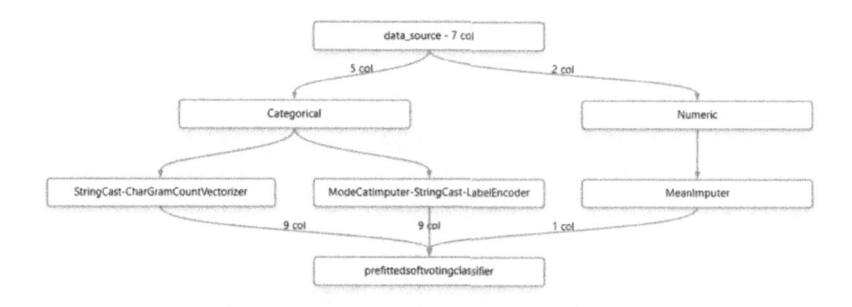

Figure 5.33 – The data transformation process implemented by AutoML

7. The run details can be viewed directly in the notebook by leveraging the `RunDetails` widget as shown in the code in *Figure 5.34*:

```
1   from azureml.widgets import RunDetails
2   RunDetails(remote_run).show()
```

Figure 5.34 – The RunDetails widget

8. With the widget, you can visualize the value of the metric at each iteration of the training run for the primary metric (and other metrics as well), as seen in the following figure:

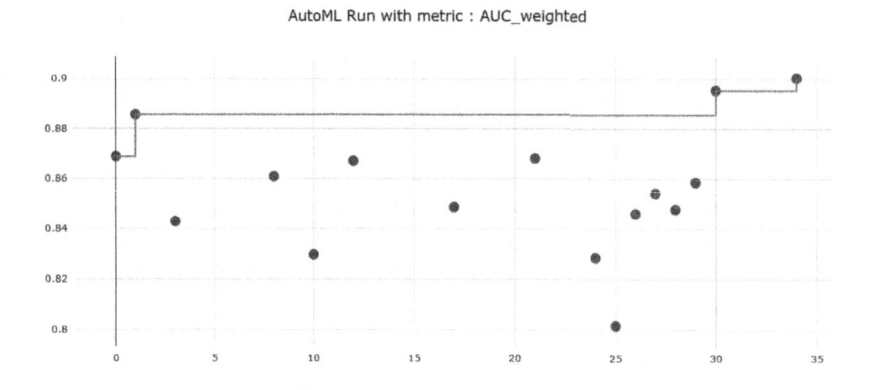

Figure 5.35 – Training iteration for the AutoML experiment run

9. For the training run, we are able to pull out the best run and the fitted model programmatically through the SDK as shown here:

```
1    best_run, fitted_model = remote_run.get_output()
2    print(best_run)
3    print(fitted_model)
```

Figure 5.36 – Retrieving the best model

10. We are also able to retrieve the estimator leveraged by AutoML as shown here. `estimator` is a class that helps organize the execution and configuration used for a particular run. It also allows us to configure the scale and compute used for the modeling. There are multiple steps inside `estimator` to be the code, and `[-1]` goes back to the previous steps:

```
1    estimator = fitted_model.steps[-1]
2    print(type(estimator))
3    print(estimator)
```

Figure 5.37 – Retrieving the estimator

11. Given the model has been retrieved, we are able to leverage it for predictions directly as shown in *Figure 5.38*:

```
1    X_test = pd.read_csv('./automl_train/test.csv')
2
3    Y_test = X_test.pop("Survived")
4
5    y_predict = fitted_model.predict(X_test)
6    print(y_predict[:10])
```

Figure 5.38 – Leveraging the AutoML model directly

12. We can leverage the test dataset to obtain metrics for the experiment, but we can also view a child run for the run that the best model was created for and retrieve the primary metrics for the test dataset:

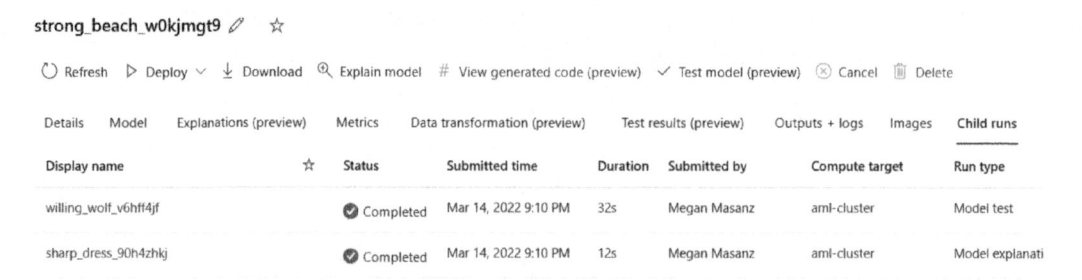

Display name	☆	Status	Submitted time	Duration	Submitted by	Compute target	Run type
willing_wolf_v6hff4jf		Completed	Mar 14, 2022 9:10 PM	32s	Megan Masanz	aml-cluster	Model test
sharp_dress_90h4zhkj		Completed	Mar 14, 2022 9:10 PM	12s	Megan Masanz	aml-cluster	Model explanati

Figure 5.39 – Best model child run

13. Clicking on the run for the model test displays the metrics that were computed for the test dataset provided. This is on the unseen data that was not leveraged for model creation:

Tags

No tags

Metrics

AUC_binary
0.873

AUC_weighted
0.873

AUC_macro
0.873

accuracy
0.81

AUC_micro
0.894

≡ View all metrics

Figure 5.40 – Best model child run metrics

14. As an output of the model, a `scoring` file is generated that can be leveraged for model deployment. This `score.py` file can be downloaded from the best run as shown in *Figure 5.41*:

```
1   model_name = best_run.properties['model_name']
2
3   print(model_name)
4
5   script_file_name = 'inference/score.py'
6
7   best_run.download_file('outputs/scoring_file_v_1_0_0.py', 'inference/score.py')
```

Figure 5.41 – Downloading the scoring file

15. Leveraging the AML Python SDK, the model can be registered to the AML workspace to enable the model deployment as shown in *Figure 5.42*:

```
1   description = 'AutoML Model trained on data to predict survival'
2   tags = None
3   model = remote_run.register_model(model_name = model_name, description = description, tags = tags)
4
5   print(remote_run.model_id) # This will be written to the script file later in the notebook.
```

Figure 5.42 – Registering the AutoML model

16. Given that the model is registered and the scoring script is defined, we can deploy the model as an ACI service as shown in *Figure 5.43*. Once the model has been deployed, which usually takes a few minutes, we can then use Postman or another REST- or HTTP-based client to call the inferencing API to test or consume other applications:

```
from azureml.core.model import InferenceConfig
from azureml.core.webservice import AciWebservice
from azureml.core.model import Model

inference_config = InferenceConfig(environment = best_run.get_environment(), entry_script=script_file_name)

aciconfig = AciWebservice.deploy_configuration(cpu_cores = 2,
                                                memory_gb = 2,
                                                tags = {'type': "automl_classification"},
                                                description = 'sample service for Automl Classification')

aci_service_name = 'automl-titanic'
print(aci_service_name)
aci_service = Model.deploy(ws, aci_service_name, [model], inference_config, aciconfig)
aci_service.wait_for_deployment(True)
print(aci_service.state)
```

Figure 5.43 – Model deployment

17. We are then able to call the test endpoint for real-time inferencing as shown in *Figure 5.44*:

```
1   import requests
2
3   X_test_json = X_test.to_json(orient='records')
4   data = "{\"data\": " + X_test_json +"}"
5   headers = {'Content-Type': 'application/json'}
6
7   resp = requests.post(aci_service.scoring_uri, data, headers=headers)
8
9   y_pred = json.loads(json.loads(resp.text))['result']
10  print(y_pred)
```

Figure 5.44 – AutoML best model deployment

Next, let's summarize the chapter.

Summary

In this chapter, we gave you an overview of Azure AutoML. We talked about how featurization, which can be an extremely time-consuming task, is handled by AutoML. We then explored how to use AutoML via AMLS for a no-code experience. Finally, we walked you through writing code using AutoML via the AML Python SDK and how to view and parse the output.

In the next chapter, we will show you how to deploy your ML models for real-time inference – for example, calling a REST API exposing the trained model – and for batch scoring.

Part 2: Deploying and Explaining Models in AMLS

In *Part 2*, readers will learn how to deploy models in AMLS in batches and in real time. Additionally, they will learn how to explain ML models and mitigate bias using AMLS.

This section has the following chapters:

- *Chapter 6*, *Deploying ML Models for Real-Time Inferencing*
- *Chapter 7*, *Deploying ML Models for Batch Scoring*
- *Chapter 8*, *Responsible AI*
- *Chapter 9*, *Productionizing Your Workload with MLOps*

6
Deploying ML Models for Real-Time Inferencing

In this chapter, we will look at how data scientists and ML professionals can make predictions available through a REST service hosted in Azure to support real-time predictions. Data is sent to a REST API, and the predicted result is provided in the response. This allows for a variety of applications to consume and leverage a model created with AMLS. We will explore a variety of options for making your models available in real time with AML.

So far, we have leveraged AMLS to handle feature engineering and built and registered models. In this chapter, we will focus on providing solutions that leverage your model to provide predictions on datasets in real time.

Azure Machine Learning provides several options for providing inferencing to business users to support batch and real-time inferencing use cases.

In this chapter, we will cover the following topics:

- Understanding real-time inferencing and batch scoring
- Deploying an MLflow model with managed online endpoints through AML Studio
- Deploying an MLflow model with managed online endpoints through the Python SDK v2
- Deploying a model with managed online endpoints through the Python SDK v2
- Deploying a model with managed online endpoints through the Azure CLI v2

Technical requirements

In order to access your workspace, repeat the steps from the previous chapter:

1. Go to `https://ml.azure.com`.
2. Select your workspace name.
3. On the workspace user interface on the left-hand side, click **Compute**.
4. On the **Compute** screen, select your compute instance and select **Start**.

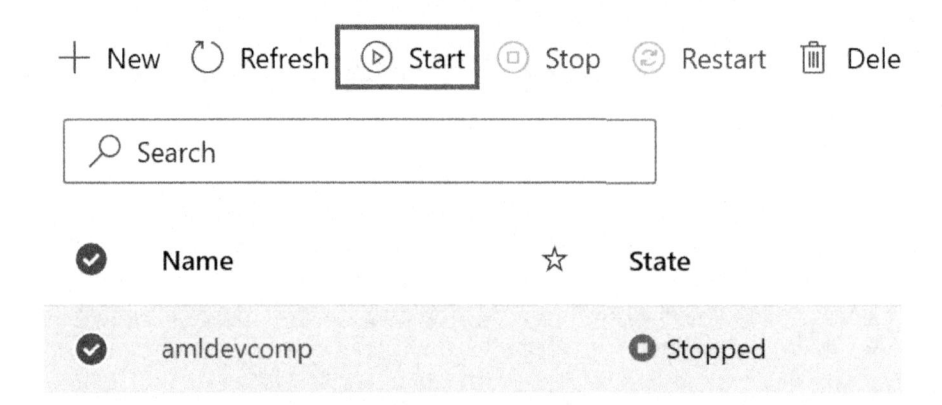

Figure 6.1 – Start compute

5. Your compute instance will change from **Stopped** to **Starting** status.
6. In the previous chapter, we cloned the Git repository; if you have not already done so, continue to follow these steps. If you have already cloned the repository, skip to *step 9*.
7. Open the terminal on your compute instance. Note the path will include your user in the directory. Type the following into the terminal to clone the sample notebooks into your working directory:

```
git clone https://github.com/PacktPublishing/Azure-Machine-Learning-Engineering.git
```

8. Clicking on the refresh icon shown in *Figure 6.2* will update and refresh the notebooks displayed on your screen.

Figure 6.2 – The refresh icon

9. Review the notebooks in your `Azure-Machine-Learning-Engineering` directory. This will display the files cloned into your working directory, as shown in *Figure 6.3*:

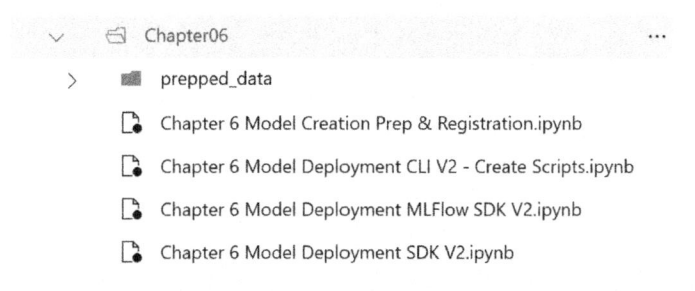

- Chapter06
  - prepped_data
  - Chapter 6 Model Creation Prep & Registration.ipynb
  - Chapter 6 Model Deployment CLI V2 - Create Scripts.ipynb
  - Chapter 6 Model Deployment MLFlow SDK V2.ipynb
  - Chapter 6 Model Deployment SDK V2.ipynb

Figure 6.3 – Azure-Machine-Learning-Engineering

Understanding real-time inferencing and batch scoring

Models can be deployed to support different use cases and different business requirements. When deploying a model in production, how you choose to deploy your model should be based on your user requirements. If you need to have a prediction available in real time to support streaming or interaction with your prediction in other applications, then real-time inferencing will be required. Real-time inferencing requires compute resources to be active and available for your model to provide a response. If your application requires less responsive predictions that are stored in a file or perhaps a database, then batch inferencing would be the correct selection. Batch inferencing allows you to spin up and down compute resources.

Before model deployment, the compute for hosting a real-time web service will need to be selected. For real-time inferencing, **Azure Kubernetes Service** (**AKS**), **Azure Container Instances** (**ACI**), and **Azure Arc-enabled Kubernetes** are compute resources supported through your AML workspace. AKS is typically used to support production workloads, and ACI is typically leveraged to support lower environments with CPU-based workloads. Azure Arc-enabled Kubernetes is typically used to run inferencing with on-premises resources where clusters are managed in Azure Arc. In this chapter, we will also explore the option of leveraging a **managed online endpoint**, which will provide a level of abstraction over the compute resources required for model deployment.

Note that there are actually two different types of compute that can be leveraged for an online endpoint. One type is the aforementioned managed online endpoints, and the other is **Kubernetes online endpoints**. Managed online endpoints provide fully managed compute provisioning, scaling, and also host OS image updates. Kubernetes online endpoints are designed for teams that want to manage those items through their own Azure Kubernetes cluster. Managed online endpoints automate the provisioning of the compute, automatically update the host OS image, and provide automatic recovery in the event of a system failure. Due to these advantages, we will focus our efforts on managed online endpoints.

Managed online endpoints not only provide a level of abstraction around the compute resources required to deploy a REST endpoint; they also support multiple deployments to a single endpoint, often referred to as **blue/green deployment**. Blue/green deployment is the practice of moving traffic from one release to another. So, when we deploy a managed online endpoint, we can have an initial model that is deployed and then deploy a new model to the same endpoint. After the new model is available on the managed online endpoint, we can move users to the new deployment with the new model. This means for each managed online endpoint, we will not only be deploying the managed online endpoint but also the endpoint deployments.

> Note
> Managed online endpoints are required to have a unique name within an Azure region. Not providing a unique name will result in a failed deployment.

We will be exploring options to make your model available to support real-time use cases leveraging managed online endpoints and deployments in this chapter. In the next section, we will explore deploying your model with AMLS Studio for a low-code experience.

Deploying an MLflow model with managed online endpoints through AML Studio

In order to deploy a model to a web service, we will be required to define the environment, which includes the Conda and `pip` dependencies, our compute resources, and a scoring script. The **scoring script**, also called an **entry script**, will load the model in an initialization function, as well as handle running predictions with the incoming data to the web service.

With MLflow models, not only is the model packaged but AML also understands how to consume the model, so there is no need to configure an environment or entry script for the model deployment with managed online endpoints; AML understands these models natively. This makes deploying the model very easy from the UI and through code.

In previous chapters, we leveraged MLflow to create and register models. Proceed to the `Chapter 6, Prep-Model Creation & Registration.ipynb` notebook to create and register a model to leverage MLflow, as we did in previous chapters.

This notebook will take you through the process of creating a model and registering it to the workspace, as discussed in previous chapters. However, there are a few points to review before creating the model.

When leveraging MLflow, we can use `autolog` to generate the model and environment information for us, but in the notebook, we actually set `log_models=False`, as shown in the following figure:

```
current_run = mlflow.start_run()
mlflow.sklearn.autolog(log_models=False)

# read in data
df = pd.read_csv(args.titanic_csv)
model = model_train('Survived', df, args.randomstate)
mlflow.end_run()
```

Figure 6.4 – Disable the logging of the model

We set logging the model to `false`, but in the training script, we explicitly package up the model and log it, as shown here:

```
# Signature
signature = infer_signature(X_test, y_test)

# Conda environment
custom_env =_mlflow_conda_env(
    additional_conda_deps=["scikit-learn==1.1.3"],
    additional_pip_deps=["mlflow<=1.30.0"],
    additional_conda_channels=None,
)

# Sample
input_example = X_train.sample(n=1)

# Log the model manually
mlflow.sklearn.log_model(model,
                        artifact_path="model",
                        conda_env=custom_env,
                        signature=signature,
                        input_example=input_example)
```

Figure 6.5 – MLflow modeling logging

This provides us with control over the packages used for deployment. When MLflow releases a new version, there may be issues between the latest version of MLflow and Azure Machine Learning managed online endpoints. Ideally, this will not happen; however, as open source continues to progress, it is a good practice to include versions when packaging up your model to ensure you are in total control of the model deployment.

After you run your `Chapter 6 Model Creation Prep & Registration.ipynb` notebook, the model will be registered in the workspace. Once we have an MLflow model registered to the workspace, we can leverage AMLS Studio to deploy the model. For this process, proceed with the following steps:

1. Select the model from **Model List**:

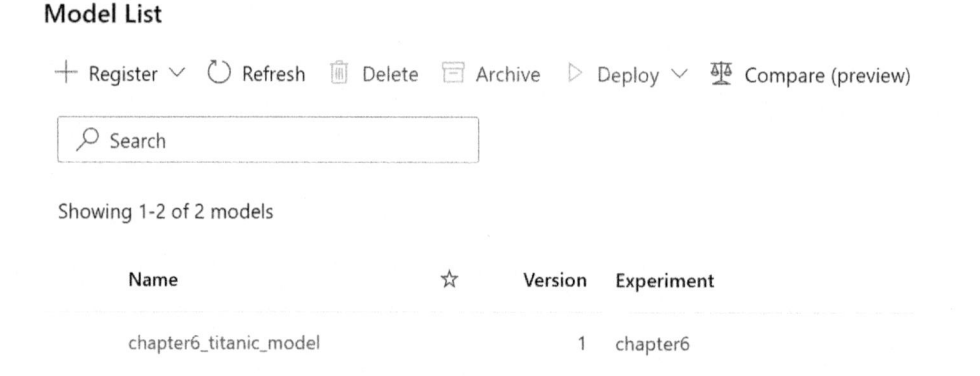

Figure 6.6 – Select the model from Model List

2. After clicking on an MLflow model, select the **Deploy** option and then the first option, **Deploy to real-time endpoint**, as shown in the following figure.

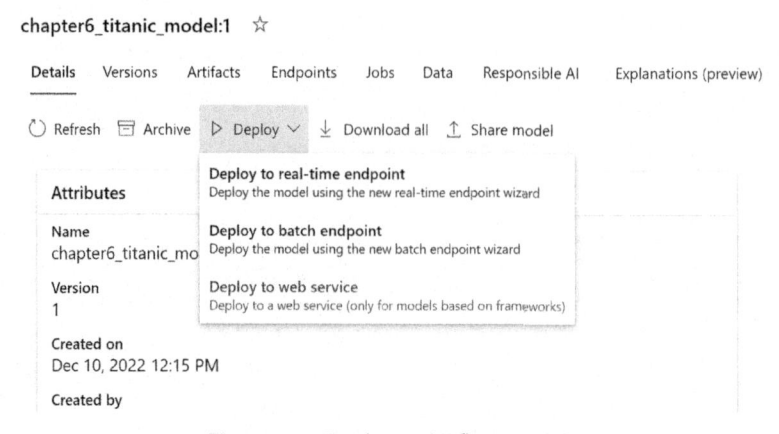

Figure 6.7 – Deploy an MLflow model

Deploying an MLflow model with managed online endpoints through AML Studio   167

3. Since the model is selected and was created with MLflow, AMLS Studio understands this is an MLflow model. After clicking on the **Deploy to real-time endpoint** option, you will be guided through creating a deployment for your model.

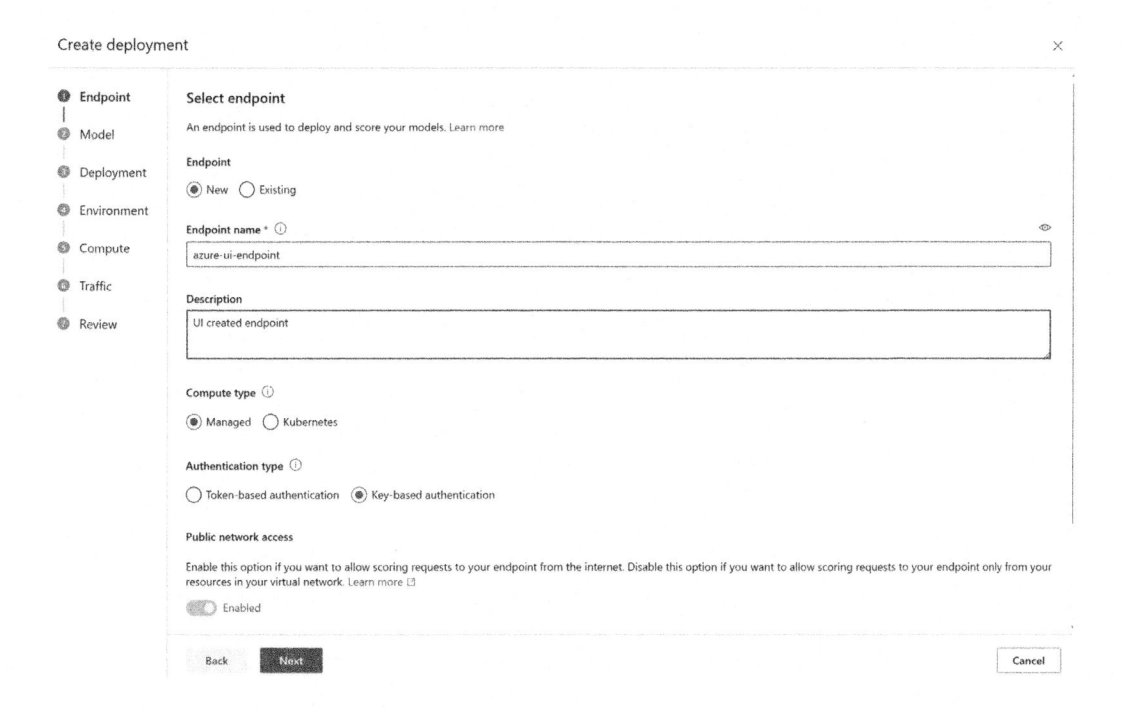

Figure 6.8 – Configure an endpoint

To create a deployment for your model, follow the options in *Figure 6.8*:

- For **Endpoint name**, enter `azure-ui-endpoint`, adding a prefix or suffix to the name to make it unique in your region.
- For **Description**, enter `UI created endpoint`
- Select **Managed** for **Compute type**
- Select **Key-based authentication**

4. Click **Next** and review the selected model, as shown in the following figure:

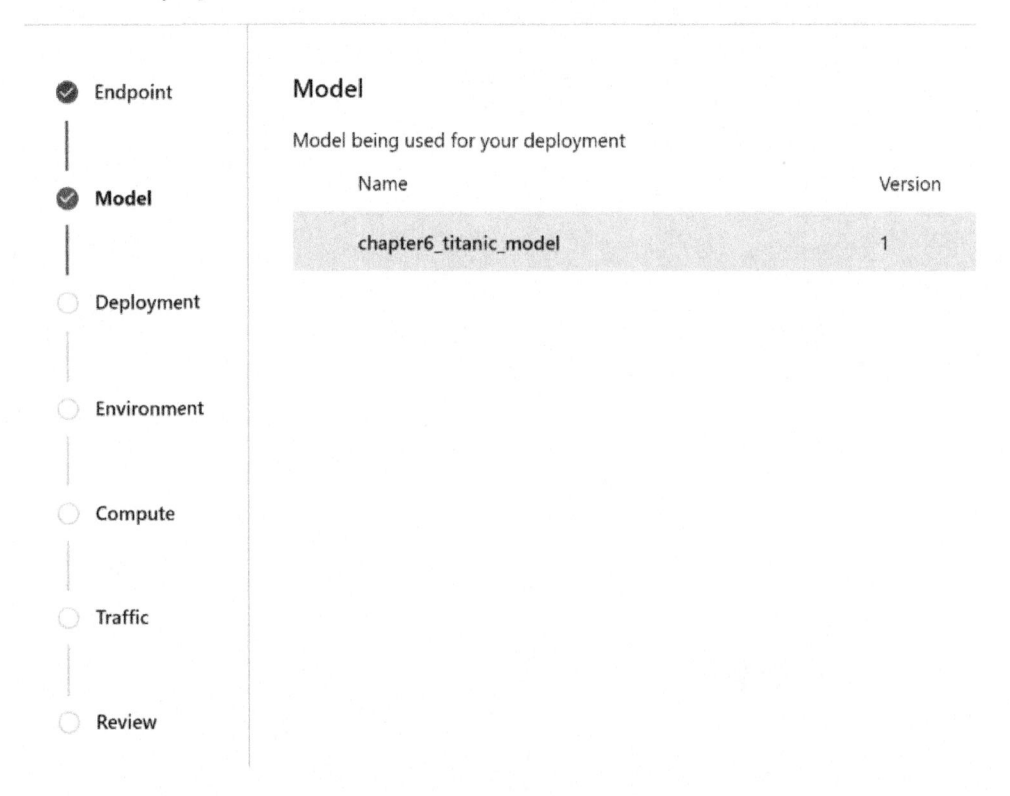

Figure 6.9 – Model selection

Since you started the deployment by selecting the model, there is no additional selection that needs to occur. As shown in *Figure 6.9*, you have configured the endpoint as well as the model selection, so the next step is to move on to deployment configuration.

5. By clicking the **Next** icon on the **Model** screen, you are brought to a screen to configure the deployment:

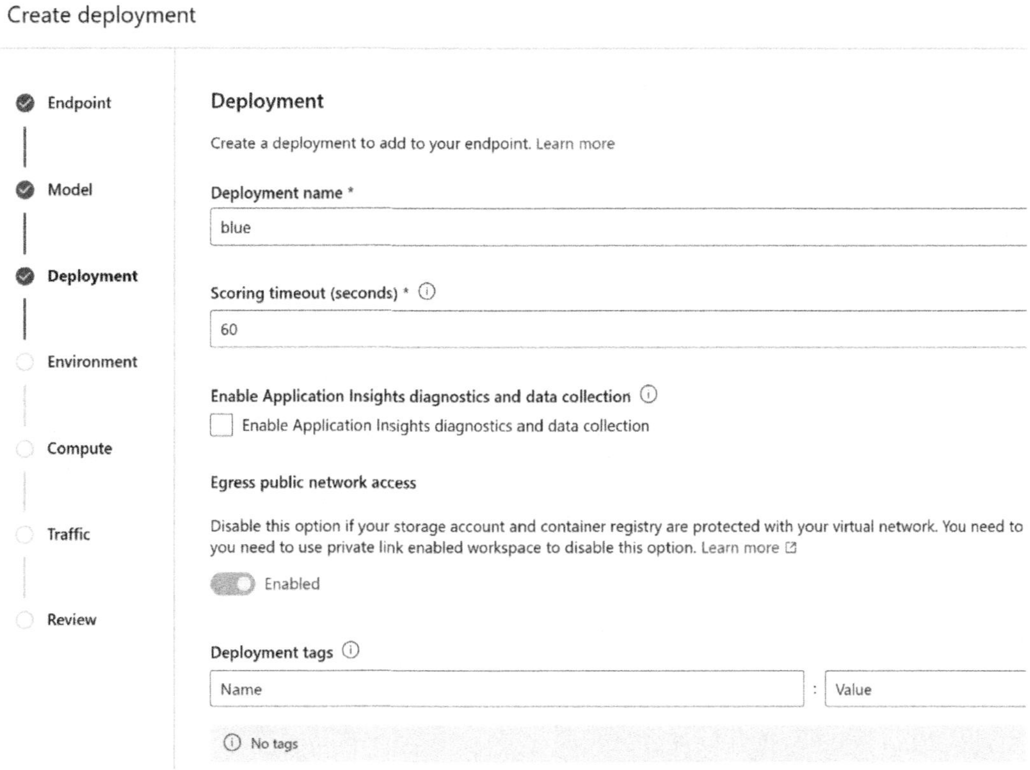

Figure 6.10 – Configure deployment

As part of the deployment configuration, a deployment name is provided. For a given endpoint, as mentioned in the *Understanding Real-Time Inferencing and Batch Scoring* section, multiple deployments can be created. This allows you to configure the traffic pattern to test out a deployed model.

In addition to the deployment name, you can configure the scoring timeout. This is the timeout to enforce scoring calls. You can also enable application insights diagnostics and data collection for the deployment. This will enable you to use the **Monitoring** tab to view activity for the managed online endpoint.

6. Once the deployment has been configured, you will be brought to the environment selection tab by again clicking **Next**. Given this model was created with MLflow, no environment selection is required.

The environment was already created for the model, as shown here:

Create deployment

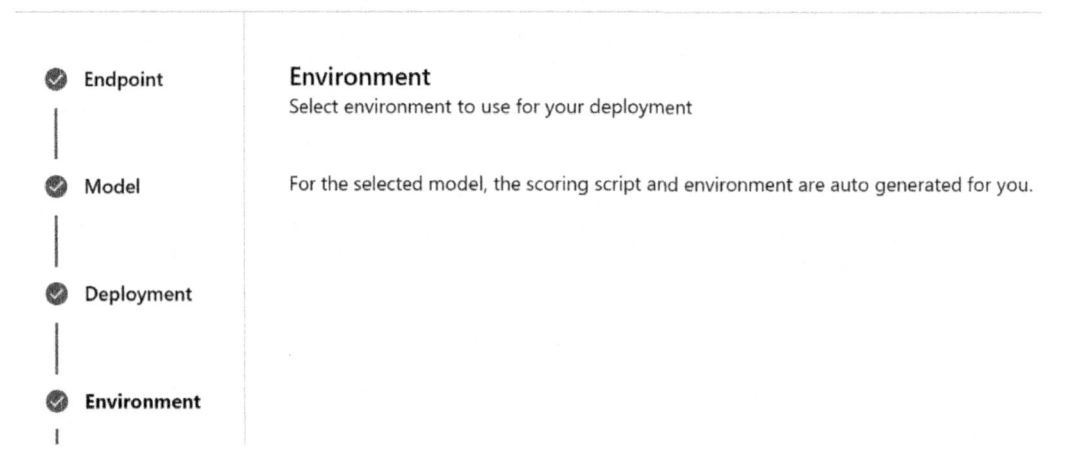

Figure 6.11 – Environment selection

7. Now that the environment has been established, the compute resources should be selected for the model. In the **Virtual machine size** dropdown, select **Standard_DS3_v2**, and under **Instance count**, enter 1, as shown in the following figure:

Create deployment

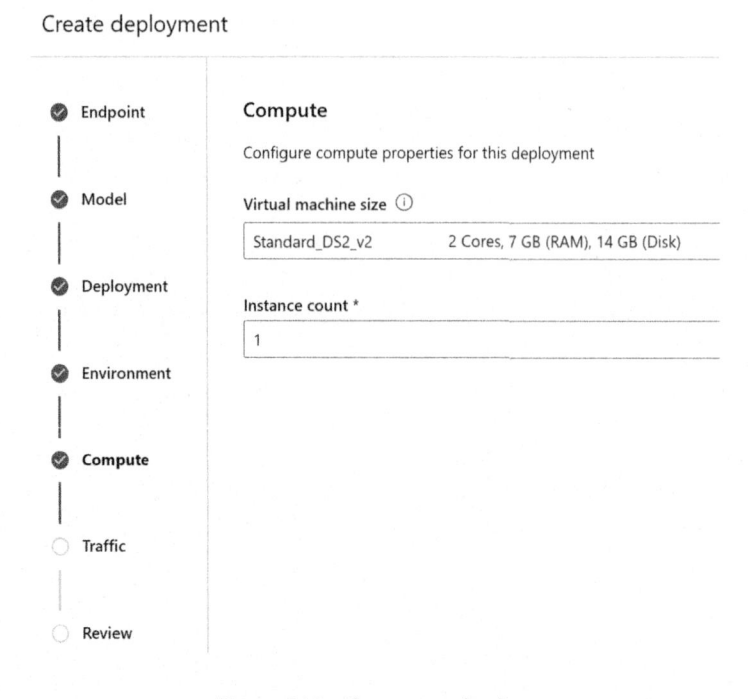

Figure 6.12 – Compute selection

8. Now that the compute has been selected, the traffic allocation for this deployment should be configured. If you have updated your model, deploy it initially with traffic set to 0, confirm it is working correctly, and then, as shown in the following figure, update the traffic to 100% on the new model, given this is our first model deployment. This should provide a seamless experience for consumers of the REST API from the old model to the new model.

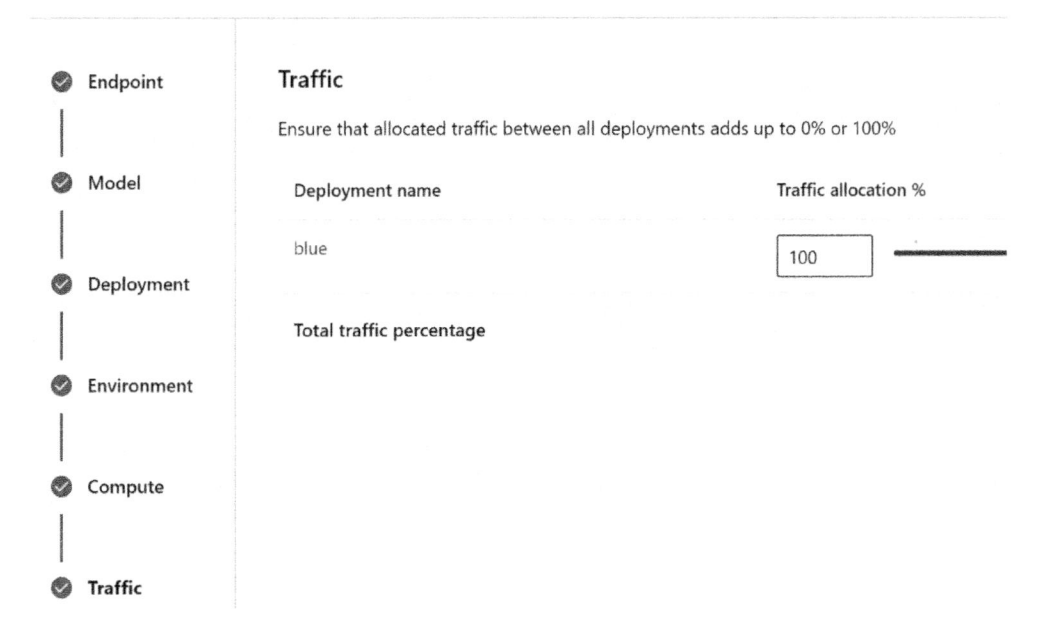

Figure 6.13 – Configure deployment traffic

172   Deploying ML Models for Real-Time Inferencing

9. After configuring the traffic, we can review the deployment that is about to occur. By clicking **Next**, AMLS Studio will bring you to the **Review** stage of the guided model deployment.

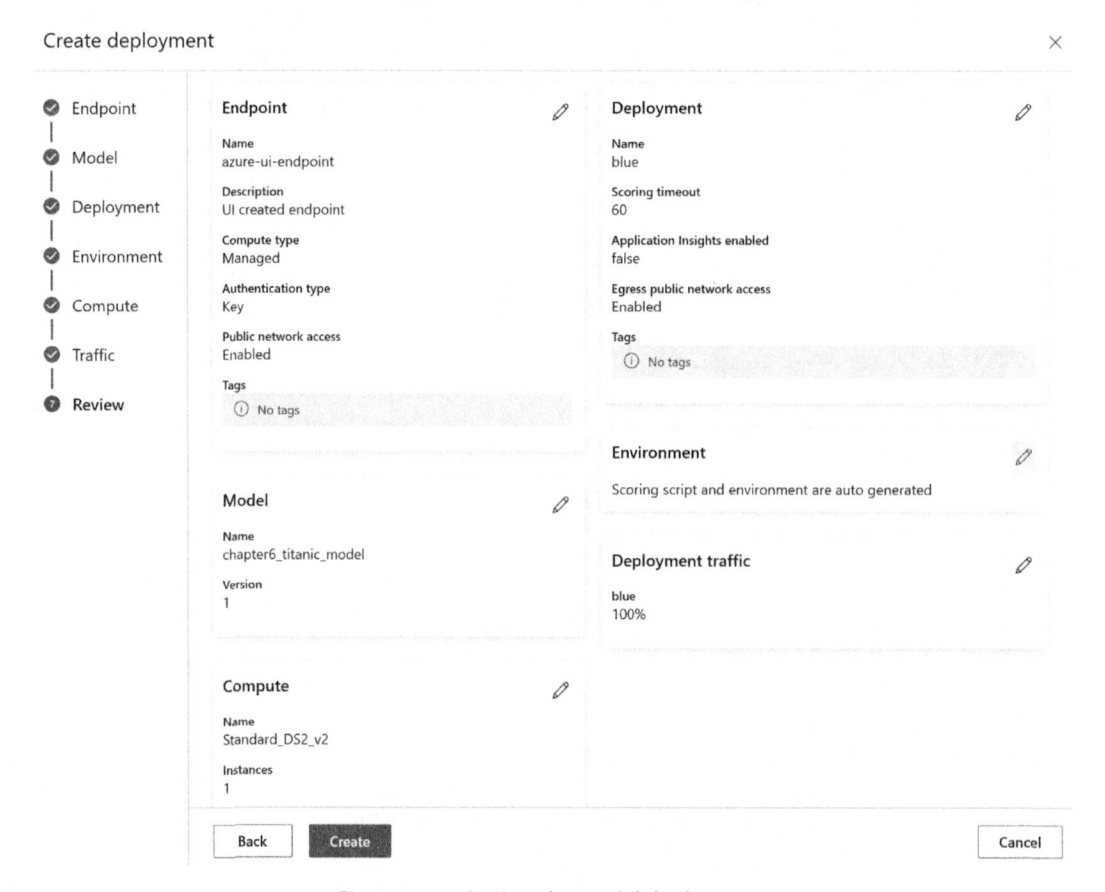

Figure 6.14 – Review the model deployment

10. The information shown on the screen will reflect the input you provided during the guided online managed deployment. After you have confirmed the settings displayed in the previous screenshot, click on the **Create** button to create the endpoint as well as the deployment.

The following figure shows the deployment progress. The managed online endpoint is being provisioned, given that the status of **Provisioning state** is **Creating**, and the blue deployment is being provisioned as well. Currently, the traffic is set to **0** for the **blue** deployment.

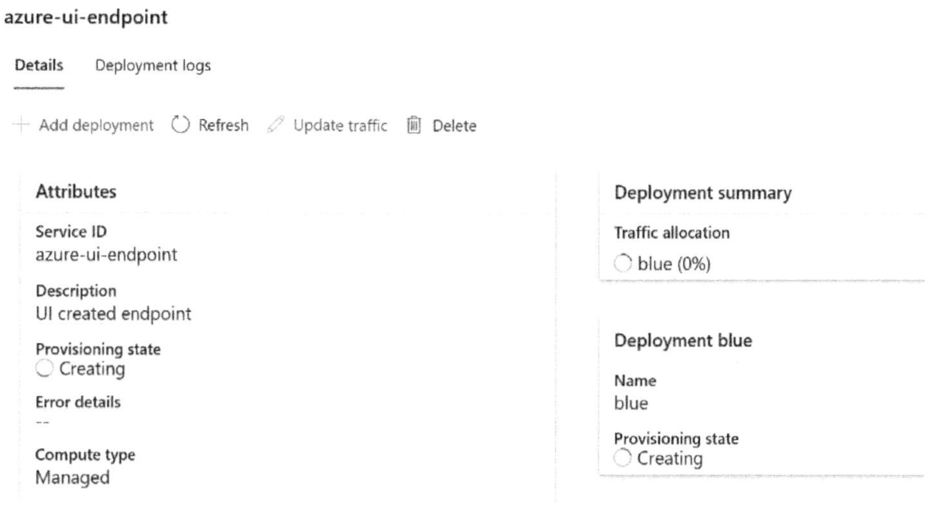

azure-ui-endpoint

Details   Deployment logs

+ Add deployment   ○ Refresh   ✎ Update traffic   🗑 Delete

Attributes

Service ID
azure-ui-endpoint

Description
UI created endpoint

Provisioning state
○ Creating

Error details
--

Compute type
Managed

Deployment summary

Traffic allocation
○ blue (0%)

Deployment blue

Name
blue

Provisioning state
○ Creating

Figure 6.15 – Managed online endpoint deployment in progress

11. Once the deployment has been completed, the endpoint will show that the status of **Provisioning state** is **Succeeded**, and **Traffic allocation** will be **100%** of the deployment, as shown in the following figure.

azure-ui-endpoint

Details Test Consume Monitoring Deployment logs

+ Add deployment   ⟳ Refresh   ✎ Update traffic   🗑 Delete

Attributes

Service ID
azure-ui-endpoint

Description
UI created endpoint

Provisioning state
Succeeded

Error details
--

Compute type
Managed

Created by
Megan Masanz

Created on
Dec 10, 2022 12:52 PM

Last updated on
Dec 10, 2022 1:06 PM

Authentication type
Key

Public network access
Enabled ⓘ

Swagger URI
https://azure-ui-endpoint.eastus.inference.ml.azure.com/swagger.json

REST endpoint
https://azure-ui-endpoint.eastus.inference.ml.azure.com/score

Metrics
View metrics

Deployment summary

Traffic allocation
● blue (100%)

Deployment blue

Name
blue

Traffic
100%

Scoring script
Auto-generated

Provisioning state
● Succeeded

Error details
--

SKU
Standard_DS2_v2

Egress public network access
Enabled ⓘ

Instance count
1

Scaling
Configure auto scaling

Model ID
chapter6_titanic_model:1

Environment
Auto-generated

Figure 6.16 – AMLS Studio deployment completed

Congratulations! You have successfully deployed a managed online endpoint for consumption. Recall that the model has columns – `Embarked`, `Loc`, `Sex`, `Pclass`, `Age`, `Fare`, and `GroupSize` – as input parameters. We can send JSON to the REST endpoint, specifying the input data columns and the data we would like to receive predictions to leverage the JSON schema leveraged by AMLS.

Deploying an MLflow model with managed online endpoints through the Python SDK V2 175

azure-ui-endpoint

Details **Test** Consume Monitoring Deployment logs

Deployment

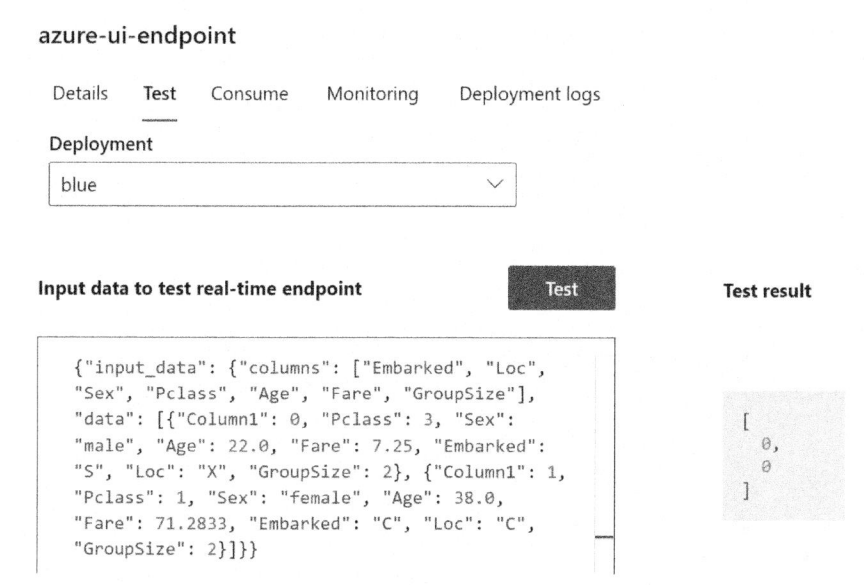

```
blue
```

Input data to test real-time endpoint   **Test**   **Test result**

```
{"input_data": {"columns": ["Embarked", "Loc",
"Sex", "Pclass", "Age", "Fare", "GroupSize"],
"data": [{"Column1": 0, "Pclass": 3, "Sex":
"male", "Age": 22.0, "Fare": 7.25, "Embarked":
"S", "Loc": "X", "GroupSize": 2}, {"Column1": 1,
"Pclass": 1, "Sex": "female", "Age": 38.0,
"Fare": 71.2833, "Embarked": "C", "Loc": "C",
"GroupSize": 2}]}}
```

```
[
  0,
  0
]
```

Figure 6.17 – Test the managed online endpoint

A sample of this request file is located in the `prepped_data` folder under the `chapter 6` folder in the Git repository. You can copy and paste this text into the studio test screen shown in *Figure 6.17*.

Now that the managed online endpoint has been tested from the AMLS Studio experience, we will next deploy a managed online endpoint through the Python SDK.

Deploying an MLflow model with managed online endpoints through the Python SDK V2

In the previous section, we leveraged AMLS Studio to deploy our MLflow model. In this section, we will explore code to deploy an MLflow model to a managed online endpoint through the SDK v2.

In order to leverage the SDK v2 for model deployment, we will leverage the `Chapter 6 MLFlow Model Deployment SDK V2.ipynb` notebook.

To deploy a managed online endpoint through the SDK V2, follow the next steps:

1. To deploy the model, we will create `ManagedOnlineEndpoint` with the appropriate configuration. In the case of an MLflow model, we will need to specify `name` and `auth_mode`. In addition, we will provide `description` as well as `tags`.

```
online_endpoint_name = "chp6-mlflow-endpt-" + datetime.datetime.now().strftime("%m%d%H%M%f")
# create an online endpoint
endpoint = ManagedOnlineEndpoint(
    name=online_endpoint_name,
    description="titanic online endpoint for mlflow model",
    auth_mode="key",
    tags={"mlflow": "true"},
)
```

Figure 6.18 – Configure ManagedOnlineEndpoint

2. After the endpoint has been configured, we are able to call the create or update method, passing in the endpoint to create the endpoint in the workspace with the create_or_update command, as shown here.

```
ml_client.begin_create_or_update(endpoint)
```

Figure 6.19 – Leveraging ml_client to create a managed online endpoint

3. Once the endpoint has been created, you are ready to create a deployment. For the deployment, we will pass a name, the endpoint name, which was created in the previous figure, the model to deploy, the instance type of the VM to leverage for compute resources, as well as the instance count.

The model can be retrieved directly from the workspace by its name and version, as shown here:

```
run_model = ml_client.models.get(name="chapter6_titanic_model", version="1")
```

Figure 6.20 – Getting the model from the registry based on name and version

4. The model is required for the managed online deployment. Now that the model has been retrieved from the workspace, it can be passed into ManagedOnlineDeployment, as shown here:

```
blue_deployment = ManagedOnlineDeployment(
    name="blue",
    endpoint_name=online_endpoint_name,
    model=run_model,
    instance_type="Standard_F4s_v2",
    instance_count=1,
)
```

Figure 6.21 – Configure deployment

Note `instance_type`, which is the compute being leveraged by our managed online endpoint. We specified here the use of `Standard_F4s_v2`, as we have great flexibility in the type of compute resources we can use to serve up our real-time prediction requests.

5. Once the deployment has been configured, leveraging `ml_client`, the managed online endpoint can be deployed with initial traffic set to 0 through the `begin_create_or_update` method, as shown here:

```
ml_client.online_deployments.begin_create_or_update(blue_deployment)
```

Figure 6.22 – Create a deployment

6. After the deployment has succeeded, the traffic for the endpoint can be set to 100% using the deployment name.

```
# blue deployment takes 100 traffic
endpoint.traffic = {"blue": 100}
ml_client.begin_create_or_update(endpoint)
```

Figure 6.23 – Update deployment traffic

7. Now that the endpoint has been deployed, the URI for the endpoint and the primary key can be retrieved to make a REST API call to retrieve a prediction. For the online endpoint, we can easily retrieve both the scoring URI as well as the primary key, as shown in the following code.

```
# Get the details for online endpoint
endpoint = ml_client.online_endpoints.get(name=online_endpoint_name)

print(endpoint)
print(' ')
# existing traffic details
print(endpoint.traffic)
print(' ')
# Get the scoring URI
print('uri: ' + str(endpoint.scoring_uri))
primary_key = ml_client.online_endpoints.get_keys(name = online_endpoint_name).primary_key
print(' ')
print('primary key: ' + str(primary_key))
```

Figure 6.24 – Retrieve the URI and primary key

8. Finally, a call can be made to the REST endpoint to retrieve predictions. The following code below takes a dataframe into the `make_predictions` function, prepares the request, and returns the results from the managed online endpoint.

```python
import json
url = endpoint.scoring_uri
api_key = primary_key  # Replace this with the API key for the web service
headers = {'Content-Type':'application/json', 'Authorization':('Bearer '+ api_key), 'azureml-model-deployment': 'blue' }
import requests

def make_prediction(df):
    strjson = str(df.to_json(orient='records'))
    endpoint_url = url
    
    request_data = {
                "input_data": {
                  "columns": [
                    "Embarked",
                    "Loc",
                    "Sex",
                    "Pclass",
                    "Age",
                    "Fare",
                    "GroupSize"
                  ],
                  "data": []
                }
              }
    request_df = X_raw.head(2)
    request_data['input_data']['data'] = json.loads(request_df.to_json(orient='records'))
    parsed = json.dumps(request_data)
    print(parsed)
    r = requests.post(endpoint_url, headers=headers, data=parsed)
    return (r.json())

results = make_prediction(X_raw.head(2))
print('')
print('predictions')
print(results)
```

```
{"input_data": {"columns": ["Embarked", "Loc", "Sex", "Pclass", "Age", "Fare", "GroupSize"], "data": [{"Embarked": "S", "Loc": "X", "Sex": "m", "Pclass": "3", "Age": "22.0", "Fare": "7.25", "GroupSize": "2"}, {"Embarked": "C", "Loc": "C", "Sex": "f", "Pclass": "1", "Age": "38.0", "Fare": "71.2833", "GroupSize": "2"}]}}

predictions
[0, 1]
```

Figure 6.25 – Making predictions

Running the preceding code allows a dataframe to be passed and prediction results to be returned. This model can be tested to leverage the sample input provided in the file located in the `prepped_data` folder under the `chapter 6` folder in the Git repository. Regardless of whether the managed online endpoint was deployed through the SDK or AMLS Studio, the functionality is the same.

You have been able to deploy a model through AMLS Studio and the SDK, as it was created as an MLflow model. In the event that MLflow is not leveraged to create a model, one can easily be deployed, but additional configuration is required to deploy it. In the next section, we will continue to deploy a model, specifying the environment and the script required for inferencing.

Deploying a model with managed online endpoints through the Python SDK v2

In the previous section, we deployed an MLflow model, but when you create a model that does not leverage MLflow, you need to provide two additional details for a successful managed online endpoint deployment. In this section, we will focus on adding functionality so that we can deploy our model without relying on MLflow to provide the environment and scoring script.

In order to deploy a managed online endpoint leveraging the SDK v2 and not relying on MLflow to provide the environment and scoring script, we will create those in this section as you leverage the notebook: Chapter 6 Model Deployment SDK V2.ipynb:

1. Our first step is to create our score.py file. This is the file that will be used to load the model and serve a request to the endpoint.

    The following code snippet provides the information required for the entry script:

```
%%writefile $script_folder/score.py

import os
import json
import joblib
from pandas import json_normalize
import pandas as pd
import logging

# Called when the service is loaded
def init():
    global model
    # Get the path to the deployed model file and load it
    model_path = os.path.join(os.getenv('AZUREML_MODEL_DIR'), 'model.pkl')
    model = joblib.load(model_path)
    logging.info("Init complete")

# Called when a request is received
def run(raw_data):
    dict= json.loads(raw_data)
    df = json_normalize(dict['raw_data'])
    y_pred = model.predict(df)
    print(type(y_pred))

    result = {"result": y_pred.tolist()}
    return result
```

Figure 6.26 – The score.py script

In the score script shown in the previous figure, there are two required functions, `init` and `run`. The `init` function tells AML how to load a model. The model will be provided as part of the deployment configuration, the model path is set, and `joblib` is leveraged to load the model. The `model` global variable is leveraged to hold the model. When the REST endpoint is called, the `run` function will be called. The data from the API call will be passed into the `run` function. Here, a dictionary is set to retrieve the information, which is transformed into a dataframe that is then passed to the `model.predict` function. The results of `model.predict` are passed to a list and returned from the function.

In addition to the score script, we will need to have the model. In the previous section, we retrieved the registered model leveraging the SDK v2 based on its name and version, but we can also search across the experiments and retrieve the model from them. The sample code provided here shows searching for the model from the experiment and downloading it.

```python
experiment = 'Chapter06'
current_experiment=dict(mlflow.get_experiment_by_name(experiment))
experiment_id=current_experiment['experiment_id']
print(experiment_id)

df = mlflow.search_runs([experiment_id])
run_id = df['run_id'].iloc[-1]
print(run_id)
print(type(run_id))

mlflow.set_experiment(experiment_name='chapter6')
client = mlflow.tracking.MlflowClient()
client.list_artifacts(run_id=run_id)

file_path = client.download_artifacts(
    run_id, path="model"
)
shutil.copytree(file_path, './model', dirs_exist_ok=True)

model = Model(path="./model/model.pkl")
```

Figure 6.27 – Find and download the model

2. In addition to the scoring script, we will need to provide an environment to use for deployment.

```
%%writefile conda-yamls/env_for_sdkv2deploy.yml
name: job_env_for_build
dependencies:
- python=3.10
- scikit-learn=1.1.3
- ipykernel
- matplotlib
- pandas
- pip
- pip:
  - azureml-defaults==1.48.0 #needed for the inferece schema
  - mlflow<=1.30.0
  - azure-ai-ml==1.1.2
  - mltable==1.0.0
  - azureml-mlflow==1.48.0
```

Figure 6.28 – A deployment environment

In the previous Jupyter notebook when we created the model, we already created an environment, but we need to add the `azureml-defaults` package for successful deployment to a managed online endpoint. Therefore, instead of using the already registered environment, we are creating a new environment to pass to the deployment.

3. In order to deploy a managed online endpoint that was not created with MLflow, the key difference is in the deployment configuration. Note that *Figure 6.21* provided the code snippet required to deploy a model created with MLflow. Compare that code to the code found in the following snippet:

```
blue_deployment = ManagedOnlineDeployment(
    name="blue",
    endpoint_name=online_endpoint_name,
    model=model,
    environment=env,
    code_configuration=CodeConfiguration(
        code="./ManagedOnlineEndpoint", scoring_script="score.py"
    ),
    instance_type="Standard_F4s_v2",
    instance_count=1,
)
```

Figure 6.29 – Managed online endpoint deployment with score script and environment

Note that in the previous code block, the `score.py` file is specified as well as the environment.

4. This managed online endpoint can again be tested. As the `score.py` file highlighted, this REST API will be expecting a different schema for its input:

```
{"raw_data": [{"Pclass":3,"Sex":"male","Age":22.0,
"Fare":7.25,"Embarked":"S","Loc":"X","GroupSize":2},
{"Pclass":1,"Sex":"female","Age":38.0,"Fare":71.2833,
"Embarked":"C","Loc":"C","GroupSize":2},
{"Pclass":3,"Sex":"female","Age":26.0,"Fare":7.925,
"Embarked":"S","Loc":"X","GroupSize":1},
{"Pclass":1,"Sex":"female","Age":35.0,"Fare":53.1,
"Embarked":"S","Loc":"C","GroupSize":2},
{"Pclass":3,"Sex":"male","Age":35.0,"Fare":8.05,
"Embarked":"S","Loc":"X","GroupSize":1}]}
```

You now have an understanding of how powerful tool-managed online endpoints are for model deployment. In addition to a guided AMLS Studio experience as well as full capabilities within the SDK, we can also leverage the Azure CLI v2 to manage the deployment process. In the next section, we will explore leveraging the Azure CLI v2 for this capability.

Deploying a model for real-time inferencing with managed online endpoints through the Azure CLI v2

In this section, we will leverage a managed online endpoint and deploy it with the Azure Machine Learning CLI v2. The CLI v2 will leverage YAML files holding the configuration required for our deployment in the commands we call. Remember the requirement for a unique managed online endpoint name, so when running the code, be sure to update your managed online endpoint name in both the YAML files and the CLI command.

To use the new Azure CLI v2 extension, we are required to have an Azure CLI version greater than 2.15.0. This can easily be checked by using the `az version` command to check your Azure CLI version:

1. On your compute instance, navigate to the terminal and type the following command: `az version`. After typing that command, you should see that the Azure CLI v2 is installed on your compute instance, as shown in the following figure.

```
{
    "azure-cli": "2.38.0",
    "azure-cli-core": "2.38.0",
    "azure-cli-telemetry": "1.0.6",
    "extensions": {
        "ml": "2.5.0"
    }
}
```

Figure 6.30 – The Azure CLI v2 with the ml extension installed

2. You can update your `ml` extension through the following command:

   ```
   az extension update -n ml
   ```

   After installing the new extensions, we can again run `az version` to confirm that the extension is installed and up to date so that we can proceed to log in.

3. You will need to log in with the Azure CLI to handle your deployment by typing `az login`. You will be prompted to open a browser and type a device login to authenticate.

4. After authenticating, you should set your default Azure subscription. Your Azure subscription ID can be easily retrieved by finding an Azure Machine Learning workspace within the portal and copying the guide displayed in the **Subscription ID** section of the **Overview** tab, as shown here.

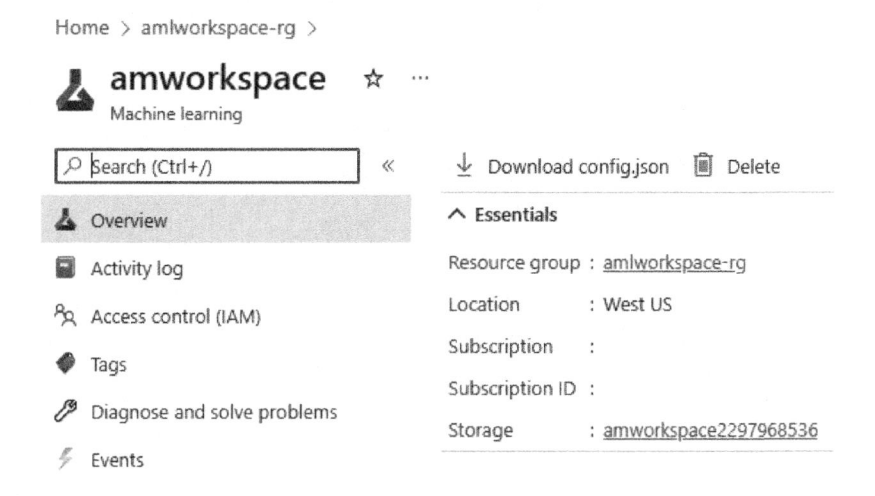

Figure 6.31 – Azure Subscription ID

5. Back in the terminal on your compute instance, set the account for the Azure CLI to leverage by typing `az account set -s XXXX- XXXX - XXXX - XXXX – XXXX`, replacing XXXX- XXXX - XXXX - XXXX – XXXX with your subscription ID. Then, set variables to hold your resource group name, the location of your AML workspace, and your workspace name:

   ```
   GROUP=amlworkspace-rg
   LOCATION=westus
   WORKSPACE=amworkspace
   ```

   Based on where your AMLS workspace is deployed, the `LOCATION` value can be found here: https://github.com/microsoft/azure-pipelines-extensions/blob/master/docs/authoring/endpoints/workspace-locations.

6. Once the variables have been set, you can run the following:

   ```
   az configure --defaults group=$GROUP workspace=$WORKSPACE
   location=$LOCATION
   ```

7. Navigate to the *Chapter 6* directory in your AML workspace.

   To create the required files, run the Chapter 6 Model Deployment CLI v2 - Create Scripts.ipynb notebook, which will create an endpoint.yml file, a deployment.yml file, and a score.py file for inferencing. The files will be generated in a folder called CLI_v2_ManagedOnlineEndpoint.

8. In the notebook, we will create the directory by running the following code:

   ```python
   import os

   # Create a folder for the experiment files
   script_folder = 'CLI_V2_ManagedOnlineEndpoint'
   os.makedirs(script_folder, exist_ok=True)
   print(script_folder, 'folder created')
   ```

   Figure 6.32 – Directory creation

9. For the managed online endpoint, we will also create a score.py file. The score script will leverage our model and provide the init and run functions that our previous score.py file provided.

   ```python
   %%writefile ./CLI_V2_ManagedOnlineEndpoint/score.py

   import os
   import json
   import joblib
   from pandas import json_normalize
   import pandas as pd
   import logging

   # Called when the service is loaded
   def init():
       global model
       # Get the path to the deployed model file and load it
       model_path = os.path.join(os.getenv('AZUREML_MODEL_DIR'), 'model/model.pkl')
       model = joblib.load(model_path)
       logging.info("Init complete")

   # Called when a request is received
   def run(raw_data):
       dict= json.loads(raw_data)
       df = json_normalize(dict['raw_data'])
       y_pred = model.predict(df)
       print(type(y_pred))

       result = {"result": y_pred.tolist()}
       return result
   ```

   Figure 6.33 – The score.py file

10. Next, we will create the endpoint .yml file. We can create a basic file that contains the required attributes of the name and the authorization mode. The authorization mode can be specified as a key or `aml_token`. Key-based authentication will not expire, but the Azure ML token-based authentication will. We will proceed with key-based authentication.

> **Note**
> When using `aml_token`, you can get a new token by running the `az ml online-endpoint get-credentials` command.

11. Run the command to generate the `endpoint.yml` file with the same key value as `auth_mode`, as shown here:

```
%%writefile ./CLI_V2_ManagedOnlineEndpoint/endpoint.yml
$schema: https://azuremlschemas.azureedge.net/latest/managedOnlineEndpoint.schema.json
name: titanic-managed-online-endpoint
description: "CLI V2 titanic online endpoint for mlflow model"
auth_mode: key
tags : {"CLIV2": "titanic"}
```

Figure 6.34 – Managed online endpoint configuration

Remember to update your name to be something unique; if `titanic-managed-online-endpoint` is already deployed in your region, your deployment will fail.

12. For the managed online endpoint deployment, we will also generate a `deployment.yml` file. In this file, we need to specify the model, the scoring script, the environment, and the instance type used for model deployment.

Creation of the `deployment.yml` file:

```
%%writefile ./CLI_V2_ManagedOnlineEndpoint/deployment.yml

$schema: https://azuremlschemas.azureedge.net/latest/managedOnlineDeployment.schema.json
name: blue
endpoint_name: titanic-online-endpoint
model: azureml:chapter6_titanic_model@latest
code_configuration:
  code: .
  scoring_script: score.py
environment: azureml:env_for_sdkv2deploy@latest
instance_type: Standard_F2s_v2
instance_count: 1
```

Figure 6.35 – Creation of the deployment.yml file

In this file, you will specify the registered model name and version, the registered environment name and version, the type of compute resources leveraged for the deployed model, and where the scoring script is located. In the `deployment.yml` file, you should update `endpoint_name` to reflect the name you chose in your `endpoint.yml` file.

After running the notebook and selecting a unique endpoint name, we can leverage CLI v2 to deploy our model.

13. In the command line, open the `CLI_v2_ManagedOnlineEndpoint` directory, and from that directory, create your `online-endpoint` with the following command:

    ```
    az ml online-endpoint create --name titanic-online-
    endpoint -f endpoint.yml
    ```

    Note that `titanic-online-endpoint` should be replaced with your managed online endpoint name.

14. After the endpoint is created, you can now create `online-deployment`, leveraging the following command:

    ```
    az ml online-deployment create --name deploytitaniconline
    --endpoint titanic-online-endpoint -f deployment.yml
    --all-traffic
    ```

    Once again, note that `titanic-online-endpoint` should be replaced with your managed online endpoint name.

15. Once the deployment is complete, the endpoint will be available for testing. The endpoint is available from the **Endpoints** section in your AML workspace, as shown here.

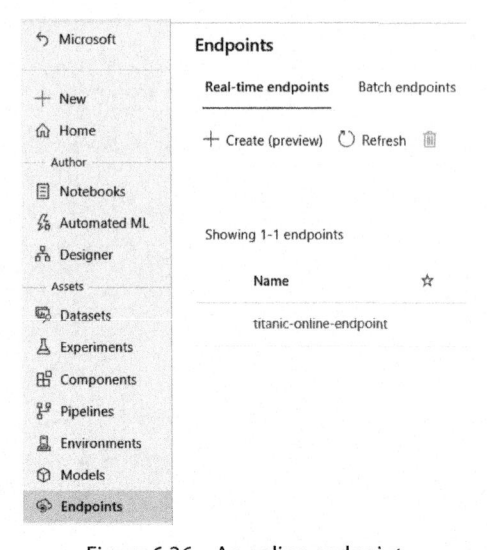

Figure 6.36 – An online endpoint

Deploying a model for real-time inferencing with managed online endpoints through the Azure CLI v2   187

16. We can test the endpoint by clicking on its name and selecting the **Test** tab on the endpoint.

17. In the test section, we can provide data for inferencing after typing into the **Test** box to retrieve results from the web service, as shown here:

    ```
    {"raw_data": [{"Embarked":"S","Loc":"X","Sex":"m",
    "Pclass":3,"Age":22.0,"Fare":7.25,"GroupSize":2},
    {"Embarked":"C","Loc":"C","Sex":"f","Pclass":1,"Age"
    :38.0,"Fare":71.2833,"GroupSize":2},{"Embarked":"S",
    "Loc":"X","Sex":"f","Pclass":3,"Age":26.0,"Fare":7.925,
    "GroupSize":1},{"Embarked":"S","Loc":"C",
    "Sex":"f","Pclass":1,"Age":35.0,"Fare":53.1,"GroupSize"
    :2},{"Embarked":"S","Loc":"X","Sex":"m","Pclass":3,"Age"
    :35.0,"Fare":8.05,"GroupSize":1}]}
    ```

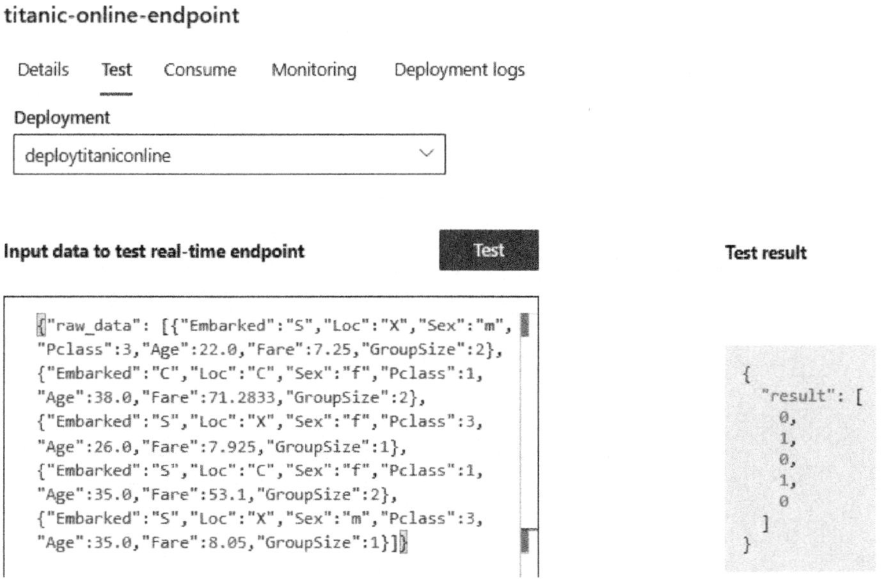

Figure 6.37 – Testing an online endpoint

This sample request can be found in the `chapter 6` folder under the `prepped_data` folder in a file named `sample_request_cli.json`.

In this section, you were able to deploy a web service utilizing a managed online endpoint in AMLS through the Azure CLI v2. This feature takes advantage of schema files to provide the deployment definitions in configuration files to enable deployment. Managed online endpoints prevent data scientists or citizen data scientists from having to be concerned about the infrastructure required to support hosting a web service, to provide real-time inferencing to support your use cases.

Congratulations on deploying a managed online endpoint through the CLI! This will be especially useful in *Chapter 9, Productionizing Your Workload with MLOps*. After testing out your managed online endpoints, be sure to delete them, as they use up compute resources.

Summary

In this chapter, the focus was on deploying your model as a REST endpoint to support real-time inferencing use cases. We saw that we are able to leverage AMLS Studio for a low-code deployment experience. We also leveraged SDK v2 to deploy models to managed online endpoints. We continued by deploying models through CLI v2 to support model deployment for real-time inferencing. These sections demonstrated deploying real-time web services through low-code, code-first, and configuration-driven approaches. These capabilities empower you to deploy in a variety of ways.

In the next chapter, we will learn how to leverage batch-inferencing to support our use cases.

7
Deploying ML Models for Batch Scoring

Deploying ML models for batch scoring supports making predictions using a large volume of data. This solution supports use cases when you don't need your model predictions immediately, but rather minutes or hours later. If you need to provide inferencing once a day, week, or month, using a large dataset, batch inferencing is ideal.

Batch inferencing allows data scientists and ML professionals to leverage cloud compute when needed, rather than paying for compute resources to be available for real-time responses. This means that compute resources can be spun up to support batch inferencing and spun down after the results have been provided to the business users. We are going to show you how to leverage the Azure Machine Learning service to deploy trained models to managed endpoints, which are HTTPS REST APIs that clients can invoke to get the score results of a trained model for batch inferencing using the studio and the Python SDK.

In this chapter, we will cover the following topics:

- Deploying a model for batch inferencing using the Studio
- Deploying a model for batch inferencing through the Python SDK

Technical requirements

In order to access your workspace, recall the steps from the previous chapter:

1. Go to https://ml.azure.com.
2. Select your workspace.

3. On the left side of the workspace's UI, on click **Compute**.
4. On the compute screen, select your compute instance and select **Start**.

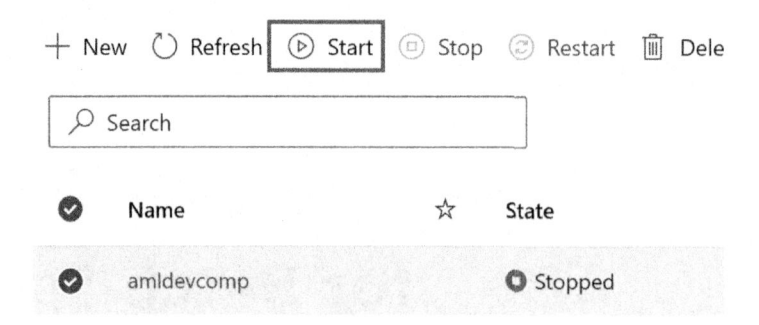

Figure 7.1 – Start compute

5. Your compute instance will change from the **Stopped** to the **Starting** status.
6. In the previous chapter, we cloned the Git repository. If you have not done this, continue with this step. If you have already cloned the repository, skip to *step 7*.

   Open the terminal on your compute instance. Note that the path will include your user in the directory. Type the following into the terminal to clone the sample notebooks into your working directory:

   ```
   git clone https://github.com/PacktPublishing/Azure-Machine-Learning-Engineering.git
   ```

7. Clicking on the refresh icon shown in *Figure 7.2* will update and refresh the notebooks displayed on your screen.

Figure 7.2 – Refresh Icon

8. Review the notebooks in your `Azure-Machine-Learning-Engineering` directory. This will display the files cloned into your working directory, as shown in *Figure 7.3*:

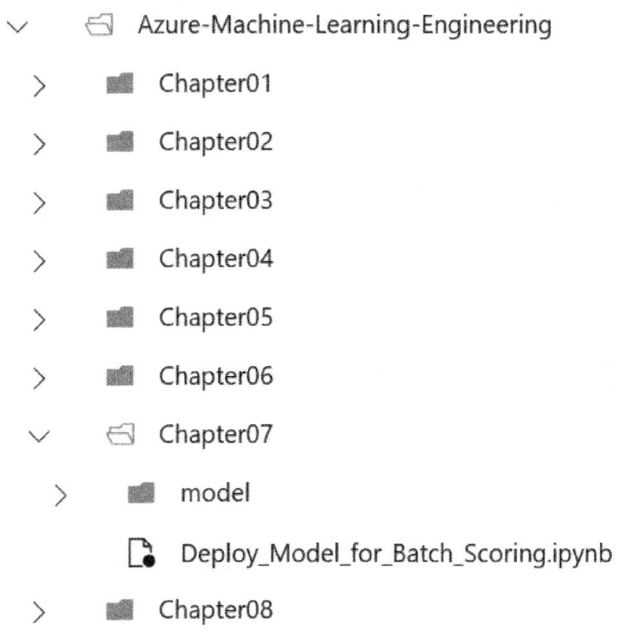

```
                  ∨    📁  Azure-Machine-Learning-Engineering
                > 📁  Chapter01
                > 📁  Chapter02
                > 📁  Chapter03
                > 📁  Chapter04
                > 📁  Chapter05
                > 📁  Chapter06
                ∨    📁  Chapter07
                    > 📁  model
                         📄  Deploy_Model_for_Batch_Scoring.ipynb
                > 📁  Chapter08
```

Figure 7.3 – Azure-Machine-Learning-Engineering

Let's start with deploying a model for batch inferencing using the studio next.

Deploying a model for batch inferencing using the Studio

In *Chapter 3*, *Training Machine Learning Models in AMLS*, we trained a model and registered it in an Azure Machine Learning workspace. We are going to deploy that model to a managed batch endpoint for batch scoring:

1. Navigate to your Azure Machine Learning workspace, select **Models** from the left menu bar to see the models registered in your workspace, and select **titanic_servival_model_**, as shown in *Figure 7.4*:

Deploying ML Models for Batch Scoring

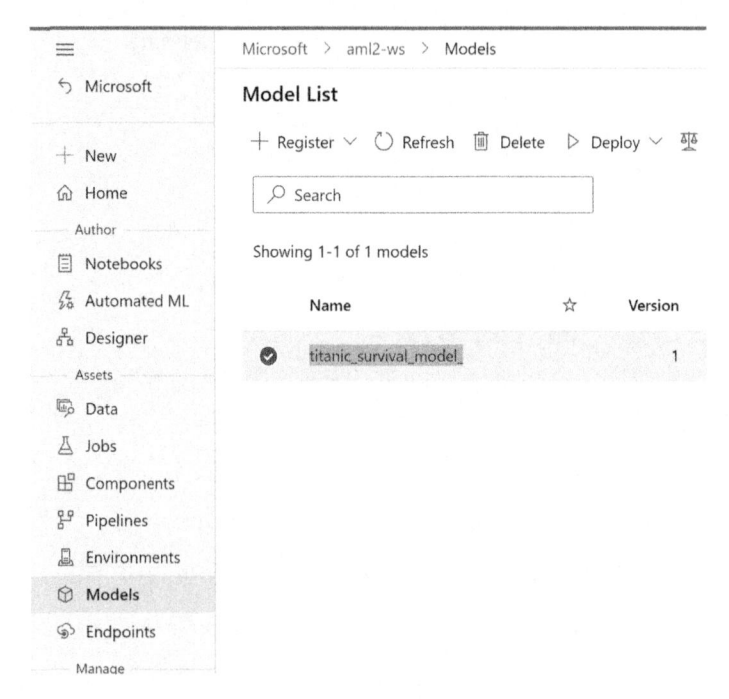

Figure 7.4 – List of models registered in the workspace

2. Click on **Deploy** and select **Deploy to batch endpoint**, as shown in *Figure 7.5*:

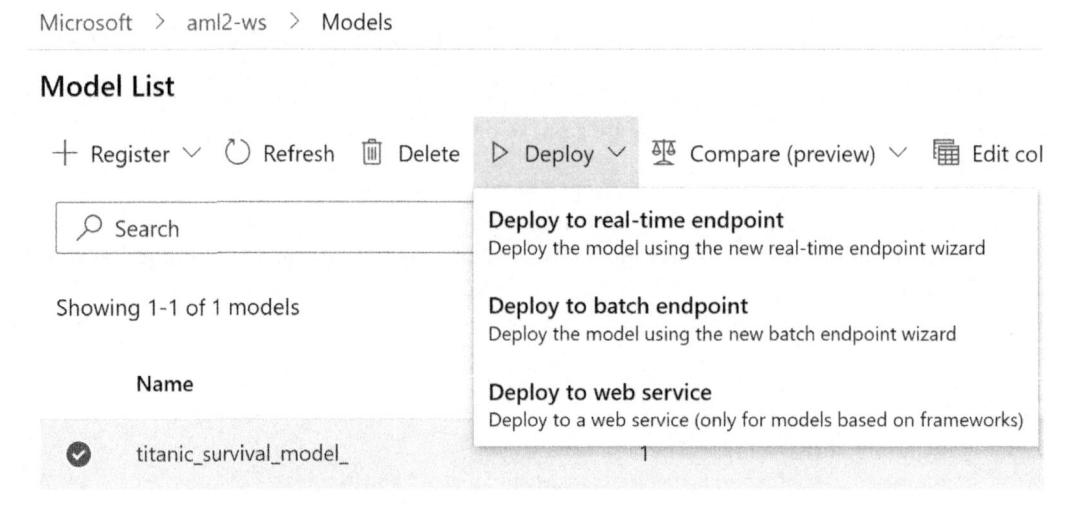

Figure 7.5 – Deploy the selected model to a batch endpoint

This opens the deployment wizard. Use the following values for the required fields:

- **Endpoint name**: `titanic-survival-batch-endpoint`
- **Model**: Retain the default of **titanic_survival_model_**
- **Deployment name**: `titanic-deployment`
- **Environment**: For the selected model, the scoring script and environment are auto-generated for you
- **Compute**: `cluster cpu-cluster`

Review your batch deployment specs and click **Create deployment**, as shown in *Figure 7.6*:

Create deployment

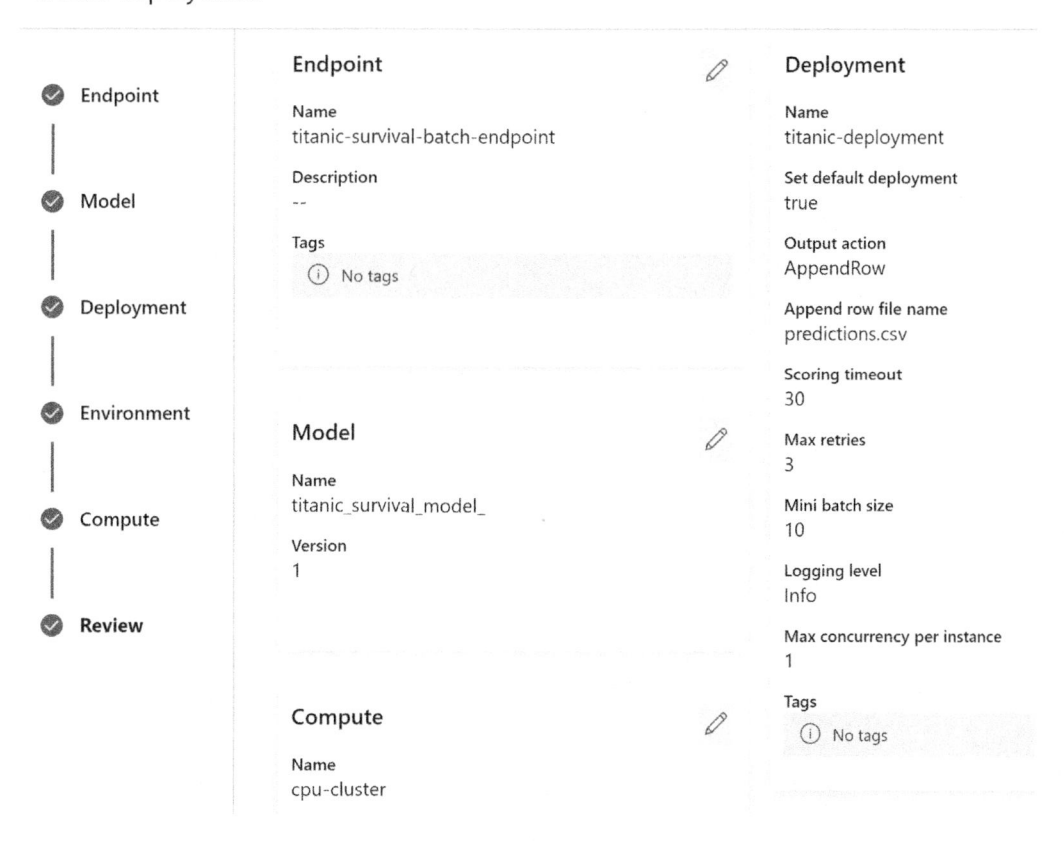

	Endpoint	Deployment
✓ Endpoint	Name titanic-survival-batch-endpoint	Name titanic-deployment
	Description --	Set default deployment true
✓ Model	Tags ⓘ No tags	Output action AppendRow
✓ Deployment		Append row file name predictions.csv
		Scoring timeout 30
✓ Environment	Model	Max retries 3
	Name titanic_survival_model_	Mini batch size 10
✓ Compute	Version 1	Logging level Info
		Max concurrency per instance 1
✓ Review		Tags ⓘ No tags
	Compute	
	Name cpu-cluster	

Figure 7.6 – Create batch deployment

3. After a minute or so, you should see a page that shows that your batch endpoint has been deployed successfully. It also has some information about your batch endpoint, as shown in *Figure 7.7*:

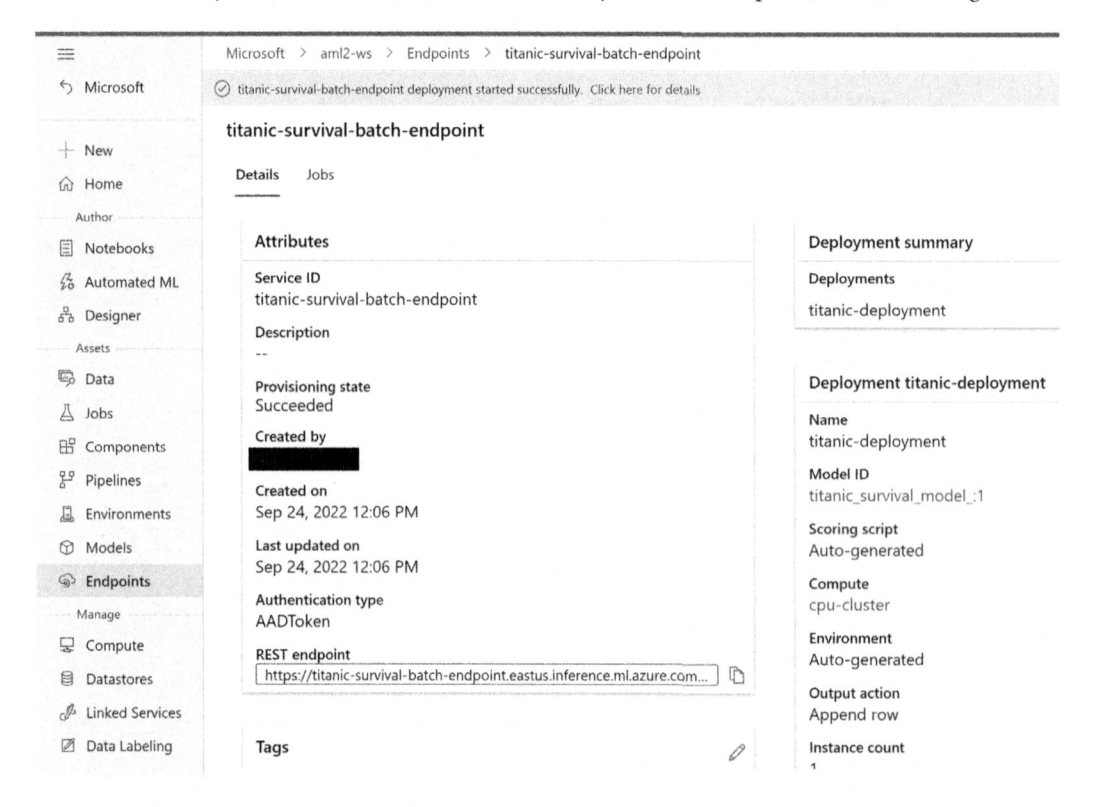

Figure 7.7 – Successful batch deployment

Now that you have a batch endpoint up and running, let's create a scoring/inferencing job that invokes your endpoint. To do so, follow these steps:

1. Click on **Endpoints** in the left menu bar and click on your recently created batch endpoint, as shown in *Figure 7.8*:

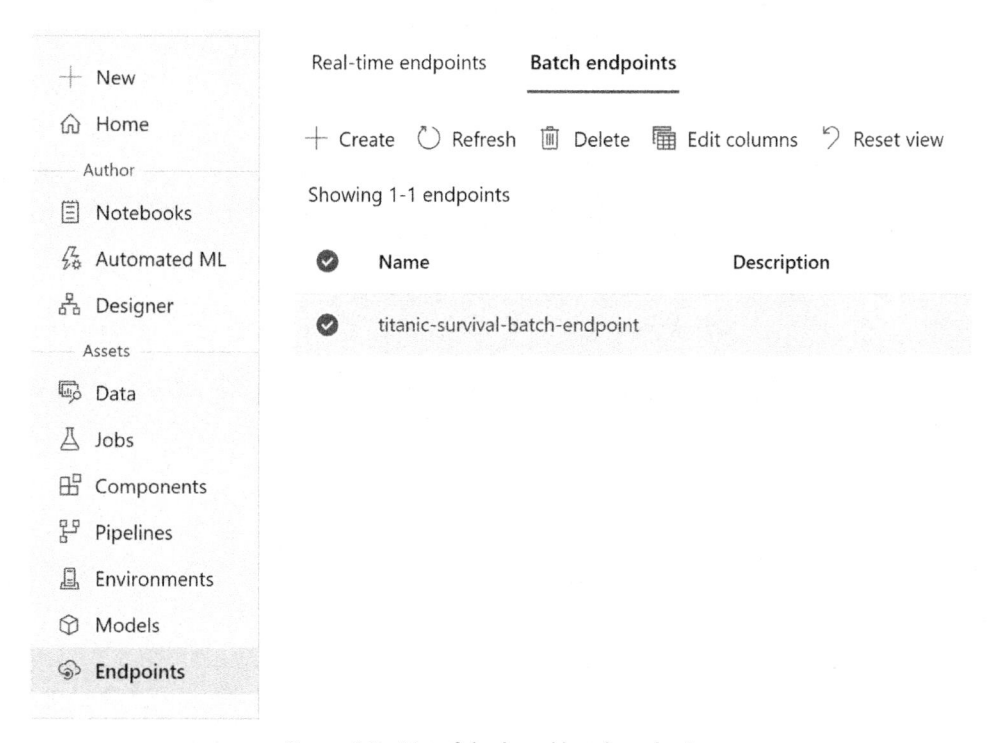

Figure 7.8 – List of deployed batch endpoints

196   Deploying ML Models for Batch Scoring

2. On the **titanic-survival-batch-endpoint** page, select the **Jobs** tab, as shown in *Figure 7.9*:

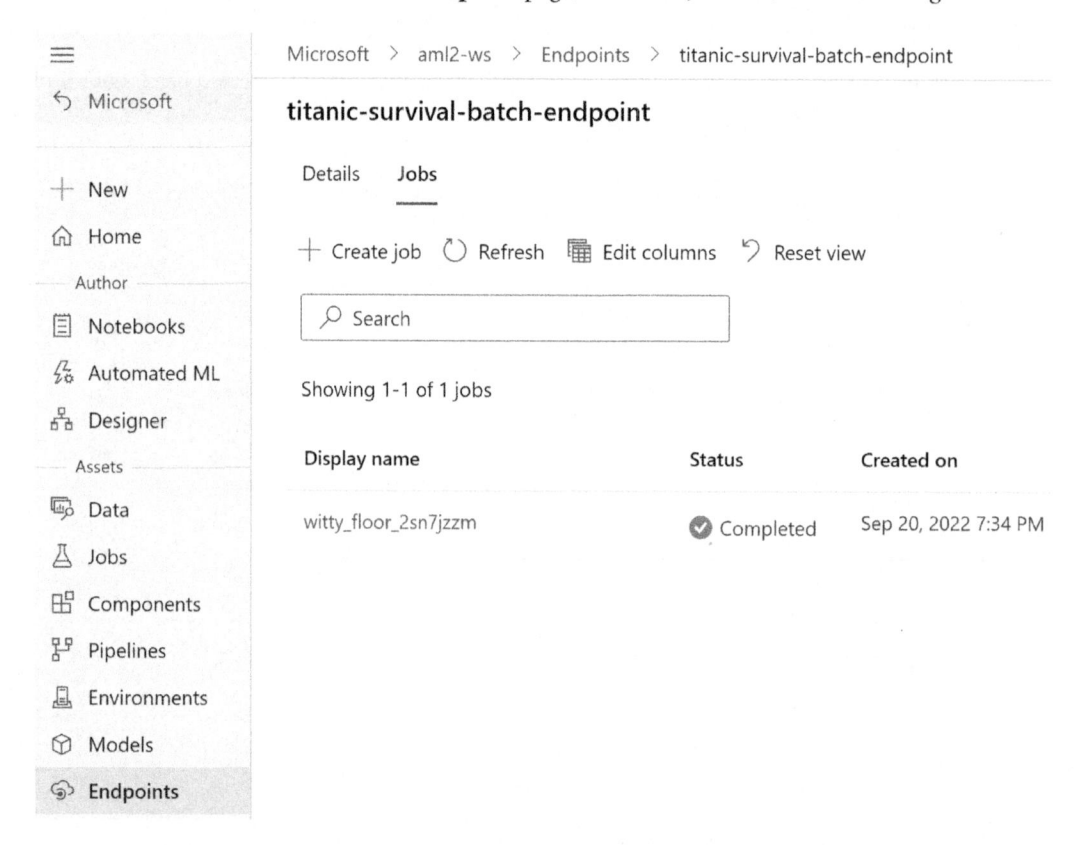

Figure 7.9 – titanic-survival-batch-endpoint Jobs tab

3. Click **Create job** and pick the corresponding values for the fields in the wizard as shown in *Figure 7.10*. Click **Create** once you're done. Please note that the deployment is pre-selected for you, but make sure the correct deployment is pre-selected. You should also have a test dataset called **titanic-test-data**, which was created in *Chapter 3, Training Machine Learning Models in AMLS*.

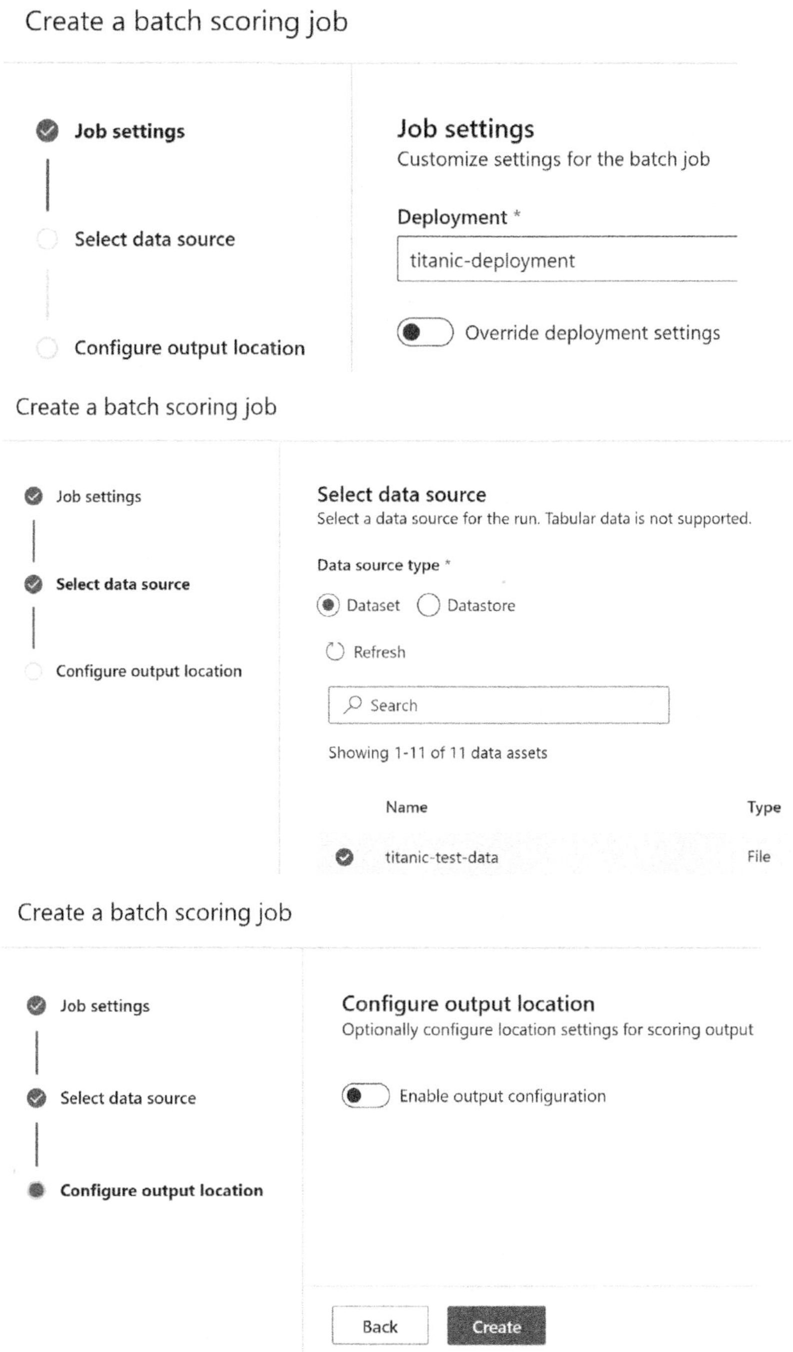

Create a batch scoring job

✓ **Job settings**

○ Select data source

○ Configure output location

Job settings
Customize settings for the batch job

Deployment *

titanic-deployment

◉ Override deployment settings

Create a batch scoring job

✓ Job settings

✓ **Select data source**

○ Configure output location

Select data source
Select a data source for the run. Tabular data is not supported.

Data source type *

◉ Dataset   ○ Datastore

○ Refresh

🔍 Search

Showing 1-11 of 11 data assets

Name	Type
✓ titanic-test-data	File

Create a batch scoring job

✓ Job settings

✓ Select data source

● **Configure output location**

Configure output location
Optionally configure location settings for scoring output

◉ Enable output configuration

Back   **Create**

Figure 7.10 – Create a batch scoring job

4. Depending on the size of the test dataset that you selected in the last step, it will take some time for the job to complete. Once it is complete, you will see a pipeline representing the batch scoring job for **titanic-survival-batch-endpoint**, as shown in *Figure 7.11*:

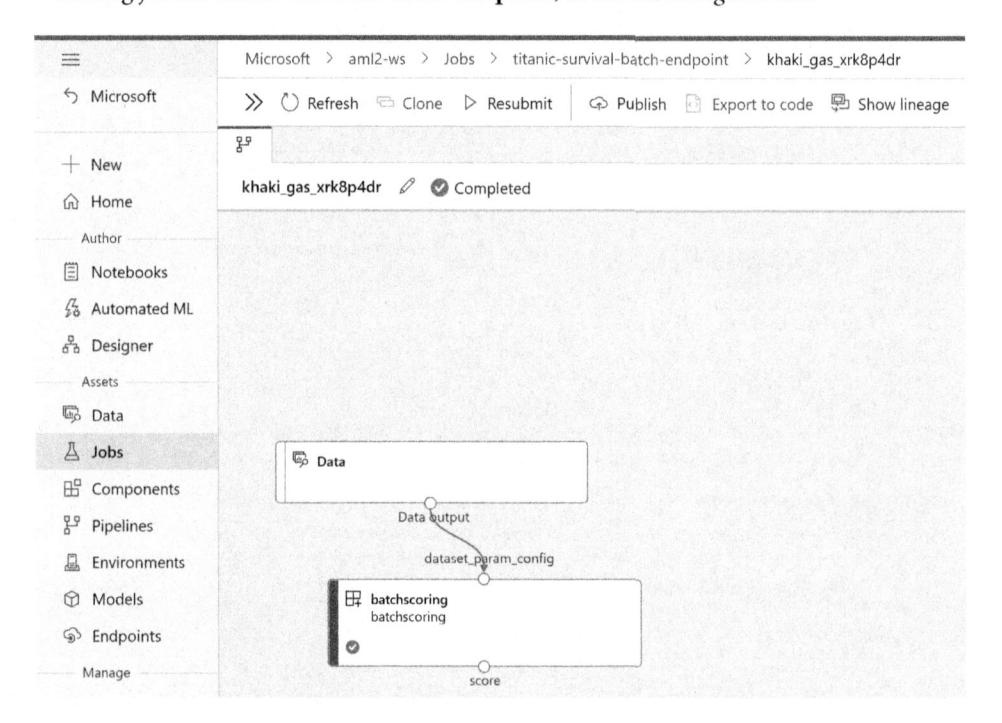

Figure 7.11 – Batch scoring job for titanic-survival-batch-endpoint

5. Now, in order to view the scoring results, click on the **batchscoring** step of the pipeline, click on **Job overview** on the right, select the **Outputs + logs** tab, and finally, click on **Show data outputs**, as shown in *Figure 7.12*:

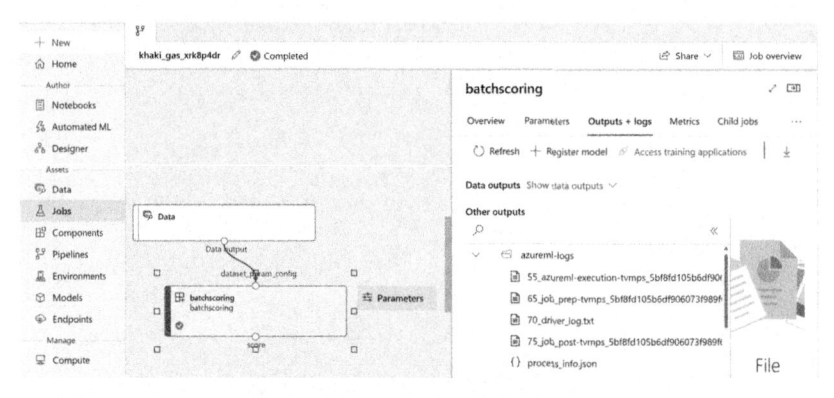

Figure 7.12 – Batch scoring results

Deploying a model for batch inferencing using the Studio   199

6. After you click on **Show data outputs**, you will see the **Access data** option, which opens the storage account where the `predictions.csv` file has been saved. Click on this file and select the **Edit** tab in order to view the scoring results, as shown in *Figure 7.13*:

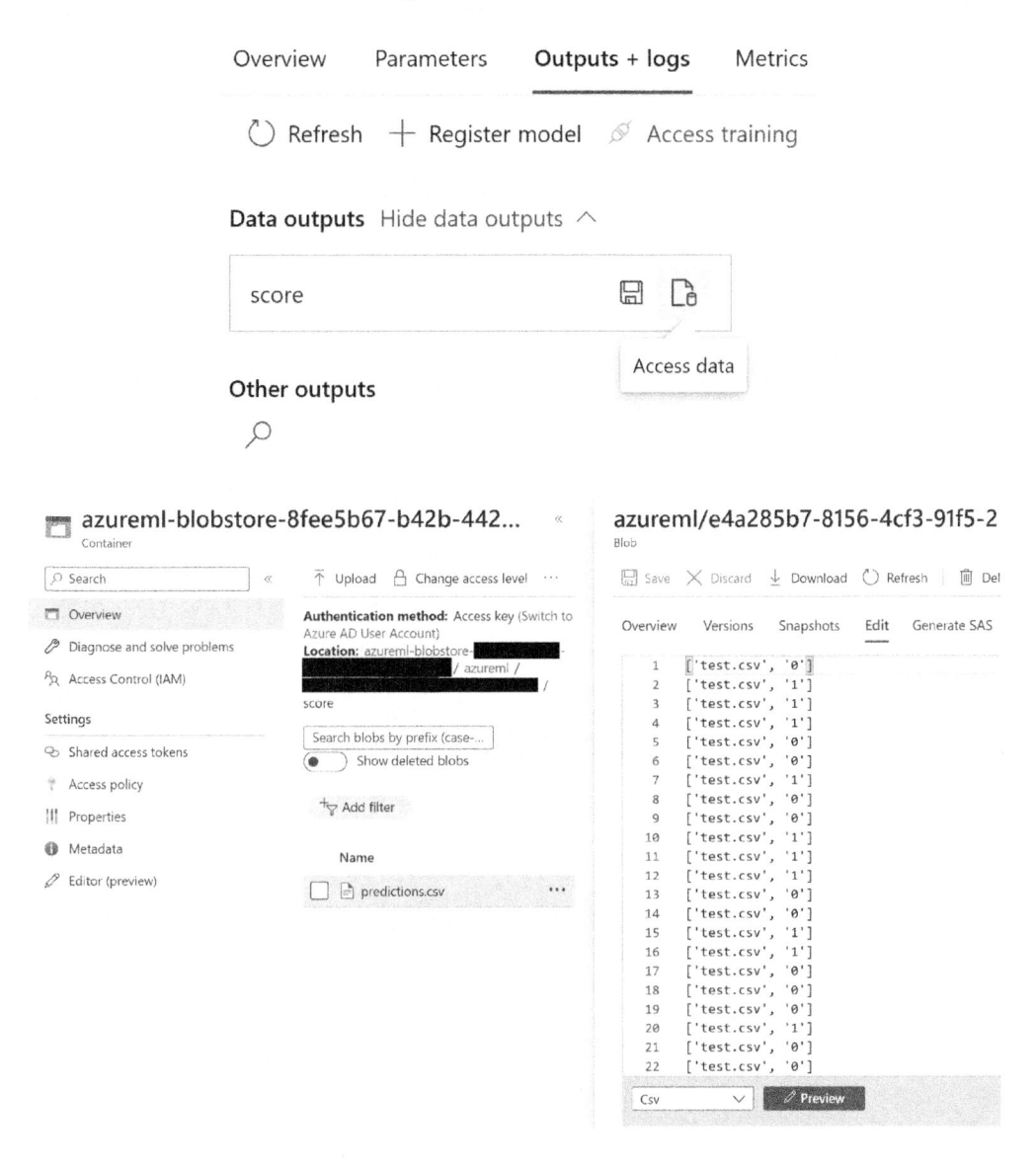

Figure 7.13 – Viewing batch scoring results

In this section, you learned how to deploy an existing model to a managed endpoint for batch inferencing using the studio. In the next section, we will show you how to deploy a model to a managed endpoint for batch scoring using the Python SDK.

Deploying a model for batch inferencing through the Python SDK

In this section, we are going to deploy an existing model to a managed endpoint for batch inferencing using the Python SDK by following these steps:

1. Go to `https://ml.azure.com`.
2. Select your workspace.
3. On the workspace user interface on the left side, click **Compute**:

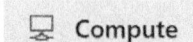

Figure 7.14 – Compute instance icon

4. On the **Compute** screen, select your compute instance and select **Start**:

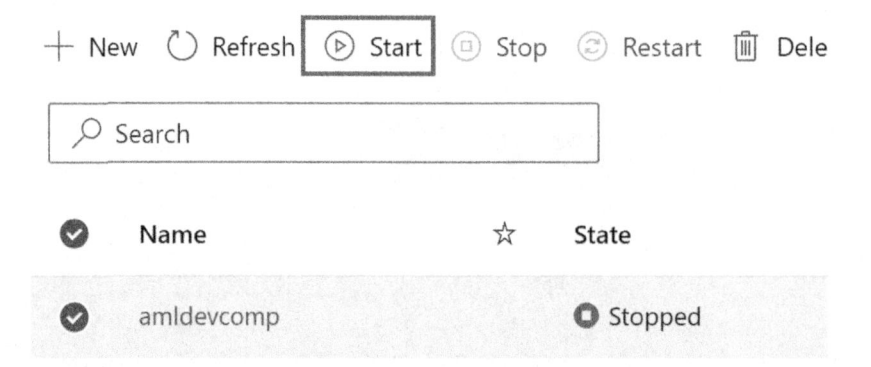

Figure 7.15 – Start compute

Your compute instance will change from **Stopped** to **Starting**. Once the compute instance moves from **Starting** to **Running**, it is ready for use, so go ahead and clone our repository, which contains some sample notebooks to walk through.

5. Click on the **Terminal** hyperlink under applications.

This will open the terminal on your compute instance. Note that the path will include your user in the directory path. Type the following into the terminal to clone the sample notebooks into your working directory:

```
git clone https://github.com/PacktPublishing/Azure-
Machine-Learning-Engineering.git
```

6. Click on the Jupyter link under applications, and this will display the folders that were just cloned. Navigate to `chapter 7` and click on `Deploy_Model_for_Batch_Scoring.ipynb` to bring up the notebook for this section.

7. The code snippet shown in *Figure 7.16* shows the libraries that need to be imported and how to connect to the Azure ML workspace in your compute instance:

Import required libraries

```python
# import required libraries
from azure.ai.ml import MLClient, Input
from azure.ai.ml.entities import (
    BatchEndpoint,
    BatchDeployment,
    Model,
    Environment,
    BatchRetrySettings,
)
# from azure.ai.ml.constants import AssetType
from azure.identity import DefaultAzureCredential
from azure.ai.ml.constants import BatchDeploymentOutputAction
import mlflow
from azure.ai.ml.entities import ManagedOnlineEndpoint, ManagedOnlineDeployment, Model
```

Configure workspace details and get a handle to the workspace

```python
# Enter details of your AML workspace
subscription_id = "                                        "
resource_group = "aml-v2-book"
workspace = "aml2-ws"
# get a handle to the workspace
ml_client = MLClient(
    DefaultAzureCredential(), subscription_id, resource_group, workspace
)
```

Figure 7.16 – Import required libraries and connecting to the Azure Machine Learning workspace

8. The code snippet shown in *Figure 7.17* shows how to create a batch endpoint:

Create a batch endpoint for inferencing

```python
import datetime

batch_endpoint_name = "titanic-batchendpoint-sdk"

# create a batch endpoint
endpoint = BatchEndpoint(
    name=batch_endpoint_name,
    description="this is a sample batch endpoint created using sdk",
    tags={"tag1": "val1"},
)
```

```python
ml_client.begin_create_or_update(endpoint)
```

Figure 7.17 – Creating a batch endpoint for inferencing

9. The code snippet shown in *Figure 7.18* shows how to retrieve an existing model from the workspace and how to create a batch deployment. The batch deployment must specify the batch endpoint, the trained model, and the compute cluster that is used for scoring, along with other deployment parameters:

Retrieving an existing registered model from the workspace

```python
model = ml_client.models.get("titanic_survival_model_", label="latest")
```

Creating a batch deployment

```python
# create a batch deployment
deployment = BatchDeployment(
    name="titanic-deployment-sdk",
    description="titanic deployment created using sdk",
    endpoint_name="titanic-batchendpoint-sdk",
    model=model,
    compute="cpu-cluster",
    instance_count=1,
    max_concurrency_per_instance=2,
    mini_batch_size=10,
    output_action=BatchDeploymentOutputAction.APPEND_ROW,
    output_file_name="predictions.csv",
    retry_settings=BatchRetrySettings(max_retries=3, timeout=30),
    logging_level="info",
)
```

```python
ml_client.begin_create_or_update(deployment)
```

Figure 7.18 – Creating a batch deployment

10. Now, that your batch endpoint is ready to be invoked, you are going to pass some test data to the endpoint, as shown in *Figure 7.19*:

Invoke your batch endpoint with a registered dataset

```python
data = ml_client.data.get("titanic-test-data", version=7)

job = ml_client.batch_endpoints.invoke(
    endpoint_name="titanic-batchendpoint-sdk",
    input=Input(path=data.id, type="uri_file"),
    deployment_name="titanic-deployment-sdk",   # name is required if default deployment is not set
    params_override=[{"mini_batch_size": "1"}, {"compute.instance_count": "1"}],
)
```

Figure 7.19 – Creating a batch deployment

11. The code snippet shown in *Figure 7.20* shows the Python code required to monitor the batch scoring job that was submitted in the previous step:

Monitor the batch scoring job

```python
# get the details of the job
job_name = job.name
batch_job = ml_client.jobs.get(name=job_name)
print(batch_job.status)
# stream the job logs
ml_client.jobs.stream(name=job_name)
```

```
Running
RunId: 3109449d-7dc4-41e7-9a02-3b158e9ea856
Web View: https://ml.azure.com/runs/3109449d-7dc4-41e7-■■■■-3b158e9ea856?wsid=/subscriptions/■■■■
■■■■/resourcegroups/aml-v2-book/workspaces/aml2-ws
```

Figure 7.20 – Creating a batch deployment

12. Clicking on the output link from the previous step will open the workspace displaying the batch scoring job, as shown in *Figure 7.21*. You can follow *steps 9* and *10* from the last section to see the results.

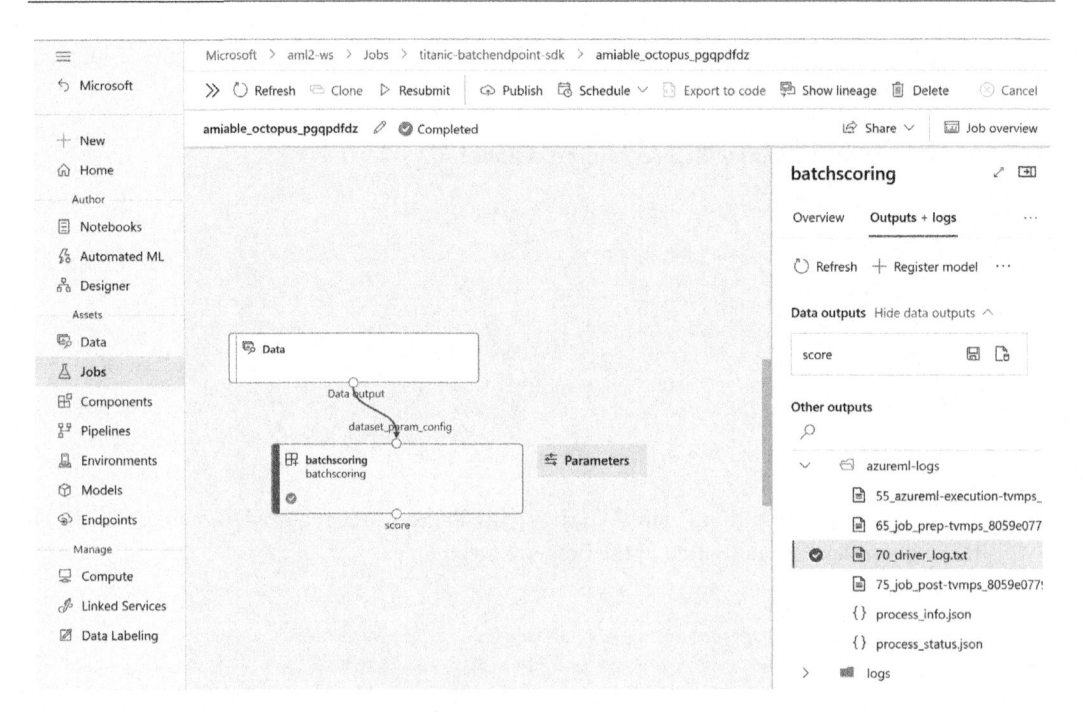

Figure 7.21 – Batch scoring results

Let's summarize the chapter next.

Summary

We have covered a lot of topics in this chapter. We have shown you how to deploy a model for batch scoring using the studio and through the Python SDK. We also showed you how to pass some test data to be scored by the deployed model by invoking the batch endpoint.

In the next chapter, you will learn about responsible AI and the capabilities within Azure Machine Learning that allow you to develop, assess, and deploy models more responsibly to minimize unwanted bias in your AI systems.

8
Responsible AI

One of the recent research areas to emerge in **artificial intelligence** (**AI**) is making models responsible and accountable, thus producing accurate results, as opposed to biased or incomplete results. This is a new area of computer science, but it is also something many in the data science field are looking into. Microsoft is concentrating its efforts on a number of areas, including **Fairness**, **Reliability and Safety**, **Privacy and Security**, **Inclusiveness**, **Transparency**, and **Accountability**. Microsoft has provided a toolbox that can be used and applied to datasets and models to address these topics. In this chapter, we will be exploring what these terms mean and how Microsoft's Responsible AI Toolbox can be leveraged to address these concerns.

In this chapter, we will cover the following topics:

- Responsible AI principles
- Response AI Toolbox overview
- Responsible AI dashboard
- Error analysis
- Interpretability dashboard
- Fairness dashboard

Responsible AI principles

As mentioned, there are six core principles – Fairness, Reliability and Safety, Privacy and Security, Inclusiveness, Transparency, and Accountability – that Microsoft has incorporated into their Responsible AI Toolbox. We will briefly explain these as follows:

- **Fairness** in the context of AI systems is a sociotechnical challenge that scientists and developers need to address to ensure that people are treated equally and to reduce unfairness relating to the specific use case we are building the model for. In a variety of domains and use cases, AI systems can be used to provide resources and opportunities, and through checking fairness we can ensure that we are not reinforcing existing stereotypes.

For example, if we are predicting what ethnic groups there are in a certain segment of the population and what their food preferences are, not all customer segments of cities or states have the same ethnic diversity. So, when we design the model, we have to take into consideration all ethnic groups, giving each equal distribution within the data, building fairness into the model. Otherwise, the model might be skewed by the ethnic group with the highest population available in the test set. This is also hard because all cities and states have unequal distributions of ethnic groups.

- **Reliability and Safety**: One important thing to keep in mind is to ensure models are safe for others to consume and that the output creates no harm. When a model makes predictions, make sure those predictions lead to safe and reliable decisions for all consumers. Understand that a wrong prediction can have an adverse negative effect when applying the model's outcome. Spend time making the model's outcome safe and reliable for the use case that it has been designed and developed for.

- **Privacy and Security**: Use cases that depend on human-related data, such as predicting patient diagnosis or attrition analysis for companies, use a lot of personal data. Proper precautions should be in place to protect **personally identifiable information** (**PII**) and privacy. Depending on where the model is run, try to run the model closer to where data is stored, and do not move it or copy it to ensure privacy. Also, make sure permission is granted individually to each person who needs access to the data and not everyone. In some cases, we can either encrypt the data or convert PII into something unidentifiable before building the model, if possible. There is also talk about synthetic data creation for modeling. Depending on the use case, the business problem we are attempting to solve must drive the decision on how to protect privacy and apply security.

- **Inclusiveness** is a core value stating that systems should empower all people, users and customers alike. The ability of the AI system to work with every human being on the planet regardless of who they are is always the goal. Inclusiveness is very similar to fairness. The question to ask is how we can include all of the various groups or include all ethnic minority communities in the model, ensuring no one is left out. Our dataset should represent all communities so that everyone gets proper representation when building our model.

- **Transparency** in a system is key to ensuring a system can be trusted. The system should be transparent, allowing users to know what is going on at any given time. This improves trust in the system. We can talk about two different categories of transparency:

    - **Transparency on how AI systems are built**: We need to be transparent on how the AI systems are built and provide proper documentation on the process and purpose of the model we've built. Anyone using the model should feel comfortable and able to trust the model.

    - **Transparency on pitfalls of the models**: Using interpretability to explain how the decision was made and what features were used is also an important way to gain trust in the model to be consumed.

- **Accountability**: Given that model building is somewhat unpredictable, we must be accountable for what we are building. Proper processes must be in place in order for us to accept accountability for the model we build. We should make sure that what we build takes privacy into account and that we accept responsibility for the trustworthiness of the model. For example, a data scientist who is building a model is responsible for building the model by following all of these principles and will be held accountable for that model. First and foremost, every organization has to have the following:

  - A responsible AI strategy
  - A methodology to develop AI/**machine learning** (**ML**) responsibly

In order to have a responsible AI strategy, you need to develop business guidelines relating to how AI/ML can be used to drive business outcomes, establish how teams can apply responsible AI and build better model outcomes, and decide what tools and techniques need to be in place to ensure responsible AI. This strategy should be the foundation of all AI/ML model development and should be used in any other systems. You should also create a framework around which to report and monitor risks or leaked AI/ML behavior.

In the next section of this chapter, we will discuss how to leverage **raiwidgets** (or the **Responsible AI Toolkit SDK**) and how we can analyze the six core principles. Not all of these principles are covered by the SDK. For example, while Fairness and Transparency are covered by the SDK, Privacy and Security, Reliability, and Accountability will be covered by other programming mechanisms.

Follow this URL for more details and up-to-date information: `https://www.microsoft.com/en-us/ai/responsible-ai`.

Responsible AI Toolbox overview

One of the biggest challenges we face in data science is understanding what the model does. For example, if the algorithms we use are all black boxes, it's not that easy to know how the decisions are made. To discern how our algorithms make decisions, we can make use of responsible AI. This will give us the opportunity to explain the model's decisions, find the features that contribute to the prediction, do error analysis on the dataset, and also ensure fairness in the dataset.

Microsoft recently developed a Responsible AI Toolbox that encompasses interpretability, fairness, counterfactual analysis, and causal decision-making through three dashboards: a **fairness dashboard**, an **error analysis dashboard**, and an **interpretability dashboard**.

Dashboards simplify the **user interface** (**UI**) by bringing all the toolkit output into one UI. Before the toolbox, it was hard because we needed to download a separate library and build code for each of the dashboards. Now, it's very easy, and I will show some code to achieve this with the Responsible AI Toolbox.

Responsible AI dashboard

> **Note**
> The toolbox is in public preview, and there are new developments on the way. Make sure your libraries are updated often to check which new features are available for you.
>
> The Toolbox is available here: `https://github.com/microsoft/responsible-ai-toolbox`.

To leverage the Toolbox, we will create a model to apply the Toolbox to. Let's look at the process of creating and analyzing responsible AI.

Let's go through the steps to create a model in the Azure ML service:

1. Go to the Azure ML Studio UI.
2. Start the compute instance.
3. Click on **Notebook** in the **Author** section.
4. Create a new notebook with Python 3.8 with Azure ML as the kernel.
5. Name the notebook `RAIDashboard.ipynb`.
6. Now, we need to install or upgrade libraries. Only install libraries if they aren't already on your system. At the time of writing, Python 3.8 with the Azure ML kernel was used, and it already has `raiwidgets` installed. If there is an older version, please use the following upgrade command to upgrade to the latest version:

```
1   !pip install raiwidgets
```
Press shift + enter to run

```
1   !pip install --upgrade raiwidgets
```
Press shift + enter to run

Figure 8.1 – Install or upgrade the Responsible AI Toolbox

7. Now, let's upgrade the dependencies:

```
1    !pip install --upgrade pandas
```
Press shift + enter to run

Figure 8.2 – Upgrade the pandas libraries to the newest version

8. Restart the kernel and clear all the outputs. Once the libraries are installed, it's always a good practice to restart the kernel to reflect the installed libraries. Some packages force us to restart the kernel to be effective.

9. We are now going to load the libraries for us to consume in the notebook. The Responsible AI dashboard is used to generate a nice UI to interact with and do **what-if analysis**, as well as other types of analysis, including **error analysis**, **feature permutation**, and **counterfactual analysis**, on the model created.

   For RAIInsights, this is where we calculate all the calculations to generate the dashboard. It usually takes time to execute and analyze the model and get insights into what the model is doing. Whatever is displayed on the Responsible AI dashboard will be calculated by the RAIInsights libraries.

```
1    from raiwidgets import ResponsibleAIDashboard
2    from responsibleai import RAIInsights
```

Figure 8.3 – Importing the Responsible AI libraries

10. Next, we create a sample regression model to which to apply Responsible AI. Let's import the shap and sklearn libraries for our model. Here, we are going to load the ML libraries and also the library required to split the data for training and testing. Later, we will split the dataset into two parts: one for training and one for testing. Usually, 80% is used for training and 20% is used for testing.

```
1    import shap
2    import sklearn
3    import pandas as pd
4
5    from sklearn.model_selection import train_test_split
6    from sklearn.ensemble import RandomForestRegressor
```

Figure 8.4 – Importing the model's libraries

11. Now, let's load the sample datasets and split the data for training and testing. Also, let's assign the column that is used for the target feature, or label the column to be predicted. Here, we are loading a sample dataset for diabetes. Then, we are going to assign the column to predict, which is `'y'`. Sometimes, it's called `target_feature`. Then, we use the remaining columns as features to train the model.

```
1    data = sklearn.datasets.load_diabetes()
2    target_feature = 'y'
3    continuous_features = data.feature_names
4    data_df = pd.DataFrame(data.data, columns=data.feature_names)
5
```

Figure 8.5 – Loading the sample dataset

12. Split the data and assign it to different dataframes for modeling. Usually, when modeling, the training data is split into two datasets, one for training and one for testing. Next, the predicting column, which is called the label or target, is also split into training and testing. The following screenshot shows the features used for modeling.

```
1    X_train, X_test, y_train, y_test = train_test_split(data_df, data.target, test_size=0.2, random_state=7)
2
3    train_data = X_train.copy()
4    test_data = X_test.copy()
5    train_data[target_feature] = y_train
6    test_data[target_feature] = y_test
7    data.feature_names
```

['age', 'sex', 'bmi', 'bp', 's1', 's2', 's3', 's4', 's5', 's6']

Figure 8.6 – Splitting data for training and testing

Now that we have made our model, we need to run it. This is necessary before we analyze the model using the Responsible AI Toolbox for fairness, privacy, reliability, and bias. Bias means we want to have equal records for the categories we use. For example, if we use a dataset that contains ethnicity or sex features, we have to make sure we have an equal amount of data for each represented group to avoid bias.

Let's now create the responsible AI code by following these steps:

1. First, we need to train the model before we pass it to `RAIInsights` to calculate the fairness, bias, and other error analyses.

```
1    model = RandomForestRegressor()
2    model.fit(X_train, y_train)
```

```
2022/04/18 23:32:34 INFO mlflow.utils.autologging_utils: Created MLflow autologg
cb7cf761b9b0', which will track hyperparameters, performance metrics, model arti
sklearn workflow
RandomForestRegressor(bootstrap=True, ccp_alpha=0.0, criterion='mse',
                      max_depth=None, max_features='auto', max_leaf_nodes=None,
                      max_samples=None, min_impurity_decrease=0.0,
                      min_impurity_split=None, min_samples_leaf=1,
                      min_samples_split=2, min_weight_fraction_leaf=0.0,
                      n_estimators=100, n_jobs=None, oob_score=False,
                      random_state=None, verbose=0, warm_start=False)
```

Figure 8.7 – Model configuration and training

2. The model is ready. The next step is to apply responsible AI. Let's configure the `RAIInsights` details.

   We need to pass the following parameters: `model`, `train_data`, `test_data`, `target_feature`, the model type (for example, `regression` or `classification`), and `categorical_features`.

   With this, `RAIInsights` is going to produce the following:

   - An error analysis dashboard
   - An interpretability dashboard
   - A fairness dashboard
   - A Responsible AI dashboard

```
1    rai_insights = RAIInsights(model, train_data, test_data, target_feature, 'regression',
2                               categorical_features=[])
```

Figure 8.8 – Invoking RAIInsights

3. The next step is to invoke interpretability, error analysis, and fairness and build the dashboard:

- **Interpretability**: `IntepretML` is used to understand how the columns affect the prediction made by the model. `IntepretML` is an open source package. Here, we combine all the open source package output, making it seamless, and show it in `ResponsibleAIDashboard`.

- **Error analysis**: Error analysis allows us to identify high error rates with respect to the benchmarked error rate to find any errors in the model. It also allows us to conduct root cause analysis in combination with interpretability to see how the model characteristics are performing. We use the open source `Error Analysis` package for this.

- **Counterfactuals**: This accepts the total number of counterfactuals to generate and the range that their labels should fall within. Counterfactual analysis allows us to analyze the model's performance with various outcomes by changing parameters. We can use this section to do what-if analysis to understand how the model performs. `DiCE` is the open source package that we use to do this analysis.

- **Causal analysis**: This is performed by the `EconML` open source package. This package allows us to change conditions and see the impact. For example, what would the impact be if we introduced a new product to a customer segment or if we introduced new strategies into the company?

```
# Interpretability
rai_insights.explainer.add()
# Error Analysis
rai_insights.error_analysis.add()
# Counterfactuals: accepts total number of counterfactuals to generate,
# and a list of strings of categorical feature names
rai_insights.counterfactual.add(total_CFs=20, desired_range=[50, 120])
```

Figure 8.9 – Adding explainer, error analysis, and counterfactual packages

Now, let's carry out interpretability, error, and counterfactual analysis:

1. Usually, it will take some time to do all the calculations. Depending on the model type and the size of the dataset, be prepared to spend a little while here. Depending on the ML type, causal analysis using `EconML` will also be computed for what-if analysis.

```
     ▷           1    rai_insights.compute()
   [19]          ✓ 38 sec

    ...    100%|██████████| 89/89 [00:36<00:00,  2.42it/s]
```

Figure 8.10 – Compute responsible AI calculation insights

2. Next, we need to build the Responsible AI dashboard. The Toolbox consolidates all the output in a dashboard and provides one place to conduct analysis. Please remember that not all the principles have been implemented yet, and research and development is still an ongoing process with the SDK. *Figure 8.11* shows the creation of the Responsible AI dashboard.

```
    1    ResponsibleAIDashboard(rai_insights)
         ✓ 1 sec
```

ResponsibleAI started at https:/.   centralus.instances.azureml.ms
<raiwidgets.responsibleai_dashboard.ResponsibleAIDashboard at 0x7f6b0ec0c358>

Figure 8.11 – Responsible AI dashboard

3. Once the dashboard is built, click on the hyperlink to open it. For each type of analysis, please see the heading in the dashboard link.

The link is available here: responsible-ai-toolbox/tour.ipynb at main · microsoft/responsible-ai-toolbox (https://github.com/microsoft/responsible-ai-toolbox/blob/main/notebooks/responsibleaidashboard/tour.ipynb).

The dashboard created from the preceding code will have a few options to customize and work with cohorts:

- **Dashboard navigation**: Allows us to filter any analysis
- **Cohort settings**: Allows us to work with cohorts
- **Switch global cohort**: Allows us to switch between cohorts and also display statistics in popups
- **Create new cohort**: Allows us to create new cohorts as needed

Next, we are going to deep dive into the error analysis dashboard to understand feature errors.

Error analysis dashboard

Error analysis allows us to analyze where the model is underperforming and also find errors in the decision-making process.

Error analysis can be done as either a tree map or a heat map. Based on the analysis, red represents an error. If you click one of the insight bubbles, you'll see the path the model traversed.

Dashboard analysis will be based on the type of ML modeling we choose. The two types are classification and regression. In our example, we chose regression. The following are two of the accuracy metrics used:

- **Mean squared error**
- **Mean absolute error**

The following screenshot shows the error analysis dashboard UI created by the Responsible AI SDK.

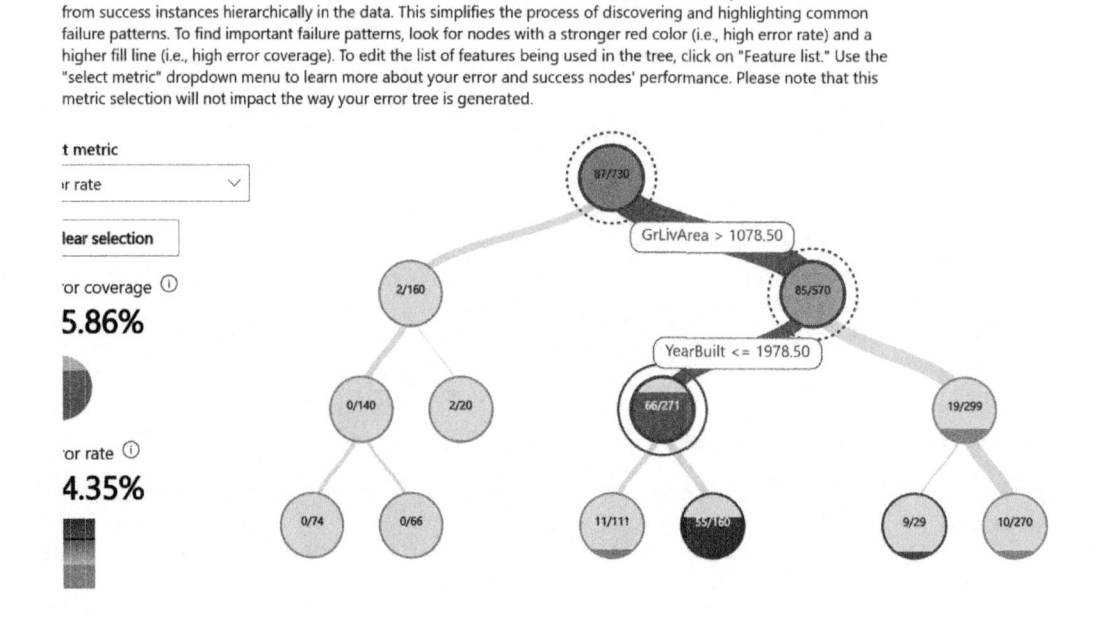

Figure 8.12 – Error analysis dashboard

This dashboard provides options to save the error analysis for further analysis or share it with others. This feature is very helpful if we need to share information with other data scientists or subject matter experts to understand a model's performance.

The following screenshot shows the error analysis screen with **Heat map** selected:

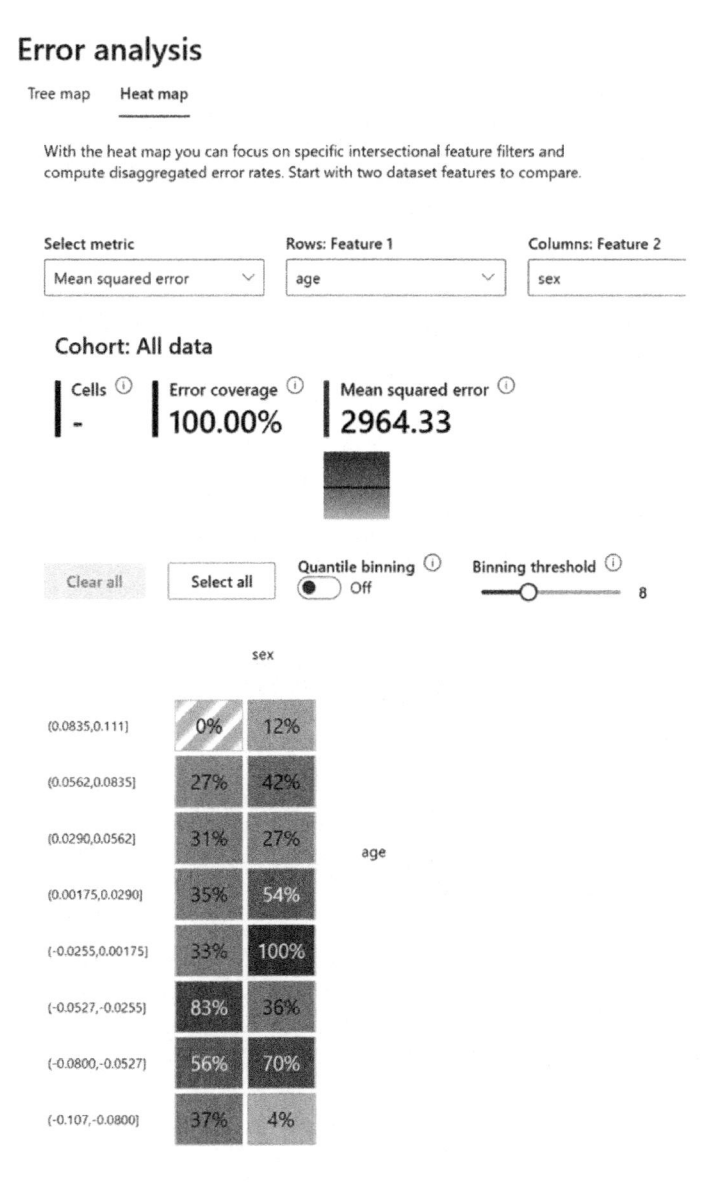

Figure 8.13 – Heat map error analysis

In this heat map, we need to select the features for which we want to do error analysis. Once we select the features, the system will analyze the error percentage.

Options are available for **Quantile binning** and **Binning threshold**.

216　　Responsible AI

The following screenshot shows us **Feature List**. This section shows which features have been selected and how important each one is to the prediction.

Feature List

To retrain the tree map, select and save the features below. The feature importances were calculated using mutual information with the error on the true labels. Please use it as a guideline for training the tree map.

Features	Importances
s1	▬▬▬▬▬▬▬
bmi	▬▬▬▬▬▬
s5	▬▬▬
s4	▬▬
s3	▬▬
age	▬▬▬▬▬▬
sex	▬▬▬▬▬
bp	▬▬▬▬▬
s2	▬▬▬▬▬
s6	▬▬▬▬▬

Maximum depth 　4
Number of leaves 　21
Minimum number of samples in one leaf 　21

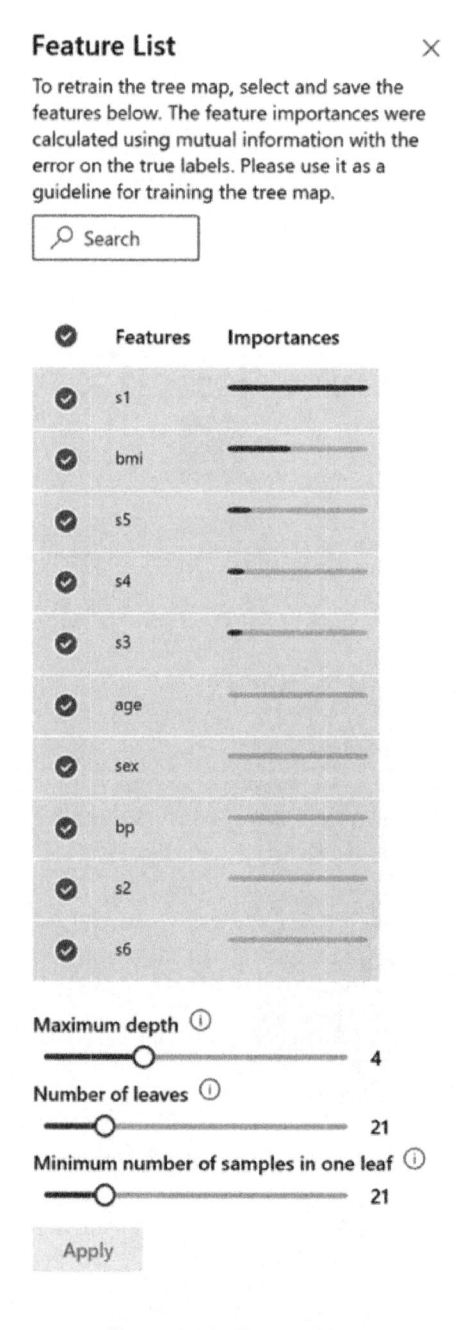

Apply

Figure 8.14 – Feature List

This feature illustrates the importance of the columns or features to the predictions. There are options to change the maximum depth and leaves of the decision tree created by the responsible AI dashboard, as well as how the minimum number of samples in one leaf is analyzed.

Interpretability dashboard

Now let's look at the interpretability section of the dashboard. This is where each feature is analyzed and the importance and impact of the features are shown. The top features are either aggregated or available individually for analysis.

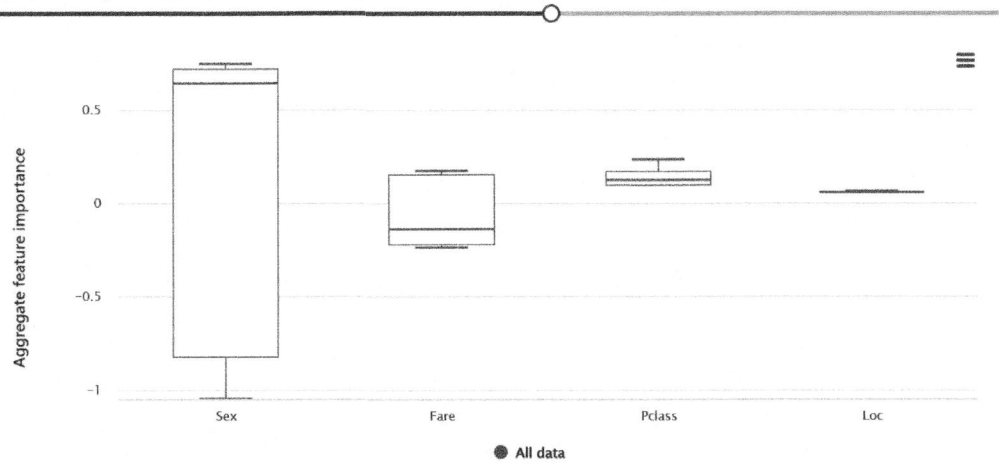

Figure 8.15 – Aggregated feature importance

In the preceding screenshot, you can see the aggregated feature importance.

Select **Individual feature importance** to analyze the data row by row. Then, select the rows to analyze, as follows:

Index	TrueY	PredictedY	Pclass	Sex	Age	Fare
Correct predictions (19)						
0	0	0	3	1	20	8.6625
1	0	0	2	1	21	11.5
2	0	0	3	1	39	7.925
3	0	0	3	1	25	15.5
4	1	1	1	2	21	77.9583
6	0	0	3	1	32	7.75

Figure 8.16 – Selecting data points for feature importance

Once the feature data points are selected, scroll down to see the charts. The following chart shows the feature importance and its impact on the row that is selected. For every row in the dataset, you can analyze the dataset by selecting a row.

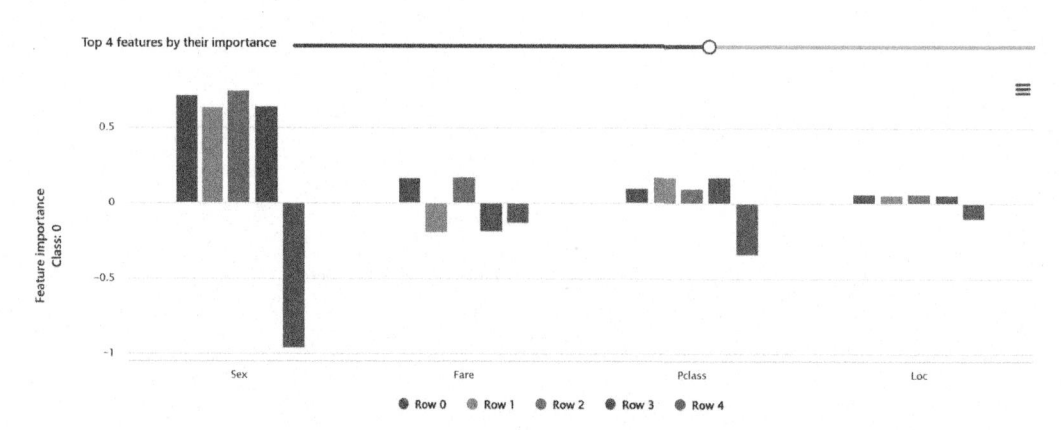

Figure 8.17 – Individual feature importance plot

Now click **Individual conditional expectations (ICE) plot** to change the plot. The ICE plot will show all the rows with respect to the feature selected and show how much impact each row had on the model.

On selecting **Individual conditional expectation (ICE) plot**, you should see what is shown in *Figure 8.17*. The *x* axis should be the feature selected and the *y* axis the prediction. Click the **Feature** dropdown and select the feature to see the impact. Also, options to set minimum and maximum steps are available. To get more information, click **How to read this chart**.

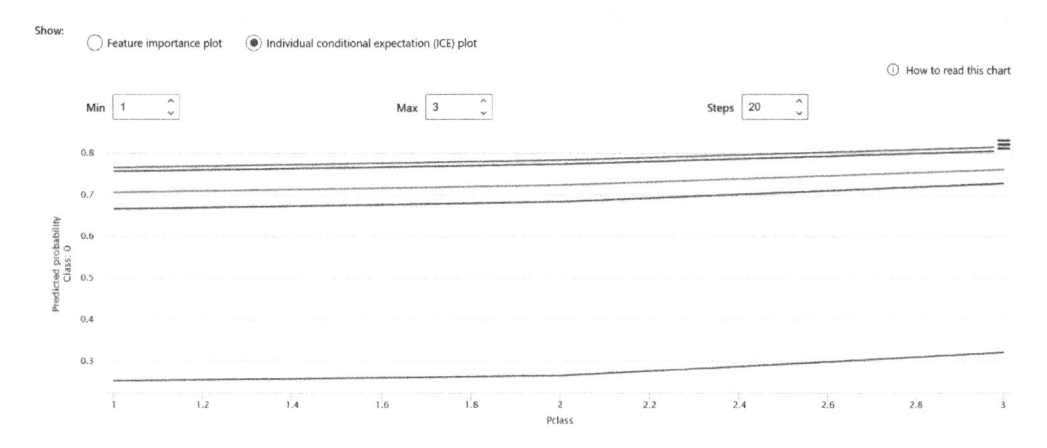

Figure 8.18 – Individual conditional expectation (ICE) plot

Now let's look at model statistics.

Model statistics allow us to analyze distribution across prediction values, the model's performance, and model metrics. Options to switch between a cohort and a dataset are also available. Select the *y* value to see the error in the dataset, the predicted Y value (the label for the column that the model predicted), and what the true Y value (label for the column provided in the training dataset) was. These options allow us to understand the model performance.

You can also swap the axes to show errors on the x axis and predictions on the Y axis. Also, if you click **Cohort**, there is the option to select a dataset and the features to plot and see how the model performed.

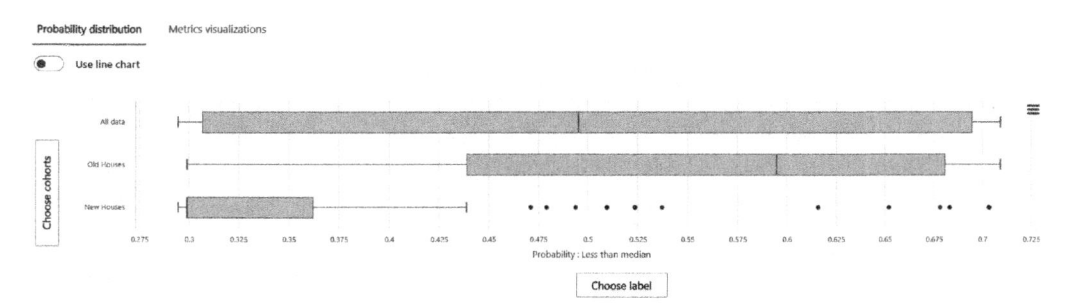

Figure 8.19 – Model statistics

Next, we are going to look into the **Data explorer** feature on the Responsible AI dashboard.

Data explorer

Data explorer is another visual tool for analyzing the predicted value, error, and features. You can use either aggregated or individual features. It also allows you to select predicted features and training features for what-if analysis.

Figure 8.20 shows a box plot of how age is grouped or binned into chunks. The *x* axis is the index and the *y* axis is the age groups, which can be age data points or bins of ages. You have the choice to select either **Aggregate plots** or **Individual datapoints** to visualize the difference between aggregated and individual plots. Box plots provide a clear visualization of where the outliers are and show the range of plotted points.

We can change the *x* axis from the index to the predicted *y* or true *y* value to see the patterns. There is also the option to change the number of bins. In the following example, we chose five bins. Also, if you click **age**, there is the option to change the feature as well to see how the prediction value changes.

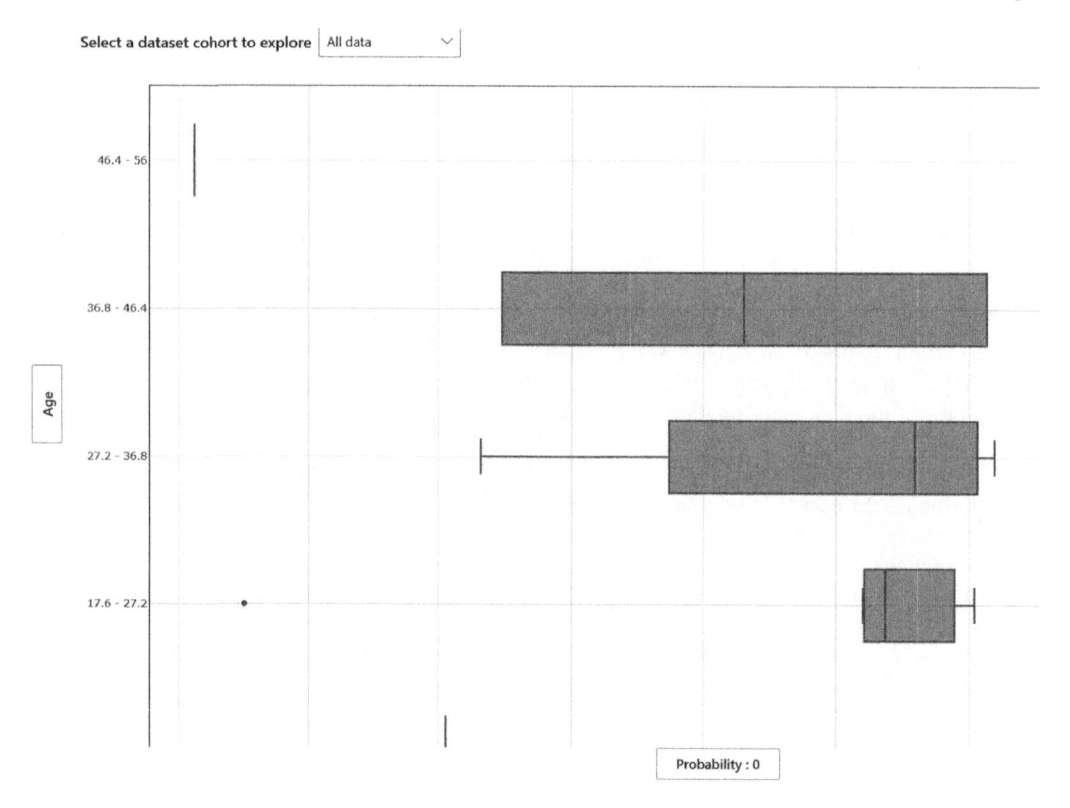

Figure 8.20 – Aggregated plots

Data explorer allows us to select the predicted and original values and plot either aggregated or individual scatter plots to see how the values align or intersect. In the following chart, the *y* axis is the age and the *x* axis is the index, and the predicted outcome is a scatter plot. You can change the cohort to see various values.

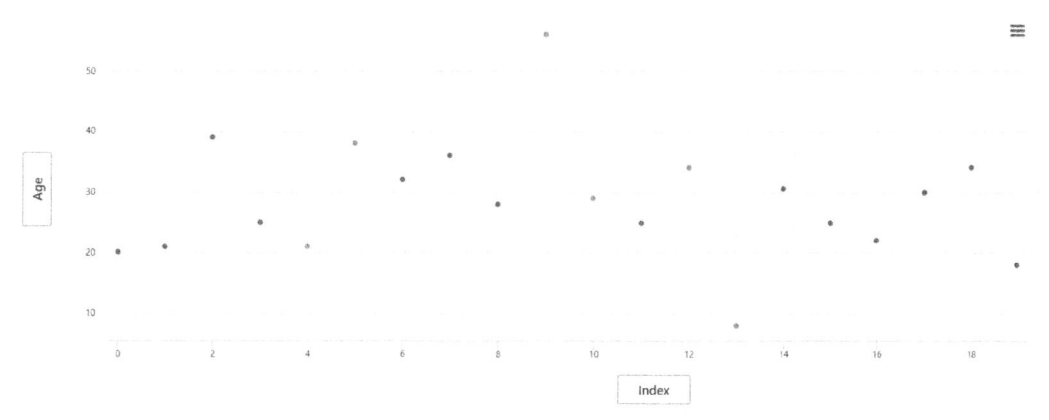

Figure 8.21 – Scatter plot for individual values

The preceding charts provide a way to visualize the predicted and error values of our model. This enables us to build a better model with more accuracy that is more realistic.

What-if counterfactuals

Now, we can change the datapoints and click **Create what-if counterfactuals**. What-if analysis allows us to select the predictor and compare with features to see the impact on the outcome. We can also change the index and age and switch to see predicted *y* or true *y* values and the features to see the counterfactuals. Then, we can select the index value and select one to see how the charts change.

We can see a counterfactual chart in the following screenshot and analyze the chart by changing features.

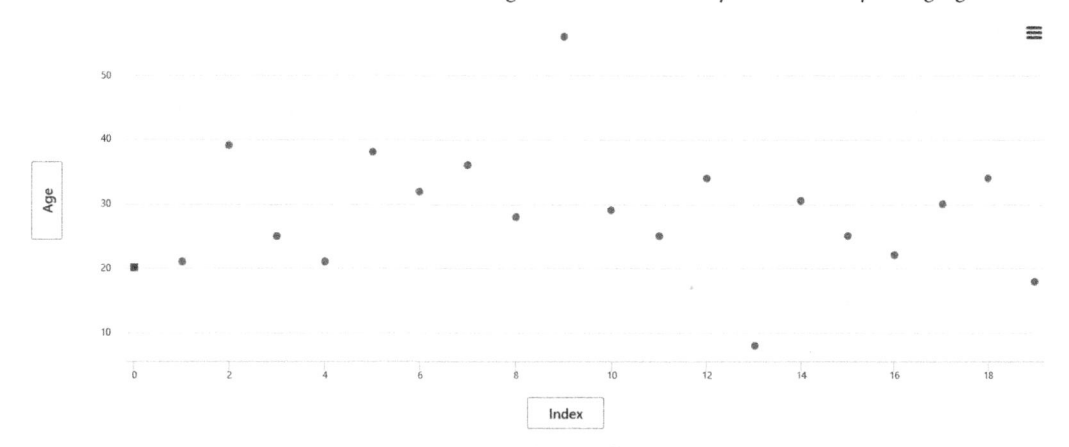

Figure 8.22 – Counterfactuals

Responsible AI

Select the index and then click **Create what-if counterfactual** to see the features percentage in the distribution chart. You can also save the chart.

	Predicted value (Survived)	Sex	Fare	Loc	Pclass
Reference datapoint: Row 0 Set Value	0	1	8.6625	9	3
Counterfactual Ex 1 Set Value	1	2	89.606	-	-
Counterfactual Ex 2 Set Value	1	2	131.209	-	-
Counterfactual Ex 3 Set Value	1	2	-	-	1
Counterfactual Ex 4 Set Value	1	2	96.194	-	-
Counterfactual Ex 5 Set Value	1	2	164.137	-	-
Counterfactual Ex 6 Set Value	1	2	-	7	-
Counterfactual Ex 7 Set Value	1	2	109.633	-	-
Counterfactual Ex 8 Set Value	1	2	-	2	-
Counterfactual Ex 9 Set Value	1	2	205.397	-	-
Counterfactual Ex 10	1	2	151.774	-	-

Figure 8.23 – What-if counterfactuals

In the next section, we are going to see how fairness can be analyzed using the SDK.

Fairness

Fairness is a topic that we need to investigate in use cases where people are involved. Proper precautions should be taken to figure out whether the dataset is fair or not. In Azure ML, with the Responsible AI Toolbox, we can create a fairness dashboard. To do that, first, we need to know which features need to be fair, such as sex and race. Once we know that, we can create a dashboard, as shown in *Figure 8.24*.

In this section, we are going to create a fairness dashboard with a sample dataset:

1. Go to the Azure ML Studio UI.
2. Start the compute instance.
3. Click on **Notebook** in the **Author** section.
4. Create a new notebook with Python 3.8 with Azure ML as the kernel.
5. Create a new notebook called `FairnessDashboard`.
6. Import all the required libraries:

    ```python
    from raiwidgets import FairnessDashboard

    from fairlearn.reductions import GridSearch
    from fairlearn.reductions import DemographicParity
    from fairlearn.metrics import MetricFrame, selection_rate

    from sklearn import svm, neighbors, tree
    from sklearn.metrics import accuracy_score
    from sklearn.preprocessing import LabelEncoder, StandardScaler
    from sklearn.linear_model import LogisticRegression
    from sklearn.datasets import fetch_openml

    import pandas as pd

    import numpy as np
    ```

    Figure 8.24 – Fairness imports

7. Next, we are going to load the sample dataset:

    ```python
    data = fetch_openml(data_id=1590, as_frame=True)
    X_raw = data.data
    y_true = (data.target == '>50K') * 1

    X_raw["race"].value_counts().to_dict()
    ```

    Figure 8.25 – Getting the sample data

8. Then, we are going to specify the sensitive features and then use categorical columns and label encoder to convert strings to numbers:

```
sensitive_features = X_raw[['sex','race']]
X = X_raw.drop(labels=['sex', 'race'],axis = 1)
X = pd.get_dummies(X)

sc = StandardScaler()
X_scaled = sc.fit_transform(X)
X_scaled = pd.DataFrame(X_scaled, columns=X.columns)

le = LabelEncoder()
y_true = le.fit_transform(y_true)
```

Figure 8.26 – Feature engineering

9. Now that we have feature engineering taken care of, the next step is to split the dataset for training and testing. We will split the dataset into 80% for training and 20% for testing:

```
from sklearn.model_selection import train_test_split
X_train, X_test, y_train, y_test, sensitive_features_train, sensitive_features_test = \
    train_test_split(X_scaled, y_true, sensitive_features,
                     test_size = 0.2, random_state=0, stratify=y_true)

# Work around indexing bug
X_train = X_train.reset_index(drop=True)
sensitive_features_train = sensitive_features_train.reset_index(drop=True)
X_test = X_test.reset_index(drop=True)
sensitive_features_test = sensitive_features_test.reset_index(drop=True)
```

Figure 8.27 – Splitting data for training and testing

10. Next, configure the training:

```
unmitigated_predictor = LogisticRegression(solver='liblinear', fit_intercept=True)

unmitigated_predictor.fit(X_train, y_train)
```

Figure 8.28 – Training

Train the model with the dataset. Here, we are using logistic regression for modeling.

11. Next, let's create a fairness dashboard. A fairness dashboard needs these three parameters at a minimum:

- **Sensitive features** – columns that have sensitive data, such as sex or race
- **Original label value**
- **Predicted value to analyze**

Click the URL created by the responsible AI SDK. A new web page will open. Follow the navigation in the dashboard to select the sensitive column and see how the data is distributed across those features. The main aim here is to provide insights into how the features are balanced with sensitive information. For example, if we have data with male and female datapoints, we want to make sure that men and women have the same amount of representation in the dataset.

```
y_pred = unmitigated_predictor.predict(X_test)

FairnessDashboard(sensitive_features=sensitive_features_test,
                  y_true=y_test,
                  y_pred=y_pred)
```

Fairness started at https:/.   instances.azureml.ms

Figure 8.29 – Creating the fairness dashboard

Here is the main page of the dashboard:

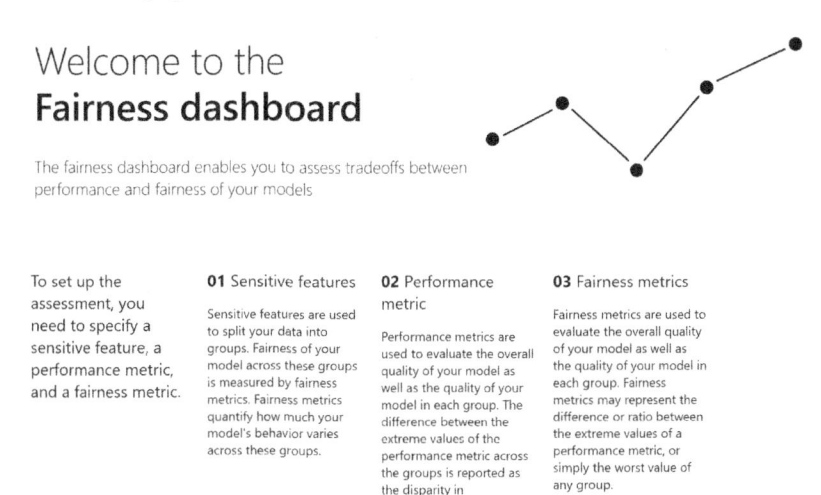

Welcome to the
Fairness dashboard

The fairness dashboard enables you to assess tradeoffs between performance and fairness of your models

To set up the assessment, you need to specify a sensitive feature, a performance metric, and a fairness metric.

01 Sensitive features

Sensitive features are used to split your data into groups. Fairness of your model across these groups is measured by fairness metrics. Fairness metrics quantify how much your model's behavior varies across these groups.

02 Performance metric

Performance metrics are used to evaluate the overall quality of your model as well as the quality of your model in each group. The difference between the extreme values of the performance metric across the groups is reported as the disparity in performance.

03 Fairness metrics

Fairness metrics are used to evaluate the overall quality of your model as well as the quality of your model in each group. Fairness metrics may represent the difference or ratio between the extreme values of a performance metric, or simply the worst value of any group.

Get started

Figure 8.30 – Fairness dashboard – intro page

12. Click on **Get started** to view the options to analyze fairness.

13. The first step of the process is to select the sensitive features. In the following screenshot, we have two columns, **sex** and **race**. In the **sex** column, we have two categories, **male** and **female**. For **race**, we have **white**, **black**, **Asian-Pac-Islander**, **Other**, and **Amer-Indian-Eskimo**. Let's first select **sex** to examine the sensitive features, and then click **Next**.

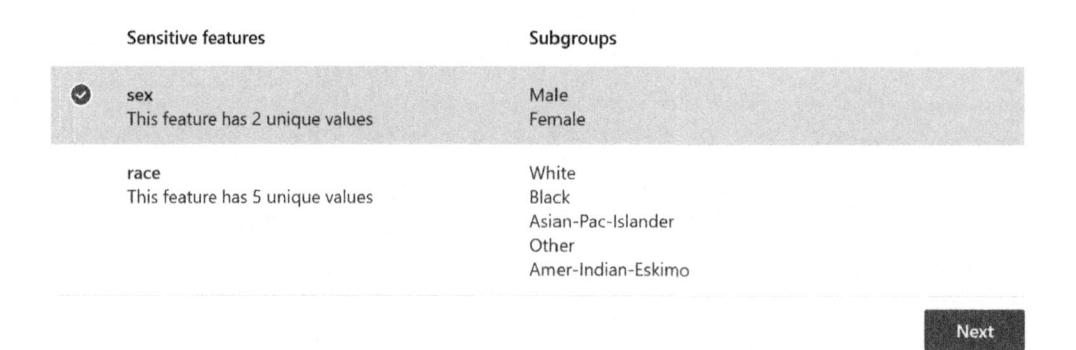

Figure 8.31 – Fairness dashboard – 01 Sensitive features

14. Now let's choose which performance metric to use for our analysis. Options for performance metrics are as follows:

    - **Accuracy**
    - **Balanced accuracy**
    - **F1-score**
    - **Precision**
    - **Recall**

    The definitions of these metrics are provided in *Figure 8.32*. For our purposes, we are going to choose **Accuracy** as the metric, with **Sex** as the sensitive column for us to analyze. Click **Next** to go to **Fairness metrics**.

How do you want to measure performance?

Your data contains binary labels and your model makes binary predictions. Based on that information, we recommend the following metrics. Please select one metric from the list.

Data statistics
2 sensitive features
9769 instances

●	Accuracy	The fraction of data points classified correctly.
○	Balanced accuracy	Positive and negative examples are reweighted to have equal total weight. S...
○	F1-score	F1-score is the harmonic mean of precision and recall.
○	Precision	The fraction of data points classified correctly among those classified as 1.
○	Recall	The fraction of data points classified correctly among those whose true label...

Figure 8.32 – Fairness dashboard – 02 Performance metrics

15. Next is one of the most important screens. Select the appropriate fairness metric for our analysis. In the following screenshot, you can see the choice. For our example, we are choosing **Demographic parity difference**. Then click **Next** to see the charts to analyze.

How do you want to measure fairness?

Fairness metrics quantify variation of your model's behavior across selected features. There are several kinds of fairness metrics that are based on a variety of performance metrics. They either capture the difference or ratio between the extreme values across the groups, or simply the worst value of any group.

Data statistics
2 sensitive features
9769 instances

> Accuracy / error rate (6)

∨ Demographic Parity / Selection rate (2)

● Demographic parity difference — The maximum difference in selection rate, that is the fraction with pred...
○ Demographic parity ratio — The minimum ratio of selection rates, that is the fraction with predicte...

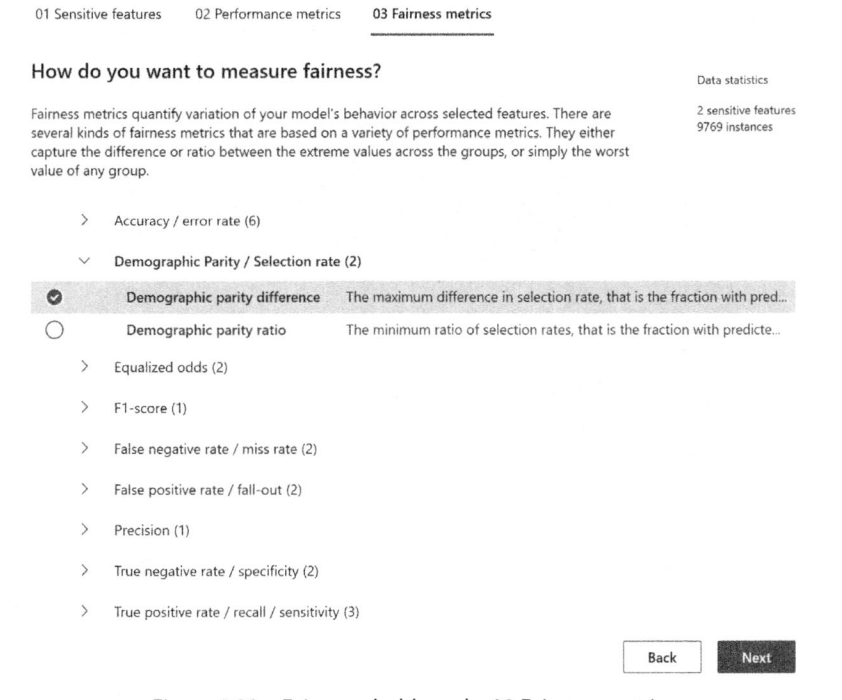

> Equalized odds (2)
> F1-score (1)
> False negative rate / miss rate (2)
> False positive rate / fall-out (2)
> Precision (1)
> True negative rate / specificity (2)
> True positive rate / recall / sensitivity (3)

Figure 8.33 – Fairness dashboard – 03 Fairness metrics

16. On the next screen, we can change these selections, see how the fairness metrics are calculated, and examine which sensitive features are selected and how fair they are.

Assessment results for **Model 0**

Sensitive feature	Performance metric	Fairness metric
sex	Accuracy	Demographic parity difference

	Accuracy	Selection ...	Demogra...	False posi...	False neg...
Overall	85.4%	19.6%	18.3%	6.74%	39.5%
Male	81.6%	25.7%		9.75%	38%
Female	93.1%	7.36%		2.01%	48%

Charts

Selection rate

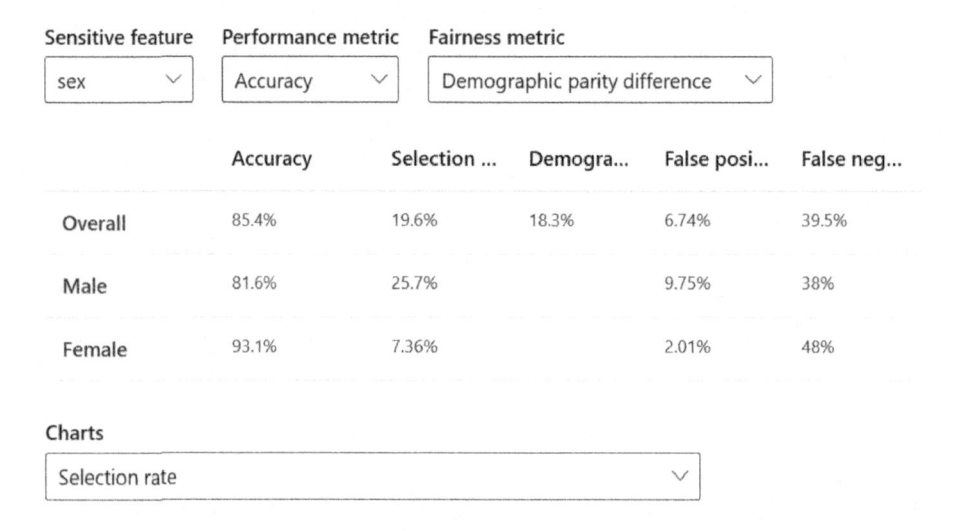

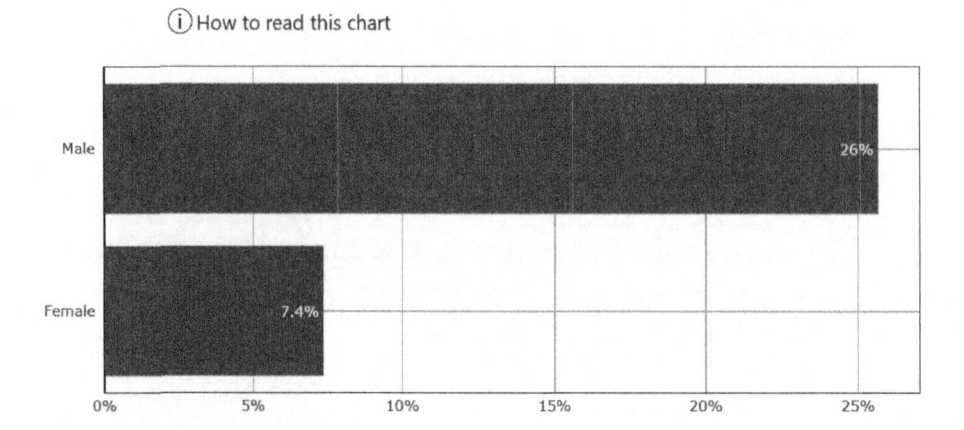

(i) How to read this chart

Male — 26%
Female — 7.4%

Figure 8.34 – Fairness results

The preceding chart shows that women are underrepresented in the model, which also suggests the model might be biased toward men. So, now we can go back and see whether we can get a more balanced dataset to make our model fairer. Try to switch the charts to false positive and false negative rates to drill down and see the rates of false positives and negatives. You can also change **Performance metric**, **Sensitive feature**, and **Fairness metric** and analyze the fairness. As these options change, the charts will reflect the changes. This tool provides a single place to analyze data for bias and fairness.

Charts

False positive and false negative rates

ⓘ How to read this chart

	False negative rate	False positive rate
Male	38%	9.7%
Female	48%	2%

False negative rate
(predicted = 0, true = 1)

False positive rate
(predicted = 1, true = 0)

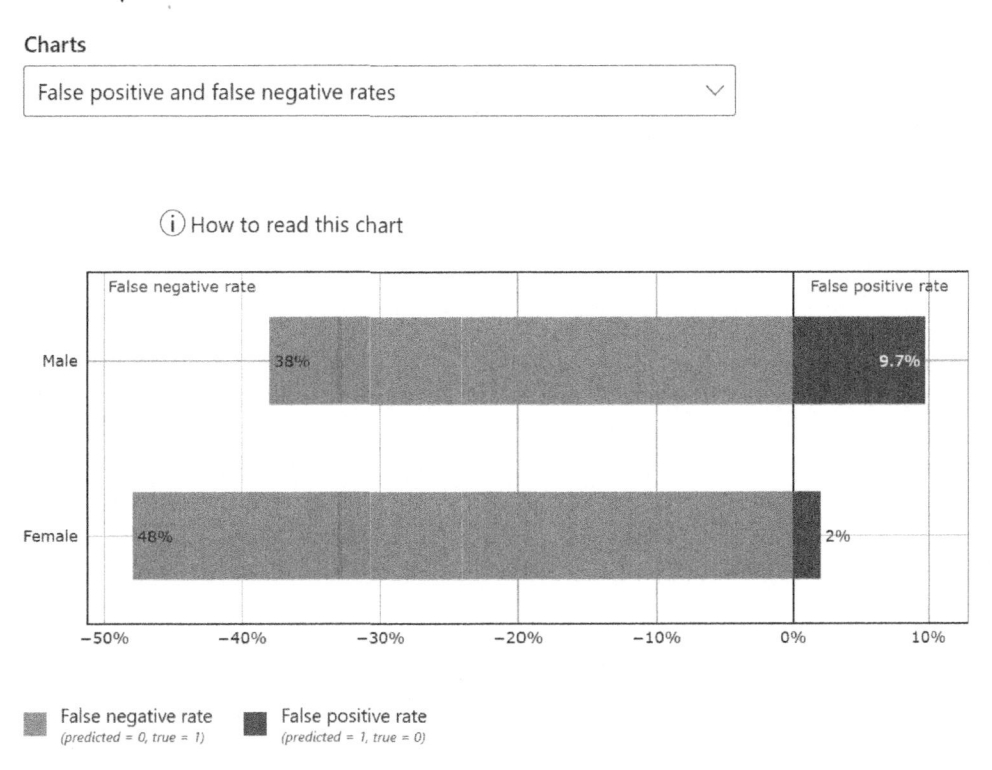

Figure 8.35 – Fairness results – False positive and false negative rates

We can now drill deeper into black-box models and see how the model made decisions, and also analyze the dataset for any bias or errors and ensure fairness.

Summary

By using the Responsible AI Toolbox SDK, we can analyze data for fairness and errors and look deep into decision trees to understand how the model makes decisions. Note that there is work to be done in this field. The SDK is still going through development, and features are being added, so please remember that the functionality will change and new features will be added. At the time of writing, we tested with the LightGBM, XGBoost, and PyTorch algorithms for fairness. The Toolbox allows us to open black-box models and see how decisions are made, and also produce output that is fair and unbiased.

In the next chapter, we will learn how to productionalize ML models.

9
Productionizing Your Workload with MLOps

MLOps is a concept that enables **machine learning** (ML) workloads to scale through the automation of model training, model evaluation, and model deployment. MLOps enables traceability with code, data, and models. MLOps allows data scientists and ML professionals to make predictions available to business users at scale with the **Azure Machine Learning** (**AML**) services.

MLOps is built on the concepts of **CI/CD**. CI/CD is a term that stands for **continuous integration/ continuous delivery** and has been used for software development for decades. CI/CD enables companies to scale their applications and by leveraging those same concepts, we can scale our ML projects, which will rely on CI/CD practices for our MLOps implementation.

One of the challenges of this domain is its complexity. In this chapter, we will go through the scenario of retrieving data, transforming data, building a model, evaluating the model, deploying a model, then pending approval, registering it to a higher environment, and publishing the model as a managed online endpoint, routing traffic to the latest version of the model. This process will leverage Azure DevOps, AML SDK v2, and v2 of the CLI.

In this chapter, we will cover the following topics:

- Understanding the MLOps implementation
- Preparing your MLOps environment
- Running an Azure DevOps pipeline

Technical requirements

To proceed with this chapter, the following are the requirements:

- Two AML workspaces
- An Azure DevOps organization, or the ability to create one

- An Azure DevOps project within an Azure DevOps organization, or the ability to create one
- The ability to assign permissions in the AML-deployed key vaults
- The ability to create Azure DevOps variable groups
- Permission to link an Azure DevOps variable group to Azure key vault
- Two service principals, or permissions to create service principals
- Two service connections, one for each environment, or permissions to create service connections
- The ability to create an Azure DevOps pipeline within an Azure DevOps project
- The ability to create an environment within an Azure DevOps project

Understanding the MLOps implementation

As mentioned, MLOps is a concept, not an implementation. We will provide an implementation of MLOps as the foundation for this chapter. We will establish an Azure DevOps pipeline to orchestrate an AML pipeline for transforming data in the dev environment, create a model leveraging MLflow, and evaluate whether the model is performing better or equal to the existing model. Following this pipeline, if a new model is registered, we will deploy this new model in the dev environment leveraging **blue/green deployments**. Blue/green deployments enable high availability. As a new model is deployed, the existing endpoint deployment is available during the new model deployment. After the new model is deployed to the managed online endpoint, we swap traffic over to the new model. After the model is deployed in the dev environment, we will trigger an approval process to then register and deploy the new model into the qa environment, which will leverage blue/green deployments as well.

Some organizations would choose not to register a model if it was performing just as well as the existing model, especially if the training data had not changed, but this will allow us to see how powerfully AML can handle updating a managed online endpoint. After a solid foundation has been applied, you can update the code to only register a model when it performs better than the existing model, but improving a model is an exercise left to you.

In this chapter, we will leverage an AML pipeline with AML SDK v2, v2 of the CLI, Azure DevOps organizations, and Azure DevOps projects, and take advantage of Azure Key Vault, which has been automatically deployed for you when deploying your environment. You will leverage two AML workspaces. For this chapter, we will refer to them as dev and qa.

Understanding the MLOps implementation

In order to break down the MLOps implementation, the following diagram represents the flow that we will create for your MLOps implementation:

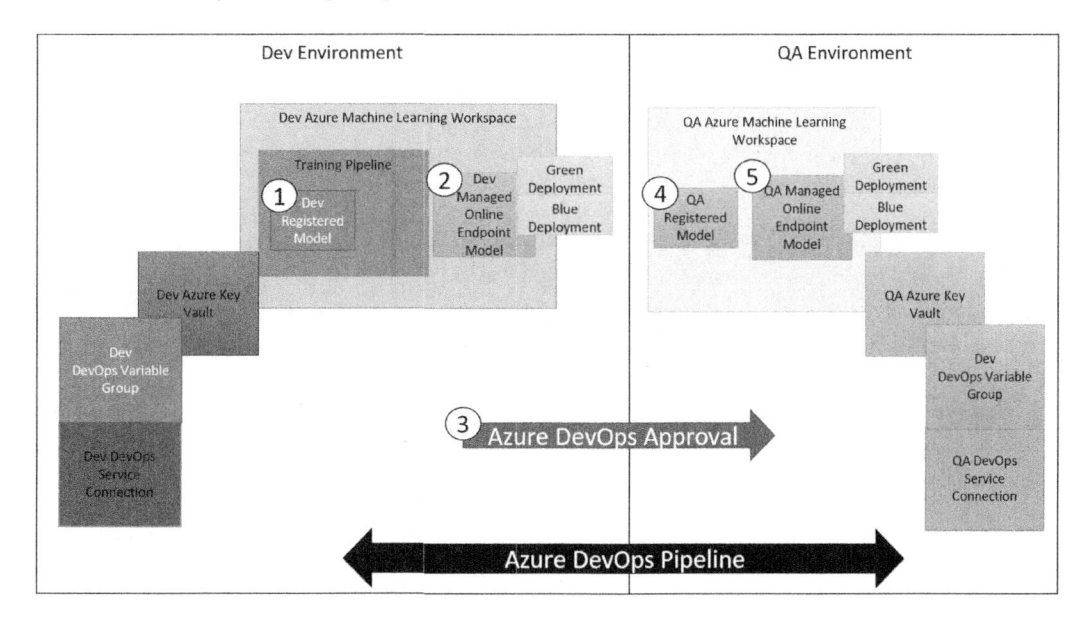

Figure 9.1 – MLOps implementation

In the preceding figure, Azure DevOps is the orchestrator. When code is checked into the **main** branch, Azure DevOps will trigger off the Azure DevOps pipeline.

We will create an Azure DevOps pipeline that consists of two stages. One stage is `dev stage`, and one will be `qa stage`. In `dev stage`, we will leverage the AML CLI to first get the initial model version and place it into a variable in the DevOps pipeline. After retrieving the model version, we will run the AML pipeline that handles the model creation and registration. After running the AML pipeline, we will retrieve the model version again in the Azure DevOps pipeline. If the model version has not changed, we know that no new model has been registered. If the model version has increased, then we know we want to deploy this model in the `dev` environment through Azure DevOps and proceed to deploy this model to the `qa` environment. Given the qa environment is a higher environment, we will include an approval process. The registration and deployment into the `qa` environment must first be approved. Once it is approved, the registration and deployment into the `qa` environment will proceed.

As part of the managed online endpoint, we can deploy a new model to an existing managed online endpoint through blue/green deployments. When a model is first deployed to a managed online endpoint, we set the traffic to 100%. In the case of a new version of a model being deployed, we initially set the traffic to 0 for the new model, wait for it to be successfully deployed, and for the given managed online endpoint, we will then swap the traffic to the latest version of the model to 100% and delete the old model deployment. This ensures the uptime for a given managed online endpoint. Users of the rest endpoint will not be interrupted during the model deployment process once a managed online endpoint is deployed.

To set up our MLOps pipeline we will leverage several key resources. During the MLOps automation pipeline, we will leverage a **service connection** to gain access to the appropriate workspaces. A service connection will leverage an Azure service principal to connect to our AML workspace. We will create a service connection for connecting to the `dev` AML workspace, and one for connecting to the `qa` AML workspace. In addition to the service connections, we will leverage the **key vaults** for each of the environments storing sensitive information. We will link these key vaults using **variable groups** in Azure DevOps. This will keep our Azure DevOps pipelines clean and easy to understand. Refer to *Figure 9.1* for a visual overview of the resources we are going to leverage.

This chapter is an opportunity to leverage your understanding of the functionality implemented so far in this book and put it all into practice. Let us get started looking at the technical requirements for a successful MLOps pipeline implementation leveraging the AML CLI v2 and SDK v2 with Azure DevOps.

Preparing your MLOps environment

In this section, we will go through ensuring that the technical requirements are fulfilled, given you have permission to do so. To prepare your environment, we will be doing the following:

1. Creating a second AML workspace
2. Creating an Azure DevOps Organization and Project
3. Confirming the code in the `dev` AML workspace
4. Moving the code to your Azure DevOps Repo
5. Setting up variables in Azure Key Vault
6. Setting up Azure DevOps environment variable groups
7. Creating an Azure DevOps environment
8. Setting your Azure DevOps service connections
9. Creating an Azure DevOps pipeline
10. Running an Azure DevOps pipeline

Creating a second AML workspace

Up to this point, you have been working in a single AML workspace. With our MLOps pipeline implementation, we will be using two workspaces. For information on deploying a second AML workspace, see *Chapter 1, Introducing the Azure Machine Learning Service*. After you have created a second AML workspace, continue to the next step: *Creating an Azure DevOps organization and project*.

Creating an Azure DevOps organization and project

An Azure DevOps pipeline is held within an **Azure DevOps project**. An Azure DevOps project is held within an **Azure DevOps organization**. You will be required to have an Azure DevOps project to host your code repository that you can write code to and create Azure DevOps pipelines, create service connections, create variable groups, and link to your key vaults. You may already have an Azure DevOps organization set up. Your administrator will have chosen either to have a single project in an Azure DevOps organization that supports many repositories and many Azure DevOps pipelines or to have many projects with one or many repositories in an Azure DevOps organization. If your administrator has already created an Azure DevOps organization, you can either request a new Azure DevOps project within the Azure DevOps organization, or access to an existing Azure DevOps project with a repository to hold your code, and the ability to create Azure DevOps pipelines. If you already have an Azure DevOps organization and project, continue to the next subsection, *Confirming code in the dev AML workspace*.

We will continue with setting up an Azure DevOps organization through the web portal. An Azure DevOps organization will host your project, and a project will hold your source code in a repository, as well as Azure DevOps pipelines for automating your MLOps pipeline.

If you do not have an Azure DevOps organization, please follow the following steps to create one:

1. Sign in to Azure DevOps at `https://dev.azure.com/`.
2. In the left-hand menu, select **New organization** as shown in the following screenshot:

Figure 9.2 – New organization

3. This will bring up a new window for getting started with the process of creating an Azure DevOps organization. Then, click on the **Continue** button.

Preparing your MLOps environment   237

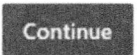

Figure 9.3 – Get started with Azure DevOps

4. This brings you to the next screen for creating your Azure DevOps organization:

Figure 9.4 – Creating your Azure DevOps organization

238   Productionizing Your Workload with MLOps

Azure DevOps organizations are required to be unique, so you need to create yours with a name that has not already been taken. As shown in *Figure 9.4*, populate the following information:

   I. Name your organization. A unique organization is required. In the preceding example, we have opted for `mmxdevops`.

   II. The location at which to host your projects – we have selected **Central US**.

   III. Enter the characters you see on the screen – we have typed `Dp5Ls` for validation.

   IV. Click on the **Continue** button.

5. The next screen will ask you to fill in the **Project name** field for where your code and MLOps pipelines will be held. As shown in *Figure 9.5*, we have selected a **Private** project. If you are working in an organization, you may see an option for an **Enterprise** project. If this option is not available to you, create a **Private** project. Creating a **Public** project will allow public access to your project. A private project will give you the ability to add users that you choose to your project if you would like to share it. Finally, click on the **+ Create project** button.

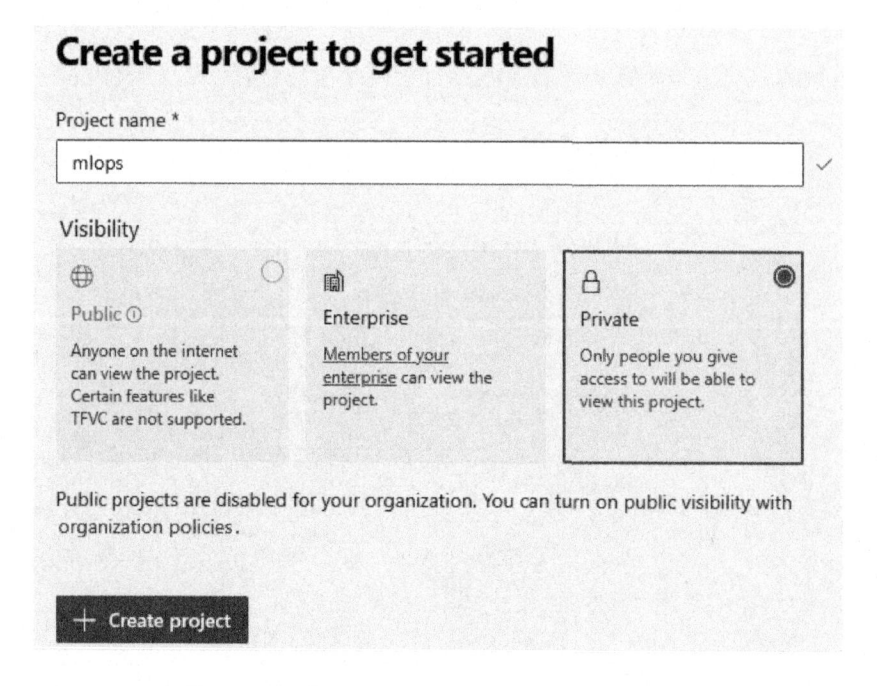

Figure 9.5 – Creating an Azure DevOps organization

6. Now that your project has been created, you will have a place to hold key resources required for MLOps.

   The Azure DevOps project includes the following two key components:

   - **Repos**: A place to store your code
   - **Pipelines**: A place to create your MLOps pipeline automation

   We will leverage these as shown in *Figure 9.6*:

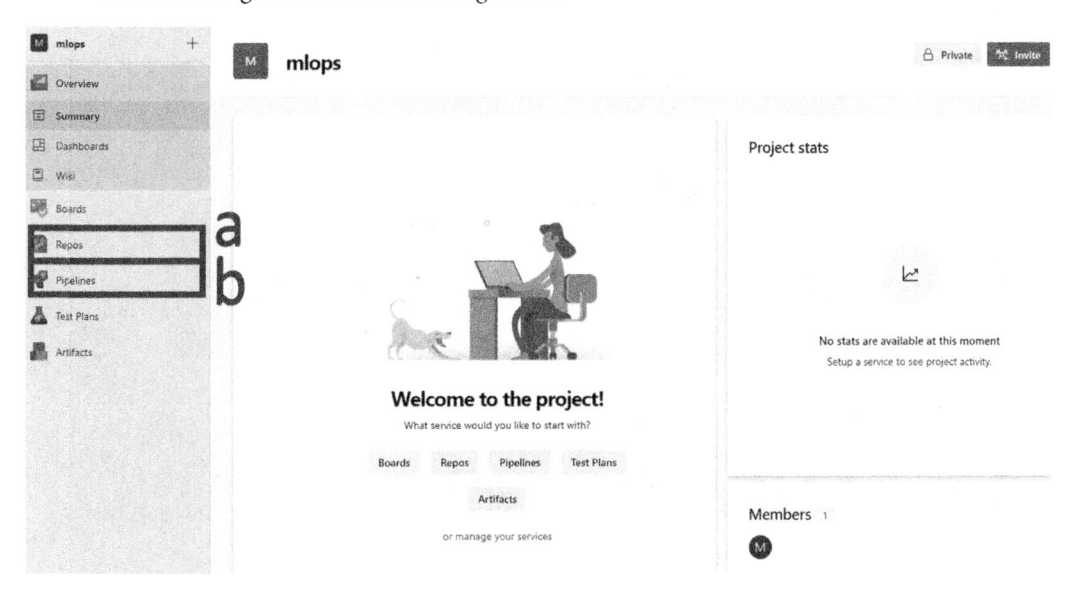

Figure 9.6 – Creating an Azure DevOps organization

We will explore leveraging both **Repos** and **Pipelines** later in the chapter.

Congratulations – you have set up an Azure DevOps organization and project. Now it is time to dig into creating the repository for holding your code.

In *Figure 9.6*, you can see that **Repos** is one of the menu options. Select this to enter the repository section of your Azure DevOps project as shown in *Figure 9.7*:

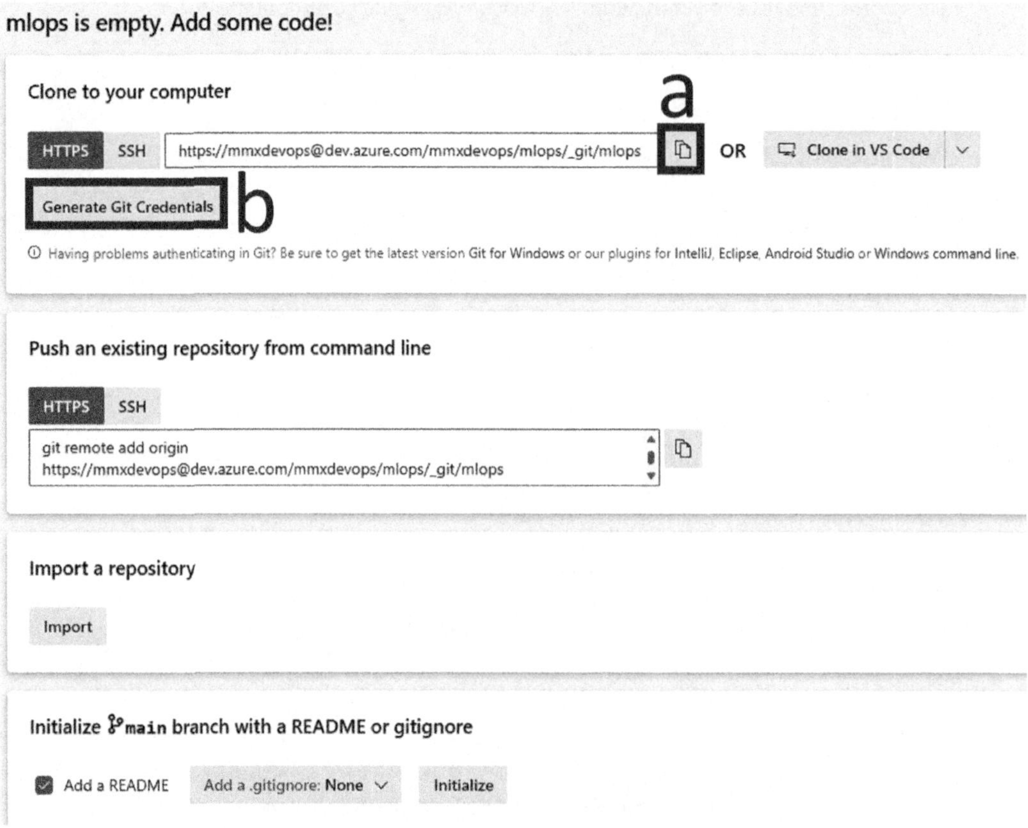

Figure 9.7 – Empty repository

There are three important items that we will copy and save for future use. Selecting the copy button, as shown in *Figure 9.7* marked as **a**, will copy the URL to your Git repository. Selecting the **Generate Git Credentials** button, marked as **b** in the figure, will give you a user and password. We will provide the information to link the code in your AML workspace to your Azure DevOps repository in the AML terminal.

> **Tip**
> At any time, to head to your DevOps Project, you can enter the following URL: `https://dev.azure.com/<organization_name>/<project_name>`.

Now that we have copied the URL, the user, and the password for connecting to your Azure DevOps project, we are ready to review the next requirement for your AML workspace.

Connecting to your AML workspace

In addition to your Azure DevOps organization and project, we will need to connect to your AML workspace to leverage SDK v2 and the AML CLI v2 to implement an MLOps pipeline, as done in previous chapters.

In the previous chapter, we cloned the Git repository. If you have not already done so, continue to follow the steps provided ahead. If you have already cloned the repository, skip ahead to the next section:

1. Open the terminal on your **Compute** instance. Note that the path will include your user in the directory. Type the following into the terminal to clone the sample notebooks into your working directory:

   ```
   git clone https://github.com/PacktPublishing/Azure-Machine-Learning-Engineering.git
   ```

2. Clicking on the refresh icon will update and refresh the notebooks displayed on your screen.
3. Review the notebooks in your `Azure-Machine-Learning-Engineering` directory. This will display the files cloned into your working directory as shown in *Figure 9.8*:

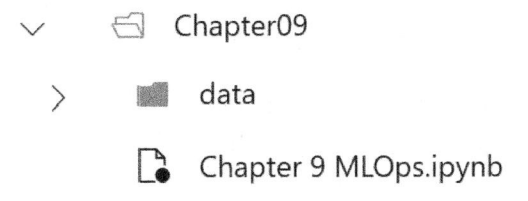

> Chapter09
>> data
>> Chapter 9 MLOps.ipynb

Figure 9.8 – Azure-Machine-Learning-Engineering directory

Now that your code is in your dev AML environment, you are ready to move your code to your Azure DevOps repo. At this point, the code required to build your MLOps pipeline is in your AMLS workspace. In the next subsection, we will move your code from the AML workspace into the DevOps repo in your Azure DevOps project. This connection will simulate the work a data scientist or MLOps engineer would do. Write code in your AML workspace, and commit that code to your Azure DevOps repo.

Moving code to the Azure DevOps repo

We already have your code in our first AML workspace, which is referred to as our dev AML workspace. Now, we will move your code over to our Azure DevOps repo.

Navigate to a terminal session in your dev AML workspace:

1. In your terminal, navigate to your `Azure-Machine-Learning-Engineering` folder as follows:

   ```
   cd Azure-Machine-Learning-Engineering
   ```

2. First, we will need to specify that the directory is safe by typing the following command:

   ```
   git config --global --add safe.directory '*'
   ```

3. We will want to update your origin, which specifies the remote location your code resides in, into a repository in your Azure DevOps project. In the following command, we will replace the URL with that of your Azure DevOps repo. This will be the URL you copied from *Figure 9.7*. The command to do this, in general, is the following:

   ```
   git remote set-url origin https://<organization_name>@dev.azure.com/ <organization_name> /<project_name>/_git/mlops
   ```

4. To review that your origin has been set correctly, you can type the following command in your terminal:

   ```
   git remote -v
   ```

5. To enable your Git user information to be saved, you can set the following:

   ```
   git config --global credential.helper store
   ```

6. Next, we will set the Git user information as follows:

   ```
   git config --global user.email <username_from_azuredevOps>
   git config --global user.name "Firstname Lastname"
   git config --global push.default simple
   ```

7. To push to the origin, which is the repo in your Azure DevOps project, you can type the following command:

   ```
   git status
   git add -A
   git commit -m "updated"
   git push origin main
   ```

8. This will prompt a password, which was provided when you clicked on the credentials for your Azure DevOps project, referred to in *Figure 9.9*.

   After using the preceding command, the code will now be copied from your AML workspace, over to the repo in your Azure DevOps project as shown in the following screenshot:

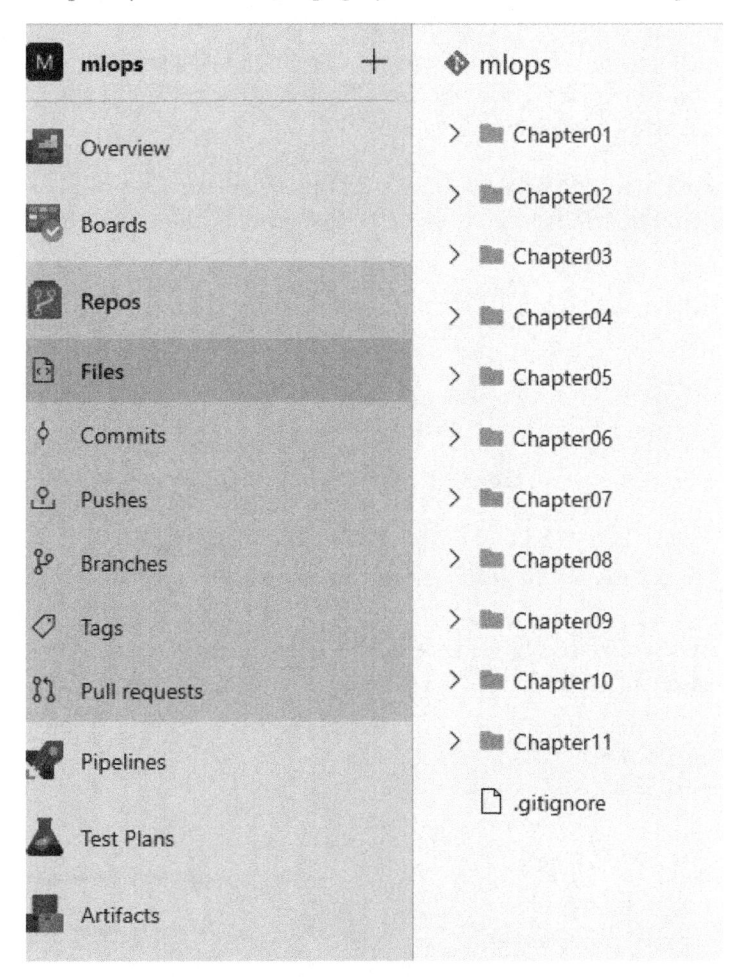

Figure 9.9 – Azure DevOps MLOps project

At this stage, you have successfully moved your code over to your Azure DevOps repository. Changes made to the code on an AML compute resource that are committed to your repository will be reflected and updated in your Azure DevOps repository.

In the next subsection, we will be setting up variables in Azure Key Vault for each of the AML workspace environments.

Setting up variables in Azure Key Vault

When your AML workspace was deployed, Azure Key Vault was also deployed for each of your workspaces. We will leverage each key vault to store sensitive information related to each workspace so Azure DevOps can connect and run the AML pipeline and AML CLI v2 commands on an Azure DevOps build agent. We could have chosen not to leverage the default key vaults deployed with the AML workspace and spun up two separate key vaults for this task, but given the resources are already available, we will choose to continue with leveraging the default deployed key vaults. To set up variables in Azure Key Vault, follow these steps:

1. Head over to the Azure portal by going to `https://portal.azure.com/` and locate your AML workspace. Click on the resource, as shown in the following figure:

Figure 9.10 – AML workspace icon in the Azure portal

2. Clicking on the resource, we can see the overview of the AML workspace includes **Key Vault** information:

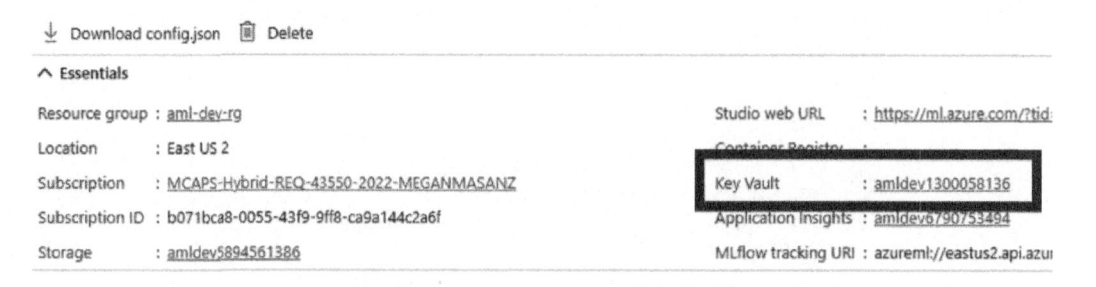

Figure 9.11 – AML workspace overview

Clicking on the **Key Vault** name will bring us directly to the Azure key vault, as shown here:

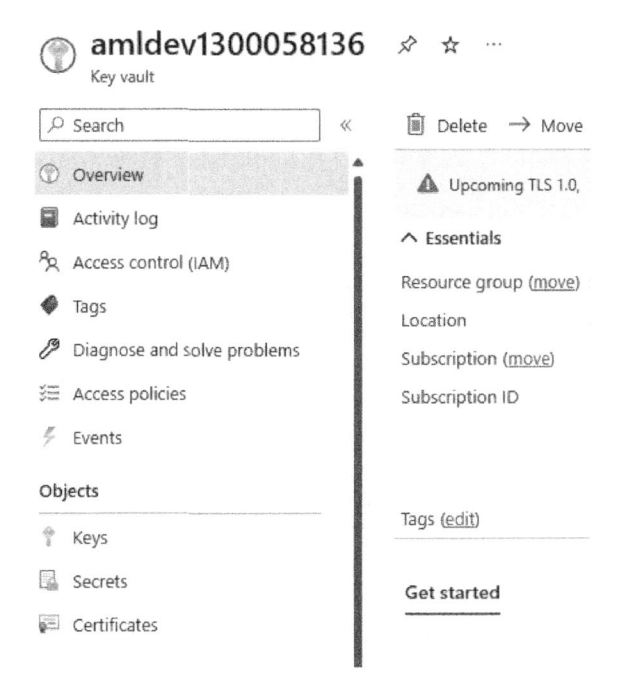

Figure 9.12 – Azure Key Vault overview

3. Currently, you are not authorized to view **Secrets**, so click on the **Access polices** menu on the left as shown in the preceding figure. This will bring up the **Access policies** options as shown here:

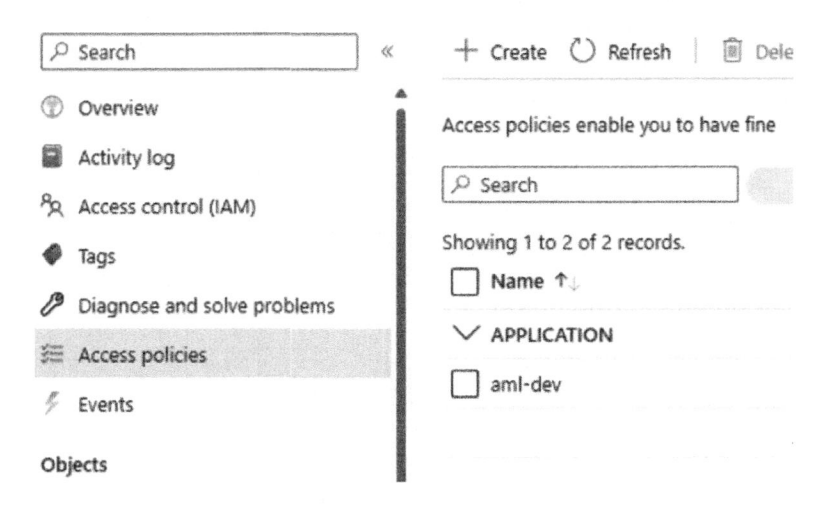

Figure 9.13 – Azure Key Vault access policies

4. Clicking on + **Create** as shown in *Figure 9.14* will present you with options for assigning permissions. Under **Secret permissions**, check **Get**, **List**, **Set**, and **Delete**, and click on **Next**:

Secret permissions

Secret Management Operations

☐ Select all

☑ Get

☑ List

☑ Set

☑ Delete

☐ Recover

☐ Backup

☐ Restore

Figure 9.14 – Setting secret permission options

5. You will then search for yourself either by name or email address to assign yourself the permissions, as shown in the following figure:

Create an access policy
amldev1300058136

✓ Permissions ❷ Principal ③ Application (optional) ④ Review + create

Only 1 principal can be assigned per access policy.
Use the new embedded experience to select a principal. The previous popup experience can be accessed

🔍 Search by object ID, name, or email address

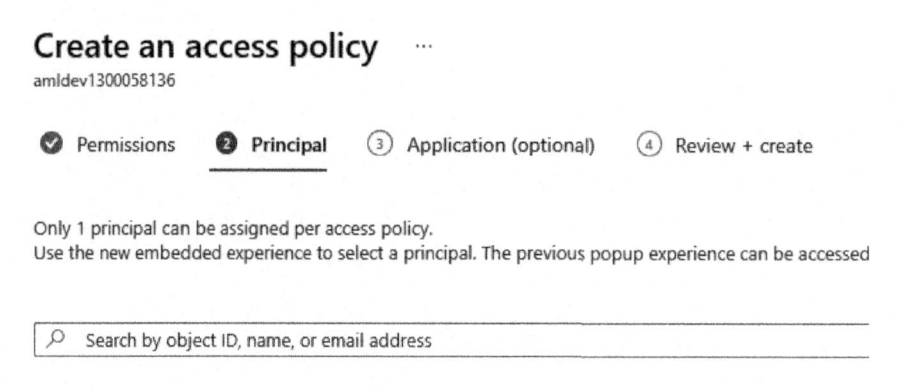

Figure 9.15 – Searching by email to assign Azure Key Vault selected permissions

6. In the text box shown in *Figure 9.16*, type your email address and find yourself to assign access:

Figure 9.16 – Locating your email address

7. After you have found yourself, select your name, and click on the **Next** button.
8. You will then be given the option to select an application – do not select anything in the **Application (optional)** section and click **Next**.

Figure 9.17 – Skipping Application (optional)

9. Finally, click on the **Create** button under the **Review + create** section.

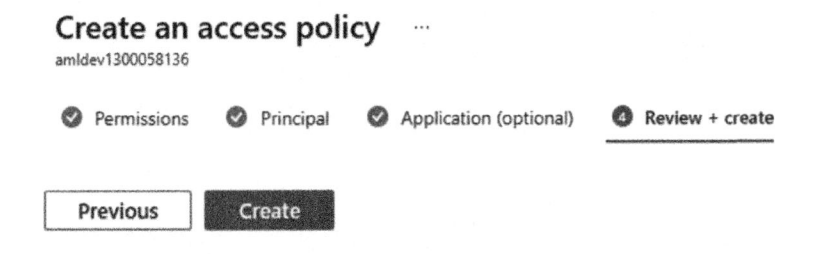

Figure 9.18 – Creating Azure Key Vault permissions

10. Now that you have permission to view and create secrets, head to the **Secrets** option in the left-hand menu:

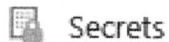

Figure 9.19 – Secrets option in the left-hand menu

11. Click on the + **Generate/Import** button, as shown here:

Figure 9.20 – Generating a new secret

12. This brings up the screen for **Create a secret**, as shown in the following figure:

Figure 9.21 – Create a secret

Populate a secret and click on the **Create** button for each of the values listed in the following table, as they will be leveraged by your Azure DevOps pipeline. The table provided here gives you sample information in the **Value** column. This sample information should be taken from the overview of your AML workspace as shown in *Figure 9.11*, except for the location. Based on where your AML workspace is deployed, the location value can be found here – `https://github.com/microsoft/azure-pipelines-extensions/blob/master/docs/authoring/endpoints/workspace-locations`:

Key Vault variable	Value
`resourceGroup`	`aml-dev-rg`
`wsName`	`aml-dev`
`location`	`eastus`

Figure 9.22 – Azure key vault variables for the dev Azure key vault

Now that you have set up the Azure key vault for your first AML workspace, we will follow the same *steps 1 to 13* to set up the Azure key vault and values for your second AML workspace. This information should be taken from the overview of your second qa AML workspace, as shown in *Figure 9.11*:

Key Vault variable	Value
`resourceGroup`	`aml-qa-rg`
`wsName`	`aml-qa`
`location`	`eastus`

Figure 9.23 – Azure key vault variables for the qa Azure key vault

> **Note**
> In a real scenario, we would typically see either a non-prod and prod environment, or `dev`, `qa`, and `prod`. This code can be extended to support *n* number of environments.

Once you have completed this for both environments, you are ready to move on to the next step – setting up your environment variable groups.

Setting up environment variable groups

Now that your variables are securely in Azure Key Vault, we will set up variable group to hold your settings to be leveraged inside your Azure DevOps pipeline. An variable group is a collection of variables that are leveraged together in an Azure DevOps pipeline task. This means that each task can use variables that specify whether we are going to the `dev` environment with the `dev` service connection or connecting in the `qa` environment, leveraging the `qa` service connection.

We will be creating two variable groups, `devops-variable-group-dev` and `devops-variable-group-qa`, to simulate moving from one environment to another:

1. From the left-hand menu, select the **Pipelines** blue rocket icon, and select the **Library** option as shown:

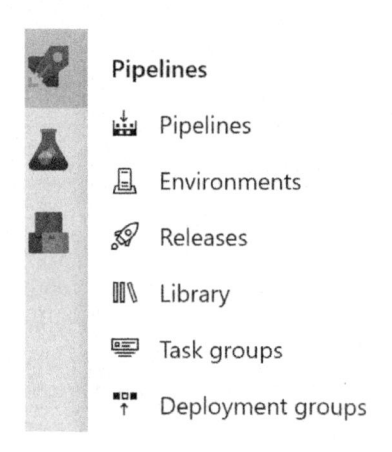

Figure 9.24 – Library option

2. Selecting the **Library** option, you will be prompted to create a new variable group as shown here:

Figure 9.25 – New variable group

3. Clicking on the **+ Variable group** button will allow you to create a variable group. The name of the variable group will be leveraged by the Azure DevOps pipeline, so you will want to name it `devops-variable-group-dev`, and enable the **Link secrets from an Azure key vault as variables** option, as shown in the following screenshot:

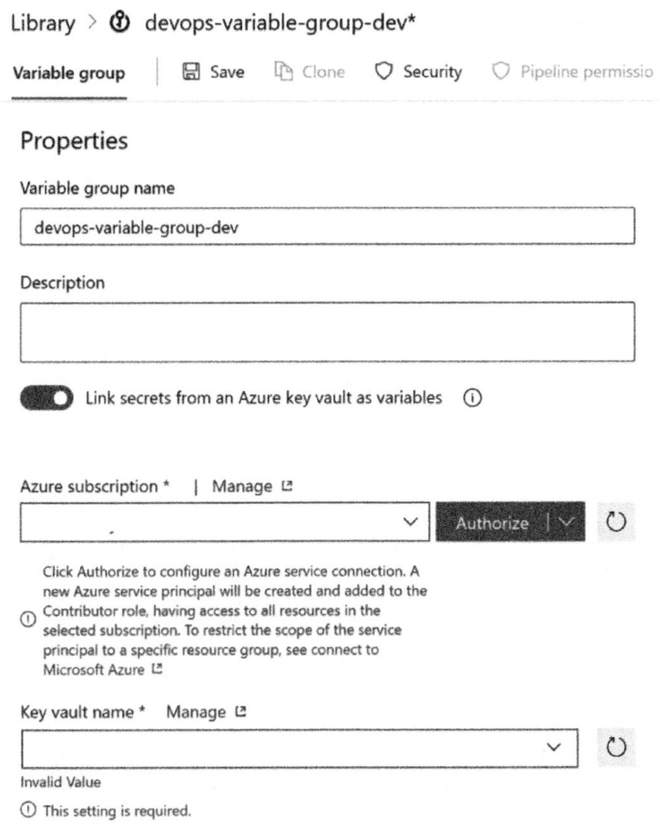

Figure 9.26 – Variable group creation

4. You will need to click on the **Authorize** button for your Azure subscription.

5. When selecting the Azure key vault to link with your variable group, make sure that you link the `dev` key vault with the `devops-variable-group-dev` variable group, and the `qa` key vault with the `devops-variable-group-qa` variable group.

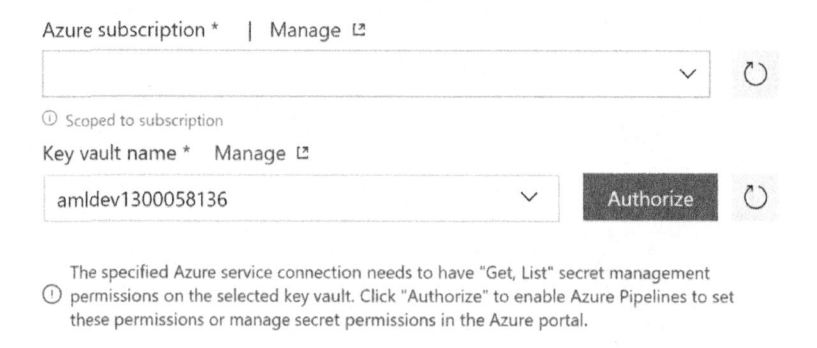

Figure 9.27 – Variable group link to Azure Key Vault

6. After the authorization for the key vault has been completed, click on the + **Add** icon to add the secrets from your key vault into your Azure DevOps variable group shown as follows:

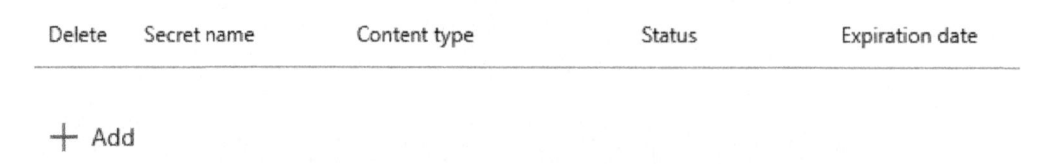

Figure 9.28 – Adding variables to the Azure DevOps variable group

7. Clicking on the + **Add** icon, you will be prompted to select secrets from the Azure key vault you have linked to the variable group, as shown here:

Choose secrets

Choose secrets to be included in this variable group

Sel...	Secret name	Content type	Status	Expiration date
☐	36d9f560-8df6-4966-a429-8adfec61...	application/vnd.ms-Stora₍	Enabled	10/15/2024 9:12:22 PM
☐	36d9f560-8df6-4966-a429-8adfec61...	application/vnd.ms-Stora₍	Enabled	10/15/2024 9:12:22 PM
☐	36d9f560-8df6-4966-a429-8adfec61...	application/vnd.ms-Stora₍	Enabled	10/15/2024 9:12:22 PM
☐	36d9f560-8df6-4966-a429-8adfec61...	application/vnd.ms-Stora₍	Enabled	10/15/2024 9:12:22 PM
☑	location		Enabled	Never
☑	resourceGroup		Enabled	Never
☑	wsName		Enabled	Never

[Ok] [Cancel]

Figure 9.29 – Selecting Azure key vault variables

Select the three variables you populated from *Figure 9.22* and *Figure 9.23*, and click on the **Ok** button. Remember, `devops-variable-group-dev` should be linked to your dev Azure key vault, and `devops-variable-group-qa` should be linked to your qa Azure key vault.

8. Do remember to click on the **Save** icon for each of your variable groups:

Library > 🕐 devops-variable-group-dev*

Variable group | 💾 Save | 📋 Clone | 🛡 Security

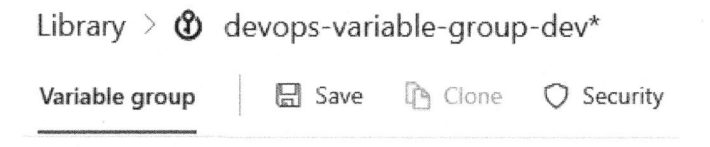

Figure 9.30 – Saving an Azure DevOps variable group

At this point, you should ensure you have linked two variable groups, and each variable group should be linked to the key vault specific to that environment.

9. Clicking on the **Library** icon in the left-hand menu within Azure DevOps will bring up **Variable groups** that you have populated as shown here:

Library

Variable groups Secure files	+ Variable group	○ Security	ⓘ Help
Name			Date modified
fx devops-variable-group-dev			just now
fx devops-variable-group-qa			just now

Figure 9.31 – Azure DevOps variable groups

Congratulations – you have set up two variable groups pointing to two different key vaults, each holding information regarding the specific workspace. Note that this is very extensible. Any variable that holds sensitive information that you would like to pass to your pipeline can leverage a secret in Key Vault stored in a variable group. Azure Key Vault provides you with the flexibility to have unique secure information per AML workspace in your MLOps pipeline.

The next Azure DevOps component we will set up is the environment for providing approval for the model registration and model deployment in the qa AML workspace.

Creating an Azure DevOps environment

In this subsection, we will create an Azure DevOps environment called qa so we can apply governance to the model deployment in the qa environment. An Azure DevOps environment requires approvers. We will be able to reference this environment in our Azure DevOps pipeline as we progress to the qa environment:

1. In the **Pipelines** section in the left-hand pane in your Azure DevOps project, select the **Environments** icon, and select **New environment**.

Preparing your MLOps environment | 255

This will pull up a new popup, as shown in this screenshot:

Figure 9.32 – Azure DevOps environment

2. For the name, type qa, leave Resource set to **None**, and select the **Create** button.
3. On the top-right side of the environment, you will see an **Add resource** button with three dots next to it, shown in the following figure. Click on the three dots:

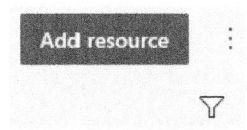

Figure 9.33 – Add resource

4. Clicking on the three dots, go to **Approvals and checks**, as shown in the following screenshot:

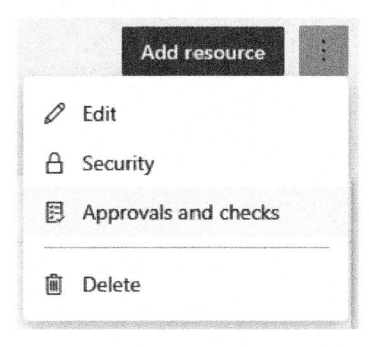

Figure 9.34 – Approvals and checks

5. After clicking on the **Approvals and checks** option, a new screen will be displayed that will allow you to enter your approvers.

   A screen will be displayed, **Add your first check**, as shown here:

   ## Add your first check

   Checks allow you to manage how this resource is used.

   Changes made to checks are effective immediately, applicable to all existing and new pipelines.

   Approvals
   Approvers should grant approval for deployment

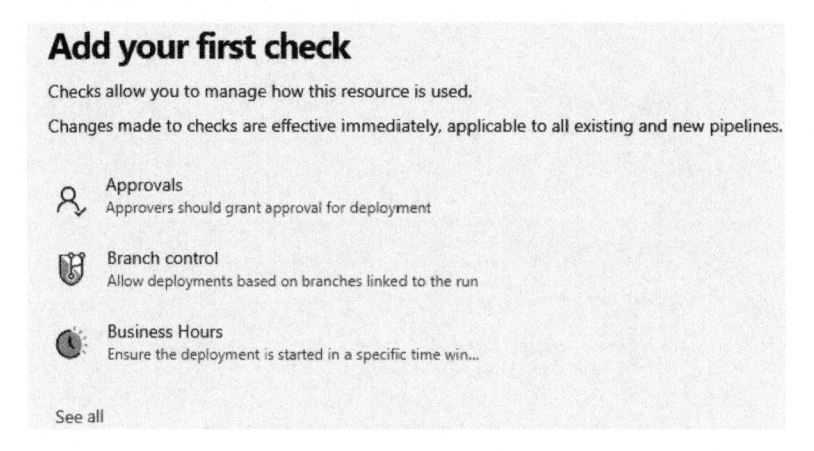

   Branch control
   Allow deployments based on branches linked to the run

   Business Hours
   Ensure the deployment is started in a specific time win...

   See all

   Figure 9.35 – Approvals and checks

6. Select **Approvals**, which will bring up the **Approvals** configuration shown here:

   ## Approvals

   Approvers

   Add users and groups

   Instructions to approvers (optional)

   Advanced

   ☑ Allow approvers to approve their own runs

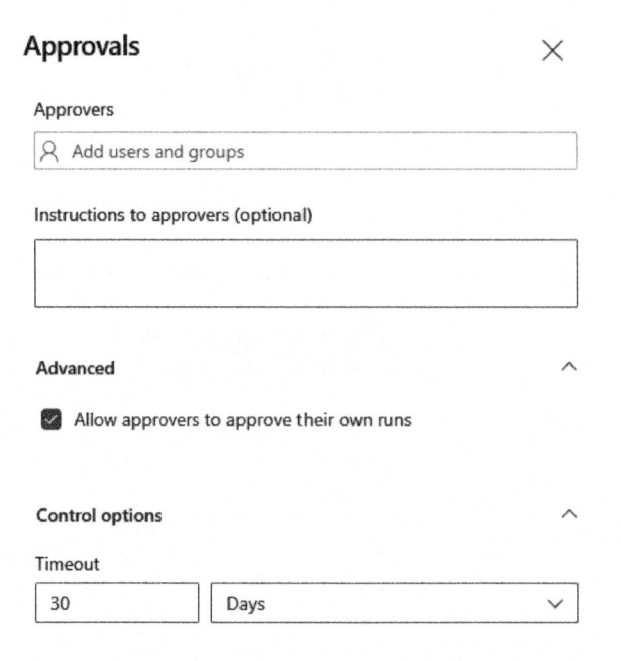

   Control options

   Timeout

   30   Days

   Figure 9.36 – Setting approvers

7. Add yourself to **Approvals**, ensure under that **Advanced**, you have checked **Allow approvers to approve their own runs**, and select **Create**.

Now that you have created your Azure DevOps environment, we are ready to create an Azure DevOps service connection.

Setting your Azure DevOps service connections

An Azure DevOps service connection uses a service principal to connect and gain access to run code on your behalf. The service connection will run your Azure DevOps pipeline as the service principal specified in the service connection. An AML service connection allows you to connect Azure DevOps to your workspace. This means that we will create two service connections, one for each AML workspace.

There is a special kind of service connection that specifies that it is an ML workspace service connection. This extension is not required, so if there is an administrator for your Azure DevOps organization, they can provide you with a service principal and not use this extension, but it is ideal, as it indicates what the service principal will be leveraged for.

We will begin by installing an AML extension for your Azure DevOps organization. To install this into your Azure DevOps environment, perform the following steps:

1. Navigate to `https://marketplace.visualstudio.com/`, and select the **Azure DevOps** tab at the top. In the search box, type `Azure Machine Learning`, as shown in the following screenshot:

Figure 9.37 – Visual Studio Marketplace

2. This will bring up the AML Azure DevOps extension shown as follows:

Figure 9.38 – Azure DevOps ML extension

3. Clicking on the icon shown in *Figure 9.38* will bring up detailed information about the extension.
4. Click on the **Get it free** button to begin the installation process. This will bring you to the next screen where it is verifying that you have permission to install the extension in your Azure DevOps organization, as shown in the following screenshot:

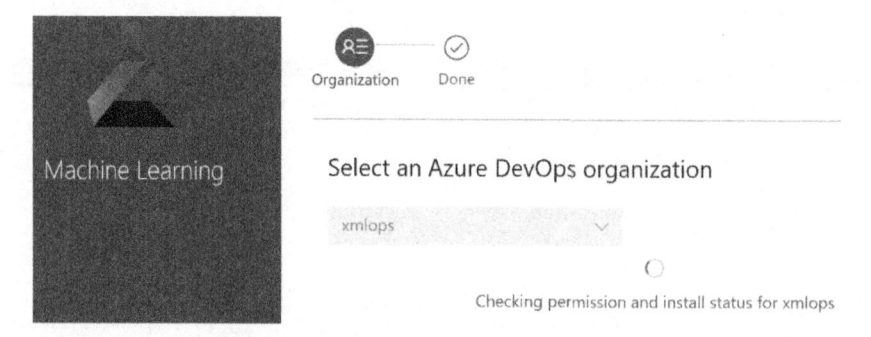

Figure 9.39 – Verifying installation permissions

5. After the permissions have been confirmed, you will be prompted to install for your Azure DevOps organization, as shown here:

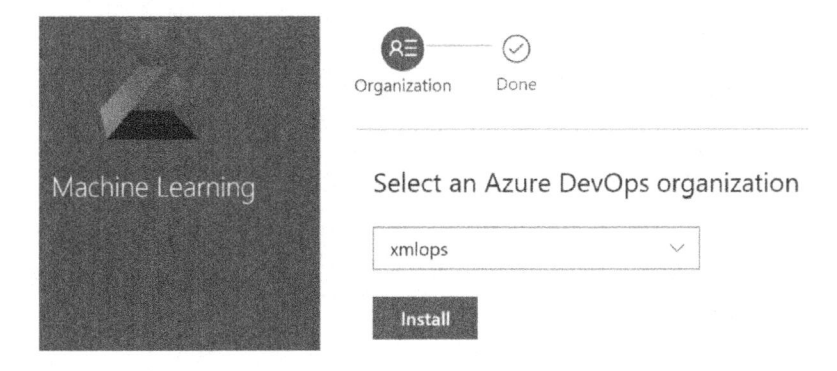

Figure 9.40 – Install option

6. Click on the **Install** button and you will be prompted to head over to your Azure DevOps organization now that the extension has been installed, as shown in the following screenshot:

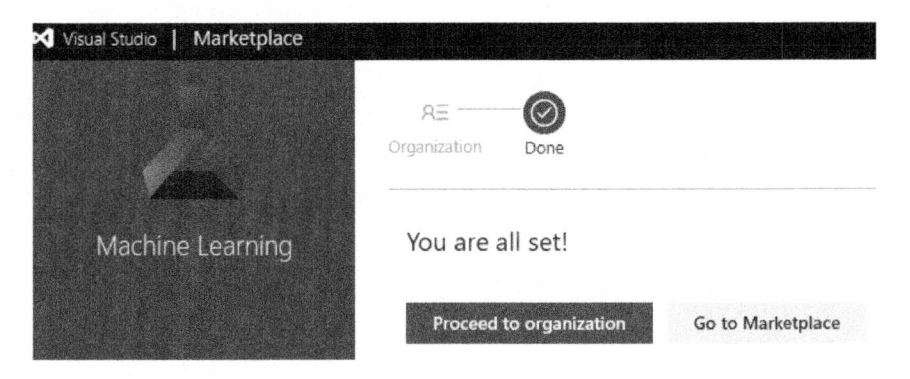

Figure 9.41 – Installation confirmation

7. Click on the **Proceed to organization** button, as shown in the preceding screenshot. This will bring you to your Azure DevOps organization.

8. Then, click on your project inside your Azure DevOps organization as shown in the following screenshot:

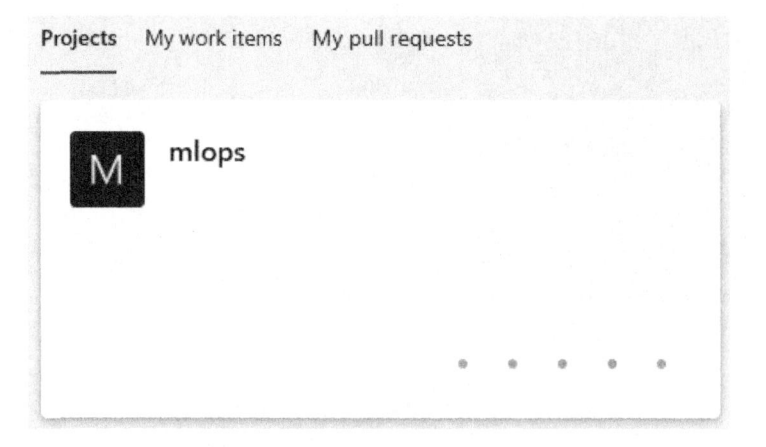

Figure 9.42 – Azure DevOps project

9. Inside your project, in the left-hand menu, you can see **Project settings** in the menu. Click on the **Project settings** icon.
10. Clicking on **Project settings**, you will see **Service Connections** in the menu. Click on the icon for **Service Connections**.
11. Click on the **Create service connection** icon on the top left of your screen; this will bring up the **New service connection** window, as shown in the following screenshot:

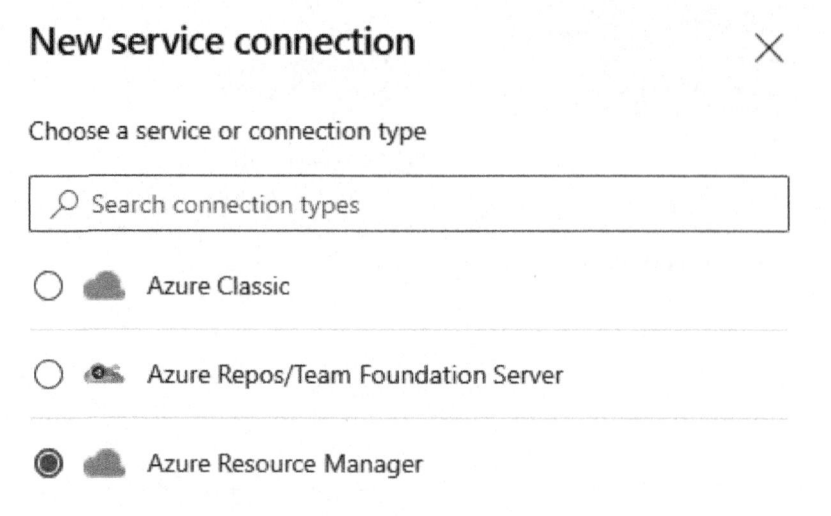

Figure 9.43 – New service connection

12. Click on the **Azure Resource Manager** option here, scroll to the bottom, and click **Next**.

    This will bring up another screen, as follows:

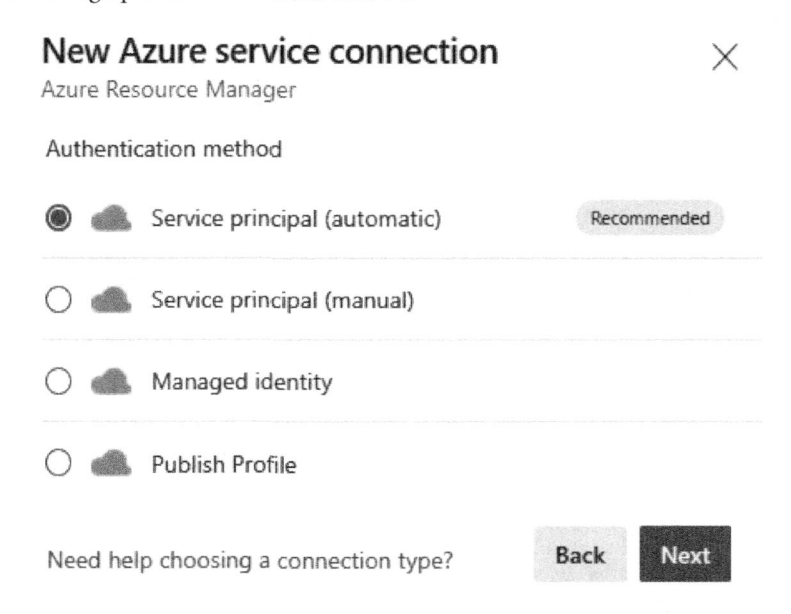

Figure 9.44 – Automatic creation of a service principal

In order to leverage the **Service principal (automatic)** option, you will be required to have the authorization in your Azure subscription to create **Service Principal** instances. If you are working in an environment where this option is not authorized, you will be able to request a service principal from your Azure subscription administrator, and they can provide you with the information required to create a service connection manually. Refer to the following screenshot:

New Azure service connection

Azure Resource Manager using managed identity

Environment

Azure Cloud

Scope Level

○ Subscription
○ Management Group
● Machine Learning Workspace

Subscription Id

Subscription Id from the publish settings file

Subscription Name

Subscription Name from the publish settings file

Resource Group

aml-dev-rg

Resource Group for connecting to the endpoint. Refer to link on how to create a resource group.

ML Workspace Name

aml-dev

Machine Learning Workspace name for connecting to the endpoint. Refer to link on how to create a ML workspace.

ML Workspace Location

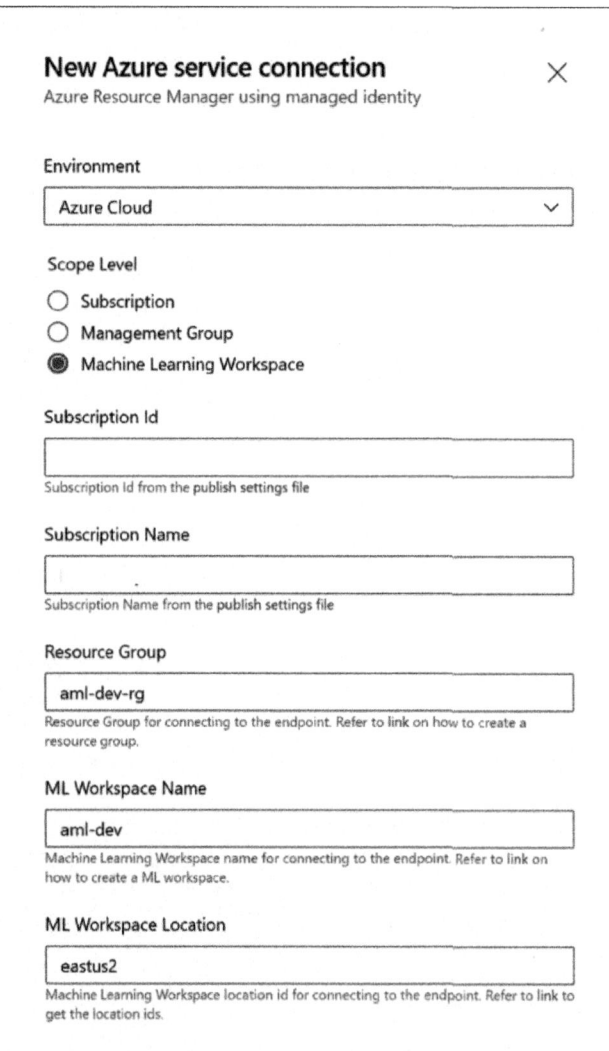

eastus2

Machine Learning Workspace location id for connecting to the endpoint. Refer to link to get the location ids.

Figure 9.45 – Service connection information

13. Populate the information on the screen as shown in *Figure 9.45*. The **Subscription Id**, **Subscription Name**, **Resource Group**, and **ML Workspace Name** information is all available on the AML resource overview screen shown in *Figure 9.11*. **ML Workspace Location** is based on where the resource is deployed. To confirm that you use the right value, a table is available here: https://github.com/microsoft/azure-pipelines-extensions/blob/master/docs/authoring/endpoints/workspace-locations.

Be sure to check **Grant access permission to all pipelines** before hitting **save** on your Azure service connection.

The `.yml` file that defines your Azure DevOps pipeline will expect certain values for the service connection. Create your service connection to the `dev` environment as `aml-dev`, and your service connection to the `qa` environment as `aml-qa`.

Congratulations – you have set up two service connections, one pointing to your `dev` AML workspace, and one pointing to your `qa` AML workspace. We will continue to the next subsection on creating your Azure DevOps pipeline.

Creating an Azure DevOps pipeline

To setup your Azure DevOps pipeline, we are going to generate some code. Recall that your code is in your `dev` AML workspace. In order to walk you through creating the Azure DevOps pipeline, we have created a sample notebook in `Chapter 09`, `Chapter 9 MLOps.ipynb`, shown in the following screenshot.

Inside your `dev` instance of your AML workspace, you will see the notebook as follows:

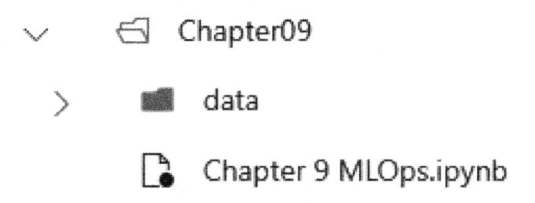

Figure 9.46 – Chapter 9 MLOps notebook

Open the notebook and slowly walk yourself through the code, executing each cell and creating the required files for your MLOps pipeline.

We start with the notebook by connecting to our AML workspace and ensuring our data is ready to be leveraged by our MLOps pipeline. Often, demos include the data that you are going to be leveraging as part of the pipeline, but in a real-world pipeline, your data is going to reside somewhere that is not in your MLOps folder, so we will take the data from the folder and register it if it is not registered already.

We are going to create an AML pipeline, to facilitate that, we create separate folders for each of the steps in the pipeline. We are going to create a step for data preparation, model training, and model evaluation. We will leverage our Azure DevOps pipeline to handle the deployment, but we will create a `.yml` file definition for the AML pipeline, and we also create a folder to hold that pipeline definition, as well as a folder to hold our `conda` environment `.yml` file.

We will create a compute cluster for the AML pipeline to leverage. We could argue that this should have been included in the MLOps pipeline, but this resource will automatically scale up and down as required by our pipelines, so we left this resource outside of the Azure DevOps pipeline – however, you certainly can take this pipeline and extend it to include this functionality.

After creating the conda.yml file to handle the environment, and a script for each step in the AML pipeline, we stitch the code together in an AML pipeline job, which was covered in *Chapter 7, Deploying ML Models for Batch Scoring*.

Here's the script for creating the environment for the pipeline to leverage:

```
%%writefile ./src/conda-yamls/pipeline_conda_env.yml
name: job_env
dependencies:
- python=3.10
- scikit-learn=1.1.3
- ipykernel
- matplotlib
- pandas
- pip
- pip:
  - azureml-defaults==1.48.0 #needed for the inferece schema
  - mlflow<=1.30.0
  - azure-ai-ml==1.1.2
  - mltable==1.0.0
  - azureml-mlflow==1.48.0
```

Figure 9.47 – conda .yml file for the environment information

Review each step in the pipeline and the code in the notebook of this chapter, as it creates an AML job pipeline to create a model and register the model.

Note that the first step will expect the raw data parameter that will tell the code where to find the titanic.csv file. In addition to the source location, the pipeline definition indicates where the data will be stored. This script is quite helpful in providing a generic solution for your pipeline to leverage data. Each step within the AML pipeline has a set of defined input and output parameters that are captured within the pipeline definition .yml file, aml_train_and_eval_pipeline.yml, which the notebook generates in the pipeline directory under src in the chapter folder directory. Reviewing this code, you can see how the inputs and outputs in the script are specified in the pipe definition:

```
 1  %%writefile ./src/pipeline/aml_train_and_eval_pipeline.yml
 2
 3  $schema: https://azuremlschemas.azureedge.net/latest/pipelineJob.schema.json
 4  type: pipeline
 5  display_name: Training_and_eval_pipeline
 6  compute: azureml:cpu-cluster
 7
 8
 9  jobs:
10    prep_job:
11      type: command
12      code: ../prep
13      command: >-
14        python prep.py
15        --raw_data ${{inputs.raw_data}}
16        --prep_data ${{outputs.prep_data}}
17      inputs:
18        raw_data:
19          type: uri_file
20          path: azureml:titanic_raw:1
21          mode: ro_mount
22      outputs:
23        prep_data:
24          type: uri_file
25          path: azureml://datastores/workspaceblobstore/paths/titanic_prep_data/titanic_prepped.csv
26          mode: rw_mount
27      environment:
28        conda_file: ../conda-yamls/pipeline_conda_env.yml
29        image: mcr.microsoft.com/azureml/openmpi3.1.2-ubuntu18.04:latest
```

Figure 9.48 – AML pipeline definition

> **Note**
> Pipeline job definitions include great flexibility. The schema for defining a job can be reviewed here: https://azuremlschemas.azureedge.net/latest/commandJob.schema.json.

In the pipeline definition here, we have specified the type for the prep job as `command` as per the schema definition. We have specified where the code can be found for the step. For the command itself, we specify to run Python and provide the file and the parameters that will be passed to the Python script from our defined inputs and outputs. We can see that the input was defined as `ro_mount`, or a read-only mount to the specified file, and the output was defined as `rw_mount`, or a read-write mount with a specified file location. In addition, the environment was specified as the `conda .yml` file generated, and an Ubuntu image is also specified.

This initial `prep_job` combined with a `train_job` and an `eval_job` make up the AML pipeline.

Now that we have reviewed the AML pipeline, we will look at the files required for the model deployment in both the `dev` and `qa` environments.

> **Note**
> Managed online endpoint names must be unique in each Azure region.

In addition to the AML pipeline definition, the notebook also generates files for handling the managed online endpoint deployment. When running the notebook, be sure to update the name value for `create-endpoint.yml` and the name value for `create-endpoint-dev.yml`; in `model_deployment.yml`, provide the `endpoint_name` value as the one you specified in `create-endpoint.yml`; and in `model_deployment-dev.yml`, provide the `endpoint_name` value you specified in the `create-endpoint-dev.yml` file.

Here is a screenshot of the `create-endpoint-dev.yml` file:

```
1  %%writefile ./src/deploy/create-endpoint-dev.yml
2  $schema: https://azuremlschemas.azureedge.net/latest/managedOnlineEndpoint.schema.json
3  name: xmmchapter9titanicendpointdev
4  auth_mode: key
```

Figure 9.49 – dev AML workspace managed online endpoint .yml file

This file shown here provides the name and authorization mode that your managed online endpoint will leverage during deployment in the `dev` environment. Be sure to update **line 3**, as the name must be unique in the Azure region into which the AML workspace is deployed.

The following is a screenshot of the `model_deployment-dev.yml` file used for the deployment to the managed online endpoint. The `endpoint_name` value here should match the name specified for the managed online endpoint:

```
1  %%writefile ./src/deploy/model_deployment-dev.yml
2  $schema: https://azuremlschemas.azureedge.net/latest/managedOnlineDeployment.schema.json
3  name: green
4  endpoint_name: xmmchapter9titanicendpointdev
5  model: azureml:mmchapter9titanic@latest
6  instance_type: Standard_DS2_v2
7  instance_count: 1
```

Figure 9.50 – dev AML workspace deployment to the managed online endpoint yml file

Just as the names should match for the managed online deployment in the `dev` environment, they also need to match up in the `qa` environment.

Here is a screenshot of the `create-endpoint.yml` file. This is the file used to create the managed online endpoint deployment in the qa AML workspace:

```
1  %%writefile ./src/deploy/create-endpoint.yml
2  $schema: https://azuremlschemas.azureedge.net/latest/managedOnlineEndpoint.schema.json
3  name: xmmchapter9titanicendpoint
4  auth_mode: key
```

Figure 9.51 – qa AML workspace Managed Online Endpoint .yml file

As shown in the figure here, **line 3** includes the name of the endpoint, which must be unique in a given Azure region. Be sure to select a unique name for your endpoints in the qa environment and the dev environment.

Here is a screenshot of the `model_deployment.yml` file:

```
1  %%writefile ./src/deploy/model_deployment.yml
2  $schema: https://azuremlschemas.azureedge.net/latest/managedOnlineDeployment.schema.json
3  name: green
4  endpoint_name: xmmchapter9titanicendpoint
5  model: azureml:mmchapter9titanic@latest
6  instance_type: Standard_DS2_v2
7  instance_count: 1
```

Figure 9.52 – qa AML workspace deployment to managed online endpoint yml file

As shown in the figure here, this file will be leveraged for online deployment in the qa environment, and it will go to endpoint_name to create a deployment, so be sure to update **line 4** in this file to match up with **line 3** in the `create-endpoint.yml` file.

These files are leveraged within the Azure DevOps pipeline definition, which we will discuss next.

The following is a snippet of the `AzureDevOpsPipeline.yml` file that orchestrates the MLOps pipeline:

```yaml
%%writefile ./src/AzureDevOpsPipeline.yml

resources:
  containers:
  - container: mlops
    image: mcr.microsoft.com/mlops/python:latest

pr: none
trigger:
  branches:
    include:
    - main

variables:
- group: devops-variable-group-dev
- group: devops-variable-group-qa
- name: model_name
  value: mmchapter9titanic

- name: ENDPT_NAME
  value: xmmchapter9titanicendpoint

- name: DEV_ENDPT_NAME
  value: xmmchapter9titanicendpointdev


pool:
  vmImage: ubuntu-latest

stages:
- stage: 'DevRunPipline'
```

Figure 9.53 – Azure DevOpsPipeline.yml file definition

The `AzureDevOpsPipeline.yml` file starts by specifying the image that an Azure DevOps build agent will leverage. The pipeline will trigger when there is a code change to `main`. The pipeline is leveraging both `devops-variable-group-dev` and `devops-variable-group-qa`, which we set up earlier.

In this `.yml` file, be sure to update the value for `ENDPT_NAME` to be the value you specified in `create-endpoint.yml` and `endpoint_name` in your `model_deployment.yml` files.

Be sure to also update `DEV_ENDPT_NAME` to be the value for the `name` variable you specified in your `create-endpoint-dev.yml` file and the `endpoint_name` `model_deployment-dev.yml` file.

The code here shows that in the `AzureDevOpsPipeline.yml` file, the values that will need to be replaced for your MLOps deployment:

```
variables:
- group: devops-variable-group-dev
- group: devops-variable-group-qa
- name: model_name
  value: mmchapter9titanic

- name: ENDPT_NAME
  value: xmmchapter9titanicendpoint

- name: DEV_ENDPT_NAME
  value: xmmchapter9titanicendpointdev
```

Figure 9.54 – Azure DevOps pipeline variable replacement

The DevOps pipeline is broken into two stages – one stage for the `dev` environment pipeline run and model deployment in the `dev` environment, and the second stage for the model promotion and deployment into the `qa` environment.

Inside the Azure DevOps stages, we leverage a set of jobs, which are CLI tasks that leverage v2 of the AML CLI for retrieving the initial model version in the `dev` environment, running the AML pipeline, and then retrieving the final model version. This final model version indicates whether a model should be registered in the `qa` environment:

```
az ml model list -w $(wsName) -g $(resourceGroup) -n $(model_
name) --query "[0].version" -o tsv
```

The preceding code is retrieved from the first stage and the first step within your Azure DevOps pipeline. Running this with Azure DevOps, we will retrieve the latest version of the model with the model name specified by the variable that is defined in your Azure DevOps pipeline as shown in the figure here. As you can see in the code, not only do we leverage the variable groups but we can also leverage variables defined directly in an Azure DevOps pipeline, as is the case with the `model_name` variable. Given this value does not change on the basis of the environment, we have added it to the pipeline definition itself, but we could have included it in the key vaults and retrieved it through our Azure DevOps variable groups as well.

The command run in Azure DevOps is modified slightly when placed into the Azure DevOps pipeline yml file, shown as follows:

```
if [[ -z "$(az ml model list -w $(wsName) -g $(resourceGroup)  -n $(model_name) --query '[0].version' -o tsv)" ]]; then
    echo "no model was found, set value to 0"
    echo "##vso[task.setvariable variable=modelversion;isOutput=true]0"
    echo "model does not yet exist in this environment, set the value of the model version to 0"
    exit 0
else
    echo "model was found"
    echo "##vso[task.setvariable variable=modelversion;isOutput=true]$(az ml model list -w $(wsName) -g $(resourceGroup)
    exit 0
fi
```

Figure 9.55 – Checking whether the model exists

Inside our Azure CLI task in the Azure DevOps pipeline, we are checking whether the result of querying for the model in the workspace comes back as an empty string, and then we set the `modelversion` variable to 0; otherwise, we retrieve it and set the `modeldeversion` variable in the Azure DevOps pipeline.

This will place the model version into an Azure DevOps variable that can be evaluated later in the pipeline, by running the following command:

```
echo 'initial model version'$(setversion.modelversion)
```

After setting the initial model version, we run the AML workspace pipeline from the Azure DevOps pipeline by leveraging the following code:

```
az ml job create --file 'Chapter09/src/pipeline/aml_train_and_
eval_pipeline.yml' --stream --set settings.force_rerun=True
```

Note that we set `force_rerun` to `True` here. AML knows the data has not changed, and if the code has not changed, then it reuses steps instead of rerunning them, which is great in a production workload. However, in a demo for updating a model, we would like to see the model version consistently updating, so we have set that value to `True`.

In the first stage, we check whether the final model version and the initial model version are equal or not. The code here depicts checking the model version and setting an output variable, `runme`, to either `true` or `false`:

```
echo 'initial model version '$(setversion.modelversion)
echo 'final model version   '$(setfinalversion.finalmodelversion)
if [[ $(setversion.modelversion) == $(setfinalversion.finalmodelversion) ]]; then
    echo "##vso[task.setvariable variable=runme;isOutput=true]false"
    exit 0
else
    echo "deploy updated model"
    echo "##vso[task.setvariable variable=runme;isOutput=true]true"
    az ml model download  -w $(wsName) -g $(resourceGroup) -n $(model_name) -v $(setfinalversion.finalmodelversion)
fi
```

Figure 9.56 – Checking the model version

If they are different, then we would like to deploy the new model in the dev environment, and we deploy the model with the AML CLI command:

```
az ml online-endpoint create --file 'Chapter09/src/deploy/
create-endpoint-dev.yml' -g $(resourceGroup) -w $(wsName) -n
$(DEV_ENDPT_NAME)
```

In the code here, we reference the endpoint .yml file, the resource group, the workspace name, and the endpoint name. After the endpoint is created, we can create an online deployment, as shown here:

```
az ml online-deployment create --name $NEW_DEPLOYMENT_
NAME -f 'Chapter09/src/deploy/model_deployment-dev.yml' -g
$(resourceGroup) -w $(wsName)
```

Finally, we can update the traffic to the endpoint to be 100% by leveraging the following command:

```
az ml online-endpoint update -n $DEV_ENDPT_NAME --set tags.
prod=$NEW_DEPLOYMENT_NAME  --traffic "$NEW_DEPLOYMENT_NAME=100"
-g $(resourceGroup) -w $(wsName)
```

Note that we are tagging the endpoint with the deployment. By tagging the endpoint, we can quickly see which deployment is being used by our endpoint. This means the next time a new model is registered, we can create a new deployment to an existing managed online endpoint, ramp up its traffic, and then delete the old deployment.

In the Azure DevOps pipeline, before handling the deployment, we check whether an endpoint already exists with our specified name by leveraging this command:

```
ENDPOINT_EXISTS=$(az ml online-endpoint list -g
$(resourceGroup) -w $(wsName) -o tsv --query "[?name=='$DEV_
ENDPT_NAME'][name]" |  wc -l)
```

Therefore, the second time, the endpoint will exist, and we will not create an endpoint, but we will still deploy an endpoint.

The second stage in the pipeline is the QAPromoteModel pipeline. It connects to the dev AML workspace and retrieves the model, downloads it, and then uses it in the qa environment. Once the model is downloaded onto the Azure DevOps build agent, we can register that in the qa AML workspace:

```
az ml model create --name $(model_name) -v
$(vardevModelVersion) --path ./$(model_name)/$(model_name)
--type mlflow_model -g $(resourceGroup) -w $(wsName)
```

Once the model is registered in the qa environment, we can check whether a managed online endpoint exists in the qa environment. If it has not yet been deployed, an online endpoint will be created leveraging the create-endpoint.yml file through the use of the AML CLI v2 as shown in the following code:

```
az ml online-endpoint create --file '$(Pipeline.Workspace)/
drop/Chapter09/src/deploy/create-endpoint.yml' -g
$(resourceGroup) -w $(wsName)
```

If this managed online endpoint does exist, then we will then use az ml online-deployment to create a deployment in the managed online endpoint to leverage the model. After it is deployed, we can set the traffic on the managed online endpoint deployment to 100% traffic for our new deployment.

If the model has already been deployed in this environment, there is no need to deploy the managed online endpoint, but we will want to swap from the previous deployment to our new deployment. This means we should create a new online deployment, and update a tag on the managed online endpoint that specifies which deployment is being used. This allows us to consistently create new deployments and swap from the previous online deployment to our next deployment, updating the traffic and then deleting the old deployment in the qa environment, as was done in the dev environment.

Once you run your pipelines, you will be able to see the tag information for your managed online endpoint in the dev or qa environment from its details as shown in this figure.

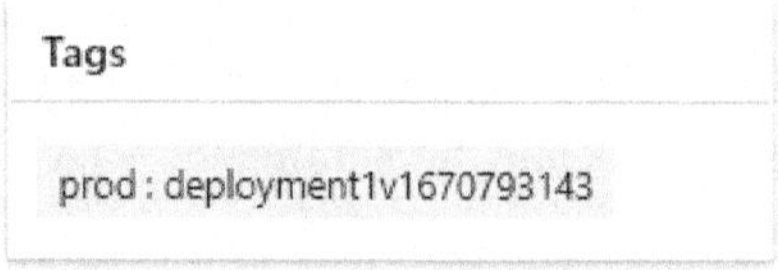

Tags

prod : deployment1v1670793143

Figure 9.57 – Managed online endpoint tag

Each time this code runs, a new deployment name is generated, leveraging the epoch of the deployment time. This ensures that we have a unique name for a given deployment. Having this unique name ensures no conflicts will occur when deploying your online deployment. After the online deployment succeeds, we update the traffic to the latest online deployment, and then delete the old online deployment. This figure shows a deployment to a managed online endpoint:

Traffic allocation
● deployment1v1670793143 (100%)

Deployment deployment1v1670793143

Name
deployment1v1670793143

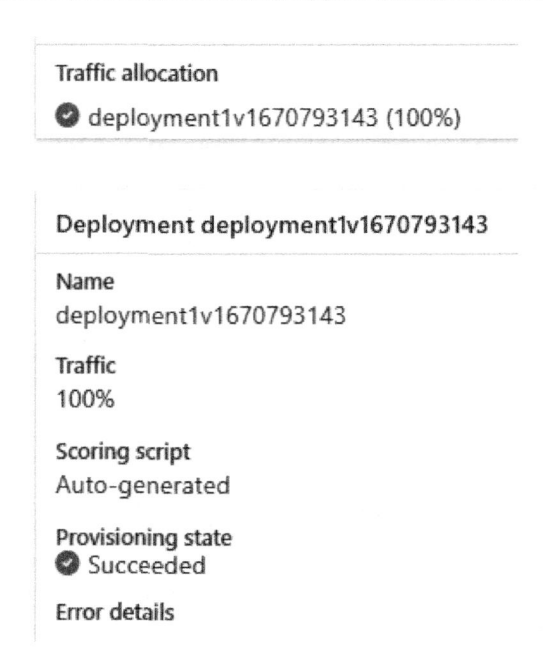

Traffic
100%

Scoring script
Auto-generated

Provisioning state
● Succeeded

Error details

Figure 9.58 – Deployment to a managed online endpoint

Note that in the figure, in the name after deployment, we include the model version number before **v** to quickly identify the model version for a given deployment.

Now that you have reviewed the code and executed the notebook, generating the files needed for the Azure DevOps pipeline, a check-in of your code to the remote origin now pointing to your Azure DevOps repository will ensure the proper files are in place to create your Azure DevOps pipeline, which is our next step in the process. To check this code in, you can run the following commands:

```
git status
git add -A
git commit -m "updated"
git push origin main
```

Congratulations – your Azure DevOps environment is now linked with your AML workspaces. You have made it through the required steps for preparing your MLOps environment. You created an Azure DevOps organization and project. You moved your code into Azure DevOps, set up your Azure key vault, and linked it to your Azure DevOps variable groups. You also created an Azure DevOps environment to handle the approval process. You created your Azure DevOps service connections and, finally, committed the code required to create and run an Azure DevOps pipeline. In the next section, you will set up your Azure DevOps pipeline, which will trigger running an Azure DevOps pipeline.

Running an Azure DevOps pipeline

We will start this section by creating an Azure DevOps pipeline. Your Azure DevOps pipeline will be kicked off any time you make a change to your code and push it to the **main** branch:

1. Inside Azure DevOps on the left-hand pane, select **Pipelines** and you will see the following screen:

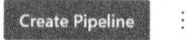

Figure 9.59 – Creating your first Azure DevOps Pipeline

2. Click on the **Create Pipeline** button to begin the process, which will bring up the following window:

Figure 9.60 – Selecting where your code is located

3. In the previous section, *Preparing your MLOps environment*, you placed your code into a code repository in Azure DevOps. Select the **Azure Repos Git** option from the preceding screenshot and this will ask you to select your repository, as shown in the following screenshot. Select your **mlops** repository here.

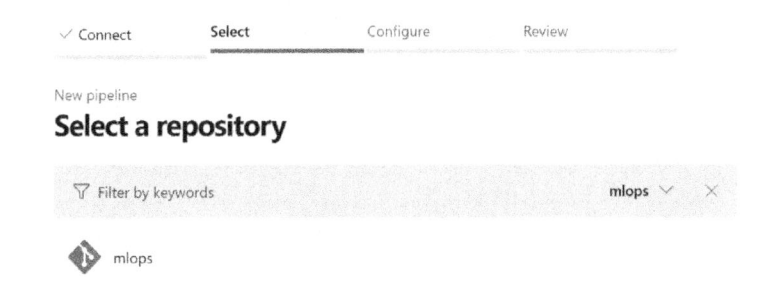

Figure 9.61 – Selecting your repository

4. Next, select the **Existing Azure Pipelines YAML file** option to use the pipeline you created by running your notebook and checking it into your Git repository:

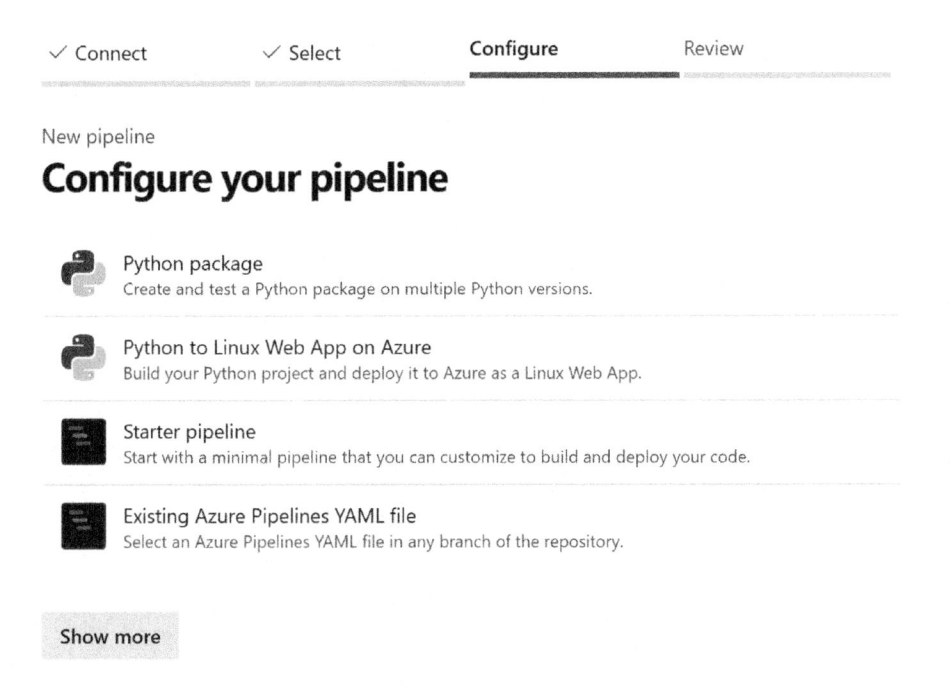

Figure 9.62 – Configure your pipeline

5. Selecting this will take you to the next screen, as shown here:

Select an existing YAML file

Select an Azure Pipelines YAML file in any branch of the repository.

Branch

> main

Path

Select a file from the dropdown or type in the path to your file

mlops

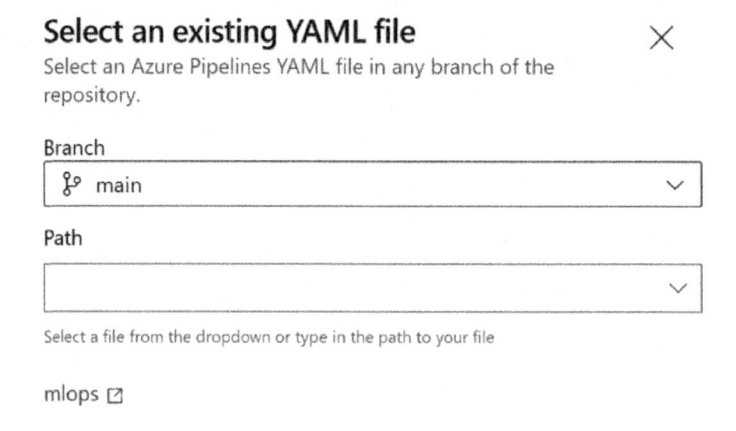

Figure 9.63 – Selecting your YAML file

6. In the **Path** dropdown, navigate to the **/Chapter09/src/AzureDevOpsPipeline.yml** file as shown here:

Select an existing YAML file

Select an Azure Pipelines YAML file in any branch of the repository.

Branch

> main

Path

/Chapter09/src/AzureDevOpsPipeline.yml

Select a file from the dropdown or type in the path to your file

mlops

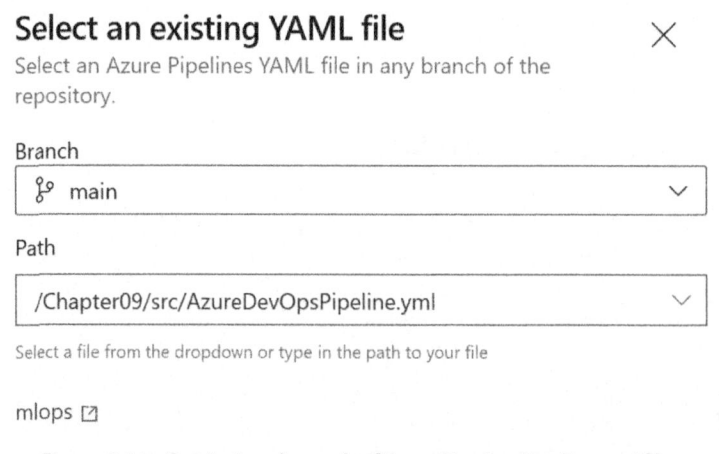

Figure 9.64 – Retrieving the path of AzureDevOpsPipeline.yml file

7. Click on the **Continue** option after selecting the **AzureDevOpsPipeline.yml** file. This will bring up the source code for the Azure DevOps pipeline, as follows:

Running an Azure DevOps pipeline 277

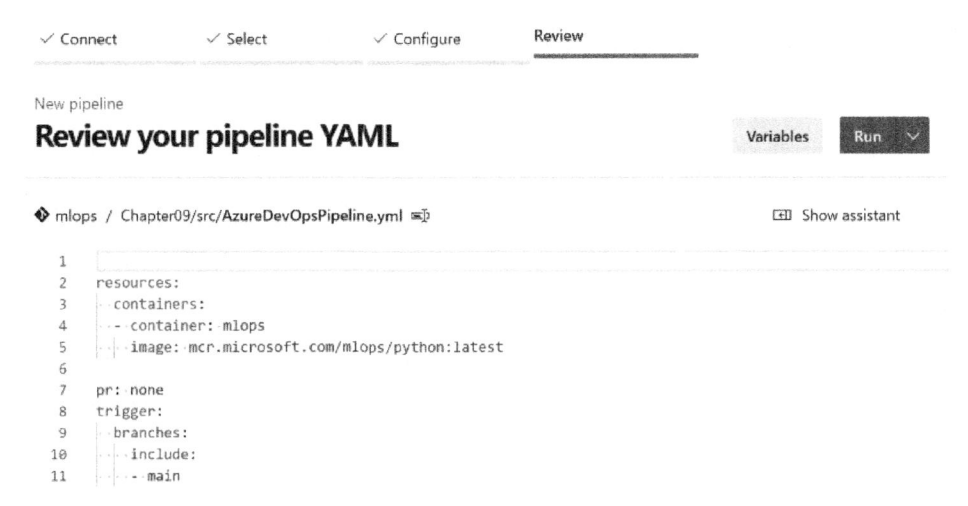

```
resources:
  containers:
  - container: mlops
    image: mcr.microsoft.com/mlops/python:latest

pr: none
trigger:
  branches:
    include:
    - main
```

Figure 9.65 – Retrieving your YAML

In the preceding screenshot, click on the **Run** button. When this pipeline runs, it will leverage your service connections. To use your service connections, you will need to provide permission for them to run.

8. Click on the **View** option to provide permission for the first stage to leverage the `aml-dev` service connection:

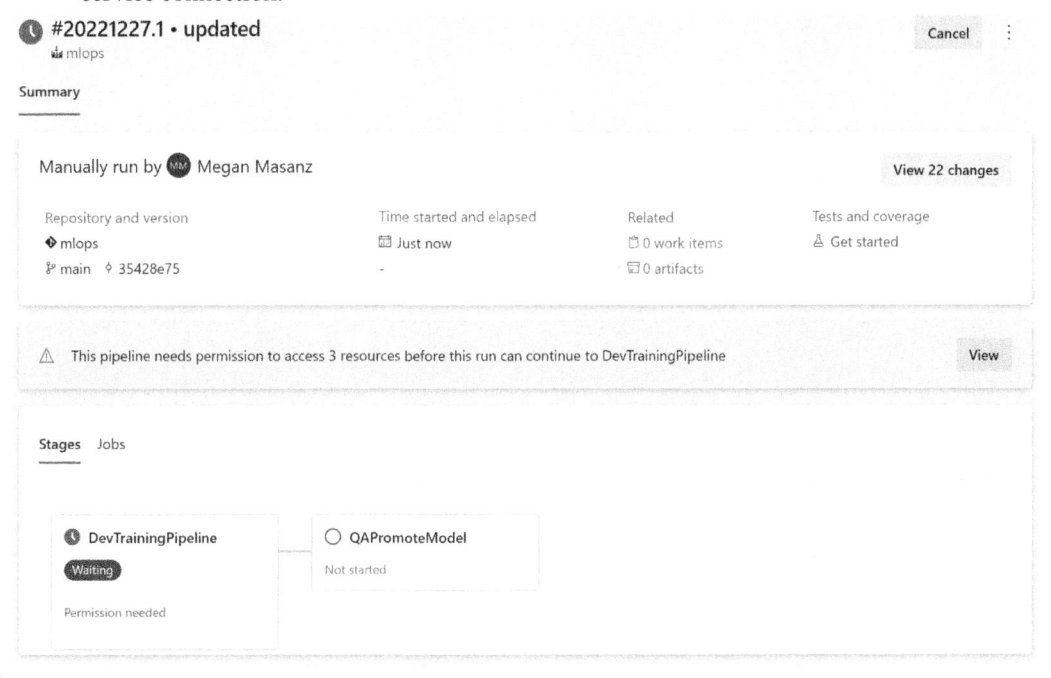

Figure 9.66 – Providing Azure DevOps with permission

9. After clicking on the **View** option, you will provide permission for the pipeline to run. Click on the **Permit** button, as shown in the following screenshot:

Figure 9.67 – Permitting the pipeline to use the service connection

10. Provide the appropriate permissions so the pipeline can execute by selecting **Permit** for each of the permissions needed as the pipeline progresses.

11. As the pipeline executes, you can see the icons displaying that the workload is progressing, as shown in the following screenshot:

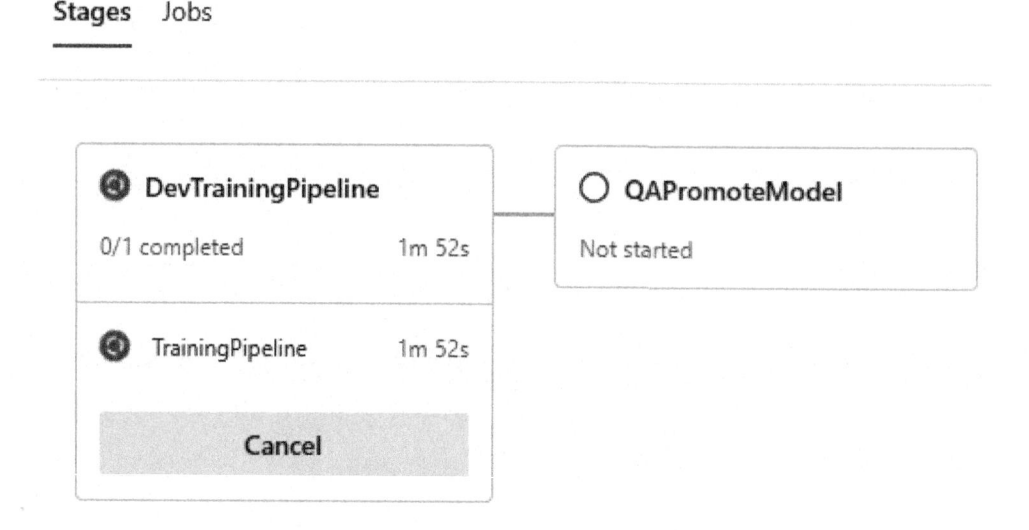

Figure 9.68 – Pipeline execution

12. Clicking on the **DevTrainingPipeline** stage will bring you to the details of the run, as shown here:

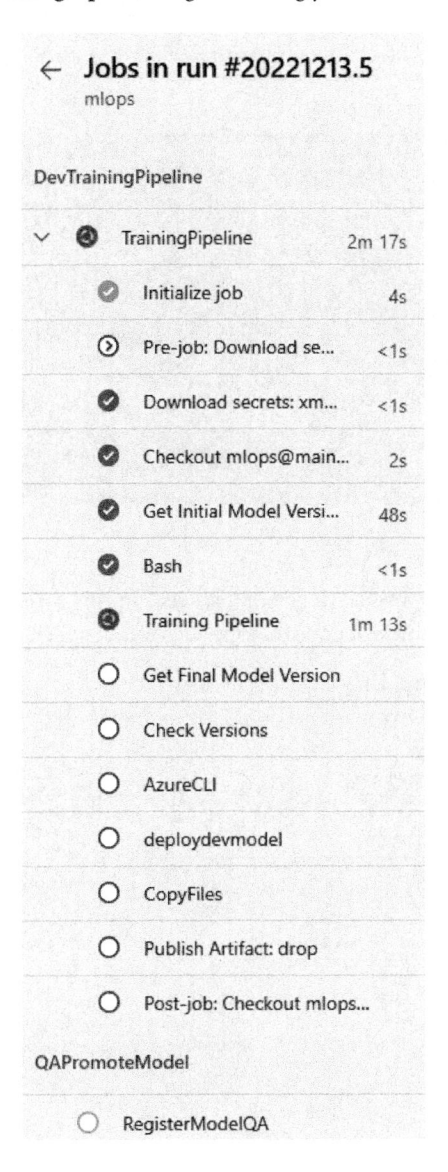

Figure 9.69 – Pipeline details

13. As the initial pipeline kicks off, the model named `mmchapter9titanic` may not exist yet, depending on whether you ran the pipeline from your AML workspace. In this case, inside Azure DevOps, if you click on the **Get Initial Model Version** task, you will see the following error message:

```
ERROR: (UserError) The specified resource was not found.
Code: UserError
Message: The specified resource was not found.
Exception Details:      (ModelNotFound) Model container with name: mmchapter9titanic not found.
        Code: ModelNotFound
        Message: Model container with name: mmchapter9titanic not found.
ERROR: (UserError) The specified resource was not found.
Code: UserError
Message: The specified resource was not found.
Exception Details:      (ModelNotFound) Model container with name: mmchapter9titanic not found.
        Code: ModelNotFound
        Message: Model container with name: mmchapter9titanic not found.
```

Figure 9.70 – Initial model find

This is correct given the model does not yet exist. In this case, we set the model version to 0 in the pipeline to continue a successful pipeline run.

14. Note that as **TrainingPipeline** kicks off in Azure DevOps, we can see it running in the `dev` instance of your AML workspace as a pipeline as shown in the following screenshot:

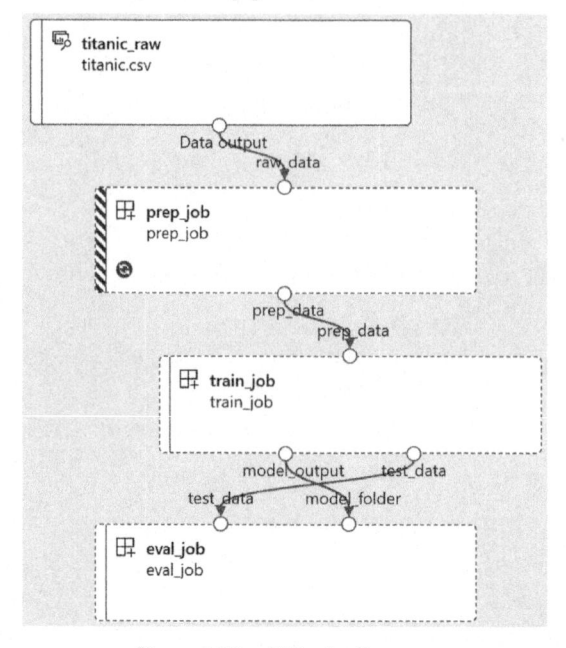

Figure 9.71 – AML pipeline run

As your Azure DevOps pipeline hits `deploydevmodel`, if it fails, it will likely be due to the fact your endpoint name in your region is already taken. If you have a failed task on the `deploydevmodel` task, look at the contents of the message in Azure DevOps. It is likely to say, **There is already an endpoint with this name, Endpoint name needs to be unique within a region. Try some other name.**

If that is the case, update your `.yml` files to leverage a different endpoint name.

After the model deployment completes in the `dev` environment, the pipeline will request approval to promote the model to the next environment.

Once the `dev` stage is complete, approval will be requested, as shown here:

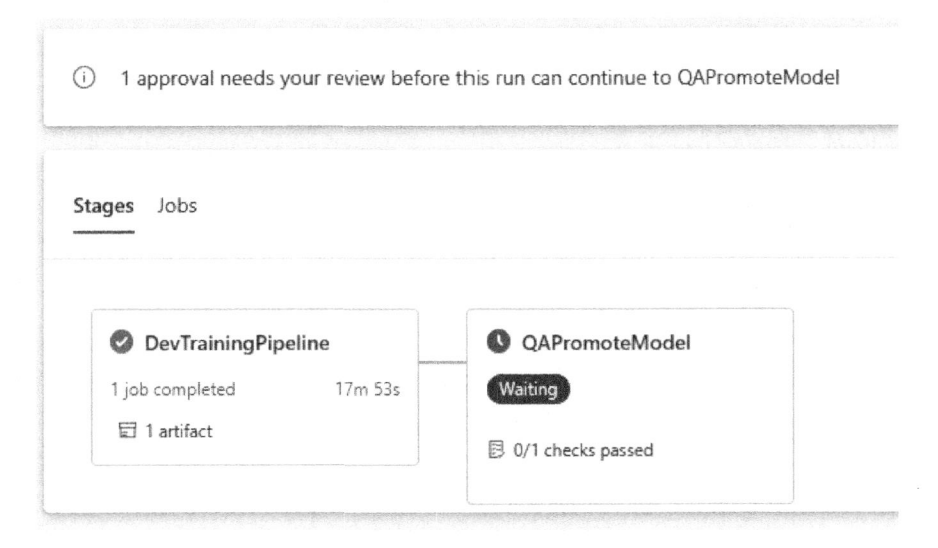

Figure 9.72 – Azure DevOps pipeline request for permission

15. Clicking on **QAPromoteModel** as shown here will allow us to drill into the `QAPromote` model stage to retrieve the pending stage and approve or reject moving the model to the `qa` environment.

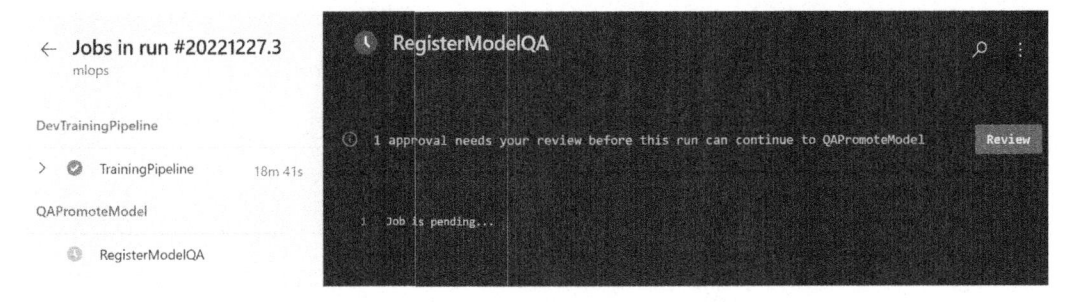

Figure 9.73 – Pending QA promotion approval

16. Clicking on the **Review** button, you will be able to either select **Reject** or **Approve** for the model promotion, as shown here:

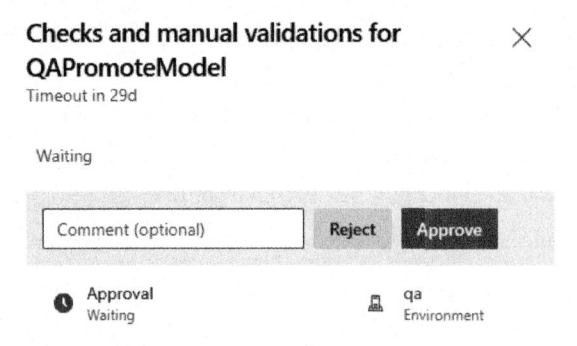

Figure 9.74 – QA promotion approval

Once the QA promotion is approved, the model can be deployed to the qa environment.

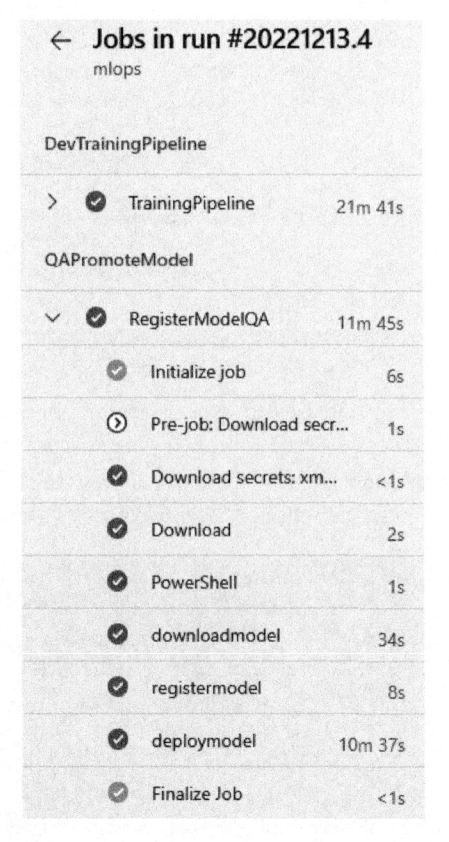

Figure 9.75 – qa environment deployment

17. As your pipeline runs, you can review the model registered in your `dev` AML workspace. As the pipeline executes, head over to your `qa` AML workspace and you will see a registered model, shown as follows:

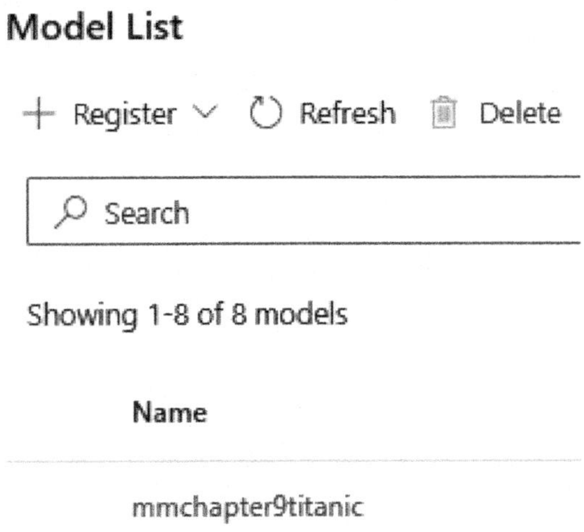

Model List

+ Register ∨   ⟳ Refresh   🗑 Delete

🔍 Search

Showing 1-8 of 8 models

Name

mmchapter9titanic

Figure 9.76 – Registered model for the qa environment

18. In addition to the registered model, you can review your managed online endpoint, as follows:

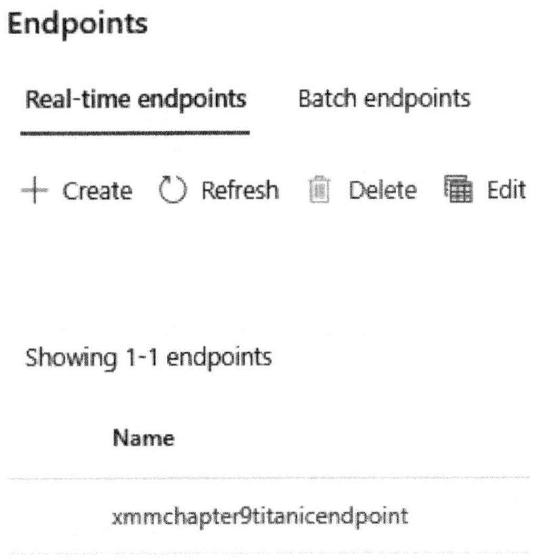

Endpoints

Real-time endpoints   Batch endpoints

+ Create   ⟳ Refresh   🗑 Delete   📝 Edit

Showing 1-1 endpoints

Name

xmmchapter9titanicendpoint

Figure 9.77 – Deployed online endpoint for the qa environment

19. The figure here demonstrates reviewing the managed online endpoint in the `qa` environment. Clicking on the name on the screen provides you with detailed information about the managed online endpoint.

    Inside the managed online endpoint, you will see the deployed instance of your model as shown here:

    xmmchapter9titanicendpoint

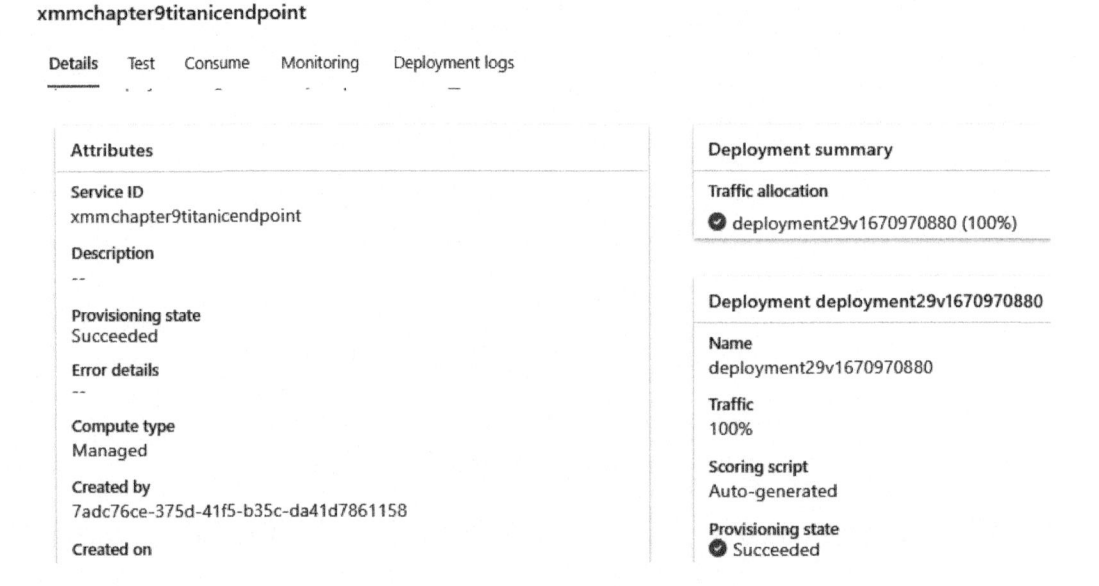

    Details | Test | Consume | Monitoring | Deployment logs

Attributes	Deployment summary
Service ID xmmchapter9titanicendpoint	**Traffic allocation** ● deployment29v1670970880 (100%)
Description --	
Provisioning state Succeeded	**Deployment deployment29v1670970880**
Error details --	**Name** deployment29v1670970880
Compute type Managed	**Traffic** 100%
Created by 7adc76ce-375d-41f5-b35c-da41d7861158	**Scoring script** Auto-generated
Created on	**Provisioning state** ● Succeeded

    Figure 9.78 – Managed online endpoint deployment in a qa environment

20. The deployment name is based on the epoch. Each time a model is deployed in the `qa` AML workspace, it checked the tag property:

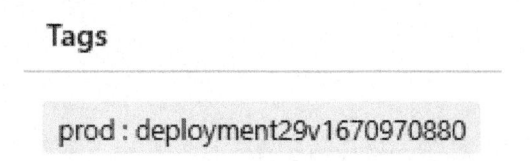

    Tags

    prod : deployment29v1670970880

    Figure 9.79 – Tag property of the managed online endpoint

Provided there is a model deployed, it creates a new deployment, updates the tag, and deletes the old deployment. This ensures that users will experience minimal interruption as the new endpoint is deployed.

In this chapter, you set up your MLOps pipeline by leveraging Azure DevOps to automate the orchestration of data preparation, model development, and model evaluation and registration; deploying the model by leveraging blue/green deployments; and promoting it from one environment to the next.

You are encouraged to leverage your `dev` AML workspace, make code modifications and review the process of your Azure DevOps pipeline, kick off your `dev` AML workspace pipeline, register the model in the `qa` environment, and update the managed online endpoints. Now that you have deployed managed online endpoints through an MLOps pipeline, take caution, as the endpoints are leveraging compute. You should delete the endpoints when you are not using them to keep your costs down. Congratulations – you have successfully implemented an MLOps pipeline!

Summary

In this chapter, the focus was on deploying your model as a managed online endpoint to support real-time inferencing use cases in an automated fashion.

This chapter brought together the concepts that you learned about in previous chapters, as well as introducing you to Azure DevOps and the orchestration it makes possible. Leveraging Azure DevOps, code and deployments are traceable. Azure DevOps pipelines automate triggering the orchestration of the `dev` environment pipeline, moving the registered model to the higher environment. Leveraging Azure Key Vault, we can securely hold information to support multiple environments, linking those to your Azure DevOps environment groups. With MLflow integration, metrics are captured for the model generated in the `dev` environment, and that model number is registered in a higher environment and then added to the managed online endpoint. We implemented an MLOps pipeline to automate data transformation, model creation, evaluation, and model deployment.

In the next chapter, we will explore leveraging Deep Learning in your AML workspace. This will be a guide to leveraging object detection with AutoML to solve your object detection objectives.

Further reading

As mentioned, in this chapter, we tried to provide a basis for creating your own MLOps pipeline. We encourage you to check out two additional resources for building your MLOps pipelines with AML:

- `https://github.com/Azure/mlops-v2`
- `https://github.com/microsoft/MLOpsPython`

Part 3: Productionizing Your Workload with MLOps

In this section, readers will learn how to integrate AMLS jobs with Azure DevOps and Github to achieve an MLOps solution.

This section has the following chapters:

- *Chapter 10, Using Deep Learning in Azure Machine Learning*
- *Chapter 11, Using Distributed Training in AMLS*

10
Using Deep Learning in Azure Machine Learning

Deep learning is a subclass of machine learning. It is based on artificial neural networks, a programming paradigm inspired by the human biological nervous system, and it enables a computer to learn from a very large amount of observational data.

There are some machine learning problems – such as image recognition, image classification, object detection, speech recognition, and natural language processing – that traditional machine learning techniques do not provide performant solutions for, whereas deep learning techniques do. This chapter will show you the deep learning capabilities available within AML that you can use to solve some of the previously mentioned problems.

In this chapter, we will cover the following topics:

- Labeling image data for training an object detection model by using the AML Data Labeling feature
- Training an object detection model using Azure AutoML
- Deploying an object detection model to an online endpoint using the AML Python SDK

Technical requirements

To access your workspace, recall the steps from the previous chapter:

1. Go to https://ml.azure.com.
2. Select your workspace name.
3. On the workspace user interface on the left side, click **Compute**.

4. On the **Compute** screen, select your compute instance and select **Start**:

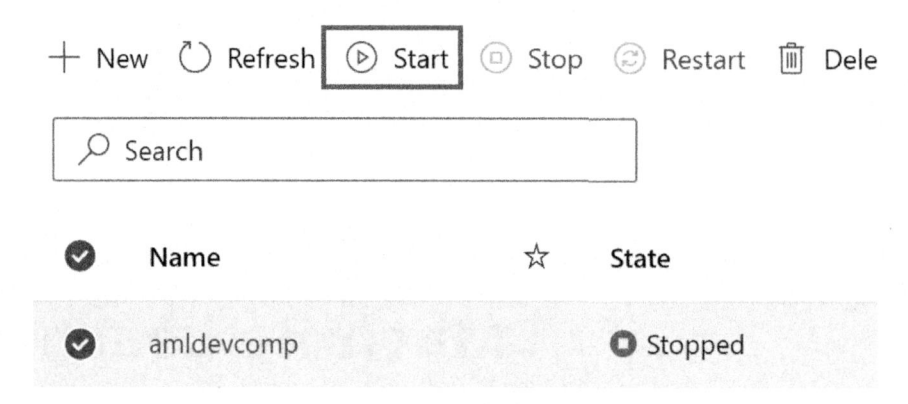

Figure 10.1 – Start compute

5. Your compute instance status will change from **Stopped** to **Starting**.
6. In the previous chapter, we cloned the Git repository; if you have not already done so, continue to follow these steps. If you have already cloned the repository, skip to *step 7*.
7. Open the terminal on your compute instance. Note the path will include your user in the directory. Type the following into the terminal to clone the sample notebooks into your working directory:

```
git clone https://github.com/PacktPublishing/Azure-Machine-Learning-Engineering.git
```

8. Clicking on the refresh icon shown in *Figure 10.2* will update and refresh the notebooks displayed on your screen:

Figure 10.2 – Refresh icon

9. Review the notebooks in your `Azure-Machine-Learning-Engineering` directory. This will display the files cloned into your working directory, as shown in *Figure 10.3*:

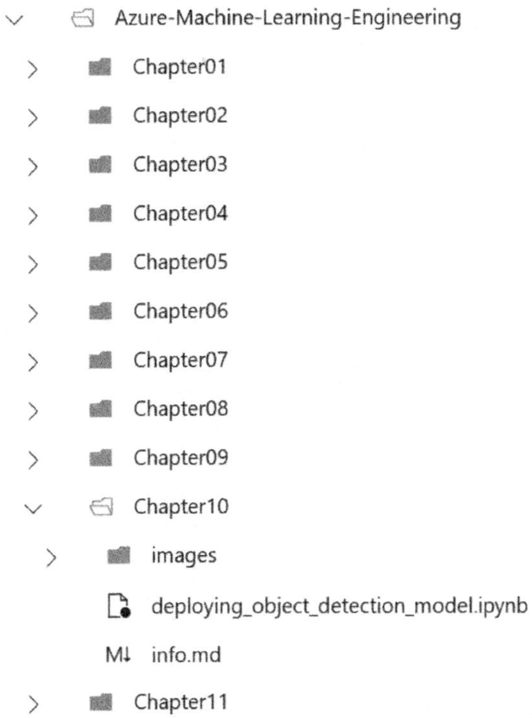

```
v  📁 Azure-Machine-Learning-Engineering
   >  📁 Chapter01
   >  📁 Chapter02
   >  📁 Chapter03
   >  📁 Chapter04
   >  📁 Chapter05
   >  📁 Chapter06
   >  📁 Chapter07
   >  📁 Chapter08
   >  📁 Chapter09
   v  📁 Chapter10
      >  📁 images
         📄 deploying_object_detection_model.ipynb
         M↓ info.md
   >  📁 Chapter11
```

Figure 10.3 – Azure-Machine-Learning-Engineering

Labeling image data using the Data Labeling feature of Azure Machine Learning

In the field of computer vision, object detection is a challenging task for predicting the location of objects in an image and predicting the object types. Just like any other supervised machine learning task, in order to train an object detection model, we need to have training data and, in this case, a lot of labeled data, as deep learning works best on a large labeled dataset. Data scientists who develop computer vision models know how tedious and time-consuming it can be to label images, and even more time-consuming when it comes to labeling images for object detection models. The **Azure Machine Learning** (**Azure ML**) service has a powerful feature called **Data Labeling**, which significantly enhances the user experience for image labeling, leveraging built-in capabilities such as ML-assisted labeling by automatically training a model to pre-label images for you to review, accelerating the labeling process.

In this section, you will learn how to label your images for training an object detection model by leveraging the Data Labeling feature of Azure ML by following these steps:

1. Go to the `chapter 10` folder of the cloned repository of this book that you have been using. You will see the `images` folder, which has two subfolders: `train` and `test`. You will be using the images in the `train` folder in the next step. Please note that these images were cloned to our repository from the public repository hosted at `https://github.com/EdjeElectronics/TensorFlow-Object-Detection-API-Tutorial-Train-Multiple-Objects-Windows-10`.

2. Navigate to the Azure ML workspace and select **Data Labeling** from the left menu bar and then click **Add project**, as shown in *Figure 10.4*:

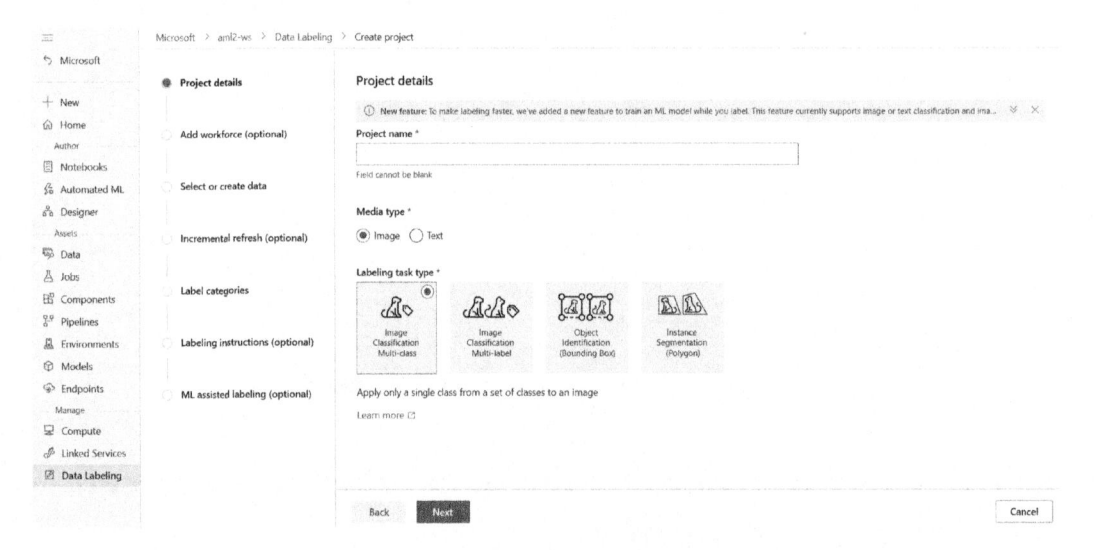

Figure 10.4 – Creating a new Data Labeling project

3. Go ahead and give your project a name, then select **Image** for **Media type** and **Object Identification (Bounding Box)** for **Labeling task type**, and click **Next**, as shown in *Figure 10.5*:

Labeling image data using the Data Labeling feature of Azure Machine Learning   293

Project details

ⓘ New feature: To make labeling faster, we've added a new feature to train an ML model while you label. This feature currently supports image or text classification and ima...   ✕

Project name *

playing_cards

Media type *

◉ Image   ◯ Text

Labeling task type *

| Image Classification Multi-class | Image Classification Multi-label | Object Identification (Bounding Box) | Instance Segmentation (Polygon) |

Assign a class and a bounding box to each object within an image

Learn more ↗

Back   **Next**   Cancel

Figure 10.5 – Filling out the project details

4. You can skip the next step and go to **Select or create data** and click **Create** to create your dataset. Pick a name and type in a description for your image data asset and then click **Next**, as shown in *Figure 10.6*:

Create data asset

● Data type   Set the name and type for your data asset

                Name *
○ Data source   playing-cards-images

                Description
                Data asset description

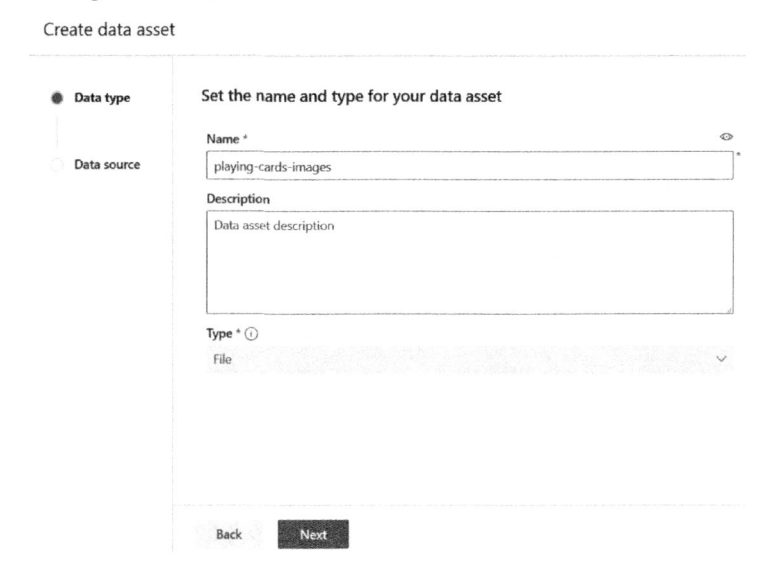

                Type * ⓘ
                File   ⌄

                Back   **Next**

Figure 10.6 – Creating an image data asset

5. Select **From local files**, as shown in *Figure 10.7*:

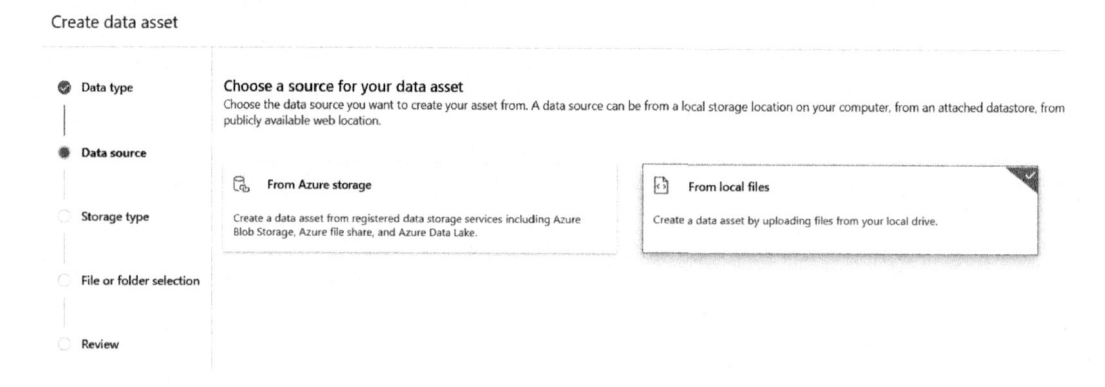

Figure 10.7 – Selecting the image data source

6. Select a datastore for uploading your images, as shown in *Figure 10.8*:

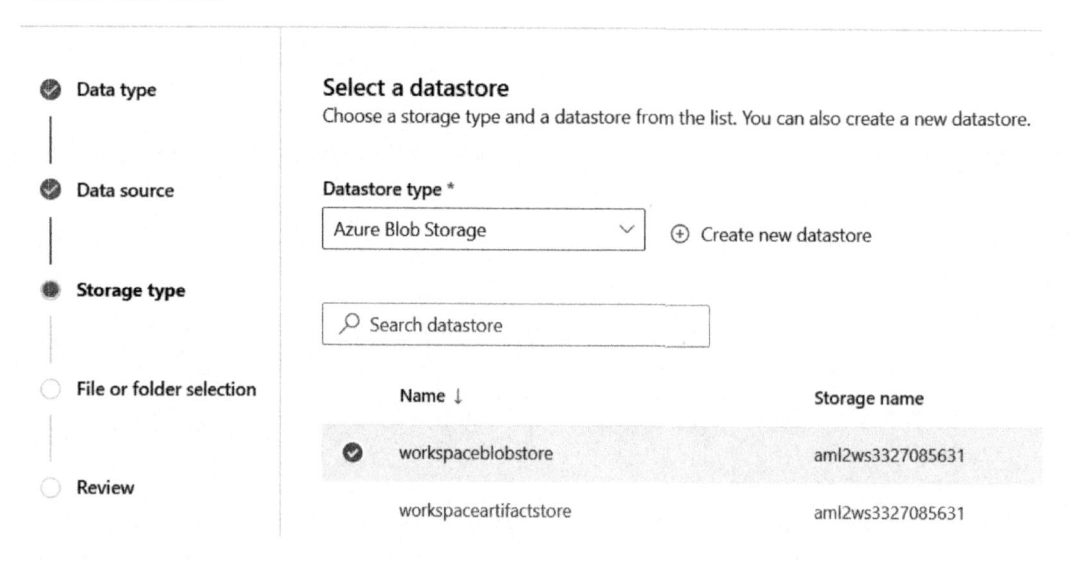

Figure 10.8 – Selecting the storage type and the datastore for your images

7. Click **Upload**, navigate to the `train` folder from *step 1*, select all the images as shown in *Figure 10.9*, and click **Next**:

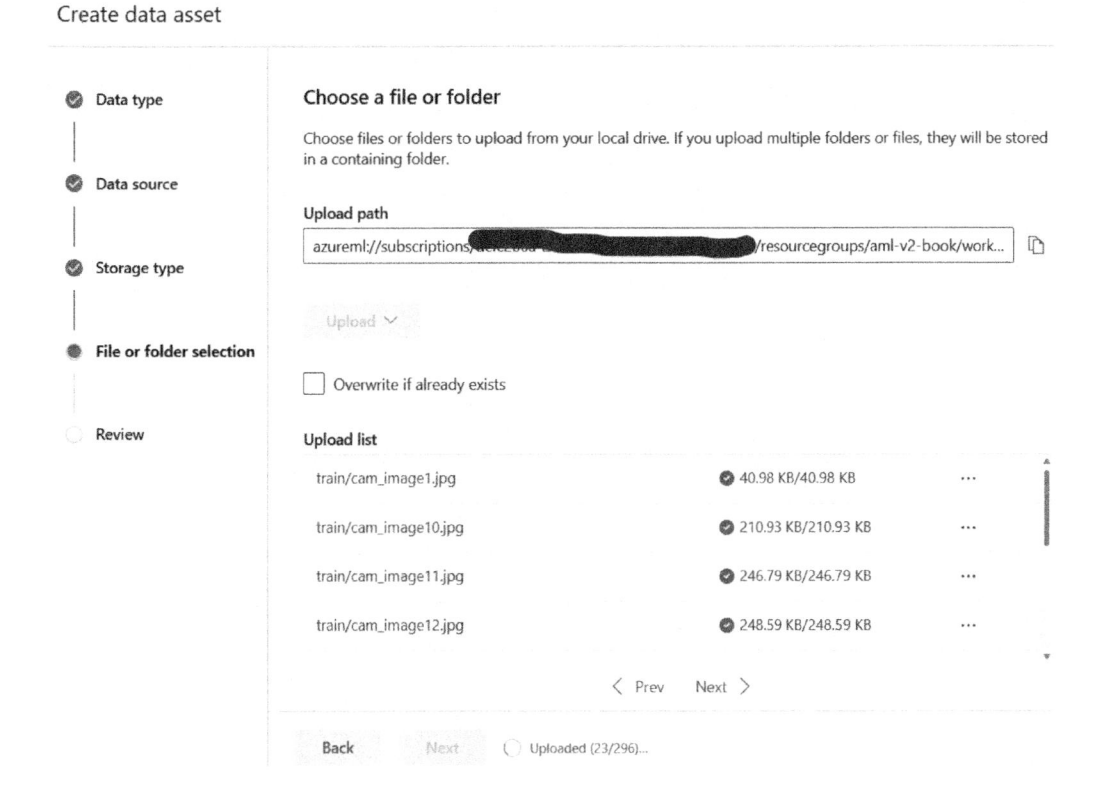

Figure 10.9 – Uploading image files from your local drive

8. Review the details for your image data asset and click **Create**.

Using Deep Learning in Azure Machine Learning

9. In this step, you need to add labels for each object found in the images, which in this case will be `Two`, `Three`, `Four`, and so on up to `Ten`, as well as `Soldier`, `Queen`, and `King`, as shown in *Figure 10.10*. Then click **Next**:

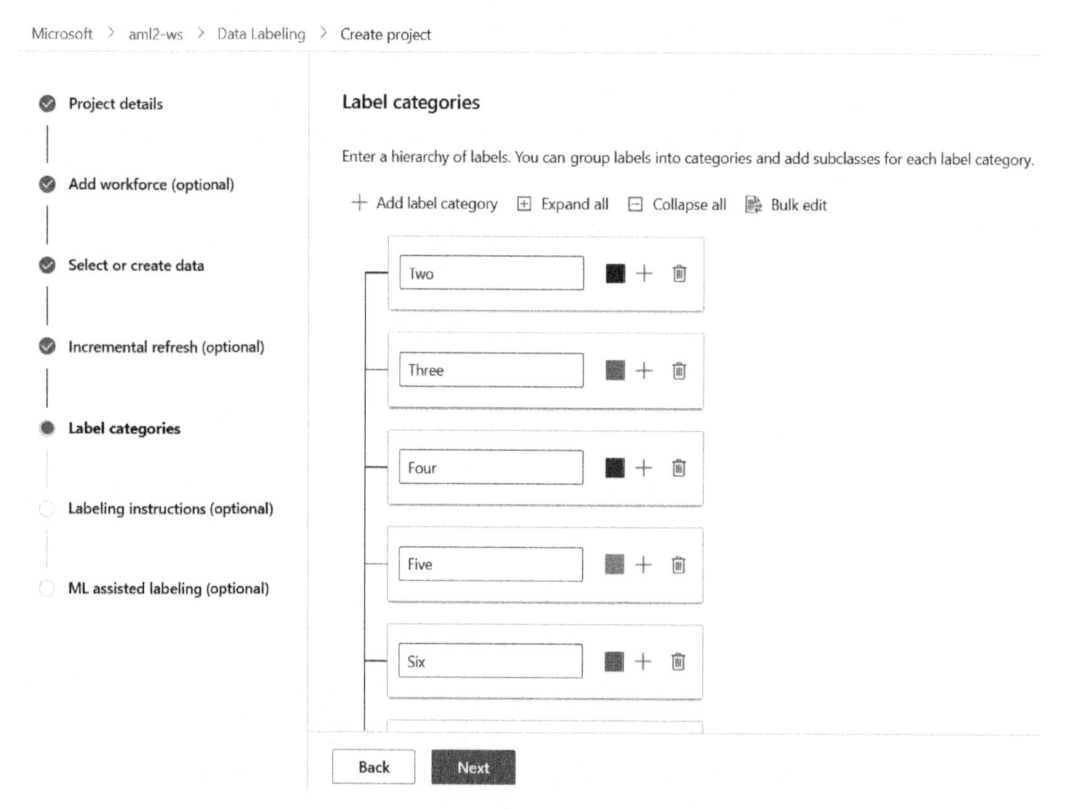

Figure 10.10 – Adding labels for the objects in all images

10. You can skip **Labeling instructions (optional)** and go to **ML assisted labeling (optional)**. Make sure **ML assisted labeling (optional)** is enabled, as shown in *Figure 10.11*, and then click **Create project**:

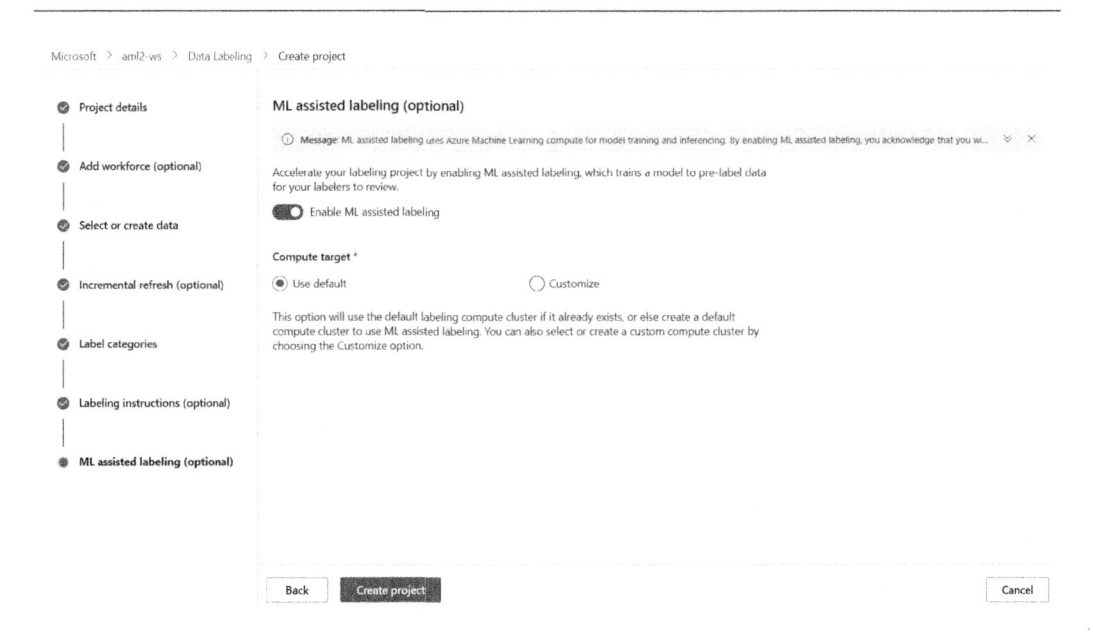

Labeling image data using the Data Labeling feature of Azure Machine Learning   297

Figure 10.11 – Reviewing and creating the data labeling project

11. Click on the project you just created from the project list, as shown in *Figure 10.12*:

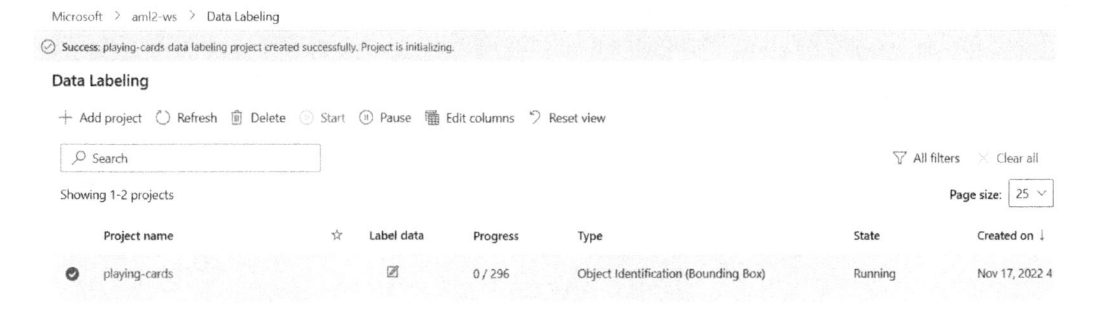

Figure 10.12 – Data labeling project list

298   Using Deep Learning in Azure Machine Learning

12. You can see the dashboard with the different options that the **Data Labeling** feature gives you to assist with the labeling process. Go ahead and click on **Label data** near the top, as shown in *Figure 10.13*:

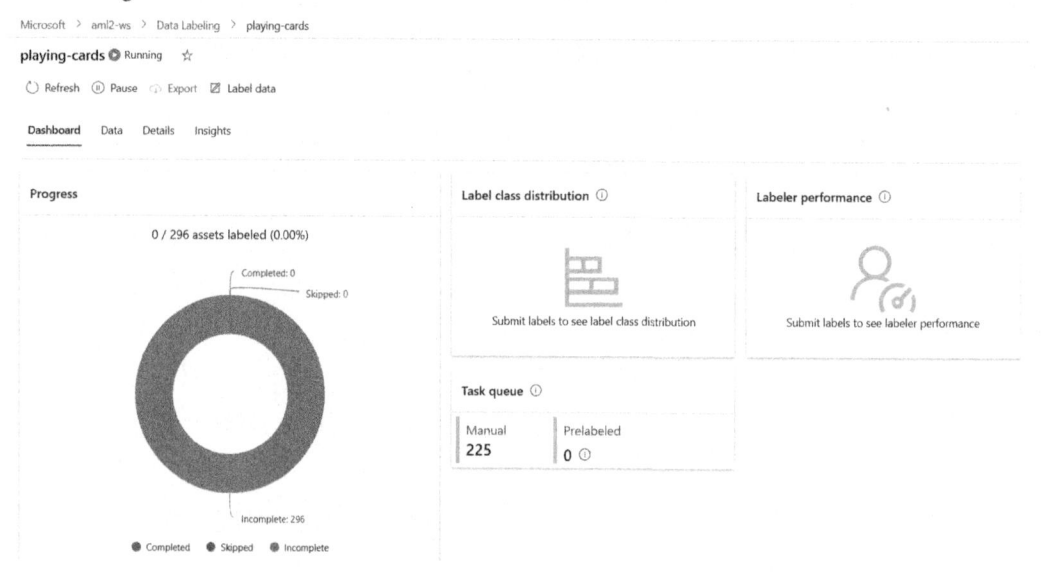

Figure 10.13 – Data labeling dashboard

13. In this step, you will start labeling the images by drawing bounding boxes around objects found in the images and assigning labels associated with them, as shown in *Figure 10.14*:

Figure 10.14 – Drawing bounding boxes around the objects and assigning them labels

Labeling image data using the Data Labeling feature of Azure Machine Learning 299

14. Once enough images have been labeled, ML-assisted labeling will start, and you will see that the next images are pre-labeled for you to quickly review the bounding boxes around the objects and their labels. After you are done labeling all the images, you will see the summary of your labeled data, such as **Label class distribution** and so on, as shown in *Figure 10.15*:

Microsoft > aml2-ws > Data Labeling > playing_cards

playing_cards ● Running ☆

◯ Refresh ⏸ Pause ⊕ Export ✎ Label data

Dashboard Data Details Insights

Progress

45 / 45 assets labeled (100.00%)

Skipped: 0
Incomplete: 0
Completed: 45

● Completed ● Skipped ● Incomplete

Label class distribution ⓘ

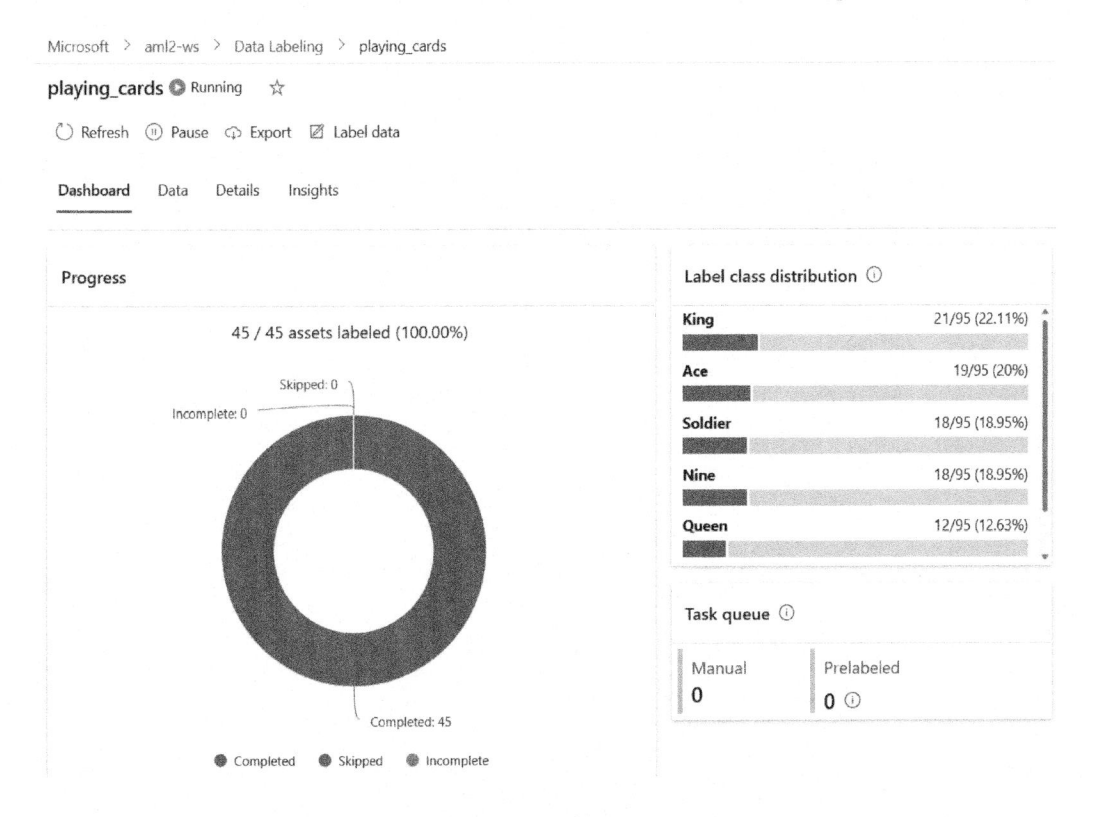

King   21/95 (22.11%)
Ace   19/95 (20%)
Soldier   18/95 (18.95%)
Nine   18/95 (18.95%)
Queen   12/95 (12.63%)

Task queue ⓘ

Manual   Prelabeled
0   0 ⓘ

Figure 10.15 – Label class distribution

15. Next, click **Export** and select **Labeled** for **Asset type** and **Azure ML dataset** for **Export format**, as shown in *Figure 10.16*:

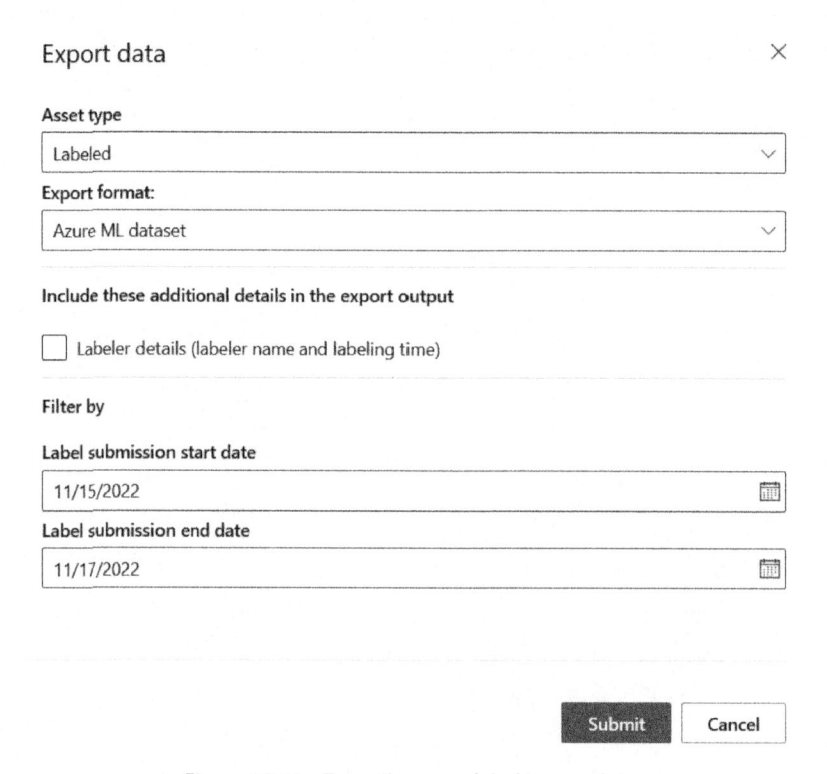

Figure 10.16 – Exporting your label image data

16. You should see a message indicating that your data was exported successfully, as shown in *Figure 10.17*:

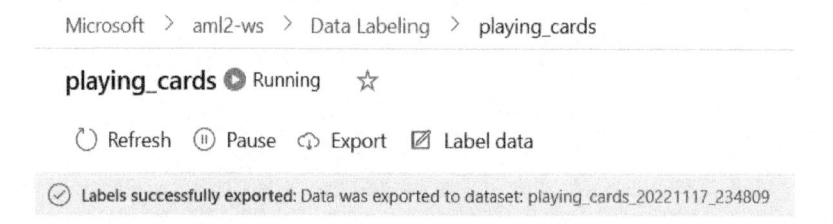

Figure 10.17 – Labeled data exported successfully

In this section, you learned how to leverage Azure ML-assisted labeling to accelerate the labeling of your images for training an object detection model, which we will train in the next section.

Training an object detection model using Azure AutoML

In this section, we will show you how to use Azure **Automated Machine Learning (AutoML)** to train an object detection model by following these steps:

1. Click on **Automated ML** from the left navigation bar and then click **New Automated ML job**.

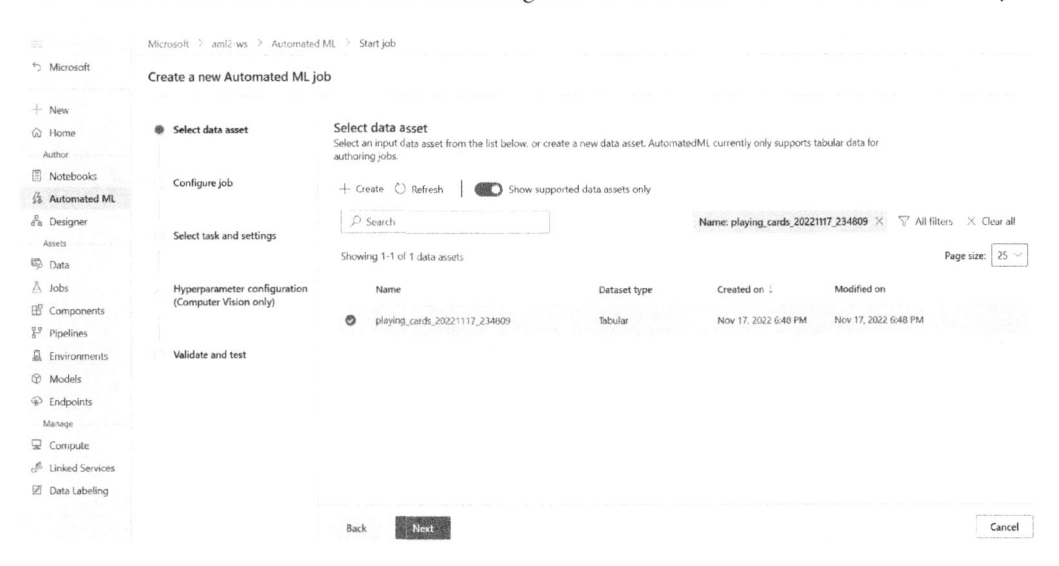

Figure 10.18 – Creating a new Automated ML job

2. Select the image data asset that you created in the last section and click **Next**.
3. In this step, you will configure the training job, as shown in *Figure 10.19*. The first thing to notice is that AutoML has automatically set the task type to **Object Detection** based on the selected dataset. Since you don't have an existing experiment, select **Create new** to create a new experiment and call it `playing_cards_experiment`. For **Target column**, select **label (List)**, and for the compute type, select **Compute cluster**. Since you do not have a GPU cluster (which is needed for deep learning tasks such as object detection), you will need to create one by selecting **+ New** and following the steps in the cluster creation wizard. Once your GPU compute cluster is created, it can be selected, and then you can click **Next**:

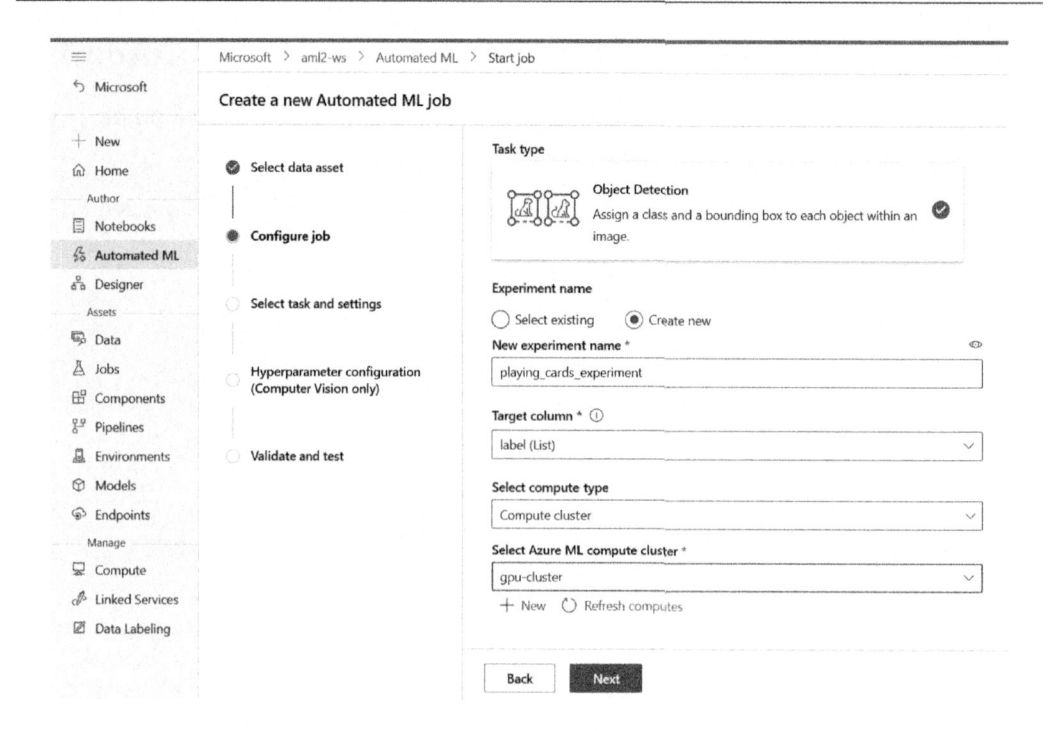

302   Using Deep Learning in Azure Machine Learning

Figure 10.19 – Configuring the object detection job

4. You can leave the default values that are selected for the algorithm details and the hyperparameter tuning settings, as shown in *Figure 10.20*, and then click **Next**:

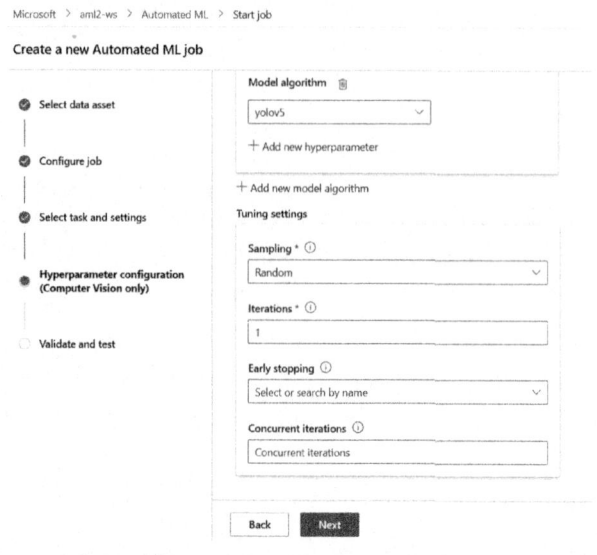

Figure 10.20 – Selecting the model and configuring the hyperparameter tuning

5. In this final step, you will set your validation type. We will again keep the default selected value, which is **Auto**, as shown in *Figure 10.21*. Then, click **Finish** to start the model training:

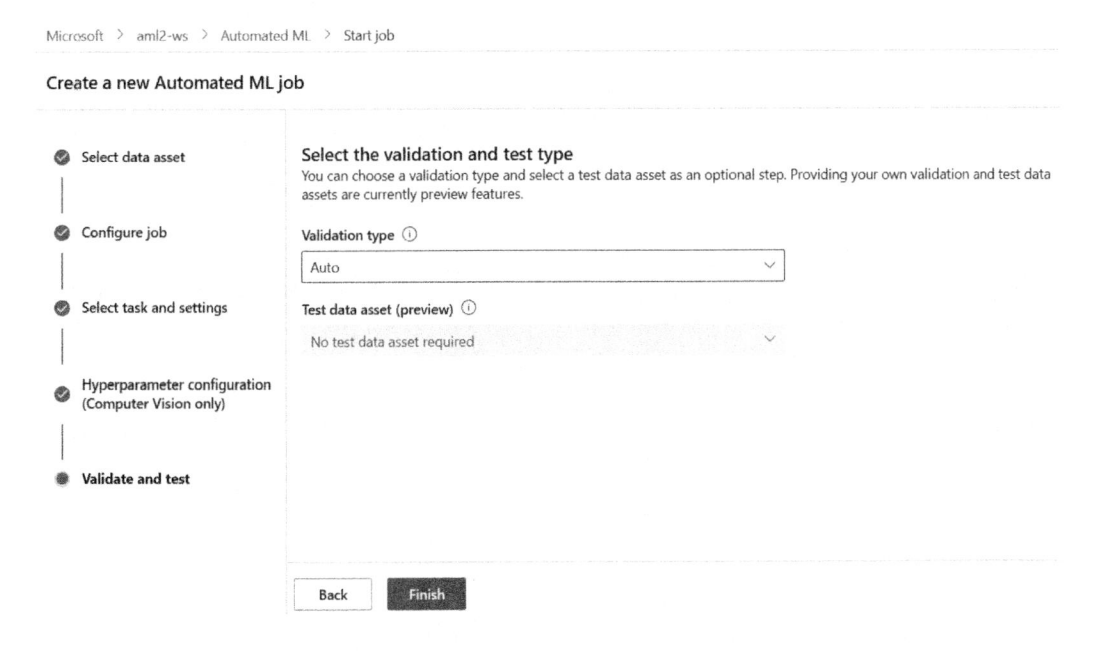

Figure 10.21 – Selecting the validation type

6. Depending on the size of your dataset, it can take anywhere between 15 minutes to a couple of hours for the model training to complete. Once the training job is completed, you can see it under **Recent Automated ML jobs**, as shown in *Figure 10.22*:

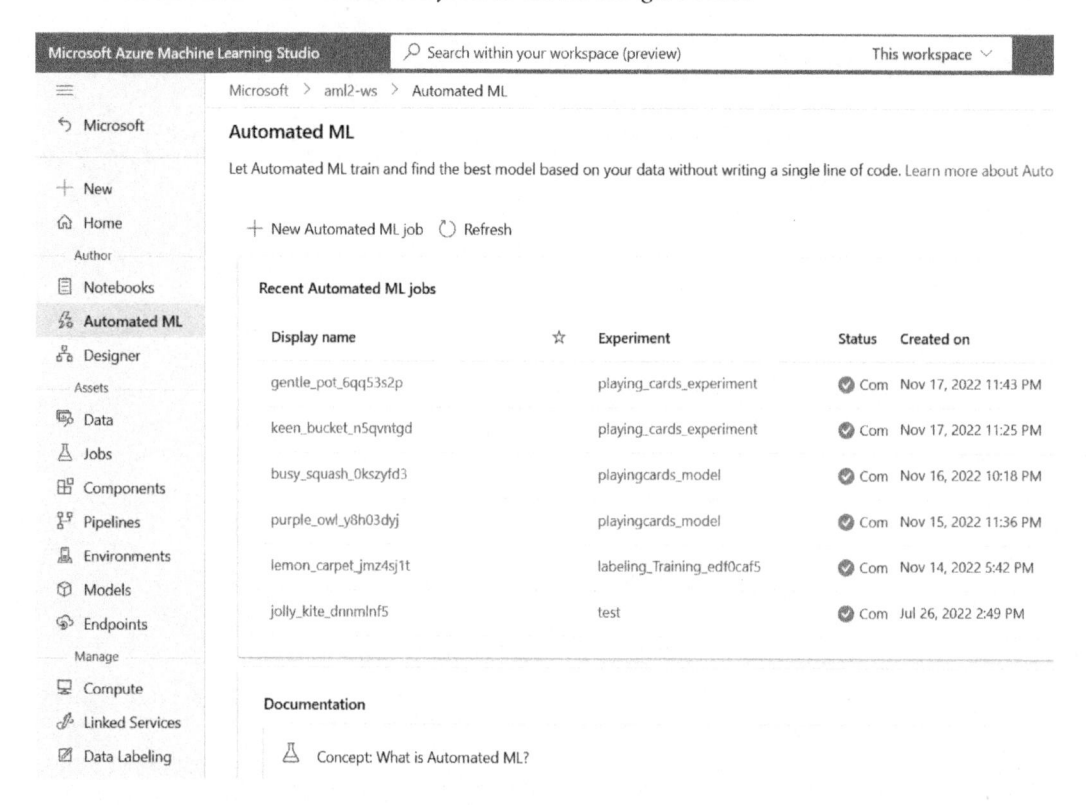

Figure 10.22 – Automated ML jobs

7. Select your latest run to see some statistics, such as **Best model summary**, **Primary metric**, **Algorithm name**, and **Duration**, as shown in *Figure 10.23*:

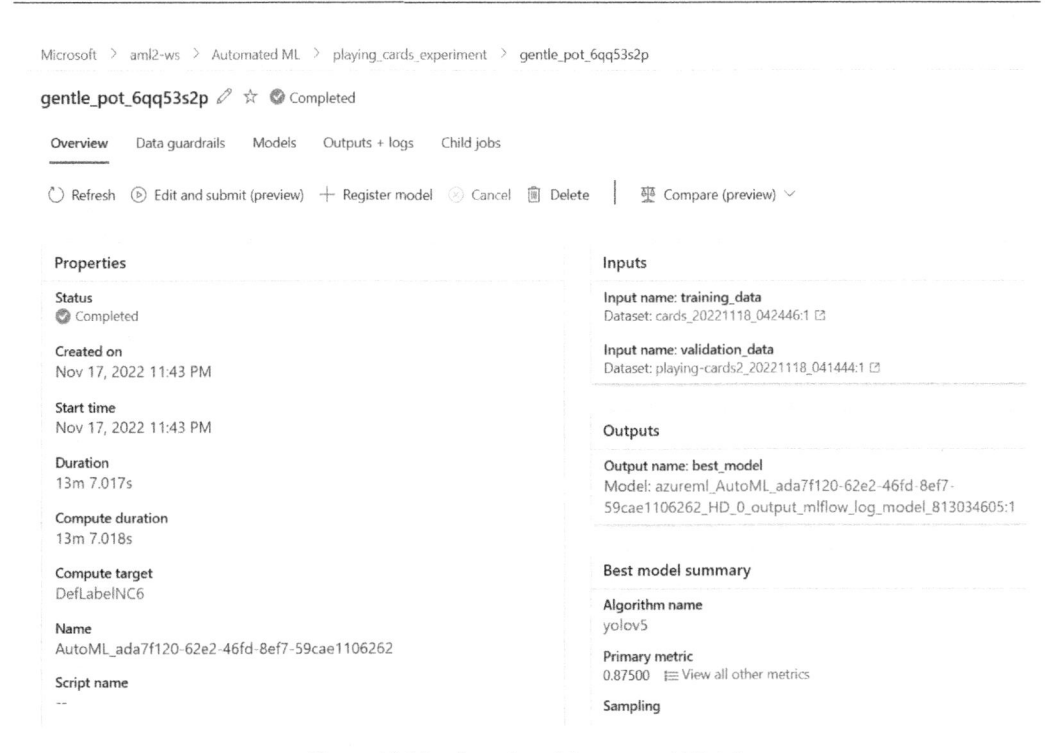

Figure 10.23 – Completed Automated ML job

In this section, you learned how to leverage Azure AutoML to train an object detection model using the image data that you had labeled by leveraging another tool called **Data Labeling**. In the next section, you will learn how to deploy the trained model to a managed online endpoint for consumption by client applications.

Deploying the object detection model to an online endpoint using the Azure ML Python SDK

Just like any other ML model, a deep learning model is not useful unless it is deployed and consumers can send data for inference. In our case, it would be sending image data and getting results back containing object types and locations within the raw image.

In this section, we will show you how to use the Azure ML Python SDK to register your previously trained model and deploy it to an online endpoint for real-time inference by following these steps:

1. Open the `chapter 10` notebook, which is inside the repository that you cloned by following the steps in the *Technical requirements* section of the chapter. Please note that our repository for this chapter uses most of the code from the original repository hosted at `https://github.com/Azure/azureml-examples`.

2. The first couple of cells import the required libraries and connect your notebook to the Azure ML workspace, as shown in *Figure 10.24*:

```
# Import required libraries
from azure.identity import DefaultAzureCredential
from azure.ai.ml import MLClient

from azure.ai.ml.automl import SearchSpace, ObjectDetectionPrimaryMetrics
from azure.ai.ml.sweep import (
    Choice,
    Uniform,
    BanditPolicy,
)

from azure.ai.ml import automl
```

```
credential = DefaultAzureCredential()
ml_client = None
try:
    ml_client = MLClient.from_config(credential)
except Exception as ex:
    print(ex)
    # Enter details of your AML workspace
    subscription_id = "XxXx"
    resource_group = "XxXx"
    workspace = "aml2-ws"
    ml_client = MLClient(credential, subscription_id, resource_group, workspace)
Found the config file in: /config.json
```

Figure 10.24 – Importing the required libraries and connecting to the Azure ML workspace

3. You are going to use the MLflow library (in particular, the MLflow client) to access the models and other artifacts generated by AutoML. The next couple of cells show how to install the latest version of the MLflow packages, how to obtain the URI for the MLflow tracking server, and how to initialize the MLflow client, as shown in *Figure 10.25*:

```
!pip install azureml-mlflow
!pip install mlflow
```

```
import mlflow

# Obtain the tracking URL from MLClient
MLFLOW_TRACKING_URI = ml_client.workspaces.get(
    name=ml_client.workspace_name
).mlflow_tracking_uri

print(MLFLOW_TRACKING_URI)
```

azureml://eastus.api.azureml.ms/mlflow/v1.0/subscriptions/dcfc206a-203b-4c00-a236-bdf576a37896/resourceGroups/aml-v2-book/providers/Microsoft.MachineLearningServices/workspaces/aml2-ws

```
# Set the MLFLOW TRACKING URI

mlflow.set_tracking_uri(MLFLOW_TRACKING_URI)

print("\nCurrent tracking uri: {}".format(mlflow.get_tracking_uri()))
```

Current tracking uri: azureml://eastus.api.azureml.ms/mlflow/v1.0/subscriptions/dcfc206a-203b-4c00-a236-bdf576a37896/resourceGroups/aml-v2-book/providers/Microsoft.MachineLearningServices/workspaces/aml2-ws

```
from mlflow.tracking.client import MlflowClient

# Initialize MLFlow client
mlflow_client = MlflowClient()
```

Figure 10.25 – Setting up the MLflow client to access the AutoML-trained model

Deploying the object detection model to an online endpoint using the Azure ML Python SDK   307

4. Go to the Azure ML workspace and click on the **Automated ML** tab from the left navigation bar. Then, click on the latest job to see the job details and make a note of the job name, which is `AutoML_ada7f120-62e2-46fd-8ef7-59cae1106262`, as shown in *Figure 10.26*. We will use the job name in the next step:

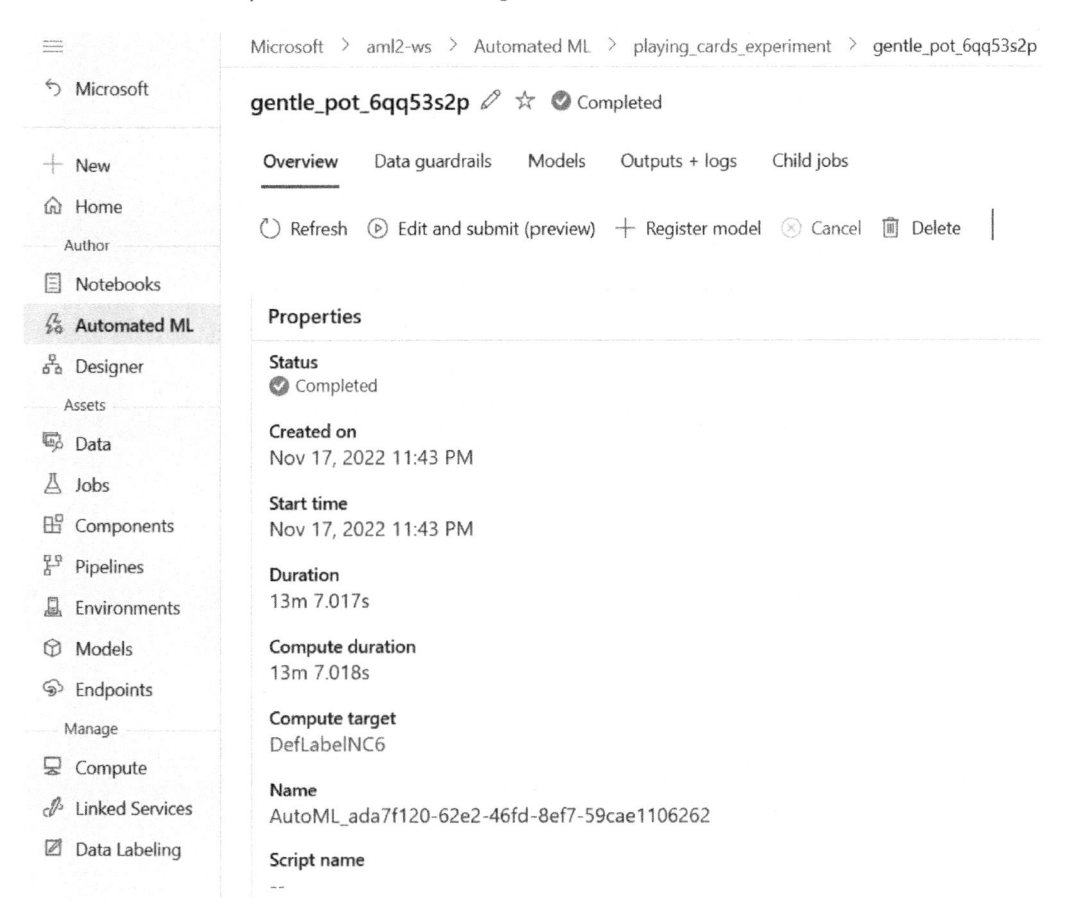

Figure 10.26 – Getting the AutoML job name

5. Now that we have the AutoML job name, we can get the AutoML best model ID, as shown in *Figure 10.27*. This will be used in a later step to retrieve the actual trained model:

```python
# Get the AutoML parent Job

job_name = "AutoML_ada7f120-62e2-46fd-8ef7-59cae1106262"


mlflow_parent_run = mlflow_client.get_run(job_name)

print("Parent Run: ")
print(mlflow_parent_run)
```

```python
# Print parent run tags. 'automl_best_child_run_id' tag should be there.
print(mlflow_parent_run.data.tags)
```

```python
# Get the best model's child run

best_child_run_id = mlflow_parent_run.data.tags["automl_best_child_run_id"]
print("Found best child run id: ", best_child_run_id)

best_run = mlflow_client.get_run(best_child_run_id)

print("Best child run: ")
print(best_run)
```

Figure 10.27 – Getting the AutoML best model ID

6. The next cell creates a local folder and downloads the best model and its artifacts into this folder, as shown in *Figure 10.28*:

```python
# Create local folder
local_dir = "./artifact_downloads"
if not os.path.exists(local_dir):
    os.mkdir(local_dir)
```

```python
# Download run's artifacts/outputs
local_path = mlflow_client.download_artifacts(
    best_run.info.run_id, "outputs", local_dir
)
print("Artifacts downloaded in: {}".format(local_path))
print("Artifacts: {}".format(os.listdir(local_path)))
```

```python
import os

# Show the contents of the MLFlow model folder
os.listdir("./artifact_downloads/outputs/mlflow-model")
```

]: ['artifacts',
    'conda.yaml',
    'MLmodel',
    'python_env.yaml',
    'python_model.pkl',
    'requirements.txt']

Figure 10.28 – Downloading the best model in a local folder

7. The next cell creates a managed online endpoint for the model to be invoked from, as shown in *Figure 10.29*:

```python
# import required libraries
from azure.ai.ml.entities import (
    ManagedOnlineEndpoint,
    ManagedOnlineDeployment,
    Model,
    Environment,
    CodeConfiguration,
    ProbeSettings,
)
```

```python
# Creating a unique endpoint name with current datetime to avoid conflicts
import datetime

online_endpoint_name = "playing-cards-" + datetime.datetime.now().strftime(
    "%m%d%H%M%f"
)

# create an online endpoint
endpoint = ManagedOnlineEndpoint(
    name=online_endpoint_name,
    description="this is a sample online endpoint for deploying model",
    auth_mode="key",
    tags={"foo": "bar"},
)
print(online_endpoint_name)
```

playing-cards-11182014325540

```python
ml_client.begin_create_or_update(endpoint).result()
```

Figure 10.29 – Creating an online endpoint for the model to be invoked from

8. The next cell registers the model to the workspace, as shown in *Figure 10.30*:

```python
from azure.ai.ml.constants import AssetTypes, InputOutputModes
model_name = "playing-cards-mlflow-model"
model = Model(
    path=f"azureml://jobs/{best_run.info.run_id}/outputs/artifacts/outputs/mlflow-model/",
    name=model_name,
    description="playing cards object detection model",
    type=AssetTypes.MLFLOW_MODEL,
)

registered_model = ml_client.models.create_or_update(model)
```

Figure 10.30 – Registering the best model to the Azure ML workspace

9. The next cell creates a deployment, which contains settings such as an ID for the model to be deployed, the compute cluster type, the number of cluster nodes, and the name of the endpoint that was created a couple of steps ago, as shown in *Figure 10.31*:

```python
deployment = ManagedOnlineDeployment(
    name="playingcards-mlflow-deploy",
    endpoint_name=online_endpoint_name,
    model=registered_model.id,
    instance_type="Standard_DS3_V2",
    instance_count=1,
    liveness_probe=ProbeSettings(
        failure_threshold=30,
        success_threshold=1,
        timeout=2,
        period=10,
        initial_delay=2000,
    ),
    readiness_probe=ProbeSettings(
        failure_threshold=10,
        success_threshold=1,
        timeout=10,
        period=10,
        initial_delay=2000,
    ),
)
```

```python
ml_client.online_deployments.begin_create_or_update(deployment).result()
```

```python
# Get the details for online endpoint
online_endpoint_name = "playing-cards-11170337875894"

endpoint = ml_client.online_endpoints.get(name=online_endpoint_name)

# existing traffic details
print(endpoint.traffic)

# Get the scoring URI
print(endpoint.scoring_uri)
```

```
{'playingcards-mlflow-deploy': 0}
https://playing-cards-11170337875894.eastus.inference.ml.azure.com/score
```

Figure 10.31 – Registering the best model to the Azure ML workspace

10. The next couple of cells show you how to invoke the endpoint and pass a test image to the model for inference, as shown in *Figure 10.32*:

```python
# Create request json
import base64

sample_image = "./images/test/cam_image9.jpg"

def read_image(image_path):
    with open(image_path, "rb") as f:
        return f.read()

request_json = {
    "input_data": {
        "columns": ["image"],
        "data": [base64.encodebytes(read_image(sample_image)).decode("utf-8")],
    }
}
```

```python
import json

request_file_name = "sample_request_data.json"

with open(request_file_name, "w") as request_file:
    json.dump(request_json, request_file)
```

```python
resp = ml_client.online_endpoints.invoke(
    endpoint_name=online_endpoint_name,
    deployment_name=deployment.name,
    request_file=request_file_name,
)
```

Figure 10.32 – Sending a test image to the model for inference

11. Finally, let's see how well the model scored the test image (which is how well it was able to find an object, identify its type, and find its location within the image). *Figure 10.33* shows the Python code to help you to visualize the model output that was returned by the endpoint:

```python
%matplotlib inline
import matplotlib.pyplot as plt
import matplotlib.image as mpimg
import matplotlib.patches as patches
from PIL import Image
import numpy as np
import json
IMAGE_SIZE = (18, 12)
plt.figure(figsize=IMAGE_SIZE)
img_np = mpimg.imread(sample_image)
img = Image.fromarray(img_np.astype("uint8"), "RGB")
x, y = img.size
fig, ax = plt.subplots(1, figsize=(15, 15))
# Display the image
ax.imshow(img_np)
# draw box and label for each detection
detections = json.loads(resp)
for detect in detections[0]["boxes"]:
    label = detect["label"]
    box = detect["box"]
    conf_score = detect["score"]
    if conf_score > 0.6:
        ymin, xmin, ymax, xmax = (
            box["topY"],
            box["topX"],
            box["bottomY"],
            box["bottomX"],
        )
        topleft_x, topleft_y = x * xmin, y * ymin
        width, height = x * (xmax - xmin), y * (ymax - ymin)
        print(
            "{}: [{}, {}, {}, {}], {}".format(
                detect["label"],
                round(topleft_x, 3),
                round(topleft_y, 3),
                round(width, 3),
                round(height, 3),
                round(conf_score, 3),
            )
        )

        color = np.random.rand(3)    #'red'
        rect = patches.Rectangle(
            (topleft_x, topleft_y),
            width,
            height,
            linewidth=3,
            edgecolor=color,
            facecolor="none",
        )
        ax.add_patch(rect)
        plt.text(topleft_x, topleft_y - 10, label, color=color, fontsize=20)
plt.show()

Nine: [98.045, 162.37, 206.062, 284.502], 0.686
```

Figure 10.33 – Python code to visualize the model output

12. *Figure 10.34* shows the model output with a bounding box around the identified object:

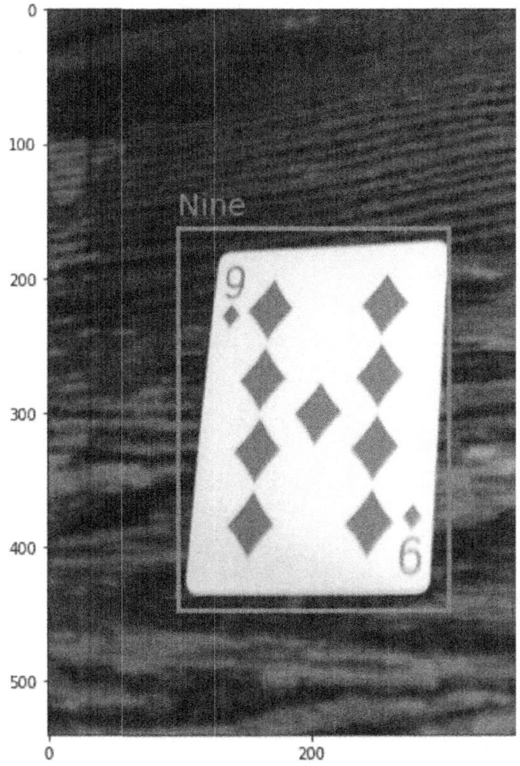

Figure 10.34 – Model output showing the bounding box around the identified object

Let's summarize the chapter next.

Summary

In this chapter, we covered a quick introduction to deep learning and the importance of having a lot of labeled data for the model to perform well. We then showed you how to use the Azure ML Data Labeling capability to assist with labeling image data to train an object detection model. We then showed you how to use AutoML to train an object detection model, and finally, you learned how to deploy your model to an online endpoint and score a test image, all using Azure ML.

In the next chapter, we will show you how to do distributed model training in Azure ML.

11
Using Distributed Training in AMLS

An interesting topic is how we can process large-scale datasets to train machine learning and deep learning models. For example, large-scale text-based mining, entity extraction, sentiments, and image or video-based, including image classification, image multiclassification, and object detection, are all very memory intensive and need large compute resources to process, which may take hours or sometimes days and weeks to complete.

In addition, if you have big data that contains business information and want to build machine learning models, then distributed learning can help. This chapter will cover how we can run large-scale models with large datasets. You will see different ways of computing large, distributed models.

There are different ways to distribute compute and data and achieve faster and better performance for large-scale training. Here, we are going to learn about a few techniques.

Data parallelism is widely used when there is a large volume of data that can be partitioned. We can run parallel computing to achieve better performance. CPU-based computing also performs well when scaled horizontally and vertically. The goal would be to process each partition and compute in groups, such as one partition, and then apply compute, and do that in parallel across all partitions.

Model parallelism is another area where you can scale the model training in deep learning modeling. Model parallelism is heavily compute based and, in most cases, GPU-based computing is needed to get better performance and time. In this chapter, we will look at some distributed training libraries available for us to use in the **Azure Machine Learning** service.

There are two main types of distributed training: data and model parallelism.

We will cover the following topics in this chapter:

- Data parallelism
- Model parallelism
- Distributed training with PyTorch
- Distributed training with TensorFlow

Technical requirements

You can review all the code for this chapter at `https://github.com/PacktPublishing/Azure-Machine-Learning-Engineering`.

To access your workspace, recall the steps from the previous chapter:

1. Go to `https://ml.azure.com`.
2. Select your workspace name from what has been created.
3. From the workspace user interface, on the left-hand side, click **Compute**.
4. On the **Compute** screen, select your last used compute instance and select **Start**.
5. Your compute instance will change from **Stopped** to **Starting**.
6. In the previous chapter, we cloned this book's GitHub repository. If you have not already done so, continue to follow the steps provided. If you have already cloned the repository, skip to *step 9*.
7. Open the terminal on your compute instance. Note that the path will include your user in the directory. Type the following into your terminal to clone the sample notebooks into your working directory:

    ```
    git clone https://github.com/PacktPublishing/Azure-Machine-Learning-Engineering.git
    ```

8. Clicking on the refresh icon.
9. Now, create a compute cluster called `gpu-cluster` with two nodes and select one of the GPU's available VMs, such as the NC6 or NC24 series.
10. Review the notebooks in your `Azure-Machine-Learning-Engineering` directory.

Data parallelism

Data parallelism is widely used when there is a large volume of data that can be partitioned. We can run parallel computing to achieve better performance. CPU-based computing also performs well when scaled horizontally and vertically. The goal would be to process each partition and compute in groups, such as one partition, and then apply compute, and do that parallel across all partitions.

Model parallelism

Model parallelism is another way to scale the model training in deep learning modeling. Model parallelism is heavily compute-based and, in most cases, GPU-based computing is needed to get better performance and time. Let's look at some distributed training libraries available for us to use in the **Azure Machine Learning** service.

In Azure Machine Learning, we can perform distributed learning in various ways:

- **Distributed training with PyTorch**: PyTorch is one of the most well-known and widely used machine learning libraries for large-scale vision, text, and other unstructured data machine learning. It uses deep learning, such as convolutional neural network or recurrent neural network-based development. PyTorch is a deep learning framework developed by Meta (Facebook).

    PyTorch implementations are very simple and easy to use and tend to eliminate the complications of other libraries in the marketplace.

- **Distributed training with TensorFlow**: TensorFlow is a deep learning library created by Google. Given that the science is difficult, it was designed to make deep learning development simple and easy to implement. In the beginning stages, TensorFlow's implementation was very difficult and required excessive lines of code. Another project called Keras was created to simplify this process; then, they were joined together.

The most current version is much more simple and easier to use compared to older versions. We have just covered the most popular frameworks used in the industry for distributed learning in the deep learning world.

> **Note**
> Both of the aforementioned SDKs are being continuously developed and improved, and new functionality is always being added since the artificial intelligence field and the number of algorithms used are growing.

Distributed training with PyTorch

In this chapter, we will learn how to use PyTorch while performing deep learning model training before distributing that training within multiple cores and running it.

Let's look at how we can write some simple PyTorch code that can be run in Azure Machine Learning.

Distributed training code

In this section, we will learn how to write code to perform distributed training using the PyTorch framework for vision-based deep learning algorithms. We will be using Python code to create the model and then train it with a compute cluster. All the code is available in this book's GitHub repository for learning and execution purposes.

Creating a training job Python file to process

Follow these steps to create a dataset while leveraging the user interface:

1. Go to `https://ml.azure.com` and select your workspace.
2. Go to **Compute** and click **Start** to start the compute instance.
3. Wait for the compute instance to start; then, click **Jupyter** to start coding.
4. If you don't have a compute cluster, please follow the instructions in the previous chapters to create a new one. A compute instance with a CPU is good for development; we will use GPU-based content for model training.
5. If you don't have enough quotas for your GPU, please create a Service Ticket in the Azure portal to increase your quotas.
6. Now, create a new folder for this chapter. I am calling mine `Chapter 11`. Also, create a subfolder called `PyTorchDistributed`.
7. Inside, I am also creating a new directory for the `src` folder, where all the Python code training files will be stored. The `PyTorchDistributed` folder (`root` folder) will be used for submitting Python files.

   We can use the terminal to run our Python code.

8. Now, we need to write our training code. So, navigate into the `src` folder and create a new text file called `train.py`.
9. For the sample code in this chapter, we will be using an open source dataset; it has no **Personally Identifiable Information** (**PII**) or privacy or legal issues.

10. Let's import all the libraries needed for the code:

```python
# imports
import torch
import torchvision
import torchvision.transforms as transforms
import torch.nn as nn
import torch.nn.functional as F
import torch.optim as optim
import os, argparse
```

Figure 11.1 – Library imports

11. Next, we must create the neural network architecture. A neural network architecture is what is used for training to create the brain. Depending on the accuracy required, you can build your network based on how many layers are needed. The neural network architecture is not the focus of this book, but there are a lot of resources available for designing one:

```python
# define network architecture
class Net(nn.Module):
    def __init__(self):
        super(Net, self).__init__()
        self.conv1 = nn.Conv2d(3, 32, 3)
        self.pool = nn.MaxPool2d(2, 2)
        self.conv2 = nn.Conv2d(32, 64, 3)
        self.conv3 = nn.Conv2d(64, 128, 3)
        self.fc1 = nn.Linear(128 * 6 * 6, 120)
        self.dropout = nn.Dropout(p=0.2)
        self.fc2 = nn.Linear(120, 84)
        self.fc3 = nn.Linear(84, 10)

    def forward(self, x):
        x = F.relu(self.conv1(x))
        x = self.pool(F.relu(self.conv2(x)))
        x = self.pool(F.relu(self.conv3(x)))
        x = x.view(-1, 128 * 6 * 6)
        x = self.dropout(F.relu(self.fc1(x)))
        x = F.relu(self.fc2(x))
        x = self.fc3(x)
        return x
```

Figure 11.2 – Neural network architecture

12. Now, let's write the training code:

```python
# define functions
def train(train_loader, model, criterion, optimizer, epoch, device, print_freq, rank):
    running_loss = 0.0
    for i, data in enumerate(train_loader, 0):
        # get the inputs; data is a list of [inputs, labels]
        inputs, labels = data[0].to(device), data[1].to(device)

        # zero the parameter gradients
        optimizer.zero_grad()

        # forward + backward + optimize
        outputs = model(inputs)
        loss = criterion(outputs, labels)
        loss.backward()
        optimizer.step()

        # print statistics
        running_loss += loss.item()
        if i % print_freq == 0:    # print every print_freq mini-batches
            print(
                "Rank %d: [%d, %5d] loss: %.3f"
                % (rank, epoch + 1, i + 1, running_loss / print_freq)
            )
            running_loss = 0.0
```

Figure 11.3 – Training code

13. Next, we will evaluate the model metrics. Model evaluation is an important step in the training process as it validates model performance in terms of accuracy:

```python
def evaluate(test_loader, model, device):
    classes = (
        "plane",
        "car",
        "bird",
        "cat",
        "deer",
        "dog",
        "frog",
        "horse",
        "ship",
        "truck",
    )

    model.eval()

    correct = 0
    total = 0
    class_correct = list(0.0 for i in range(10))
    class_total = list(0.0 for i in range(10))
    with torch.no_grad():
        for data in test_loader:
            images, labels = data[0].to(device), data[1].to(device)
            outputs = model(images)
            _, predicted = torch.max(outputs.data, 1)
            total += labels.size(0)
            correct += (predicted == labels).sum().item()
            c = (predicted == labels).squeeze()
            for i in range(10):
                label = labels[i]
                class_correct[label] += c[i].item()
                class_total[label] += 1

    # print total test set accuracy
    print(
        "Accuracy of the network on the 10000 test images: %d %%"
        % (100 * correct / total)
    )

    # print test accuracy for each of the classes
    for i in range(10):
        print(
            "Accuracy of %5s : %2d %%"
            % (classes[i], 100 * class_correct[i] / class_total[i])
        )
```

Figure 11.4 – Evaluation code

14. Next, we need to create a `main` function that will gather the data for the model, then invoke the `main` function and start to process the training code. Then, it will evaluate the model. Please refer to the following sample code for the details:

```python
def main(args):
    # get PyTorch environment variables
    world_size = int(os.environ["WORLD_SIZE"])
    rank = int(os.environ["RANK"])
    local_rank = int(os.environ["LOCAL_RANK"])

    distributed = world_size > 1

    # set device
    if distributed:
        device = torch.device("cuda", local_rank)
    else:
        device = torch.device("cuda:0" if torch.cuda.is_available() else "cpu")

    # initialize distributed process group using default env:// method
    if distributed:
        torch.distributed.init_process_group(backend="nccl")
```

Figure 11.5 – Sample main code

Here is the code that specifies the distributed dataset:

```python
if distributed:
    train_sampler = torch.utils.data.distributed.DistributedSampler(train_set)
else:
    train_sampler = None
```

Figure 11.6 – Distributed dataset code

This is where the model is distributed:

```python
    # wrap model with DDP
    if distributed:
        model = nn.parallel.DistributedDataParallel(
            model, device_ids=[local_rank], output_device=local_rank
        )
```

Figure 11.7 – Model distribution code

15. Next, we will create a `job.py` file that downloads the data needed for the experiment.

16. Now, let's create a dataset for further training processes. This dataset will invoke the compute cluster needed for the distributed training. The following sample code invokes the workspace and gets the dataset:

```python
# get workspace
ws = Workspace.from_config()

# get root of git repo
prefix = Path(__file__).parent

# training script
source_dir = str(prefix.joinpath("src"))
script_name = "train.py"

# azure ml settings
environment_name = "AzureML-PyTorch-1.6-GPU"  # using curated environment
experiment_name = "pytorch-cifar10-distributed-example"
compute_name = "gpu-cluster"

# get environment
env = Environment.get(ws, name=environment_name)

# download and extract cifar-10 data
url = "https://www.cs.toronto.edu/~kriz/cifar-10-python.tar.gz"
filename = "cifar-10-python.tar.gz"
data_root = "cifar-10"
filepath = os.path.join(data_root, filename)
```

Figure 11.8 – Job file dataset code

The following code parallelizes the training process:

```python
# create distributed config
distr_config = PyTorchConfiguration(process_count=4, node_count=2)

# create args
args = ["--data-dir", dataset.as_download(), "--epochs", 25]

# create job config
src = ScriptRunConfig(
    source_directory=source_dir,
    script=script_name,
    arguments=args,
    compute_target=compute_name,
    environment=env,
    distributed_job_config=distr_config,
)
```

Figure 11.9 – Job file invoking distributed training

17. As shown in the preceding screenshot, the code is distributed during model training, and this process is very simple. PyTorchConfiguration, along with process_count and node_count, are the configurations we must provide to distribute the model training process.

PyTorchConfiguration takes three parameters:

   I. communication_backend: This can be set to Nccl or Gloo. Nccl is selected by default.

   II. process_count: This parameter configures how many processes run inside the nodes for parallelization purposes.

   III. node_count: This is where we specify how many nodes to use for the job. node is based on how many cores are available. The higher the number of nodes, the faster the processing.

18. Run the job and wait for it to finish. Once the job has been submitted, navigate to your workspace's user interface, click on **jobs**, and go to **details** to see how this works.

Figure 11.10 – Job output

In this section, we learned how to run distributed training using the PyTorch framework for a large dataset for custom vision-based deep learning modeling.

Now, we are going to look at the TensorFlow framework and see how we can achieve distributed learning with a large dataset for custom vision-based deep learning models.

Distributed training with TensorFlow

In this section, we are going to learn how to take large image files and build custom deep learning models such as object detection or image classification using TensorFlow. By doing so, we'll learn how to distribute across multiple virtual machines to achieve faster performance for training.

Creating a training job Python file to process

Follow these steps to create a dataset that leverages the user interface:

1. Go to https://ml.azure.com and select your workspace.
2. Go to **Compute** and click **Start** to start the compute instance.
3. Wait for the compute instance to start; then, click **Jupyter** to start coding.
4. If you don't have a compute cluster, please follow the instructions in the previous chapters to create a new one. A compute instance with a CPU is good for development; we will use GPU-based content for model training.
5. If you don't have enough quotas for your GPU, please create a Service Ticket in the Azure portal to increase your quotas.
6. Now, create a new folder for this chapter. I am creating a folder called Chapter 11. Then, create a subfolder called TensorflowDistributed.
7. Inside, I am also creating a new directory for the src folder where all the Python code training files will be stored. TensorflowDistributed (root folder) will be used for submitting Python files. If the TensorflowDistributed folder doesn't exist, please create one. Create the preceding folder under the Chapter 11 folder from *step 6*.

    We can use the terminal to run our Python code.

8. Now, we need to write our training code. So, navigate to the src folder and create a new text file called train.py.
9. For the sample code in this chapter, we are using an open source dataset; it contains no PII and doesn't have any privacy or legal issues.
10. Let's import all the libraries needed for the code:

    ```
    import tensorflow as tf
    import numpy as np

    import argparse
    import os, json
    ```

    Figure 11.11 – Library imports

11. Next, we must perform dataset processing:

```python
def mnist_dataset(batch_size):
    (x_train, y_train), _ = tf.keras.datasets.mnist.load_data()
    # The `x` arrays are in uint8 and have values in the range [0, 255].
    # We need to convert them to float32 with values in the range [0, 1]
    x_train = x_train / np.float32(255)
    y_train = y_train.astype(np.int64)
    train_dataset = (
        tf.data.Dataset.from_tensor_slices((x_train, y_train))
        .shuffle(60000)
        .repeat()
        .batch(batch_size)
    )
    return train_dataset
```

Figure 11.12 – Dataset processing

12. Now, let's create a model. We will use the Keras library to simplify the neural network architecture. The layers depend on your use case and accuracy. I have seen large network architectures with low accuracy and too few layers produce poor results. So, we have to find the right balance in terms of layers through experimentation and build the neural network architecture from there:

```python
def build_and_compile_cnn_model():
    model = tf.keras.Sequential(
        [
            tf.keras.Input(shape=(28, 28)),
            tf.keras.layers.Reshape(target_shape=(28, 28, 1)),
            tf.keras.layers.Conv2D(32, 3, activation="relu"),
            tf.keras.layers.Flatten(),
            tf.keras.layers.Dense(128, activation="relu"),
            tf.keras.layers.Dense(10),
        ]
    )
    model.compile(
        loss=tf.keras.losses.SparseCategoricalCrossentropy(from_logits=True),
        optimizer=tf.keras.optimizers.SGD(learning_rate=0.001),
        metrics=["accuracy"],
    )
    return model
```

Figure 11.13 – Model neural network

13. Now, let's create the `main` function, which will run the model training process in a distributed manner. The `main` function is where all the logic flow is tied together to get the training process working. As you can see, `tf.distribute` specifies the distribution strategies:

```
tf_config = json.loads(os.environ["TF_CONFIG"])
num_workers = len(tf_config["cluster"]["worker"])

strategy = tf.distribute.experimental.MultiWorkerMirroredStrategy()

# Here the batch size scales up by number of workers since
# `tf.data.Dataset.batch` expects the global batch size.
global_batch_size = args.per_worker_batch_size * num_workers
multi_worker_dataset = mnist_dataset(global_batch_size)

with strategy.scope():
    # Model building/compiling need to be within `strategy.scope()`.
    multi_worker_model = build_and_compile_cnn_model()

# Keras' `model.fit()` trains the model with specified number of epochs and
# number of steps per epoch.
multi_worker_model.fit(
    multi_worker_dataset, epochs=args.epochs, steps_per_epoch=args.steps_per_epoch
)

# Save the model
task_type, task_id = (tf_config["task"]["type"], tf_config["task"]["index"])
write_model_path = write_filepath(args.model_dir, task_type, task_id)

multi_worker_model.save(write_model_path)
```

Figure 11.14 – TensorFlow distribution code

`Tf.distribute.experimental.MultiWorkerMirroredStrategy` synchronously replicates all the variables and computation across the worker nodes to process. It mainly uses GPU (given the large-scale processing). The preceding implementation allows multiple workers to work together to achieve better performance to complete the training run faster.

14. Next, we will have to create some Python code called `job` in the root folder, which we will execute in a terminal window to execute the TensorFlow code in the command line.

15. Now, we must create an `environment.yaml` file. This will create the environment to run the model training. Here is the sample code:

```yaml
channels:
    - conda-forge
dependencies:
    - python=3.6
    - pip:
        - azureml-defaults
        - azureml-mlflow
        - tensorflow-gpu==2.3.0
```

Figure 11.15 – environment.yaml code

16. Next, we must create the `jobtensorflow.py` file, which uses an Azure Machine Learning SDK to configure the training process and then execute it once the job has been submitted.

17. In the `code` section, specify a workspace environment to use and a training Python file to use for the experiment. There are a few changes you need to make to execute the code. The workspace, environment, and training Python files' names can change depending on how you are implementing them:

```python
# get workspace
ws = Workspace.from_config()

# get root of git repo
prefix = Path(__file__).parent

# training script
source_dir = str(prefix.joinpath("src"))
script_name = "train1.py"

# environment file
environment_file = str(prefix.joinpath("environment.yml"))

# azure ml settings
environment_name = "tf-gpu-example"
experiment_name = "tf-mnist-distributed-example"
compute_name = "gpu-cluster"

# create environment
env = Environment.from_conda_specification(environment_name, environment_file)

# specify a GPU base image
env.docker.enabled = True
env.docker.base_image = (
    "mcr.microsoft.com/azureml/openmpi3.1.2-cuda10.1-cudnn7-ubuntu18.04"
)
```

Figure 11.16 – Sample environment and experiment

18. Next, we must create some code that will set the distribution strategy and then invoke the training experiment. We can use the `TensorflowConfiguration` class to configure how to parallelize the training job.

    `TensorflowConfiguration` takes two parameters, as follows:

    I.   `worker_count`: The number of worker nodes used to parallelize. The default value is 1.

    II. `parameter_server_count`: This parameter is set for a number of tasks to run the previous `worker_count`:

```python
# create distributed config
distr_config = TensorflowConfiguration(worker_count=2, parameter_server_count=0)

# create args
model_path = os.path.join("./outputs", "keras-model")

args = ["--epochs", 30, "--model-dir", model_path]

# create job config
src = ScriptRunConfig(
    source_directory=source_dir,
    script=script_name,
    arguments=args,
    compute_target=compute_name,
    environment=env,
    distributed_job_config=distr_config,
)

# submit job
run = Experiment(ws, experiment_name).submit(src)
run.wait_for_completion(show_output=True)
```

Figure 11.17 – Distribution strategy and job submission

19. Wait for the experiment to run. This will take a few minutes to a few hours, depending on the dataset's size. Once the experiment has finished running, navigate to your workspace's user interface, go to the **job** section, and select the job to view its output:

Display name	☆	Experiment	Status	Created on ↓	Duration
upbeat_grass_r15twztv		tf-mnist-distributed-ex...	✓ Completed	Sep 24, 2022 9:41 AM	3m 40s

Figure 11.18 – Job output

In this section, you learned how to create code that will run large-scale TensorFlow distributed training for a large custom vision-based deep learning model. The code is structured to run for a long time and report backlogs for us to check and validate. These jobs can be submitted as batch jobs so that we don't have to keep watching what happens. Instead, we can submit the job and come back after a few hours to see how the model run performed.

Summary

We have covered a lot of topics in this chapter. We learned how to create code to distribute PyTorch and TensorFlow deep learning models using the Azure Machine Learning service's Python SDK. We also saw how easy and seamless it is to build code that performs in a timely fashion by distributing the model training with large volumes of data.

The goal of this chapter was to show you how to build seamless code that can execute large-scale models via batch processing without you having to watch them run. The Azure Machine Learning SDK allows us to submit the job and then come back later and check the output.

This is the last chapter of this book; I hope you had an amazing time reading and learning about Azure Machine Learning and how to build machine learning models. We would like to hear about your experience in applying machine learning or deep learning in your organization. Azure Machine Learning will make your journey simple and easy with open source in mind.

Thank you so much for reading this book. This book will help you study for certifications such as AI 102 (AI Engineer – Training | Microsoft Learn: `https://learn.microsoft.com/en-us/certifications/roles/ai-engineer`) and DP 100 (Exam DP-100: Designing and Implementing a Data Science Solution on Azure – Certifications | Microsoft Learn: `https://learn.microsoft.com/en-us/certifications/exams/dp-100`).

Index

A

AML notebooks
  using 35, 36
AMLS GUI
  compute instance, creating through 29-31
AML Studio (AMLS) 3, 131
  Data Labeling 27, 28
  Linked Services 28, 29
  MLflow model with managed online endpoints, deploying through 164-175
  model, deploying for batch inferencing 191-199
  navigating 11-27
  VS Code, connecting to 37-40
AMLS workspace
  creating 5, 235
  creating, through ARM templates 10
  creating, through Azure CLI 7-9
  creating, through Azure portal 5-7
AML workspace
  connecting to 241
Application Insights 3
Area Under the Curve (AUC) 142
ARM templates
  AMLS workspace, creating with 10
  compute instance, adding with 33, 34

AutoML 129-131
  results, parsing via AMLS 151-158
  results, parsing via AML SDK 151-158
  used, for training object detection model 301-304
  with AML Python SDK 144-151
  with AMLS 133-144
Azure CLI
  AMLS workspace, creating through 7-9
  compute instance, adding through 32
  ml extension 3
Azure CLI v2
  model for real-time inferencing, deploying with managed online endpoint 182-187
Azure Container Instance (ACI) 19, 163
Azure Container Registry 3
Azure Databricks 27
Azure DevOps environment
  creating 254-257
Azure DevOps organization
  creating 235-239
Azure DevOps pipeline
  creating 263-273
  running 274-285
Azure DevOps project
  creating 235

Azure DevOps repo
  code, moving to 241-243
Azure DevOps service connections
  setting 257-263
Azure Key Vault 3
  variables, setting up 244-249
Azure Kubernetes Service (AKS) 19, 163
Azure Machine Learning (AML) 3
  command-line interface (CLI) 42
  data assets, creating 52
  data assets, creating with Python SDK 59-61
  data assets, creating with UI 52-59
  data assets, using 61
  datastore overview 42, 43
  default datastore review 43, 44
Azure Machine Learning CLI
  blob storage account datastore, creating through 51
Azure Machine Learning SDK for Python (AML SDK v2) 17
Azure Machine Learning Studio
  blob storage account datastore, creating through 45-47
Azure ML Python SDK
  object detection model, deploying to online endpoint 305-313
Azure portal 4
  AMLS workspace, creating through 5-7
Azure Resource Management (ARM) 3
Azure storage account 3
Azure subscription 7

B

bandit policies 115
batch endpoints 26
batch inferencing 163, 189

Bayesian sampling 111
  sweep job, setting up for 120
Bidirectional Encoder Representations from Transformers (BERT) 132
blob storage account datastore
  creating 45
  creating, through Azure Machine Learning CLI 51
  creating, through Azure Machine Learning Studio 45-47
  creating, through Python SDK 48-50
blue/green deployment 164, 232

C

causal analysis 212
Central Processing Unit (CPU) 27
code-free models
  training, with Designer 68
command-line interpreter (CLI) 8
Command Prompt (CMD) 8
compute 27
compute cluster 27, 70
  model, training on 93-105
compute instance 27-29
  adding, through Azure CLI 32
  adding, with ARM templates 33, 34
  creating, through AMLS GUI 29-31
  model, training on 81-93
  schedule, adding to 32
confusion matrix 80
continuous integration/ continuous delivery (CI/CD) 231
counterfactual analysis 209, 212

Index

D

dashboards 207
data assets, Azure Machine Learning
 creating 52
 creating, with Python SDK 59-61
 creating, with UI 52-59
 data, reading in job 62-65
 using 61
Data explorer 220, 221
Data Labeling 27, 28
 used, for labeling image data 291-300
data parallelism 315-317
deep learning 289
Designer
 code-free models, training 68
 dataset, creating with user interface 68-80
distributed learning, with PyTorch 317, 318
 training job Python file, creating to process 318-324
distributed learning, with TensorFlow 317, 324
 training job Python file, creating to process 325-329

E

entry script 164
environments 24
environment variable groups
 setting up 249-254
error analysis 209, 212, 214
error analysis dashboard 207, 214-217

F

fairness 223
fairness dashboard 207
 creating 223-229
feature permutation 209
featurization concepts 132, 133

G

Graphics Processing Unit (GPU) 27
grid sampling 111
 sweep job, setting up with 116-118
Guided User Interface (GUI) 3

H

HDInsights 27
hyperparameters 107
 sampling 110-112
hyperparameter tuning 109, 110

I

image data
 labeling, Data Labeling feature used 291-300
Integrated Development Environments (IDE) 3
interpretability 212
interpretability dashboard 207, 217, 218

J

jobs 61
 data, reading 62-65
Jupyter 34
Jupyter Lab 3, 34

Index

Jupyter Notebook 3
   Python code, developing with 34, 35

K

key vaults 234
Kubernetes online endpoints 164

L

Linked Services 28, 29
linting 34
logistic regression model 120

M

Machine Learning (ML) 3, 41
managed online endpoint 163, 164
median policies 115
MLflow model, with managed online endpoints
   deploying, through AML Studio 164-175
   deploying, through Python SDK V2 175-178
MLOps 3, 231
   implementation 232-234
MLOps environment
   preparing 234
model
   creating 208-210
   training, on compute cluster 93-105
   training, on compute instance 81-93
model, deploying for batch inferencing
   with Python SDK 200-204
   with Studio 191-199
model for real-time inferencing, deploying with managed online endpoints
   through Azure CLI v2 182-187

model parallelism 315-317
model parameters 109
model statistics 219
model tuning 107
model, with managed online endpoints
   deploying, through Python SDK V2 179-182

N

nodes 27

O

object detection model
   deploying to online endpoint, with Azure ML Python SDK 305-313
   training, with AutoML 301-304
Open Neural Network Exchange (ONNX) 131

P

pandas DataFrame 29
personally identifiable information (PII) 206
primary metric 109
Principle Component Analysis (PCA) 132
Python code
   developing, with Jupyter Notebook 34, 35
Python IDE 34
Python SDK
   blob storage account datastore, creating through 48-50
   data asset, creating with 59-61
   model, deploying for batch inferencing 200-204

Python SDK V2
MLflow model with managed online endpoints, deploying through 175-178
model with managed online endpoints, deploying through 179-182
PyTorch 317
distributed learning 317

R

raiwidgets 207
random sampling 111
sweep job, setting up for 118, 119
real-time endpoints 26
real-time inferencing 163
Receiver Operating Characteristic (ROC) curve 79
resource group 5, 7
Responsible AI
URL 207
responsible AI code
creating 211, 212
Responsible AI dashboard 208-213
Responsible AI, principles
accountability 207
fairness 205, 206
inclusiveness 206
privacy and security 206
reliability and safety 206
transparency 206
Responsible AI Toolbox 207
URL 208
Responsible AI Toolkit SDK 207

S

schedule
adding, to compute instance 32

scoring script 164
search space 110
service connection 234
Singular Value Decomposition (SVD) 132
sweep job 107, 110
results, reviewing of 121-128
setting up, for Bayesian sampling 120
setting up, for random sampling 118, 119
setting up, with grid sampling 116-118
sweep jobs 112-114
Synapse Spark pools 27

T

TensorFlow
distributed learning 317
truncation policies 114

V

variable groups 234
variables
setting up, in Azure Key Vault 244-249
Virtual Machine (VM) instance 27
VS Code 3, 34, 37
AMLS, connecting to 37-40

W

what-if analysis 209
what-if counterfactuals 221, 222
Windows Powershell (Windows PS) 8
workspace 3

‹packt›

www.packtpub.com

Subscribe to our online digital library for full access to over 7,000 books and videos, as well as industry leading tools to help you plan your personal development and advance your career. For more information, please visit our website.

Why subscribe?

- Spend less time learning and more time coding with practical eBooks and Videos from over 4,000 industry professionals
- Improve your learning with Skill Plans built especially for you
- Get a free eBook or video every month
- Fully searchable for easy access to vital information
- Copy and paste, print, and bookmark content

Did you know that Packt offers eBook versions of every book published, with PDF and ePub files available? You can upgrade to the eBook version at packtpub.com and as a print book customer, you are entitled to a discount on the eBook copy. Get in touch with us at customercare@packtpub.com for more details.

At www.packtpub.com, you can also read a collection of free technical articles, sign up for a range of free newsletters, and receive exclusive discounts and offers on Packt books and eBooks.

Other Books You May Enjoy

If you enjoyed this book, you may be interested in these other books by Packt:

Machine Learning Techniques for Text

Nikos Tsourakis

ISBN: 978-1-80324-238-5

- Understand fundamental concepts of machine learning for text
- Discover how text data can be represented and build language models
- Perform exploratory data analysis on text corpora
- Use text preprocessing techniques and understand their trade-offs
- Apply dimensionality reduction for visualization and classification
- Incorporate and fine-tune algorithms and models for machine learning
- Evaluate the performance of the implemented systems
- Know the tools for retrieving text data and visualizing the machine learning workflow

Machine Learning Engineering with Python

Andrew P. McMahon

ISBN: 978-1-80107-925-9

- Find out what an effective ML engineering process looks like
- Uncover options for automating training and deployment and learn how to use them
- Discover how to build your own wrapper libraries for encapsulating your data science and machine learning logic and solutions
- Understand what aspects of software engineering you can bring to machine learning
- Gain insights into adapting software engineering for machine learning using appropriate cloud technologies
- Perform hyperparameter tuning in a relatively automated way

Packt is searching for authors like you

If you're interested in becoming an author for Packt, please visit `authors.packtpub.com` and apply today. We have worked with thousands of developers and tech professionals, just like you, to help them share their insight with the global tech community. You can make a general application, apply for a specific hot topic that we are recruiting an author for, or submit your own idea.

Share Your Thoughts

Now you've finished *Azure Machine Learning Engineering*, we'd love to hear your thoughts! Scan the QR code below to go straight to the Amazon review page for this book and share your feedback or leave a review on the site that you purchased it from.

`https://packt.link/r/1-803-23930-1`

Your review is important to us and the tech community and will help us make sure we're delivering excellent quality content.

Download a free PDF copy of this book

Thanks for purchasing this book!

Do you like to read on the go but are unable to carry your print books everywhere? Is your eBook purchase not compatible with the device of your choice?

Don't worry, now with every Packt book you get a DRM-free PDF version of that book at no cost.

Read anywhere, any place, on any device. Search, copy, and paste code from your favorite technical books directly into your application.

The perks don't stop there, you can get exclusive access to discounts, newsletters, and great free content in your inbox daily

Follow these simple steps to get the benefits:

1. Scan the QR code or visit the link below

   https://packt.link/free-ebook/9781803239309

2. Submit your proof of purchase
3. That's it! We'll send your free PDF and other benefits to your email directly

Printed in Great Britain
by Amazon